New Perspectives
in the
History of Indian Education

New Perspectives in the History of Indian Education

Edited by

Parimala V. Rao

Orient BlackSwan

NEW PERSPECTIVES IN THE HISTORY OF INDIAN EDUCATION

ORIENT BLACKSWAN PRIVATE LIMITED

Registered Office
3-6-752 Himayatnagar, Hyderabad 500 029 (T.S.), India
E-Mail: centraloffice@orientblackswan.com

Other Offices
Bengaluru, Bhopal, Chennai, Guwahati, Hyderabad,
Jaipur, Kolkata, Lucknow, Mumbai,
New Delhi, Noida, Patna, Vijayawada

First published 2014
This Paperback Edition 2016

ISBN 978-81-250-6311-7

Typeset in
Adobe Garamond Pro 11/13
by Le Studio Graphique, Gurgaon 122 001

023301
13052016

Printed in India at
Yash Printographics
Noida

Published by
Orient Blackswan Private Limited
1/24 Asaf Ali Road
New Delhi 110 002
E-Mail: delhi@orientblackswan.com

To

Professor Eleanor Zelliot

Pioneering Historian of the Dalit Movement and B. R. Ambedkar
for enriching the field of Indian history

Contents

Acknowledgements *ix*

Introduction 1
Perspectives Old and New
Parimala V. Rao

Part I
Forms of Discrimination in Education

1. Dalit Initiatives in Education, 1880–1992 45
Eleanor Zelliot

2. A College of One's Own 68
An International Perspective on the Value of Historically Dalit Colleges
Laura Dudley Jenkins

3. Silent Voices 90
Women's Perceptions about Self and Education in Late Nineteenth-century India
Radha Gayathri

4. Contested Domains 120
Restructuring Education and Religious Identity in Sikh and Arya Samaj Schools in Punjab
Mahima Manchanda

Part II
Political Context of Education

5. Compulsory Education and the Political Leadership in Colonial India, 1840–1947 — 151
Parimala V. Rao

6. Education, Missionaries and the Indian Nation, c. 1880–1920 — 176
Hayden Bellenoit

7. Re-defining Work and Education as a Means to National Self-determination — 196
A Comparative Study of Gandhian India and Peronist Argentina
Simone Holzwarth and Verónica Oelsner

8. The Genesis of Curzon's University Reforms, 1899–1905 — 224
Suresh Chandra Ghosh

9. The Transformation of Schooling in Colonial Punjab, 1854–1900 — 269
Preeti

Consolidated Bibliography 301
Notes on the Contributors 323
Index 325

Acknowledgements

I would like to thank my colleagues Professor Geetha Nambissan, Dr Srinivas Rao, Dr Saumen Chattopadhyay and Dr Arvind Kumar Mishra. They encouraged me to organise panels on the history of education at international conferences of the Comparative Education Society of India during 2010–12.

Professor Eleanor Zelliot's unending devotion to critical perspectives in historical research spanning over forty-five years has immensely inspired me. I would like to thank her and the other contributors to this volume for their patience and cooperation. Without their constant support, this volume would not have been possible.

Another source of inspiration has been my students whose persistent questioning in the classroom has contributed to furthering a critical perspective in the history of education. It is an indication of what can be achieved if freedom of questioning is entertained both within classrooms and beyond.

I am grateful to the Nehru Memorial Museum and Library for awarding me a fellowship which helped me to put together this volume. Veenu Luthria of Orient BlackSwan has been a source of strength throughout.

Introduction

Perspectives Old and New

Parimala V. Rao

> The duty of the historian of education is to rescue from oblivion those, whose voices have not yet been heard and whose stories have not yet been told.[1]

The year 2013 marks the bicentennial of the state's acknowledgement of its responsibility for education in colonial India. A budget of Rs. 100,000 or £10,000 was earmarked for the purpose. Clause number 43 of the Charter Act of 1813 specifically stated that this amount was to be 'applied to the revival and improvement of literature and the encouragement of the learned natives of India and for the introduction and promotion of a knowledge of the sciences amongst the inhabitants of the British territories in India and ... any schools, public lectures, or other institutions for the purpose aforesaid, which shall be founded at the Presidencies of Bengal, Bombay and Madras, or in any other parts of the British India'. The education clause is significant because the state had not yet accepted its responsibility for education in England. It was first accepted for India in 1813, while a long struggle led to its enactment in England in 1833. The group of people who fought for the inclusion of the education clause were also the same who did so for England—namely, the liberals, evangelical groups, and utilitarians. They were

1. Richard Aldrich, *Lessons from History of Education: the Selected Works of Richard Aldrich*, London: Routledge, 2006, p. 18.

also deeply involved in the abolition of slavery in the British-ruled territories.[2]

The education clause was drafted by Robert Percy Smith, the former advocate general of Bengal. While in India, he had 'championed the cause of people's rights and liberties'.[3] Smith, a liberal, could succeed in inserting this clause as there was pressure from three recognisable groups—the liberals who were fighting for educational and political reforms within Britain, the utilitarians resisting elite control of education in England, and Protestant missionaries like the Baptists locked in a protracted struggle with the elite Anglican church. All of them lent each other support in the political and educational reform movements of the first four decades of the nineteenth century in England, though they had different ideas about education. For the liberals—most of them sceptics and rationalists—modern education was necessary to resist superstitious practices, inculcate rational thinking, and empower the lower classes. For the utilitarians, education made masses useful members of society, while for the missionaries, education was a channel for propagating Christianity.[4] Since it was the combined effort of these groups who possessed such diverse interpretations of the usefulness of education, the educational clause of the Charter Act meant different things to them. This multiple interpretation, along with the orientalist hegemony in the field of education in India, led to an uneven and complex development. The essays in this volume attempt to analyse little-known educational debates, and the facts which resulted from such myriad developments.

Old Perspectives

The 'old perspectives' in the history of Indian education can be divided into four categories: imperialist, anti-imperialist, postmodern

2. See, C. H. Philips, *The East India Company, 1784–1834*, Manchester: Manchester University Press, 1961.
3. Surendranath Banerjee, *Speeches and Writings of Babu Surendranath Banerjea*, Madras: G. A. Natesan and Co., 1940, p. 87.
4. See, M. A. Laird, *Missionaries and Education in Bengal, 1793–1837*, Oxford: Clarendon Press, 1972.

and nationalist. All of them begin with the basic assumption that the world consists of neatly divided categories of East/West, coloniser/colonised and European/non-European. These categories are often considered to be mutually exclusive, incompatible and impermeable. For the imperialist historians, Indians were incapable of reflecting upon 'the received knowledge' or going beyond what was 'taught in the classrooms'. For the anti-imperialists and postmodernists, the East, i.e., the colonised non-Europeans were voiceless, passive recipients of Western education imposed on them by the colonial state through 'cultural imperialism' to reinforce 'European hegemony'. The anti-imperialist and postmodern interpretations highlight that this is achieved only through the coercive strategies of the Western imperial powers. For the nationalist historians, the pre-colonial education system which was inherently superior had been destroyed by the British. The anti-imperialists, postmodernists and nationalists rejected Western knowledge and education in order to assert indigenous or native superiority. In continuation of this argument, they said that the coloniser could not understand and appreciate the literature and culture of the East. They were dismissive of any counter examples and highlight them as part of vicious strategies to expand territories or as Martin Carnoy says, 'to break the existing structures of power'.

Such demarcations are artificially drawn to proclaim the superiority of particular groups. As Eric Hobsbawm argues, 'myth and inventions are essential to the politics of identity'; to claim that 'we are different from, and better than the other' is part and parcel of this process.[5] He calls the tendency to treat human societies 'as self-contained, self-reproducing and ideally self-stabilizing system' as a historical. 'No tribe or a community is or has ever been an island. The ideas produced by the Enlightenment and 'the forces which transformed the world since the fifteenth century were geographically European', but universally valid. To argue that the Enlightenment was a European historical experience and that the non-Europeans should reject also implies that Islam is an Arab experience, while Buddhism an Indian one, and the rest of the world should reject

5. Eric Hobsbawm, *On History*, London: Weidenfeld and Nicolson, 1997, p. 7.

them. Such assumptions are historically incorrect. Hobsbawm argues that 'history consists of the interaction of variously structured and geographically distributed social entities, which mutually reshape each other ... Europe and non-Europe can no more be separated than Ibn Khaldun's Beduin and sedentaries: each is the other's history'.[6] The medieval Arab historian, Ibn Khaldun, called the nomads of the Arabian Desert—the Beduins (Bedouins)—courageous, and the Arabs who took to farming and settled in cities sedentaries. But the nomadic Arabs and the city dwellers influenced each other so much that their history could only be read as one. Another important aspect is that those who reject Enlightenment do not reject nationalism which is also a modern phenomenon that emerged in Europe and spread across the world. So the rejection of Enlightenment and the ideas it produced is selective.

The imperialist interpretation of the growth of modern education is based on the assumption that modern education civilised the barbarians, and emphasises the racial superiority of the Europeans. Hobsbawm rejects such notions by arguing that 'in Europe as elsewhere the most universally acknowledged border between civilization and barbarism ran between the rich and poor, that is to say between those with access to luxuries, education and the world outside, and the rest. Consequently, the most obvious division of this sort ran across, and not between, societies, that is, primarily between the city and the countryside.[7] Bruce T. McCully in *English Education and the Origins of Indian Nationalism* documents the development of modern education across India from the promulgation of the Charter Act of 1813 up to the early decades of the twentieth century. Although he provides the earliest comprehensive analysis on the subject, his conclusion rejects most of his arguments in the book. McCully's arguments have two aspects. Firstly, he states that the rise of Indian nationalism was a result of modern education as the Hindus had 'no vital political traditions'. He does not explain it any further. By political tradition, if McCully implies the growth of modern democracy since the eighteenth century, colonial rule should be

6. Ibid., pp. 172–73.
7. Ibid., p. 222.

taken into consideration for not developing it. However, if McCully is hinting at a general political tradition of stable governments with the rule of law, India never lacked one in her 4,000-year history except during brief periods of wars and political turmoil. The earliest text on statecraft was written as far back as the third century BCE by Kautilya.[8] Secondly, McCully goes on to argue as follows:

> the liberal nationalists of India—the Banerjeas, the Naorojis, the Mehtas, the Ghoses, and others—invented little or nothing in the way of ideology. Their contribution to Indian nationalist thought consisted for the most part in expounding a modified version of doctrines which they had picked up as students in the Indian universities or acquired later while studying in England or abroad. Even the tactics of the European nationalists were imitated.[9]

He also argues that 'in its infancy Indian nationalism was synonymous with Hindu nationalism'. If the nationalism advocated by the liberal nationalists was a mere imitation of European nationalism, then, on the one hand the Naorojis and the Mehtas would have fought for a separate nation state for Parsis on the west coast of India, and the Banerjeas and Ghoshs might have also clamoured in a similar vein for the Bengalis on the east coast. The fact that Dadabhai Naoroji and Pherozeshah Mehta became the voice of millions who did not share their Parsi religion or understood their mother tongue has no parallel in the linguistic and ethnic nationalism of Europe. In a country comprising six major religions with numerous minor sects, and eleven major languages with as many scripts and innumerable dialects (most of them often incomprehensible to one another), Europe did not offer a suitable model for imagining a nation-state.

8. See, R. Shamasastri, *Kautilya's Arthasastra*, Mysore: Mysore Publishing and Printing House, 1967; Romila Thapar, *From Lineage to State: Social Formations of the Mid-First Millennium B.C. in the Ganges Valley*, Delhi: Oxford University Press, 1985; Satish Chandra, *History of Medieval India*, Hyderabad: Orient BlackSwan, 2009, and Satish Chandra (ed.), *Religion, State and Society in Medieval India*, Delhi: Oxford University Press, 2008.
9. Bruce T. McCully, *English Education and the Origins of Indian Nationalism*, Glouchester, Mass.: Peter Smith, 1966, pp. 389–94.

The leaders of the Indian National Congress who led the anti-colonial movement consciously rejected the European model of nation-building based on a single language or religion, supported by military might. They upheld 'the spirit of liberalism implied in freedom from caste, creed and regional prejudices and a steady devotion to all that seeks to do justice between man and man'.[10] They equated European nationalism with 'Kipling's hooligan spirit of patriotism'. They argued that 'the European notion of my country right or wrong is narrow and selfish and would lead to mischievous results: patriotism based on hatred of other countries and foreigners would eventually prove to be suicidal'.[11] Therefore, from the very beginning, Indian nationalism was anti-colonial, opposed to colonial exploitation, rather than being anti-British, driven by a hatred of foreigners. Indian nationalism was also liberal and secular. It was this aspect which enabled the participation of British officers like Allen Octavian Hume and William Wedderburn as well as the British missionaries on the Indian side in the anti-colonial struggle. There were a few anti-liberal, anti-reformist Hindu nationalist leaders who tried unsuccessfully to capture the Indian National Congress. It was primarily this group that looked to Europe, and Mussolini, the fascist leader of Italy, for support and inspiration.[12] The liberal Congress leaders were also aware of internal contradictions like gender and caste disabilities as well as feudal oppression of the peasantry. Gopal Krishna Gokhale insisted that Indian nationalism 'would oppose tyranny and injustice by even native tyrants with the same vehemence as injustice by foreigners'.[13] Indian nationalism was essentially a fight against tyranny, both internal and external.

10. The Deccan Sabha Circular dated 4 November 1896. See *The Deccan Sabha Papers*, Nehru Memorial Museum and Library.
11. L. V. Kaikini (ed.), *The Speeches and Writings of Sir Narayan G. Chandavarkar*, Bombay: MGPM, 1911, pp. 375–77.
12. Marzia Casolari, 'Hindutva's Foreign Tie-up in the 1930s Archival Evidence', *Economic and Political Weekly*, vol. 35, no. 4, 22 January 2000, pp. 218–28.
13. Gokhale's speech in Parimala V. Rao, *Foundations of Tilak's Nationalism: Discrimination, Education and Hindutva*, New Delhi: Orient BlackSwan, 2011, p. 297.

Martin Carnoy in *Education as Cultural Imperialism* further constructs the story of perpetual division of the coloniser-colonised based on European/non-European dichotomies. He argues that it is 'colonised knowledge' which perpetuates 'the myth' that 'schooling has served the poor to succeed'.[14] He further argues that,

> the farmer's or artisan's son who gets some schooling and then goes to work in the factory has available to him goods that were not available on the farm or village: lots of people, movies, modern clothes, and the very small possibility of getting a high-paying job. But the son also gives up control over his own time and the social conditions that surround him.... [T]he son, thanks to his schooling and migration to the city, has increased his choice of some goods but has also become dependent on working and social condition set by others and out of his control.[15]

Such an idyllic construct of a rural society is far from reality. In a highly stratified caste society like that of India, has any untouchable, marginalised peasant, agricultural labourer or artisan in a village control over his own time? And more importantly, would he like to live in perpetuity in such degrading social and economic conditions that surround him? The answer is an emphatic 'No'. Two papers by Eleanor Zelliot and Laura Dudley Jenkins in this volume completely refute such arguments.

Carnoy thus begins the analysis of Indian education: '[I]n the mercantile period of European imperialism (1500 to 1780), ... the British East India Company created Moslem colleges to elicit the cooperation of the Moslem elite. The colleges were then used to develop elites loyal to European values and norms.'[16] He also states that, 'the Indian society in the sixteenth century was headed by the Moslem absolute monarchy of the Moghul empire'.[17] This introduction is not the place to debate the nature of Mughal polity; however, considering the Mughal emperor to be the leader of Indian

14. Martin Carnoy, *Education as Cultural Imperialism*, New York: Longman, 1974, p. 3.
15. Ibid., p. 14.
16. Ibid., pp. 21–22.
17. Ibid., p. 84.

society is too far-fetched. Also, the East India Company did not set up any Muslim college until 1780. The first Muslim college, the Calcutta Madrassa, was established by Warren Hastings in 1781. Carnoy argues that 'Hastings actively encouraged Brahminism as a means of breaking the Moghul power' and founded the Calcutta Madrassa as 'he was incurring hostility from the Moslem community and this was one way of conciliating them'.[18] None of these grand statements are backed up by sources. Moreover, what is forgotten here is that Hastings was a scholar of Persian literature; he was unsuccessful in his earlier attempts to establish a professorship of Persian at Oxford. As governor-general of India, he did the next best thing, i.e., establish a great institution to teach Persian literature along with Arabic at Calcutta. Hastings also encouraged British officers to 'learn Indian languages and study its literature'. When Charles Wilkins translated Bhagavadgita, Hastings commented that 'such works would live when the British domain in India has long ceased to exist'.[19] Hastings' Madrassa, Wilkins' Bhagavadita and other such efforts earned the Company the goodwill of Indians. The motive for undertaking such ventures, however, was not just *realpolitik* but also a genuine appreciation of non-European literature by the Europeans.

Carnoy makes an attempt to prove that British administration succeeded in enforcing cultural imperialism through the missionaries. He argues that

> [U]nder the military protection of the company, missionaries could get to know a geographic area more intimately and provide essential information about the social structure, culture and economic production, and trading habits of the people. They helped to legitimate foreign presence among the natives by demonstrating the superiority of Christianity.... [C]ommitting resources, manpower, and energy to seizing new lands and building trading operations overseas was not possible without the ideology of the 'white man's burden' and it is missionaries and their reformist zeal most of all that confirmed this ideology.[20]

18. Ibid., p. 94.
19. Michael Edwards, *Warren Hastings: King of Nabobs*, London: Hart-Davis, MacGibben, 1976, p. 152.
20. Carnoy, *Education as Cultural Imperialism*, p. 88–89.

The idea of the 'White Man's Burden' was promoted and popularised by Rudyard Kipling through his similarly titled poem written in 1899. By 1860 the British expansion in India was complete. Carnoy uses the White Man's Burden as a motivating factor for British expansion in the eighteenth century, a century before it was even conceptualised. Contrary to Carnoy's assumption, missionaries often fought for the rights of the local population from the very beginning. Rev. V. Taylor, after witnessing the execution of a Kannada peasant in Dharwar district, fought for the recognition of Kannada as a court language in the Bombay Presidency in 1836. This entirely Kannada-speaking district had Marathi village and district officers due to the pre-colonial Peshwa rule. The system was continued under the colonial rule. The execution took place because the peasant charged with murder had given his testimonial in Kannada, which was recorded in Marathi by the native official, and the court proceeding was conducted in Hindustani. The prisoner, ignorant of both Marathi and Hindustani, unwillingly expressed assent to the confession. There was no circumstantial evidence against him. He was charged with murder and later executed. Taylor effectively fought for the introduction of Kannada as the language of administration and education. Within six months Kannada, was made a court language and twenty-seven Kannada primary schools were established in the district.[21]

The British government in India often treated missionaries with suspicion. In 1860, Dinabandhu Mitra wrote a Bengali play *Nil Darpan* ('Blue Mirror') which depicted the plight of the indigo peasants. It squarely accused the British indigo planters and Indian factory managers for the miseries of the peasantry. The play was performed to packed houses. Although it was just two years after the Revolt of 1857–58, the government did not object. Rev. James Long got it translated into English and published it. Immediately, the government imposed a fine on Long and imprisoned him.[22] The reason for quoting this example amidst numerous others is that

21. R. V. Parulekar, *Selections from Educational Records (Bombay), Part III: 1826–1840*, Bombay: Asia Publication House, 1957, pp. 48–50.
22. Home/Public, 8 August 1861, nos. 34–37 A.

most of the missionaries belonged to Protestant Dissenter groups like Baptists; so, an extension of conflict in England could easily be cited for such an action. Long was an Anglican missionary, the denomination to which most of the British ruling classes belonged to in India. In spite of this, the government prosecuted Long who had committed no crime. This clearly shows how the British government in India treated the missionaries. There were a few British officers who supported the missionaries in their individual capacity; but mostly they were warned and transferred by the government.[23] Hayden Bellenoit's paper in this volume emphasises that missionaries often identified with Indian socio-political realities, while they were opposed to policies of the colonial state. They also took part in India's freedom struggle against British rule.

Carnoy further argues that 'as the English found their way towards absolute power in the nineteenth century, they founded the Anglo-Indian Vidyala College in 1816'.[24] The Vidyalaya ('abode of knowledge') or the Hindu College (as called by the British) was not founded by the British at all. The people of Calcutta, both rich and poor, contributed Rs. 113,179 towards the establishment this college to teach English and modern sciences to boys of that city.[25] The amount collected was more than the East India Company's annual educational budget for India at that time. This was the first institution established in Asia to teach modern subjects, and the founders included both radical reformers like Rammohan Roy and extreme orthodox Hindus like Radha Kanta Deb. In the debates on the inhuman practice of *sati*, Roy advocated its abolition, while Deb defended it as an essential part of Hindu tradition. However, both joined hands to raise funds to establish this modern institution. The Vidyalaya taught 'Shakespeare, Milton, Bacon, Byron, Pope, Scott, and Homer's *Iliad* in English literature, Bengali grammar, prose and translation, Euclid, algebra, differential and integral calculus, and trigonometry in mathematics, astronomy, Adam

23. Minute by J. P. Grant dated 19 June 1861, Home/Public 28 June 1861, nos. 103–05.
24. Carnoy, *Education as Cultural Imperialism,* p. 98.
25. Board's Collections, 1828–1829, vol. 1015, p. 451, India Office Records, London.

Smith's *Wealth of Nations*, works of Jeremy Bentham, David Hume, John Locke, histories of India, Greece and Rome and England'. The administrative and the academic structure, standard of instruction, curriculum and examination pattern of the Vidyalaya remained a model for other colleges established in nineteenth-century India.[26] Without acknowledging these developments, Carnoy states that

> by the 1820s, the policy of cultural conquest was already bearing fruit in the person of Raja Rammohan Roy, a beef-eating Brahmin ... to create a class of cheaply paid but loyal Indian low-level bureaucrats ... Malcolm's successor Lord Clare set up an English college in Boodwar Palace (Poona) in 1833 and called it Elphinstone college.[27]

Comments on Roy belong to the realm of polemical pamphleteering rather than serious social science work. Also, by making such sensational comments one cannot draw the scholar's attention away from the factual errors that this book abounds with. Clare did not establish Elphinstone College, it was done by the people of Bombay Presidency who collected Rs. 226,172 to establish a modern institution in 1827. The Directors of the East India Company contributed an equal sum, and the Elphinstone College was established in 1835 in Bombay, not Poona. Clare instituted eighteen scholarships to enable poor students to pursue their studies in this institution. The institution that Carnoy refers to was the Sanskrit College established in 1821 by Elphinstone in Poona. The graduates of Elphinstone College with sound knowledge of 'differential and integral Calculus, Dynamics, Mechanics, trigonometry' could not be appointed as low-level bureaucrats.[28] Many graduates of Elphinstone College like K. T. Telang, M. G. Ranade and N. G. Chandavarkar went on to become judges of the Bombay High Court, and Dadabhai Naoroji became a member of the British Parliament. The low-level bureaucratic positions required little English and a thorough

26. General Committee of Public Instruction Regulation for Schools and Colleges dated 30 August 1840, *GCPI Correspondence and Proceedings*, vol. V.
27. Carnoy, *Education as Cultural Imperialism*, p. 99.
28. General Department/Education, 1839, no. 485, Maharashtra State Archives.

knowledge of vernacular languages and these positions were filled by students of vernacular schools.[29] Finally, Carnoy states that the purpose of colonial education system was to give

> some sense of vocabulary as used in law and administration. More importantly it instilled in them a respect and awe for the aristocratic virtues of the majestic English language and culture, and a corresponding contempt and disdain for their own background. Even today it is very difficult for educated Indians to break this pattern. They feel much closer bonds with British professors than with Hindu peasants, to whom they are unable even to speak.[30]

Contrary to this notion, the colonial system of education over-emphasised the importance of Hindu and Islamic traditions, and used texts like *Hitopadesa, Ramcharitmanas, Prem Sagar, Mufid-ul-Mubtidi, Daira-i-Ilm, Amud Namah, Hqquik-ul-moujudat,* and other similar books as main texts for teaching in schools.[31] Without having a clue as to what was happening in the field of education, sweeping statements on Indian students and British professors was unfortunate. Do the American students feel close to the American peasantry or British professors in their respective discipline? Students and peasants do not have a closer bond because the academics are generally as ignorant of agricultural operations as peasants are of academic debates. Normally, academics and peasants do not share a common knowledge domain to discuss anything unless one is an agricultural scientist or an activist.

Gauri Viswanathan, in *Masks of Conquest: Literary Study and British Rule in India,* attempts to apply Edward Said's thesis of orientalism to Indian history. She quotes 'T. B. Macaulay's speeches in the House of Commons dated 2 February 1835', and advises that 'this speech should not be confused with the better known minute of

29. Minute by J. P. Willoughby dated 12 January 1850, *Report of the Board of Education 1850,* p. 136
30. Carnoy, *Education as Cultural Imperialism,* p. 101.
31. Home/Education, 1869, A, nos. 3–5. Spelling of book titles used here are as mentioned in the files. Titles of the published books vary a little.

July 1835'.[32] On 2 February 1835, Macaulay was not in London, but in Calcutta, presiding over a meeting of the General Committee of Public Instruction (often wrongly referred to in the book as General Counsel of Public Instruction). This introduction does not intend to concentrate on this or similar errors, as there are possibilities of such errors creeping into a text at any stage of book production. It will simply limit itself to pointing out any misrepresentation of facts. For example, Viswanathan argues that

> English Literary text, functioning as a surrogate Englishman in his highest and most perfect state, becomes a mask for economic exploitation, so successfully camouflaging the material activities of the colonizer ... the British administrators in India were not sufficiently responsive to Indian languages and Indian tradition.[33]

The fact is that the British officers were proficient in Indian languages. They had to pass both the oral and written examinations, including translation from English to vernacular and vice versa within seven years of their appointment, after which they were not allowed to appear for these examinations and removed from service. The examinations were held on the first Monday in January and July. An officer was rarely given a third chance to pass. The officers posted in Bengal had to master three difficult texts—*Dasakumaracharita*, *Mahabharata* and *Prabodh Chandrika*. The system was even tougher under the rule of the East India Company when they had to master a classical language like Sanskrit, Arabic or Persian and a vernacular like Bengali, Marathi, and so on.[34] Even Charles Trevelyan, a staunch opponent of the Orientalists, was a gold medallist in Sanskrit

32. Gauri Viswanathan, *Masks of Conquest: Literary Study and British Rule in India*, London: Faber and Faber, 1990, p. 172. Viswanathan refers to John Malcolm as having an aristocratic background and harbouring feudal beliefs, (p. 32). Malcolm was the son of a sheep farmer in Scotland. See Jack Harrington, *Sir John Malcolm and the Creation of British India*, New York: Palgrave Macmillan, 2010, pp. 15–17.
33. Ibid., pp. 20, 28.
34. Rules for passing native languages, Home/Education 1871, nos. 2–3.

literature at Haileybury College. Yet, as he was posted in Delhi, he had to master both Persian and Hindi to remain in service.[35]

Viswanathan repeatedly refers to the Government of India Resolution of 1835 (also known as 'Bentinck's Resolution') as 'the English Education Act, which officially required the Natives of India to submit to the study of English literature, irrevocably altering the direction of Indian education'.[36] By doing so, an image is created that there was an Act which coerced Indians to study English. Let us not suspect, even for a minute, the might of the East India Company until 1857 or the British crown after that to enforce its will; it was enormous. So, how can one explain the fact that in 1881–82, i.e., after forty-six years of this apparent 'Act' was in force, the government schools had only 65,645 students studying English out of a population of 202,604,080? William Hunter, the chairman of the Indian Education Commission, thought that even this was a large number, and suggested to the provincial governments to encourage 'more vernacular schools for sound education'.[37] Even this number appears to be exaggerated as all high schools were recorded as English-teaching schools. In Punjab and North-Western Provinces and Oudh, most of the *zilla* schools did not teach English, and these schools were enumerated under the category of high schools.[38]

The Government of India Resolution of 1835 was not an Act. It suggested that a major portion of the government funds should be spent on the encouragement of the study of English. Neither Macaulay's Minute of 2 February 1835, nor the Government of India Resolution of 7 March 1835, had any support from the British officers in India. Within a few months of this resolution, John Elphinstone the governor of Madras abolished eighty English schools, and for the

35. Katherine Prior, Lance Brennan and Robin Haines, 'Bad Language: The Role of English, Persian and Other Esoteric Tongues in the Dismissal of Sir Edward Colebrooke as Resident of Delhi in 1829, ' *Modern Asian Studies*, vol. 35, no. 1, February 2001, pp. 75–112.
36. Viswanathan, *Masks of Conquest*, p. 41.
37. *The Report of the Indian Education Commission*, Calcutta: Superintendent of Government Printing, 1882, pp. x–xi, 220.
38. Home/Education 1871, 14 January 1871, nos. 1–4.

next seventeen years there were no government English schools in the presidency. The lone English school was the Pachaiyappa School established by Indians in Madras. In 1839, a petition signed by 70,000 persons promising financial support if these schools were reopened was summarily rejected. In north India, soon after the departure of Macaulay, every English school established by him was closed down.[39] The schools in the Bombay Presidency survived only because the President of the Board of Education Erskine Perry threatened to resign if the schools were closed down.[40] So, Viswanathan's claim that after 'the 1835 Act', the Natives of India had to submit to the study of English literature does not hold very true.

Viswanathan also misrepresents the concept of 'English education' which comprised the study of 'modern sciences, mathematics, political economy, geography, and history through English as a medium of instruction and English literature', as 'English studies' or 'English literature'. By doing so, she constructs an image of the colonial state as one that introduced *only* English literature. She calls 'the English Studies' 'Arnoldian' and argues that

> [I]n England, [the] Arnoldian curriculum was meant for the ruling elite, the texts that were a part of it were also taught in India.... [The] Arnoldian curriculum was adopted in India in such a way that the goal of self-improvement in this context no longer meant training a ruling elite but setting educated Indians' attention on reform of their own society, a goal repeatedly articulated by Duff in his own educational writings.[41]

How far is it correct to describe a curriculum comprising the study of Bacon, Milton, Shakespeare and Homer as Arnoldian? Thomas Arnold began his educational reforms at Rugby School from 1828 onwards, while in 1817, Rammohan Roy introduced 'Bacon,

39. Parimala V. Rao, 'Promiscuous Crowd of English Smatterers': The 'Poor' in the Colonial and Nationalist Discourse on Education in India, 1835–1912, ' *Contemporary Education Dialogue*, vol. 10, no. 2, July 2013, p. 232.
40. E. Perry to the Governor dated 21 August 1848, *Report of the Board of Education, 1848*, pp. 76–84.
41. Viswanathan, *Masks of Conquest*, pp. 56–57.

Milton, Shakespeare and Homer along with histories of Europe and India, geography, arithmetic, natural philosophy, geometry'.[42] Roy was very particular about Indian students studying Bacon, and he classified knowledge as 'pre-Baconian and Baconian'.[43] Therefore, is it plausible to term the curriculum as 'Royian'? No. Roy understood the importance of these texts for Indian students in 1817, just as Arnold did for British students a decade later. The idea of 'setting the educated Indians' attention on reform of their own society' was begun by Roy as early as 1814, i.e., sixteen years before Duff arrived in India.[44] So, the agenda of encouraging the educated to take up social reform was not a missionary agenda. The social reformers and the missionaries did, however, help each other in breaking down gender and caste inequalities. The best example is the friendship between William Adam, Rammohan Roy and Alexander Duff. In spite of such examples, Viswanathan denies that there existed cooperation and understanding between the missionaries and Indians. She states that

> [T]he parents were affected by the 'tyranny of the Bible' ... '[L]et Duff Saheb do what he can', was Lal Behari Dey's father's defiant challenge to the threat of proselytism. But Duff Saheb was a little more devious than even Dey's father imagined.[45]

The actual statement of Dey's father was thus

> [I]f it be written on my son's forehead that he will not become Christian, then he will not become Christian, let Duff Saheb do what he can, but if it be written on my son's forehead that he will become a Christian, then he will become Christian, do what I can.[46]

42. *Report of the General Committee of Public Instruction of the Presidency of Fort William in Bengal, 1841*, pp. 1–20.
43. Letter from Rammohan Roy, dated 11 December 1823, in M. R. Paranjape, *A Sourcebook of Modern Indian Education, 1797–1902*, London: Macmillan, 1938, p. 10.
44. See Bhagaban Prasad Majumdar, *First Fruits of English Education*, Calcutta: Bookland, 1973.
45. Viswanathan, *Masks of Conquest,* p. 58.
46. Lal Behari Dey, *Recollections of Alexander Duff*, London: T. Nelson and Sons, 1879, p. 47.

This was not a threat, but a resignation to fate—a very typical culturally-conditioned Hindu behaviour. Indians were not averse to the study of the Bible. Lal Behari Dey gives the example of a Brahman well-versed in Hindu scriptures and the Bible, alongside a familiarity with the Koran, who would attend Sunday lectures at Duff's school, and whose discussions with missionary teachers, including Duff, would go on till eleven o' clock at night.[47] Duff did not know any Indian language, thereby indicative of the fact that the discussions must have taken place in English. Reports that the people were ready to study the Bible as a means of learning English were common in the early years of the nineteenth century.[48] In Bombay Presidency, even in the remote villages, people were not averse to sending their children to schools where the Bible was a part of the curriculum. The officials attributed it to 'the easy tolerant spirit of Hindooism ... to use even our religious books for their children'.[49] This was not limited to Hindus; Muslims too were equally enthusiastic in pursuing modern education. The first native boy to enter the Bombay Education Society School, where the Bible was a major element of the curriculum, was a Muslim.[50] Therefore, the missionaries and the colonial state did not have to, as claimed by Viswanathan, trick the Indians to study 'animated, vivified, hallowed, and baptized', English literature.[51]

Viswanathan also argues that 'in 1844, Lord Hardinge passed a resolution assuring preference in the selection for public office for Indians who had distinguished themselves in European literature. With this act, he gave literary study a material and worldly motive that set the general aim of the intellectual and moral improvement of the subject population in a wholly new perspective.'[52] Governor-General

47. Ibid., pp. 142–43.
48. 'The Hindu Character', *Asiatic Journal*, 1828, p. 697.
49. John A. Dunlop to the Secretary to the government dated 14 September 1824, General Department, 13 of 1824, Maharashtra State Archives.
50. *First Annual Report of the Bombay Education Society*, Bombay: Samuel Rans, 1816, p. 14.
51. Viswanathan, *Masks of Conquest,* p. 80.
52. Ibid., p. 89.

Hardinge was opposed to English education. He abolished English schools established by Macaulay, and established 101 vernacular schools. These schools retained the pre-colonial curriculum of Bengali and arithmetic, and added the history of India and England.[53] Parents refused to send their children to these schools. All of them had to be closed down due to lack of students. In a resolution of 10 October 1844, Hardinge asked the English schools to forward a list of all those who had passed the Senior Scholarship Examination to the Council of Education. The list was to be circulated to the heads of the departments for future appointments.[54] The subjects for the Senior Scholarship Examination comprised not just English literature, as claimed by Viswanathan, but also 'a sound knowledge of vernacular, higher mathematics, modern sciences, political economy, world geography and histories of various countries'. This resolution was opposed by the Court of Directors who argued that appointments for public office required not 'high scholastic knowledge' but 'only a moderate knowledge of English, with a thorough command of the vernacular language and testimonials of regularity, steadiness, diligence, and good conduct'.[55] Thereafter, the Hardinge Resolution which had upheld merit and competition was effectively abandoned in favour of patronage.

Viswanathan, states that 'a thorough study of English was within the reach of only a very small proportion of Indians. What distinguished this group of people from the masses was the amount of leisure time they possessed.'[56] This was true of England, but not of India. The learned men in India often belonged to poor families, and were thereby part of the masses. The elites and landed gentry seldom

53. Extract from the reports for 1840–42 on the subject of preparing a series of vernacular class books, J. A. Richey, *Selections from the Educational Records, Part II 1840–1859*, Calcutta: Superintendent of Government Printing, 1922, p. 80.
54. Ibid., Resolution of the Government of India dated 10 October 1844, pp. 90–91.
55. Ibid., Despatch from the Court of Directors dated 12 May 1847, pp. 91–92.
56. Viswanathan, *Masks of Conquest,* p. 116.

took to education.[57] Lal Behari Dey wrote thus of the students of Sanskrit of the early nineteenth century: '[T]he students of Sanskrit schools, who live upon rice and herbs and at the same time discuss the abstruse logical doctrines of the philosopher Gotama. The latchets of the shoes of these lovers of knowledge I am not worthy to unloose.'[58] The same thing continued in the field of modern education. In 1881–82, Calcutta had 1870 college students, of whom only 150 came from affluent backgrounds, while the rest were from poor families. Many of them actually lived from hand to mouth. In Bombay Presidency, the sight of Brahman students studying under streetlights was very common.[59] Thus, most of the English-educated Indians who formed the new middle class came from either poor or extremely poor backgrounds, and were not those who possessed leisure.

The theories mooted by Martin Carnoy and Gauri Viswanathan and historical facts do not go together. During the first seventy-eight years of their rule, the British did not establish any English school, but set up institutions teaching Arabic, Persian and Sanskrit. English classes were added to these institutions after a long struggle by liberal British officers and Indians.[60] The state was well aware of the fact that the introduction of English would allow Indians to have access to

57. See Rao, 'Promiscuous Crowd of English Smatterers'.
58. Dey, *Recollections of Alexander Duff*, p. 87. Gautama was a philosopher who lived during the first century CE. He wrote the Sanskrit text *Nyaya Sutra* on logic, which explores sources of knowledge and is one of the six important branches of Hindu philosophy. The other five are *Samkhya* (atheistic school), *Yoga* (meditation), *Vaisheshika* (an empiricist school), and the two orthodox schools called *Purva Mimamsa* and *Uttara Mimamsa*.
59. McCully, *English Education and the Origins of Indian Nationalism*, p. 187.
60. Here, the schools established by Thomas Munro in Madras Presidency and the lone English school in Bombay Presidency have not been taken into account for the reason that they were established in opposition to colonial state's policy. For Elphinstone's persistent attempts to close down the school in Bombay Presidency and the official opposition Munro's schools in Madras, see Rao, 'Promiscuous Crowd of English Smatterers', pp. 231–32.

radical European literature which would undermine its position. The sight of the students of the Vidyalaya buying up a sizeable portion of Thomas Paine's *Age of Reason* when it reached the shores of Calcutta, [61] must have unnerved most of the British officials. Such anxieties were well summed up by the governor of Bombay Presidency, Mountstuart Elphinstone, when he said that 'to educate the natives is our highroad back to Europe'.[62] Every English school during this period was established by Indians, often supported by a few liberal British officers in their individual capacity and missionaries. These schools did not impart a limited knowledge of English to enable Indians to secure low-level clerical jobs as assumed by many writers, but introduced entire European curricula comprising higher mathematics, sciences, English literature and radical philosophy. So, can it be said that English education instead of being a 'mask of conquest, ' was actually a 'mask of resistance'? No. Tempting though it may be, such tall claims cannot be made for the simple reason that historical developments are complex, and common people making rational choices do not allow such assumptions. When two cultures come together voluntarily or involuntarily, conquest and resistance are not the only two factors that determine interaction. Common people are open-minded and are 'ready to assimilate anything useful that came from anywhere'. Towards the end of the revolt of 1857, Henry Woodrow the inspector of schools reported, 'our schools are absolutely the most popular of all the institutions in which government has any share. The police are detested, the courts hated, and the survey dreaded'.[63] Similarly, violin is a European instrument which was adopted by musicians of south India to play the sacred Carnatic music in Hindu temples. Today, it is impossible to even imagine Carnatic music without violin. These were done without

61. Elmer H. Cutts, The Background of Macaulay's Minute, *The American Historical Review*, vol. 58, no. 4, July 1953, pp. 828.
62. Kenneth Ballhatchet, *Social Policy and Social Change in Western India, 1817–1830*, London: Oxford University Press, 1961, p. 249.
63. Hobsbawm, *On History*, p. 220. Henry Woodrow, the inspector of schools to N. Lees, the officiating Director of Public Instruction, dated 24 August 1859, Home/Education, 17 September 1859, nos 5–7.

any cultural or imperial imposition. So people simply take what they want and reject what they do not want.

During British rule, Indians did not aspire for just a working knowledge of English which would enable them to get suitable jobs under the new regime, but new knowledge. Indians clearly envisioned new knowledge as an addition to their existing stock of knowledge. People who had studied various Indian philosophies ranging from atheism to monotheism in pre-colonial Sanskrit schools could easily show enthusiasm for engaging with modern philosophies of the West, while those who had read Sanskrit and Persian literature could easily appreciate Homer and Milton. Carnoy himself quotes Governor-General Hardinge's statement in 1844, that 'boys of 15 years of age, black in colour, recite the most favourite passages from Shakespeare, ably quoting the notes of the English and German commentators'.[64] This happened because the boys were often reciting passages from the *Mahabharata* in the pre-colonial *pathasala*s (schools) of Bengal. Even the village schoolboys who had studied arithmetic up to long division and knew how to calculate compound interest easily took to Euclid and algebra.[65] The senior students of the Vidyalaya could easily compare Pope and Dryden and Homer's *Iliad* and Virgil's *Aeneid*, and were well-versed in integral calculus and spherical trigonometry.[66]

In 1816, the chief justice of the Supreme Court in Calcutta 'was struck by the enthusiasm of the prominent pundits, Sanskrit scholars, for the introduction of Western literature and sciences'.[67] Charles Trevelyan noticed that, 'the steam boats passing up and down the Ganges are boarded by native boys, begging not for money but for

64. Carnoy, *Education as Cultural Imperialism,* p. 101.
65. For the curriculum of pre-colonial schools see, A. N. Basu (ed.), *William Adam, Reports on the State of Education in Bengal: 1835 and 1838*, Calcutta: University of Calcutta, 1941, R. V. Parulekar, *Survey of Indigenous Education in the Province of Bombay: 1820–1830*, Bombay: Asia Publishing House, 1951.
66. *Report of the General Committee of Public Instruction of the Presidency of Fort William in Bengal, 1841*, pp. 1–20.
67. David Kopf, *British Orientalism and Bengal Renaissance: The Dynamics of Indian Modernisation, 1773–1835*, Berkeley: University of California Press, 1960, p. 182.

books'.[68] So, rupture between the pre-colonial and colonial education concerned structure, and not essence. Colonial schools with dedicated schoolhouses, blackboards, writing paper and trained teachers represented structural changes; but appreciation of knowledge was a continuation of the pre-existing intellectual curiosity. If Indians only aspired for jobs under the new regime, they could simply have learnt English as a language, and not bothered to study the difficult and challenging ideas of integral calculus, and trigonometry. This shows intellectual aspirations, and not just economic ones. Almost two centuries later, a similar situation persists. In January 2012, the Critical Study Team for Secondary Education appointed by the Government of Karnataka visited Shiva Kumar Swamiji, a 105-year-old Sanskrit scholar and highly respected religious leader. The reason behind the visit was the fact that he runs a modern educational institution where the poor receive free education. Swamiji complained that in the past thirty years educational standards have fallen, particularly in science and mathematics. He said: 'Earlier there used to be 28–29 theorems in geometry, now there are only 4–5. The standard of education has really gone down.'[69] Why would a traditional Sanskrit scholar and a Hindu religious head care for theorems in geometry? It is because even to an orthodox Hindu it is immaterial where knowledge has been created, India or Europe. To a real scholar, knowledge has no geographical boundaries.

The nationalist writings on the history of education continue to emphasise the difference between European and Indian, and traditional and modern education. Krishna Kumar's *Political Agenda of Education* portrays the nationalist worldview. The entire book is an attempt to construct a history to arrive at a grand justification for the Gandhian educational programme. To achieve this end, he analyses four important aspects of education—state policy, differences in educational traditions of India and Europe, changes brought in by colonial policies, and the position of teachers. He begins by arguing that the colonial state attempted to construct the 'colonial citizen' by

68. Charles E. Trevelyan, *On the Education of the People of India*, London: Longman, Orme, Brown, Green and Longman, 1838, pp. 166–67.
69. Author's interview of the Critical Study Team on 5 February 2012 at Shikshakara Sadana in Bangalore.

emphasising on the moral role of education. The example given in this context is a minute of 1811 by Governor-General Minto.[70]

There are three problems with this. Firstly, the concept of the 'citizen' as having 'individual rights, civic equality and national identity',[71] was popularised by the French revolutionaries after the French Revolution of 1789. In 1811, when the British were still fighting wars against Napoleon in Europe, and a possible Jacobin influence in India,[72] could the colonial state have used this concept to define or even imagine its subject population? In Britain, those who campaigned for political and educational reforms at that time 'were dubbed English Jacobins, tarred with the brush of the hated extremist French Republican creed'. Britain itself was 'developing [a] notion of "Britishness" citizenship equated with national cohesion during Napoleonic wars'.[73]

Secondly, until the end of the term of Governor-General Warren Hastings, Indians held respectable positions in the East India Company. His aristocratic successors like Cornwallis and Wellesley declared that both Hindus and Muslims were 'corrupt and immoral', and dismissed them from all positions of responsibility in administration. They justified British rule as 'a moral, civilizing mission'.[74] Minto's minute which explicitly states 'the prevalence of the crimes of perjury and forgery ... in both the Mohomedans and Hindoos to the want of due instruction in the moral and religious tenets of their respective faiths', was a continuation of this 'moral civilising mission'. Kumar says that in this minute, 'Minto was talking about the moral role of education in the context of civil administration'. Viewing Minto's comments in this light also means

70. Krishna Kumar, *Political Agenda of Education: A Study of Colonialist and Nationalist Ideas*, New Delhi: Sage, 1991, p. 27.
71. Anupama Roy, *Gendered Citizenship: Historical and Conceptual Explorations*, New Delhi: Orient Longman, 2005, p. 13
72. Kopf, *British Orientalism and Bengal Renaissance*, pp. 45–48.
73. Derek Heater, *Citizenship in Britain: A History*, Edinburgh: Edinburgh University Press, 2006, pp. 80–81.
74. Thomas R. Metcalf, *Ideologies of the Raj*, Cambridge University Press, Cambridge, 1995, p. 24.

accepting the idea that Hindus and Muslims were essentially corrupt and immoral, and British rule as a civilising mission.

Finally, Minto was a student of the Scottish philosopher, David Hume. Instead of introducing the rationalist ideas of Hume, Minto's minute was a justification for his attempt to establish two Sanskrit schools at Nabadwip and Tirhoot. Sanskrit education in the nineteenth century was limited to Brahman men who constituted around 1.97 per cent of India's population.[75] Religion forbade the imparting of Sanskrit knowledge to all women and non-Brahman castes, and even Brahman men were not permitted to share it with others. How could colonial citizenship have been built by encouraging the education of such a small section of the population? The notion of the 'colonial citizen' came to be recognised only towards the end of the nineteenth century.[76]

To argue the difference between Indian and European thinking, Kumar quotes a statement by William Arnold, the Director of Public Instruction of Punjab: '[W]e found a population with their own idea of the meaning of education, and to that idea thoroughly attached; and to whom our idea of education, being inconsistent with their own, was thoroughly distasteful; as to an Asiatic everything is distasteful which is new.' Kumar points out the 'inconsistency' Arnold noticed between the Indian and English concepts of education by using examples of post-Reformation Europe and its insistence on texts in direct contrast to Indian reliance on oral tradition.[77] In India, the oral tradition was predominantly Vedic, while both the heterodox Jaina and Buddhist traditions were essentially written ones. At the beginning of the nineteenth century, all major Indian languages had their own distinctive scripts, and these scripts were taught in every pre-colonial school. This denotes that the written tradition was equally strong. There were numerous requests from Punjab for the establishment of schools as early as 1830, much before

75. Aparna Basu, *The Growth of Education and Political Development in India, 1898–1920*, Delhi: Oxford University Press, 1974, p. 123.
76. Sukanya Bannerjee, *Becoming Imperial Citizen: Indians in the Late-Victorian Empire*, Durham and London: Duke University Press, 2010, p. 4.
77. Kumar, *Political Agenda*, pp. 50–55.

the British annexation of Punjab.[78] So, it was not the difference between the two systems of education, but the high-handedness of Arnold in introducing Urdu as the official language and the medium of instruction which caused much resentment among the Hindus, Sikhs and Muslims of Punjab. It was not opposition to the teaching of geography and mathematics, but the loss of jobs faced by the teachers. In other parts of India, Marathi, Tamil and Bengali indigenous teachers were provided some training and appointed to new vernacular schools established by the colonial state. In Punjab, it could not be done as Urdu was unknown to teachers from all the three communities. Even teachers of Arabic and Persian, more likely to be comfortable with Urdu due to its script, looked down upon Urdu. Arnold himself admitted in his Second Report that 'Urdu is offensive to a learned Arabic scholar'.[79] Thus, it is not, as Kumar says, that 'written language invites contention';[80] it is the script in which it is written and how people view it that is significant. Mahima Manchanda and Preeti's essays in this volume show the effects of the educational policy pursued by Arnold.

Kumar also argues that English was first mastered by the Brahmans of Bengal, Maharashtra and Madras. Enrolment data for schools and colleges, as well as the list of teachers for the 1840s, reveal that Baidyas and Kayasthas in Bengal (notwithstanding the examples of Rammohan Roy and Dwarakanath Tagore); Kayasthas and Rajputs in Delhi and Agra; Modaliyars, Pillays and the artisanal castes in Madras, and Prabhus, goldsmiths and coppersmiths in Bombay were the first to take to English education. Most of the prizes in the Vidyalaya in Calcutta and Elphinstone College in Bombay were won by non-Brahmans.[81] Brahmans dominated only the Sanskrit colleges

78. Trevelyan, *On the Education of the People of India*, pp. 166–67.
79. Arnold's Second Report dated 25 June 1858, J. A. Richey, *Selections from Educational Records, 1840–1859*, Calcutta: Superintendent of Government Printing, 1922, pp. 300–303
80. Krishna Kumar, *Political Agenda*, p. 52.
81. For Statistics on Madras see *Public Consultations 1840*, Tamil Nadu State Archives, for Elphinstone College enrolment see, *Report of the Board of Education for the years 1840*, Maharashtra State Archives, for Bengal see, *Report of the General Committee of Public Instruction of*

at Banaras, Calcutta, Poona and Madras. However, they were the far behind others in English education. Brahmans came to dominate English education in Bombay and Madras by the 1870s, while they continued to lag behind the Kayasthas, Baidyas, Rajputs and Khatris in Bengal and North India, even at the end of the nineteenth century.[82] Regarding the position of teachers, Kumar argues that in pre-colonial India

> ... the teacher was remunerated by the community he served. Under the new system, he became a paid servant of the colonial government. This switching over of the teacher from the charge of the local population to that of the government triggered a process of estrangement of the school from the local community.[83]

This presupposes that in pre-colonial India, every village had a school just as every village had a potter or an ironsmith. Nadia district of Bengal, renowned for its Sanskrit schools, did not have vernacular schools in its 5,749 villages. In an educationally advanced district like South Konkan (Ratnagiri) in Maharashtra, only eighty-six of its 2,240 villages had schools. Vernacular teachers were not servants of the village community. They were not assigned a share of the village produce like the potter or blacksmith. They had an independent vocation and taught in return for a fixed sum paid every month (the Hindu month calculated from full moon to full moon). They were paid in both cash and kind by the parents of the boys who studied under him. In Bengal, parents paid 2–8 annas per month and gave food articles for a day's requirement, while in Bombay Presidency, it was 1 anna per month with some gifts. In Madras, the fee was higher, and the teachers were paid 6–8 annas. Many teachers taught deserving but poor children for free.[84] So, the vernacular teachers in pre-colonial India were not members of the village community

---

the Presidency of fort William in Bengal, 1840, for Delhi and Agra see General Report of Public Instruction in the North Western Province of the Bengal Presidency for 1843–44, West Bengal State Archives.

82. Aparna Basu, *The Growth of Education,* p. 152.
83. Krishna Kumar, *Political Agenda,* p. 48.
84. Minute by Thomas Munro dated 10 March 1826, *Madras Public Consultations.* One *anna* was 1/16th of a rupee.

but paid professionals. Parulekar explicitly states that 'the village community did not hire the teachers. They had no regular income. If the teacher found his income dwindling, he would move elsewhere and the school would close down.' He was paid only by the students whom he taught. The relationship between the teacher, student and his parents was entirely based on 'casual reciprocal advantages and would weaken or dissolve with slight disagreement between the two'.[85]

The position of the vernacular teachers in colonial India is contrasted by Kumar with the teachers mentioned in mythological texts composed approximately 2,000 years ago. The stories of 'the supremacy of the teacher and the modesty of the ideal disciple' in which there was 'total allegiance to authority, unquestioning obedience, capacity for enduring hardship and self-sacrifice' are up held by him. By arguing that in the Indian tradition the teacher 'was an object of worship, ' he stresses that 'the teacher inculcated these values by providing a figure of authority during the student's training'. Kumar cites the mythological stories of Upamanyu and Ekalavya to support his argument.[86] Upamanyu was deliberately starved by his teacher. Unable to bear the pangs of hunger, he ate poisonous berries and became blind. However, the teacher was pleased with Upamanyu's devotion and had his blindness cured. But the story does not say how psychologically scarred Upamanyu was after going through this ordeal, or how his parents felt betrayed by the breach of trust they had reposed in the teacher. Ekalavya was not even a student of Dronacharya; he had heard of his greatness, and made a statue of him and practiced archery before it. When Dronacharya saw the mastery Ekalavya had attained, he could not tolerate it and ended up demanding the thumb of his right hand as *gurudakshina* or payment for his teaching (or rather in this case, 'never teaching'). Due to the loss his thumb, Ekalavya, a passionate archer could never practice archery again. Upamanyu and Ekalavya were the victims of

85. See, R. V. Parulekar, *Survey of Indigenous Education in the Province of Bombay 1820–1830*, Bombay: Asia Publishing House, 1951, p. xviii; A. N. Basu, *Reports on the State of Education*, p. 21.
86. Kumar, *Political Agenda*, pp. 86–87.

egoistical and ruthless teachers. Kumar, emphasising the enormous power the teacher had on students in the Hindu tradition says that

> [In] the teaching of the fine arts, particularly music and dancing, ... the teacher had the freedom to delay the learning of one pupil, and in the case of another to permit a rapid progression through several stages. This autonomy in the pacing of pedagogy gave the teacher tremendous power over the student.[87]

Such arbitrary power in the hands of a teacher is problematic considering the caste, gender and religious diversity of students and teachers. Was it not the autonomy in the pacing of pedagogy that cost Ekalavya his thumb? Was it not the low-caste status of Ekalavya that sealed his fate? Upamanyu and Ekalavya are not the only examples available in the Hindu mythological tradition where the teacher was ruthless, and student felt helpless to the point of despair. A counter example can be found in the real-life incident of Yajnavalkya, a teenage student who had dared to question and challenge his teacher in the first century CE. He had to endure ostracism and hardship, but triumphed in the end. Yajnavalkya split the *Yajurveda* and created the *Shukla Yajurveda*. He also wrote the legal treatise, *Yagnavalkya Smriti* which the scholars consider 'more systematic than Manu'.[88] Contemporary scholarship recognised his genius, and thousands of Brahmans became his followers. This is not a lone example; the presence of multiple and conflicting philosophies ranging from agnosticism and atheism to idol-worship and extreme ritualism within the sacred ambit of Hindu philosophy demonstrate dissent; blind adherence was not the hallmark of the Hindu educational and intellectual tradition.

After arguing that in the Hindu tradition there was a 'total allegiance to authority [and] unquestioning obedience' to the teacher, Kumar defends Gandhian education, which, according to him, provided 'a new educational ideal for the system to pursue as well as a new pedagogical strategy'.[89]

87. Ibid., p. 72.
88. Pandurang Vaman Kane, *History of Dharmasatras*, Poona: Bhandarkar Research Institute, 1968, vol. I, p. 430.
89. Kumar, *Political Agenda*, p. 112.

> The epistemology of Basic Education was thoroughly radical ... it implied a radical restructuring of the sociology of school knowledge. It introduced into the school curriculum a form of knowledge on which low-caste groups had monopoly.... In a school following this curriculum, a low-caste child would feel far more at home than an upper-caste child. Both in terms of worldview and functional skills, the curriculum of a 'basic' school favoured the child belonging to the lowest stratum of society.[90]

The schools established under the 'Basic Education' programme of Gandhi introduced spinning which was practiced not only by the weaver castes, but also by many Brahmans and other upper castes. (Brahman men spun yarn to make sacred thread.) These schools did not introduce shoemaking or pottery-making which would have made an untouchable or potter's child 'feel at home'. My essay, and the one by Simone Holzwarth and Verónica Oelsner show how oppressive Gandhian education was on children.

Moreover, did the lower castes want to 'feel at home'? The main plank of Ambedkar's opposition to Gandhian education was that untouchable children did not want to remain in a degraded position to 'feel at home' which tradition had assigned to them. They aspired for a better life of dignity by taking up modern education. In Ahmedabad district of Gujarat, when the upper-caste Rajput men attacked the untouchables for sending their children to school, Gandhi did not intervene. Ambedkar asked 'why Gandhi did not advise his reformer colleague at Ahmedabad to prosecute the upper caste Hindus'. Kumar explains that 'this kind of action was of course incompatible with Gandhi's preference for reform without coercion'.[91] If prosecution was coercion, Gandhi could have easily led a *satyagraha* against the perpetrators of such oppression. Gandhi's Basic Education was firmly rooted in his absolute faith in the highly stratified caste system called *Varnashramadharma*. Gandhi said that it was 'not a human invention, but an immutable law of nature—the statement of a tendency that is ever present and at work like Newton's

90. Ibid., pp. 170–76.
91. Ibid., p. 104.

law of gravitation'.[92] By comparing the *varna* system to Newton's law, Gandhi held that gender and caste inequality was universal and eternal and could not be questioned.

The Gandhian education system was not accepted by many and did not go unchallenged. As Kumar notes, the National Planning Committee established by the Indian National Congress, openly stated that 'too much stress on vocation at such age is spiritually harmful and teaching of general subjects through such single narrow-down medium makes the knowledge of subject superficial and defective.... To a certain extent such a system will mean existence of child labour in schools.' Kumar dismisses it as 'the staple of modernist thought'.[93]

New Perspectives

The need for 'new perspectives' arises due to two important drawbacks in the 'old perspectives'; namely, factual errors and a complete silencing of the voice of the truly oppressed. This calls for discarding fashionable theories and reverting back to actual history-writing, called narrative and chronological history. This type of history-writing does not 'create [a] past' to suit a theory. It is not what Hobsbawm calls 'comforting history', a history suited for an ideology or an interest group.[94] It is a faithful recording of an historical event—*wei es eigentlich gewesen*—'as it actually happened', an ideal upheld by Leopold von Ranke. Such a history essentially presents factually accurate, chronologically documented historical events. This form of history is not an end itself, but forms the basis for further critical examination in historical research.

The second important reason for a New Perspective is the complete absence of the poor, women, untouchables and the lower castes in this saga of oppression perpetuated by the elitist Old Perspective. Eleanor Zelliot's chapter on 'Dalit Initiatives in Education' records trials and tribulations faced by the early reformers from diverse caste

92. M. K. Gandhi, *Varnashramadharma*, Ahmedabad: Navajivan Publishing House, p. 1962, pp. 13–23.
93. Krishna Kumar, *Political Agenda*, p. 179.
94. Hobsbawm, *On History*, p. 227.

backgrounds in admitting untouchable children into classrooms. The struggle against the prevailing landed Brahman hegemony in education in Poona by Jotirao Phule can be considered to be the earliest recorded resistance to caste-based inequalities in education.[95] The love of learning and the enthusiasm of the Dalit students was undeterred even though they had to sit outside the classrooms. She documents the experience of a Dalit boy 'leaning in through the window to write with rain falling behind him, ' that moved his teacher belonging to a Sonar (goldsmith) caste to tears.

To save the untouchable children from such plight, Jotirao Phule, Shivram Janaba Kamble, Kisan Phagoji Bansode and others opened schools. It was Vittal Ramji Shinde, the founder of the Depressed Classes Mission, who could mobilise funds to establish a larger network of educational institutions. These institutions supplied many of the important associates of Ambedkar. What strikes one the most about these initiatives is that many of those who had night schools and hostels were themselves not educated. Ambedkar was more than aware of the importance of modern education for Dalits to assert their identity and overcome the servitude of two millennia. He stressed that what the Dalits needed was not economic solvency, but education, which would enable them to earn their livelihood with self-respect and dignity. The institutions established in post-independent India by Ambedkar and his supporters fared much better. They got much-needed government support, though overall government educational policies lacked focus.

The difficulties faced by the marginalised and the oppressed have no geographical boundaries. This is effectively shown by Laura Jenkins in her comparative study of Dalit educational institutions in India, the educational institutions established for African Americans in the United States, and those established for non-whites in South Africa—all aimed at promoting self-respect. However, do such institutions undermine the policy of integration into the mainstream in the long run? By comparing Dalit institutions in India with institutions for African Americans in the United States and all-black institutions in

95. See Rosalind O'Hanlon, *Caste, Conflict and Ideology: Mahatma Jotirao Phule and Low Caste Protest in Nineteenth-century Western India*, Cambridge: Cambridge University Press, 1985.

South Africa, the author finds similarities between their respective, interrelated contexts and histories of education, though the forms of discriminations are different.

The effort to combine historically 'black', 'coloured' and 'white' institutions of higher education in South Africa is part of an ongoing commitment to de-segregate higher education. This step is motivated partly by economic pressures, and partly by a desire to create multiracial institutions. These efforts may erase from the public memory the anti-racist ideals of their founders. These institutions historically served as sites of resistance to racial domination. The gradual but successful integration of black institutions into mainstream ones that took place throughout the twentieth century in the United States is another available model.

Dalit colleges in India offer a distinct educational space as well as significant resources and opportunities that can facilitate the advancement of the Dalit communities. If such institutions are disbanded or absorbed, policymakers must consider how such functions might be served in more integrated institutions. In this regard, other Dalit-led initiatives, particularly study centres, offer possibilities that may serve as useful models elsewhere. The public space dominated by a hostile environment makes it imperative to maintain these institutions. She points out that Ambedkar was in fact frustrated over the lack of resources while building the Milind College. He stated that, 'the white Americans spent far more on Negro education than Hindus spent on any funds for untouchables'. He included tables of American bequests, educational funds, and religious organizations' donations, and estimated that American whites spent $85,000,000 between 1865 and 1930 on the advancement of the African Americans, whereas 'the only organization the Hindus can boast of is the Harijan Sevak Sangh.... Its annual expenditure does not go beyond a few thousand rupees on petty and insignificant and insubstantial purposes.' Thus, the need to retain Dalit institutions is crucial to not only for the benefit of Dalit students, but also for the empowerment and identity of the entire Dalit community.

Along with the Dalits, women belonging to all castes were denied education in the past two millennia. Once women got access to education in the mid-nineteenth century, how did they feel about their own position in Hindu society? Radha Gayatri's essay, 'Silent Voices', shows how educated Indian women's perceptions about themselves demonstrated their ability to critically engage and reflect on their roles within Indian society. This is explored through the writings of Pandita Ramabai, Tarabai Shinde, Rukhmabai, Anandibai Joshi, Cornelia Sorabji, Rokeya Sakhawat Hossein, Haimabati Sen and Mahadevi Varma. These writers were educated in the most adverse of times, and that heightened their awareness of their own condition and the injustice meted out to them by a patriarchal society. The inhuman practice of female infanticide in north, north-western and central India, supported by statistics, is a poignant reminder of how low the status of a girl child has always been in India. In 1868, the ninety-nine villages of Basti district in North-Western Provinces and Oudh had 1,204 boys as against 259 girls under the age of ten. Pandita Ramabai commented that families killed newborn girls 'as easily as destroying a mosquito or other annoying insect'.

In addition to this, pre-pubertal marriage for girls; an immediate post-pubertal consummation of marriage; early and frequent childbearing and secluded widowhood allowed no space for the education of girls. Ramabai explained that the seclusion of women not only ledled to the loss of their identities, it also perpetuated their ignorance. She asserted that 'men cannot, in the least, understand the wretchedness which we Hindu women have to endure'. Within this extremely patriarchal system, women were not even considered as 'daughters', 'wives' or 'mothers' with even limited rights. If a woman had the limited rights of a mother, how could she have been forced to kill her daughters soon after their birth? Women's position within the Hindu society was that of a 'daughter-in-law', who was virtually an unpaid labourer—an aspect well analysed by Rakmabai (Rukhmabai). She wrote that 'a daughter-in-law worked with the servants but was worse off than the servant as the latter had an option of refusing to work or change the masters whereas a daughter-in-law was bound for life'.[96]

Within a society which promoted the superstition that literate women would become widows, the early reformers faced almost

96. 'A Hindu Lady on Early Marriage', *The Mahratta*, 5 July 1885, pp. 1–2.

insurmountable difficulties in initiating the education of the girl child. This superstition was created and nurtured for centuries by men, in order to, as Jotirao Phule commented, 'keep women unenlightened in order to preserve their own superiority'.[97] In other words, women's illiteracy was not a part of general illiteracy of the society, but the deliberate, well thought-out, and carefully constructed strategy to keep women ignorant. Jotirao Phule and Ishwar Chandra Vidyasagar faced intense hostility when they opened schools for girls in 1850s. To contain these violent attacks, district officials suggested police protection to girl students and their parents. In such a situation, providing basic literacy was a challenge. Radical reformers like Mahadev Govind Ranade, Gopal Ganesh Agarkar and Gopal Krishna Gokhale insisted on providing equal educational opportunities to both boys and girls, through co-educational institutions. It was not the orthodox elements that intensely opposed women's education and social reform, but the newly emerging nationalist leaders. Reacting to the nationalist contention that educated women would neglect domestic responsibilities, Agarkar pointed out 'that there is no rule that all domestic work should be done by women alone, similarly one cannot prove that women should limit themselves to producing children'. He further stated that 'some men feel that if women study science they would lose faith in religion, and others oppose women's education as they fear that women will learn what is best for them and men will have to abandon the habitual oppression'.[98]

Radical reformers like Agarkar and Sayyid Mumtaz Ali insisted on equal treatment of men and women, while important leaders like Bal Gangadhar Tilak and Syed Ahmad Khan, both of whom created strong Hindu and Muslim identities, opposed education for girls.[99] In

97. Charles Heimsath, *Indian Nationalism and Hindu Social Reform*, Princeton: Princeton University Press, 1964, p. 103.
98. Sonali Sharma, 'Reformist Ideas and Emergence of Feminism in Marathi Fiction 1850s–1920s', Unpublished M.Phil. dissertation, Centre for Historical Studies, Jawaharlal Nehru University, 2008, pp. 24–26.
99. Gail Minault, 'Sayyid Mumtaz Ali and Tahzib un-Niswan: Women's Rights in Islam and Women's Journalism in Urdu', in *Religious Controversy in British India: Dialogues in South Asian Languages*, ed.

this tussle between those who wanted to educate women on par with men and those who wanted to completely deny education to women, a new group emerged that supported limited education to women to train them as educated companions with access to a very limited public space. The pressure from the nationalist leaders who opposed even this limited public space further curtailed their power to protest and negotiate. It is well documented how influential political leaders like Tilak hounded Rukhmabai and Pandita Ramabai during their lifetimes. In spite of such constraints on their lives and creativity, these women pioneered feminist protest and resistance.[100]

Mahima Manchanda's paper 'Contested Domains' brings forth how modern curricula in girls' schools reinforced pre-modern, feudal and patriarchal agendas in the field of education. The Sikh Kanya Mahavidyalaya in Jalandhar was set up with the desire to impart Sikh ideals amongst the girls who studied in this institution. Here, the desire to educate girls was intertwined with the larger question of religious identity: namely, the desire to separate Sikhism from Hinduism, and to create a *Tat Khalsa* or real Sikh identity amongst the Sikhs. The Kanya Mahavidyalaya in Jalandhar, by contrast, was an Arya Samaj school. The purpose behind the inception of this school was to create the identity of 'Arya woman' through Sanskritised Hindi. In these schools, the curricula was fixed keeping in mind religious requirements. Boys studied in government schools with a strong secular educational tradition and Urdu language as the medium of instruction, while the girls enrolled in these denominational schools, learning Punjabi and Hindi, firmly grounded in their respective religious traditions. They, thus, represented two mutually exclusive categories. Women became pallbearers of tradition. The notion of women as sole repositories of *izzat* (honour), prestige and reputation, was developed and the notion of pure 'Arya' which automatically implied an upper-caste identity was consolidated. The founders of these denominational schools prepared both the curriculum as

Kenneth W. Jones New York: State University of New York Press, 1992, pp. 180–83.

100. See 'Educated Women as Rakmabais and Ramabais,' in Rao, *Foundations*, pp. 96–137.

well as authored and published textbooks. The structure of modern schools was used in Punjab to reproduce pre-modern caste, as well as religious and gender, stereotypes.

The second set of essays investigates the political context of education. How the politics of colonialism and nationalism affected the debates concerning modern education in India. Although the state acknowledged its responsibility for education as early as 1813, the reluctance of British officers and the resistance of the bulk of the Indian political leadership prevented the expansion of modern education. Instead of advocating compulsory education, vital to the formation of a modern nation state, various activists and nationalists not only stalled such efforts but also attempted to control education in the name of defending Indian identity. This forms the backdrop to 'Compulsory Education and the Political Leadership in Colonial India, 1840–1947'. The first attempt to introduce compulsory mass education, though in a limited sense, was made by the colonial state during the 1870s, and coincided with the passing of the Elementary Education Act in England in 1870. The second attempt was made by Gopal Krishna Gokhale in 1910–11. Both these attempts were defeated by the very leaders who claimed to represent Indian aspirations. The attempt to deny education to the poor, lower castes, and women ran parallel to the unequivocal demand for political independence by the same leaders. This leads to the question: Whose nation did they represent? It is therefore necessary to investigate the parallel activities of the national leaders struggling for independence. Was their demand for freedom aimed at essentially to reinforce a pre-modern feudal order or to build a modern nation state based on democratic principles?

The activities of the national leaders in defending child labour in the textile industries and agriculture, child marriage in the society, and child workers in schools have hitherto been sidelined by focusing the historical gaze upon the colonial and anti-colonial contradiction. Their political agenda of opposing modern education in the name of defending Indian tradition appear to be hollow, as national education was meant for, in most cases, the lower castes and women, while the 'leaders of the society' enjoyed the benefits of modern education. Gandhi made rich landlords the 'trustees of the society', but he did not make them trustees of the schools, which would have given young children freedom to enjoy their childhood and not made them work for four hours a day to earn enough to pay for the salaries of the teachers and the upkeep of their schools. Gandhian opposition to modern education has been defended as a civilisational opposition to the West. Rabindranath Tagore, too, rejected the Western notion of formal schooling. In his alternative model of education, children danced, sang, and painted with gay abandon and enjoyed childhood at Shantiniketan.

Just as 'Compulsory Education' questions the myth of nationalists fighting solely for Indian national interests, Hayden Bellenoit's 'Education, Missionaries and the Indian nation, c.1880–1920' questions the postmodernist myth that Christian missionaries were instruments of colonial rule. Bellenoit argues that 'the missionaries viewed the Swadeshi Movements as an exercise in patriotism rather than a bellicose anti-foreign movement'. Charlie Andrews actively supported the freedom movement.[101]

Simone Holzwarth, and Verónica Oelsner, in their essay, 'Redefining Work', not only draw out similarities between Gandhi and the Argentinian dictator Juan Perón, but also allow greater breadth to the relationship between education and nation-building. They argue that political leaders focus on education in order to create a new social order. India and Argentina both experienced colonialism, and Argentina's independence from Spain in 1810 led to major structural changes in education. During 1865 and 1884, the two influential presidents Domingo Faustino Sarmiento and Nicolás Avellaneda, aimed to educate all social classes. They passed legislation, subsidised the construction of school buildings, established teacher training institutions, made primary education free, and restricted the teaching of religion in the national primary schools during school hours. These measures led to a massive increase in literacy and, by the end of nineteenth century, Argentina had achieved 50 per cent literacy. However, secondary education was neglected due to the lack of resources. Thus, what the country required was a systematic

101. See, Charles Freer Andrews, 'The Effect of the Japanese Victories upon India', *The East and the West*, 1905, p. 371.

expansion of secondary and collegiate education. The 1943 coup was a turning point against secular education in Argentina. Its leaders advocated 'Catholic nationalism' or religious nationalism. They suspended all schoolteachers, specialists and administrators and began a massive catholicisation of educational institutions.[102] Perón's educational policies need to be situated within this context. Gandhi, too, rejected secular education and school textbooks by declaring that 'India would never be godless'.[103] The rejection of secular education and insistence on manual work in schools by Perón and Gandhi clearly demonstrates that both political movements intended a clear rupture with the previous educational policies. The authors explain that the political leaders of both countries deliberately disseminated a new complex representations related to work and education. Both upheld the dignity of labour. According to Perón, the state had a dual role, being responsible for both economic progress as well as the protection of the weaker sections of society.[104] Hence, the schools taught mechanics, carpentry, bricklaying, and radio and telecommunication technologies. In other words all those skills required for running a modern nation. In Gandhi's schools, only spinning was taught. What would have happened if India had implemented the Gandhian

102. See Victoria Leonard, *Politicians, Pupils, and Priests: Argentine Education Since 1943*, New York: Peter Lang, 1989; Miguel Somoza Rodríguez, 'Poverty, Exclusion and Social Conflict in the Schoolbooks of Argentina during the First Peronist Period', *Paedagogica Historica*, vol. 43, no. 5, 2007, pp. 633–52; Mark D. Szuchman, 'Childhood Education and Politics in Nineteenth-Century Argentina: The Case of Buenos Aires', *Hispanic American Historical Review*, vol. 70, no. 1, 1990, pp. 109–38; Pablo Pineau, 'Peronism, Secondary Schooling and Work in Argentina, 1944–1955: An Approach through Cultural Hierarchies', *Paedagogica Historica*, vol. 40, nos. 1–2, 2004, pp. 183–91, and Marcelo Caruso, 'Latin American Independence, Education, and the Invention of New Polities', *Paedagogica Historica*, vol. 46, no. 4, 2010, pp. 409–17.
103. M. K. Gandhi, *Hind Swaraj* (Reprint Edition), Ahmedabad: Navajivan Publishing House, 1946p. 107, again in *Harijan*, 9 July 1938.
104. Monica Esti Rein, *Politics and Education in Argentina 1946–1962*, New York: M. E. Sharp, 1998, p. 21.

educational model throughout the country? Who would have manned the post and telegraph departments and the railways, or operated mikes and radios? Gandhi himself extensively used these devices to propagate his political views.

Perón's triple agenda, namely 'political sovereignty', 'social justice' and 'economic independence' have parallels in Gandhi's triple freedom: *swaraj* (political freedom), *sarvodaya* (social justice), and *swadeshi* (economic independence). The pre-Perónist political leaders in Argentina and the pre-Gandhian Congress leaders in India had an identical agenda, [105] but the foot soldiers to carry out this agenda were not little children. They were the state and adult citizens. So Gandhi and Perón transferred the burden of carrying out their political agendas onto the shoulders of children who very often, as was the case with India, poor, malnourished, and starving little souls.

The politicisation of education was not limited to school education but also, crucially, extended to higher education. Suresh Chandra Ghosh's essay entitled 'Genesis of Curzon's University Reform, 1899–1905' looks at how the Indian Universities Act of 1904 enacted by Viceroy Curzon was intended to introduce radical changes in the functioning of the five existing universities in Calcutta, Bombay, Madras, Lahore and Allahabad. Today, after a century, very few question the enlargement of the functions of the university, limiting the membership of syndicates to university teachers, and stricter conditions for the affiliation of colleges to a university. However, at that time, the response to these very changes shook the foundations of an empire.

105. Ganesh Vasudeo Joshi the founder of the Poona Sarvajanik Sabha was the first person to promote *swadeshi* or consumption of indigenous products as a means of achieving economic self-sufficiency. He wore *khaddar* or hand-spun cloth in 1860s. The Congress leaders adopted it in 1894, The Circular of the Poona Sarvajanik Sabha, quoted in *The Mahratta*, 10 February 1907, p. 61, Editorial Notes, and *Kesari*, 5 February 1907. Similarly *swaraj* or self-rule was widely advocated during the Swadeshi Movement. See Sumit Sarkar, *Swadeshi Movement in Bengal, 1903–1908*, New Delhi: Peoples Publishing House, 1973.

In the second half of the nineteenth century, Indian educationists and reformers had been criticising the nature of universities which were essentially affiliating bodies, and not teaching institutions. The Woods Despatch of 1854 had specifically recommended professorships for the purpose of the delivering lectures in various branches of learning, which had been ignored subsequently. The unofficial fellows were appointed for life. There was no upper limit to the number of fellows to be appointed, although the minimum was fixed at thirty. The number of fellows in Calcutta steadily rose from forty in 1857 to 220 in 1890. Many had left the Bengal Presidency for other provinces and even Ceylon, but continued to be fellows of the senate of the University of Calcutta. They had little stake in the matter and never took part in its deliberations. However, they voted in the elections. Affluent candidates spent a lot of resources appointed election agents to hunt down these fellows and win their votes. The university teachers with little resources could hardly think of becoming fellows of the senate.

Curzon attempted to rectify the situation. By doing so, he was also trying to remove high-ranking British officers like the lieutenant-governors of the North-Western Provinces and Punjab from the senate of the University of Calcutta. The second problem was the question of affiliated colleges. They were scattered in far-flung places. Colleges in Jaipur and Ceylon had been affiliated to the University of Calcutta. The university could hardly be expected to supervise and control the quality of teaching and functioning of these colleges. Yet, besides these technical realities, there were significant political issues. The senate committee, dominated by its Indian members, had the power to prescribe textbooks in the affiliated colleges. It refused to prescribe William Lee-Warner's *Citizen of India* as a textbook. This book introduced civics for the first time as a subject in Indian educational institutions. Though located within the larger context of substantiating colonial rule, this book was an attempt to teach the rights and duties of people in the immediate context of over 300 communal riots that had taken place across India during 1890 and 1894.[106]

106. For a complete report of communal riots see, Home/Public A 1894, nos. 258–65 and nos. 345–64.

Preeti's essay, 'Transformation of Schooling in Colonial Punjab', examines the crucial changes in schools. As a relatively late addition to the East India Company's empire in the late 1840s, Punjab presents an interesting case for analysing modern forms of educational development. The British annexation of Punjab in 1849 was very different from earlier acquisitions. By this time, the 'imperial agenda' had been crystallised and consolidated. Although the Hindu, Muslim and Sikh communities spoke Punjabi, the government took a unilateral decision in adopting Urdu as an official language, [107] and consequently, the medium of instruction in schools. The first Director of Public Instruction, William Arnold, was the third son of Thomas Arnold, the famous headmaster of the Rugby School. He had initiated a number of educational reforms like introducing modern subjects, a fixed timetable, division of teaching time into periods, and physical training. William Arnold had studied in the same school, but he did not attempt similar changes in Punjab. As Director of Public Instruction, he had a virgin field before him for educational reforms. However, all he did was carry forward the imperial agenda of opposing modern education, which was laid out by Governor-General Auckland in 1839.[108] Arnold introduced a system of circle schools with very low educational standards. He ignored the models of the vernacular primary schools in the Bombay and the Madras Presidencies, where modern sciences and mathematics were taught through the medium of the vernacular.[109] The circle school System called 'Hardinge schools' in Bengal and 'Halqbandi schools' in the North-Western Provinces and Oudh had been introduced during 1840s with disastrous results. There was widespread opposition as their standard in arithmetic was lower than the pre-colonial vernacular schools. People resisted by not sending their boys to these

107. Farina Mir, *The Social Space of Language: Vernacular Culture in British Colonial Punjab*, Los Angeles and London: University of California Press, 2010, p. 54.

108. Auckland's minute dated 24 November 1839, India Office Records, London, pp. i–xxxvii.

109. Bhudev Mukherjee's *Report on the Village Schools in North-Western Province and Punjab*, Calcutta: Calcutta Central Press, 1868, pp. 10–12.

schools. This led to the closing down of many schools as early as 1843.[110] It was virtually the grafting of the modern school system of designated schoolhouses, fixed timetables, written examinations on pre-colonial knowledge, rather than the introduction of the 'modern' sciences, mathematics and social sciences. The transformation of the school system in Punjab refers to this particular historical context. The students who had studied in the vernacular schools could not enter the English-teaching Anglo-vernacular schools meant for the local elite. So, those who went to the vernacular schools were either the sons of petty village officials like *lambardars* and *patwaris*, who sought employment as village revenue officials. The low quality of the government vernacular schools was an important reason for the popularity of the schools established by the Arya Samaj, the Anjumans and the Singh Sabha. Instead of creating secular spaces, these denominational schools perpetually divided education and society along religious lines. The part played by these schools in the formation of strong Hindu, Muslim and Sikh religious identities was the direct result of the colonial educational policy in Punjab.

This volume, by focussing on the little-known educational debates and the education of the marginalised communities and women, contests the existing old perspectives. By attempting to go beyond the existing binaries of understanding the coloniser/colonised, European/non-European and imperialist/anti-imperialist, or what Hobsbawm calls 'comforting history', it makes an effort to script a critical history. By bringing out these lesser-known debates and educational developments, an effort has been made to, as Richard Aldrich emphasises, 'rescue from oblivion, those whose voices have not yet been heard and whose stories have not yet been told'.[111]

110. Minute by Lt. Governor of Bengal F. J. Halliday dated 24 March 1859, Home/Education, 20 May 1859, nos. 7–11

111. Richard Aldrich, *Lessons from History of Education: the Selected Works of Richard Aldrich*, London: Routledge, 2006, p. 18.

Part I

Forms of Discrimination in Education

1

Dalit Initiatives in Education, 1880–1992[1]

Eleanor Zelliot

In September 1951, Dr B. R. 'Babasaheb' Ambedkar (1891–1956) welcomed Dr Rajendra Prasad, the first President of India, to the foundation stone-laying ceremony of one of his most unusual educational efforts, Milind Mahavidyalaya (Milind College). The site was Aurangabad in the Marathwada region of the former princely state of Hyderabad, a vast area with no English or Marathi college, or even a high school. Ambedkar's words on that occasion reveal an opinion just as important as the site chosen for his educational experiment:

> Coming as I do from the lowest order of the Hindu Society, I know what is the value of education. The problem of raising the lower order is deemed to be economic. This is a great mistake. The problem of raising the lower order in India is not to feed them, to clothe them and to make them serve the higher classes as [is] the ancient ideal

1. Dalit began its use as a translation of 'depressed' for the British 'Depressed Classes'. It is a very negative word meaning 'depressed', 'suppressed', 'broken', 'held down', etc. It began its current use in the 1970s, when the rather feisty Dalit writers decided to found something akin to the Black Panthers, and as 'black' is a word used for African Americans, so Dalit came to be used for untouchables, tribals, or any marginalised group. Now, it is just a general word for the marginalised. The word 'Harijan'—meaning children of God—was used by Gandhi, and was seen as very patronising by Ambedkar and his followers. However, it is now almost entirely replaced by Dalit, which no longer has the totally negative meaning.

> of this country. The problem of the lower order is to remove from them that inferiority complex which has stunted their growth and made them slaves to others, to create in them the consciousness of the significance of their lives for themselves and for the country, of which they have been cruelly robbed by the existing social order. Nothing can achieve this purpose except the spread of higher education. This is in my opinion the panacea of our social troubles.[2]

Ambedkar was speaking from his own experience. The child of a school teacher in the British Indian army, he was aided by non-Brahman reformers to achieve not only a BA in Bombay—rare for an untouchable at that time—but also an MA and Ph.D. from Columbia University, a D.Sc. from London University, and admission to the Bar from Grey's Inn in London. After several trips abroad, he returned to India in 1923 to devote the rest of his life towards promoting education and engaging in public service, not only among his own Mahar community, but in a country he never rejected in spite of its treatment of the untouchables. As Chairman of the Drafting Committee of the Constituent Assembly (1946–49), he was instrumental in the framing of the Indian constitution, and then oversaw the planning of labour laws and water projects and the drafting of the important Hindu Code Bill, as the first law minister of independent India. By starting newspapers, setting up hostels, organising conferences, establishing political parties, putting in place an educational system, and finally converting to Buddhism, he awakened and enlightened the 'Depressed Classes'. Ambedkar was the most successful of Dalit educators, building upon a century of Dalit initiatives.

2. Quoted in K. B. Talwatkar, 'Peoples' Education Society: A Glorious Heritage', in the *Siddharth College of Arts and Sciences Silver Jubilee Number*, 1973–74, pp. 77–83. The silver jubilee was postponed for two years because of the 1971 Bangladesh war. Padma Velaskar has also used this quotation as an introduction to her excellent essay, 'Ideology, Education and the Political Struggle for Liberation: Change and Challenge among the Dalits of Maharashtra', in *Education, Development and Underdevelopment*, eds. Sureshchandra Shukla and Rekha Kaul, New Delhi: Sage Publications, 1998.

The Early Educators

The first Dalit educator was not a Dalit, but is a Dalit hero. Jotiba Phule (1827–90)—called 'Mahatma' for his development of a non-Brahman worldview and efforts towards the social uplift of the lower classes—founded schools for girls and untouchables in the mid-nineteenth century, an act which illustrates not only his foresight but also an undercurrent of desire for change among the lower orders. Phule was a Mali (a gardener caste) resident of Poona (now Pune) with an affluent background, and was clearly committed to a life of both social work and protest against Brahman domination. We can trace the history of his religious organisation, the Satyashodhak Samaj (Truth-seeking Society);[3] but the history of his schools contains few facts besides the bare notes about founding, and even here the dates differ. We do not know what happened to those who were schooled, and we have only one record of a student's writing.[4] There is, however, a report of progress as of 1853. But Phule's work has acquired such significance today that many references in speeches and books are to the ideology of 'Phule-Ambedkar', and the portraits of both hang in many schools and Buddhist *vihara*s.

Towards the end of the nineteenth century, we have references to efforts by Mahars—the largest untouchable caste and the one most active in new occupations in the Vidarbha region of Maharashtra.

3. Three books deal with Phule's work: Gail Omvedt, *Cultural Revolt in a Colonial Society: The Non-Brahman Movement in Western India, 1873 to 1930*, Bombay: Scientific Socialist Education Trust, 1976; Rosalind O'Hanlon, *Caste, Conflict and Ideology: Mahatma Jotirao Phule and Low Caste Protest in Nineteenth-century Western India*, Cambridge: Cambridge University Press, 1985, and J. R. Shinde, *Dynamics of Cultural Revolution: 19th Century Maharashtra*, Delhi: Ajanta Publications, 1985. Dhananjay Keer's pioneering biography of Phule (*Mahatma Jotirao Phooley: Father of our Social Revolution*, Bombay: Popular Prakashan, 1964) deals briefly with his educational projects.
4. An essay by Muktabai, a Mang girl, called the 'Sorrows of the Mahars and Mangs', trans. Maya Pandit in *Women Writing in India: 600 B.C. to the Present* (vol. I), ed. Susie Tharu and K. Lalita, New York: Feminist Press at the City University of New York, 1991, pp. 214–16.

In Akola, a town which probably was home to many Mahar railway workers, a free boarding system was arranged by Janoji Khandare; and one of the early important Mahar leaders, G. A. Gawai, was educated there. My first informant on education in Vidarbha[5] told me that the boarding house opened around 1880 and was still in existence as a government enterprise. A printed source mentions an institution which is undoubtedly the same hostel—the Shri Janoji Free Boarding—founded in 1895 and now run by the founder's great-grandson.[6] *The Gazetteer for the Central Provinces and Berar, Akola District* (1910), fills in the picture: 'Mahars, apart from the individuals employed in the public service of the village, are almost always labourers, though a very few are shopkeepers and still fewer landholders. One of the latter, Janu Kachrya of Paras, who died about six years ago, started a boarding house at Akola so that boys of the caste coming from the villages might have the benefit of the good schools at headquarters. A night-school for adults, attended at present by 28 pupils, has also been in existence at Akola for about a year; the expenses are chiefly paid from subscriptions by men of other castes.'[7]

The gazetteer also noted that government schools for Mahars and Mangs were closed in 1902 for want of attendance: 'The need for these institutions no longer exists, as the prejudice which prevented low-caste boys from attending ordinary schools has given way to a more enlightened feeling.'[8] Unfortunately, we know nothing of these government schools; but we do know that the pattern of treatment of untouchables was not an even one, and that even much later there was still a discriminatory practice prevalent in many schools of not allowing untouchables to enter a classroom, and the lesson could be followed only while sitting on the veranda or looking through a

5. Mr Kavadi of Nagpur, interview by author, 1964.
6. R. K. Kshirsagar, *Dalit Movement in India and Its Leaders (1857–1956)*, New Delhi: M D Publications, 1992, p. 245.
7. C. Brown, *Central Provinces and Berar District Gazetteers, Akola District. Vol. A—Descriptive*, Calcutta: Baptist Mission Press, 1910, p. 121.
8. Ibid., p. 419.

window. The *Central Provinces and Berar Census of 1931* indicates that the problem of untouchable attendance was by no means solved even then:

> Mahars have won by their own efforts 'the right to be taught'. The castes against the admission of whom there is the greatest opposition are Sweepers, Basors, Mangs and Chamars ... The degree of objection taken to the various castes in schools varies with the caste, the area, the school committee and the staff. Generally speaking, the crucial person is the Head Master ... Jubbulpore Municipality treats all castes exactly alike; Bilaspur, Raipur and Nagpur maintain separate school[s] for Sweepers ... a few [schools] in the Nagpur district accept all castes and treat them much the same. The Marathi are stated to be more liberal than the Hindi districts.[9]

At the beginning of the twentieth century, a high-caste Marathi educator, Vithal Ramji Shinde (1873–1944) began an extraordinary programme of education with his Depressed Classes Mission, founded in 1906.[10] By this time, a caste Hindu reformer could state that his efforts were in response to initiatives begun by the untouchables themselves. Shinde once spent a night in Ahmadnagar and was invited by a group of untouchables to address their community in a neighbouring village at midnight, when all would be free from their work. Shripatrao Thorat, a butler; Pandurang Laxman Dangle, a head master, and Ravji Sadoba Gaikwad, a teacher, were the leaders of the group. They said that they had been advised to invite him by friends in Vidarbha who had established the Somavansh Hitachintak Samaj (Society for the Uplift of the Somavansh). (The Somavansh was a sub-caste of the Mahars.) While addressing this meeting, Shinde became convinced that he should make the education of the untouchables his life's mission.[11]

9. Ibid., p. 392.
10. For all the non-Brahman educators, see Eleanor Zelliot, 'Experiments in Dalit Education, Maharashtra, 1850–1947', in *Education and the Disprivileged: Nineteenth and Twentieth Centuries*, ed. S. Bhattacharya, New Delhi: Orient Longman, 2001, pp. 35–49.
11. M. S. Gore, *Vitthal Ramji Shinde: An Assessment of His Contribution*, Bombay: Tata Institute of Social Sciences, 1990, p. 145.

With his high-caste status and his circle of reform-minded Hindus, Shinde was able to do much more with the establishment of educational institutions than the untouchables themselves at that time. Although Shinde and Ambedkar later parted ways over political issues, including membership in the Indian National Congress, the former's Depressed Classes Mission was able to found schools and hostels that allowed Dalits in Poona a range of educational opportunities, and many of the graduates of those institutions went on to become important associates of Ambedkar. But even before Shinde began his efforts in 1906, a remarkable Mahar reformer had begun work in Poona and an equally innovative Mahar was active in Nagpur.

From these efforts we can develop 'benchmarks' for indigenous institutions of education. These may help our understanding of when and where Dalit initiatives could take place.

Benchmarks of Dalit Initiatives

1. Some economic freedom from traditional work. In the western Marathi-speaking area, the army. In the east, railroads and textile mills.
2. Some aid from higher castes, often non-Brahmans.
3. An individual's initiative.
4. A group willing to be educated.
5. A useful place in the system, such as a hostel, which allows villagers to enrol in government schools in cities.
6. A commitment to encourage pride and self-respect. Especially important was the influence of the *Bhakti* (devotional religion) saint-poet, Cokhamela.
7. A clear need, not met by Christian missions, of a reform effort.

Shivram Janaba Kamble, Kisan Phagoji Bansode and the Nagpur Activists

Shivram Janaba Kamble (1875–1940) was the acknowledged leader of the untouchables in Poona for the first third of the twentieth century. He welcomed Ambedkar to the city and joined the latter's movement, but later parted ways over the choice of candidates for the 1937 provincial elections. With good English at his command (by virtue of his position as a butler in the Masonic Hall in Poona), he was able to send petitions to the government for re-enlistment privileges in the army on the grounds of former service, English justice and human worth. He asked for posts in civil administration, noting that Britain herself had raised her working class to representation in Parliament. He began a Marathi newspaper; started a movement to abolish the *devadasi* system of dedicating girls (chiefly Mahar and Mang) to a temple; was a leader in the unsuccessful *satyagraha* to enter the Parvati Temple in Poona in 1929, and most significantly for this paper, was active in the 'anna fund'[12] night school run by literate Mahars for the less-educated.[13] The Cokhamela Vidyavardak Mandal, named after the medieval Bhakti saint from the Mahar caste, was probably started about 1900, and a proper night school was run from 1912 to 1933, when it was closed due to plague. The school taught English and the first to fourth standards were patronised by adults working during the daytime as postmen and office peons.[14]

Another pioneer with wide-ranging interests emerged on the eastern side of the Marathi-speaking territory. The first important educator in Nagpur was Kisan Phagoji Bansode (1879–1946), who may have been the first Mahar student in the area to sit inside a schoolroom. His teacher was a follower of the Brahman reformer, Gopal Ganesh Agarkar; and Bansode, probably because of his close association with high-caste reformers, was more interested in Hinduism than were other Mahar reformers. His story is remembered vividly today. I was told in Mopla that Kisan Phago at

12. Anna was a small denomination of currency. A rupee consisted of 16 annas.
13. Printed sources for the life of Shivram Janba Kamble are Kshirsagar, *Dalit Movement*, pp. 237–41 and (in Marathi) Harishchandra Narayanrao Navalkar, *S. J. Kamble yanche charitra* (also titled in English, *The Life of Shivram Janba Kamble and Brief History of the Poona Parvati Satyagraha*), Poona: S. J. Kamble, 1930.
14. N. K. Kadam of Pune, interview by author, 1964.

first had to stand outside the schoolhouse, leaning in through the window to write, with rain falling behind him. The teacher wept, and then allowed Kisan Phago in. The teacher was Rago Shivaram, a Sonar (goldsmith) by caste. Bansode's biography of the medieval saint Cokhamela is dedicated to Vithal Ramji Shinde, and he was closely associated with the Hindu Mahasabha leader, Madan Mohan Malaviya. Like Kamble in Poona, he was a very influential supporter of Ambedkar until the mid-1930s, when Ambedkar's announcement that he would not die a Hindu and that the untouchables should convert to another religion became so influential that it left Bansode almost alone with his Hindu commitments.

Bansode's family owned a small shop—a reflection of greater social mobility in the Vidarbha area. Bansode started a press and this enabled him to make a living by printing various newspapers, brochures and books related to the abolition of untouchability. He also began a library—the Sri Satchidananda Vachan Griha—in Mopla, his birthplace and where he received his early education, and got thirty trunks of books from caste Hindus interested in his efforts. It is said that the Brahman leader 'Lokmanya' Bal Gangadhar Tilak solicited books for the library. With the help of Jaibai Chaudhary, Bansode founded the Cokhamela Girls' School in 1907 and also started a number of hostels. Jaibai (1892–1964), a remarkable woman who worked in her youth as a *coolie* (porter), went on to establish another Saint Cokhamela Girls' School which is now Jaibai Choudhary Junior College. Bansode published a number of periodicals, including one for his own sub-caste, the *Somavamshiya Mitra*, started in 1908, which was closed down after three years due to 'persecution from [the] orthodox'.[15]

Bansode also organised many Mahar conferences, petitioned for re-enlistment in the army and places in government, and worked for the improvement of the conditions of Mahar life. The most unusual among his efforts was the Sanmarg Bodhak Nirashrit Samaj (Depressed Class Society Showing the Right Path) for improving hygiene, encouraging industry, and promoting good eating and

15. A. B. Shah, 'Dalit Movement and Its Historical Background', *Bulletin of the Indian Educational Institute*, vol. 11, 1981, p. 25.

drinking habits among the lower orders. He urged Mahars, Mangs and Chambhars 'not to become Christian and to obstruct conversion, not to eat what is not to be eaten, not to drink what is not to be drunk, to spread education, to acquire citizenship, to uplift their economic condition, to organize, and to create among caste Hindus a feeling that the downtrodden should be raised up'.[16]

Bansode's activities touched Mahar life in many areas. He was a labour leader in the Empress Mills in Nagpur, where a large percentage of the workers were untouchables, and published *Mazdur Patrika* (Workers' Newspaper) from 1918 to 1922 to educate the millhands. He went from house to house in the Maharwada (Mahar quarter), 'preaching self-respect among people who felt they were being punished for previous sin'.[17] He preached Mahar pride on the basis that they were the former rulers of the land. He created an anna fund to encourage Mahars to enter hotels and order tea. He made a number of trips to Pandharpur, trying to collect the songs of the poet-saint Cokhamela, which were as yet unpublished, and used this religious heritage as well as his own songs to preach a higher religion to the untouchables.

Another Vidarbha reformer, L. N. Hardas (1904–39), had as broad a range of interests as Bansode, including the founding of three night schools in 1924 and a Cokhamela Library. Unlike Bansode, he stayed in Ambedkar's movement, supporting the Nashik Temple-entry Satyagraha in 1930 and joining Ambedkar's Independent Labour Party. He urged the abandonment of humiliating religious practices in contrast to the effort to reform Hinduism that was Bansode's message.[18] His death at the age of thirty-five prevented

16. From the programme of the Sanmarg Bodhak Nirashrit Samaj, which was founded in 1903. A copy of the programme is in the possession of Bansode's son, Shamrao Bansode, translation by M. D. Panchbhai and Eleanor Zelliot. There is a short life of Bansode by N. R. Shende in a collection of Bansode's poetry *Pradip* (Illumination), Nagpur: Shamrao Bansode, 1958. A brief life appears in Kshirsagar, *Dalit Movement in India*, pp. 176–77.
17. S. V. Dahat of Nagpur, interview with author, 1964.
18. Kshirsagar, *Dalit Movement in India*, pp. 224–27.

further work, although he is well-remembered in Nagpur and his home town of Kamathi.

Nagpur was a centre for still another early educator: G. M. Thaware (1902–52) opened a primary school and library and a hostel there in 1920; and in the years that followed, founded a girls' school, night schools in several places, a sweepers' boys' school (indicating a concern for untouchables not in his own caste), and a reading room for *bidi* (handmade cigarette) makers who were generally, if illogically, untouchables. He wrote to Mahatma Gandhi in 1933 stating that a separate university should be established at Wardha for untouchable students.[19] Thaware belonged to the Mahanubhav sect, once considered heterodox, as did an even earlier reformer, Kalicharan Nandagavali (1860–1962), who in addition to supporting the Indian National Congress and the Salt Satyagraha in 1930, set up a girls' school in Gondia (then in the Central Provinces and Berar) in 1910.[20] The Mahanubhav sect was born in the thirteenth century as an egalitarian sect within the Brahmanical fold, and although it had lost much of its radical openness, may have still been a leavening influence in the Vidarbha area.

The work of Bansode, Hardas and Thaware in Nagpur and Kamble in Poona was unusually effective, but there were stirrings all over the Marathi-speaking area. *The Gazetteer for Chanda District* is perhaps representative of many districts. After describing the Mahars—nearly 12 per cent of the population—as 'a despised race, the helots of the District, whose touch is polluting', the gazetteer paints a different picture: 'The kotwars or village watchmen are mainly drawn from this caste. They are not unintelligent, and a good many of the cultivators and weavers have abandoned caste and joined the Kabirpanth. Many Mahars are anxious to have their children educated, and send their boys to school, though on account of caste prejudice they are not allowed to mingle with Hindu boys but must sit apart in the verandah or in a separate room. They are quite up to the average in ability.'[21]

19. Ibid., p. 351.
20. Ibid., pp. 285–87.
21. *The Gazetteer for Chanda District*, Allahabad: The Pioneer Press, 1909, p. 117.

Around the State of Maharashtra

While there were educational efforts initiated by Dalits in the southern area of the Marathi-speaking territory, they are not as well-documented as in Vidarbha, and probably fewer in number because of effective efforts by non-Dalits. The Hostel for Depressed Classes Students in Kolhapur founded in 1909 by the ruler of the area, Chhatrapati Shahu Maharaj, provided for the education of many would-be Dalit leaders. For many rural areas, the remarkable effort of a Jain, Bhaurao Patil (1887–1959), provided for education among all groups, with special concern for the untouchables. His Rayat Shakshan Sanstha (Peasants' Education Society) founded in Poona in 1919 continues today, with a Dr. Ambedkar College established there recently.

A rapid survey of Dalit institutions founded and run by Dalits—sometimes with the aid of Ambedkar's People's Education Society, but not always—reveals widespread initiatives. Nagpur has been an important centre for educational ventures. In addition to the early work of Bansode, Hardas, Jaibai Chaudhary and Thaware, N. K. Tirpude, social welfare minister in a Congress government in Maharashtra, established the Tirpude Institute of Social Work in Nagpur in 1965. His Yugantar Society also runs some twenty schools and hostels in various districts. Justice R. R. Bhole founded the People's Welfare Society, which established the P. W. S. Arts and Commerce College in Nagpur in 1968. Others are: Dr. Ambedkar College of Arts and Commerce at Amravati, Dr. Ambedkar College at Brahmapuri and Dr. Ambedkar College of Arts and Commerce at Chandrapur. The last was the site of tragic violence in 1994. The day after Marathwada University in Aurangabad added 'Dr. Babasaheb Ambedkar' to its name, the library at the Chandrapur college was burned. Ironically, the participants at the annual conference of a Dalit literary magazine *Asmitadarsh* (Mirror of Identity) were watching a performance of the Marathi version of the American play *Slave* by Amiri Baraka (LeRoi Jones) at the time.

Three other Nagpur area educators are mentioned briefly in the work of R. K. Kshirsagar.[22] L. S. Bhatkar founded a Shri Cokhamela

22. Kshirsagar, *Dalit Movement in India*, pp. 183–86, 229–30.

Hostel in Buldhana district in 1921; P. N. Bhatkar, a college graduate and an associate of Vithal Ramji Shinde, started a Cokhamela Boarding in Nagpur around 1917, and Raibhan Jadhav ran a boarding in Buldhana district from 1938 to 1942. The Dr. Babasaheb Ambedkar Memorial Law College near Dhule was founded by the Paschim Khandesh Dalit Shikshan Prasarak Mandal (Western Khandesh Dalit Education Society), and approved by the University of Pune in 1975. The Khandesh Mandal, founded by P. L. Lalinkar, had earlier set up a hostel for Dalit students in a remote town in Dhule district, and Lalingkar often fed the students by begging for grain until government aid was established. At Nanded, the Nagsena High School recalls the army of the Nags, a people who may have been Buddhist ancestors of the Mahars. Hanmantrao More (1901–93) initiated work in Nanded with a Milind Hostel and Milind Primary School in 1965 and 1966 respectively.[23] In Amravati, S. G. Naik, a leader of the Ambadevi Temple Satyagraha in Amravati in 1927, started a hostel and a school. And in Yavatmal, V. D. Makesar, born in 1878, started the Shri Cokhamela Free Boarding which is still in existence.

Nashik became an educational centre with contributions from D. K. 'Dadasaheb' Gaikwad (1902–71) and Shantabai Dani, both very important political figures and social workers. Gaikwad's political life is beyond the scope of this essay, but it should be said that he was so integral a part of the Ambedkarite movement that he organised a conference of untouchables at Yeola in Nashik district in 1935, at which Ambedkar declared his intention to quit Hinduism. And he embraced Buddhism along with Ambedkar in 1956. Gaikwad was the superintendent of the Ashram at Nashik (set up by Shahu Chhatrapati) from 1920 to 1926; and in 1934, he established the Ramabai Ambedkar Boarding also at Nashik. In 1957, he began the Takshashila High School and the Gautam Centre for Buddhism. He is also credited with establishing the Dr. Ambedkar College in Nagpur at the same spot where the mass conversion to Buddhism took place in 1956. Shantabai Dani, born in 1918 and still active, was a founder-member of the Republican Party of India (as was Gaikwad);

23. Ibid., p. 275.

she participated in the religious and economic activities of the Ambedkarite movement, and also founded the Ramabai Ambedkar Girls' School in 1965. She is by far the best-known female figure in the Ambedkarite political movement in Maharashtra. Another important early political leader, P. J. Roham (1905–91), was the superintendent of the Shahu Chhatrapati Boarding in Nashik from 1926 to 1934, succeeding Gaikwad. He also established a Depressed Classes Hostel in 1932 at Sangamner.

Although most educational institutions in southern Maharashtra were set up by Bhaurao Patil and his organisation, D. M. Shirke (1901–85), once a member of the former Bombay Legislative Assembly and an organiser of the Buddhist conversions in Kolhapur in 1957, also ran a school called Samata Vidyalaya (Equality School) in a Bhangi locality in Kolhapur although he was not a Bhangi.[24] In Ahmadnagar district, the area which witnessed the rise of Shinde's early Depressed Classes Mission, D. T. Rupvate continued the educational work begun much before. A hostel was started in 1946 in Sangamner, which developed into the Siddharth High School later on. Rupvate also founded the Janata High School in Poona and the Sambodhi High School in Ahmadnagar, and now his organisation runs some twenty-three hostels.

By no means was all enterprise in the Marathi-speaking area begun by Mahars. D. S. Powar, a Chambhar, started the Maharani Indumati Boarding at Kolhapur in 1924. Two other Chambhars were extremely important leaders, both in the Ambedkarite movement and outside: Sitaram Shivtarkar, secretary and treasurer of the Depressed Classes Education Society from its founding in 1928 until Ambedkar's announcement of conversion in 1935, founded the Rohidas Samaj Panchayat Sangh in 1952, named after Rohidas, the medieval Chamar saint of Varanasi. And P. N. Rajbhoj, who was injured in the Parvati Satyagraha in Poona in 1928, founded the Mahatma Phule Hostel and the Kamala Nehru Hostel, both near Poona. R. G. Khandale, who founded the All India Matang Seva Sangh in 1932, began a hostel in Dound in 1959. Much earlier, a Mang had been an important figure in Phule's movement. Lahujibuwa

24. Ibid., pp. 328–30.

Salve (1811–81) encouraged untouchable children to attend school and also opened a *talimkhana* (gymnasium and wrestling centre) in Poona where, it is said, not only Phule, but the revolutionary, Vasudeo Balwant Phadke and Bal Gangadhar Tilak were also trained in martial arts.[25]

Finally, the work of Vilas and Usha Wagh in Pune district is so unusual that it should be mentioned here. Besides a very active publishing house that deals solely with Dalit causes, the Waghs have founded and managed hostels and *ashrams* for three groups of neglected children: those of nomadic tribes, those whom the British called 'Criminal Tribes', and the children of prostitutes. They also have an organisation which aids those who, like themselves, have entered into inter-caste marriages.

Dalit Institutions outside Maharashtra

Outside Maharashtra, there are a great variety of institutions, including some 'open universities', which offer distance education to small groups of students living away from the main campus. These are usually government enterprises. At Deenapur in Andhra Pradesh, the Dalit Open University offers a one-year course on the life and mission of Ambedkar, and there is a Department of Dr Ambedkar and Jagjivan Ram Studies—a reference to the Chamar politician from Bihar who was a member of the union council of ministers in Congress governments from Independence until 1975. Babu Jagjivan Ram also encouraged scholarship about the medieval untouchable saint Ravidas, which culminated in the construction of a great Ravidas temple on the banks of the Ganga in Varanasi. One of the most ambitious projects is the medical college established in Bangalore by L. Shivalingaiah, formerly chief executive engineer in the state of Karnataka. As far as I know, there is no other medical college founded by a Dalit. Not even the People's Education Society's endeavours have been so ambitious.

25. Ibid., pp. 322–23.

In West Bengal, thousands attended a meeting of the Dalit Students' Movement in 1989.[26] There is an Ambedkar Open University in Gujarat, as well as a flourishing Gujarati Dalit literary movement. The *Bheem Patrika* for December 1994, published in Jalandhar in Punjab, notes that the Government of Punjab intends to set up a university in the name of Ambedkar soon. In Uttar Pradesh, there are numerous Dalit student groups, and also a multi-faceted university in Lucknow which is funded by the state government but established and planned by very committed Dalits. Another impressive educational venture has come up in Madhya Pradesh, planned by Dr M. L. Shahare, a retired government official. The Dr. Ambedkar National Institute is located in Mhow, the town which housed the army quarters where Ambedkar was born. Another Dalit institute is at Bhubaneshwar, Odisha—the National Institute of Social Work and Social Sciences (NISWASS)—established by Dr Radhakant Nayak, a person of broad interests since he combines a Dalit and Adivasi heritage. There are doubtless many more such institutions, but they all indicate the passion with which Dalits have taken the initiative for the furtherance of education and research.

It is hard to grasp the reach of Dalit educational institutions begun in various parts of India before the contemporary period, but it seems there was greater activity than any scholar, including myself, has so far acknowledged. R. K. Kshirsagar of the Dr. Babasaheb Ambedkar College of Arts and Commerce in Aurangabad collected a massive list of Dalit leaders from all over India by interviewing children and grandchildren when no printed sources were available. Limiting his study to those born between 1800 and 1920, he still has found 155 names worthy of mention. The briefest of references to some of the many who began educational enterprises gives us a sense of a tremendous stirring in almost all parts of India. We should note that every institution seems to have been begun by an individual, one of the 'benchmarks' established earlier. By looking at Kshirsagar's list, we find names and places that form an impressive array of Dalit initiative: M. L. Audiah started a high school in Secunderabad in the former state of Hyderabad in 1906; Ayyan Kali

26. *Dalit Voice*, 16–31 May 1989.

started a primary school (which was later burned) in Travancore in 1904, and M. V. Bhagya Reddy of Hyderabad began forty primary schools which had to be handed over to the government when there were no funds to run them. M. Chikkalingaiah, the first untouchable graduate in Mysore state, began hostels for girls and boys; Dharam Prakash founded Kumar Ashram at Meerut in 1928; Ealy Vadapally was responsible for a hostel in 1940 and later an Industrial Training School in the East Godavari district of present-day Andhra Pradesh; L. K. Guruswami started two night schools in Madras city in 1921 and later in four other areas; I. N. Iyakannu, born in 1875, taught in his Buddhist Primary School at the Kolar Gold Fields until 1942; Manikchand Jataveer, born in 1897, started a hostel, a library and schools in Agra, and M. Jayaseelan, born in 1912, started the hostel in Karnataka where L. Shivalingiah, founder of the Dr. Ambedkar Medical College in Bangalore, studied as a youth. Krishnaswamy, born in 1916, an active politician, an advocate of temple-entry, and a member of the Adi Dravida Education Society, began a free hostel in North Arcot, in the former province of Madras, and Piarelal Kureel started the Ranuva Ram Primary School and Hostel at Unnao in the United Provinces (now Uttar Pradesh) in 1940. In Bengal, two highly educated Namasudras—a community of Dalits—were concerned with educational activities: Sitanath Mondal, a doctor, began a school in his village in Khulna district (now in Bangladesh); and M. B. Mullick, a professor at the University of Calcutta, began a hostel. Clearly, Namasudras in Bengal had more opportunities than most untouchables in other areas.

B. S. Murthy founded the M. C. Rajah Hostel in Madras. Another early Tamil Buddhist, M. Y. Murugesan, started the South India Buddhist School in Marikuppam in 1932. S. Nagappa began a free hostel at Kurnool in present-day Andhra Pradesh in 1938; Pandit Palaniswami began a school for Depressed Classes in 1917 and a hostel in 1921, both in Madras; Madurai Pillai (1858–1913) of Madras, who seems to have had a financial base in Rangoon, founded a high school even earlier; Poykayil Yohannan propagated a new faith and set up schools and an industrial training centre in present-day Kerala before his death in 1939; Puranchand began a school at Agra in 1947; M. C. Rajah (1883–1947), one of the most famous

Depressed Class leaders of his day, established the Dravidian School at Nungambakkan in Madras city in 1930. The headquarters of the Adi Dharm of Mangu Ram (1886–1980) in Jalandhar in Punjab became the Ravi Das High School; and the Rev. John Rathnam began a Model School for technical and professional training in the Thousand Lights area in Madras, and a school and hostel later which do not seem to be related to any foreign mission.

Sundarlal Sagar, a man with no formal education, established the Jatav Pathshala Primary School in Agra; S. M. Siddayya of Mysore founded the Siddharth Educational Society and High School; Swami A. S. Sahajanandar established a school for untouchables in Madras in 1910, and built a Nandanar Temple, named after the untouchable saint of the Tamil country, and Tagadi Keshwan Shastri, born in 1907, started several night schools after the school he started in Kerala was burned by caste Hindus. Muldas Vaishya, a Vankar, was superintendent of the Gandhian Hostel in Ahmedabad—which seems to have been the only such Dalit institution in Gujarat—from 1921 to 1951.

Initiatives from America

VISION, a Dalit organisation based in New Jersey and New York, has a small scholarship fund for Dalit students in India, and this is probably the oldest of the American efforts. The recent work of two individuals seems to be very effective. Dr Rahul Deepankar, a medical practitioner in suburban Chicago, has begun a girls' school—Deepankar Kanya Inter-College—in the village of his birth, Unchagaon, near Bulandshahar in Uttar Pradesh. Started in 1997, the school now has 220 girls from the sixth to eighth standards, with a plan in place to add schooling up to the twelfth standard. The school was established in memory of Dr Deepankar's sister, who tragically suffered a dowry-related death. Ram Vilas Paswan, the Dalit Union railway minister at the time, was present at the inauguration of the school, an event that witnessed a gathering of 10,000 people in a village of 7,000.

According to *India Abroad* for 6 February 1998, Dr Solomon Darwin, 'from a Scheduled Caste family', founded the Riverside

School near Moti village (the Indian state is not mentioned). In this residential school of 160 students and twelve teachers, the students use computers from the third standard upward. Darwin hopes to have three Indian students studying in the United States and three American teachers in India. The school is affiliated to the Riverside Christian Schools system in Riverside, California, but Darwin stresses that there are no compulsory Bible lessons. He hopes that 90 per cent of the students will eventually go abroad for further education, a hope very different from that of Deepankar, who simply hopes for a better and more productive life for women. Darwin went to the United States in 1970 with a fifth standard education, attended Harvard University, became a banker, and in 1996, joined the University of Southern California to teach clinical accounting.

What strikes one about this recital of Dalit initiatives is the fact that many who founded night schools and hostels were themselves not educated. The other startling observation is the widespread and early initiative in the Marathi-speaking area. It is true that the compiler of much of the data from outside Maharashtra is Dr R. K. Kshirsagar, a political scientist and an academic, but his book is not in his main area of expertise, i.e., constitutional and political studies, and is clearly a labour of love as well as much personal effort on his part and that of several dozen associates. Not only education, but the history of Dalit efforts in education is important—and a cause for pride.

What was the rationale and what were the results of these efforts to initiate educational institutions? Early on, of course, hostels were established to enable an untouchable child from a village to have a place to live while attending a school, since it was unlikely that there would be relatives in the city wealthy enough to accommodate her/him. Night schools, of course, made it possible for labourers to learn to read, and were also centres for disseminating information about and the spirit of the Ambedkarite movement. When the government schools did not welcome untouchable children or accommodate girls, setting up schools in which they were respected as pupils was a genuine service. These early independent schools seem to have been chiefly in the Nagpur area, indicating greater wealth as well as greater eagerness among their patrons.

For Ambedkar, the motivation seems to have been the clear knowledge that pride and self-respect would be inculcated in a student in an institution which had been established by one of their own, and in which values were not dominated by those at the apex of the caste hierarchy. This indicates that the People's Education Society's colleges 'provide not only the freedom and space to breathe freely, but also a conducive setting in which Dalit students can develop and grow. It is here that Dalit students discover that they too can sing, dance, act, deliver speeches, play hockey and cricket, and crack jokes. They can develop egalitarian peer groups and seek sources of support.'[27] Padma Velaskar's study provides a welcome relief from the generally negative and pessimistic sociological surveys of Dalit student achievement, especially their high drop-out rate. Further study of the achievements and problems of Dalit students, specifically in these Dalit-founded institutions would be welcome. The culmination of Dalit efforts was enabled by Ambedkar's position in the pre-Independence government as a member of the viceroy's executive council and later in Nehru's cabinet. At that level, the only benchmark is individual initiative.

Ambedkar and the People's Education Society

Even before the People's Education Society was founded in 1945, a college was established in Bombay under Ambedkar's influence. As Sardar Jagjit Singh records, '[I]t was prior to 1937 that Baba Sahib Dr. B. R. Ambedkar was exploring the possibilities of opening some negotiations with the leaders of the Sikh Community and he had a mind to embrace Sikhism, which was also in turn to become the religion of all his followers. During the course of his negotiation with the Gurdwara Committee of Shri Nankana Sahib it was decided to open a College in Bombay which was to impart education to the people of all races, castes, creeds and sexes. Thus the College which is now called Khalsa College was founded in 1937. It now has more

27. Velaskar, 'Ideology, Education and the Political Struggle for Liberation: Change and Challenge Among the Dalits of Maharashtra', in *Education, Development and Underdevelopment*, eds. Shukla and Kaul, p. 117.

than two thousand six hundred students.' Singh concludes that Khalsa College is 'a living monument of the short lived honeymoon of the Sikhs and Dr. Ambedkar'.[28] I was told that when the Siddharth College was founded by Ambedkar in 1946, the administrators and faculty from the Khalsa College became its earliest staff.

The People's Education Society was founded by Ambedkar on 8 July 1945, with him as its first chairman, followed by D. G. Jadhav, Parmar Guruji, Mohiti Guruji, and Justice Bhole as chairmen successively. Parmar and Mohiti Guruji were Gujarati untouchables, representing not only their commitment to the Ambedkarite movement but also to Ambedkar's efforts to broaden the scope of his work to reach out to all untouchable castes. Higher castes were also included in Ambedkar's efforts if they believed in the People's Education Society's goals; indeed, the early colleges could not have been run without their participation. The Society's first governing body was entirely Dalit in composition. The principal of the first college and many of the administrators and professors belonged to higher castes, chiefly Chandrasena Kayastha Prabhu. A caste with high educational attainments which claimed Kshatriya status, it was nevertheless labelled as Shudra by most Brahmans. Many of them were involved in Ambedkar's early activities, from Surendranath Tipnis who participated in the historic Mahad Satyagraha demanding the opening up of public water bodies for use by the untouchables—which marked the beginning of the mass phase of the Ambedkarite movement—in 1927 to M. B. Chitnis, who later became a vital member of the People's Education Society. Similarly, many Brahmans also supported Ambedkar's movement. For instance, B. G. Gokhale, a Buddhist scholar now retired from Wake Forest University in the United States, came from the prestigious St. Xavier's College in Bombay to Siddharth College to teach Pali and the tenets of Buddhism out of his faith in the education of Dalits and conversion

28. 'A Living Monument' by Sardar Jagjit Singh, Head of the History Department at Khalsa College, printed in *Baba Saheb Dr. Ambedkar Jayanti Sandesh* (message), Agra: Siddharth Educational and Cultural Society, 1966. The late Dr S. D. Gaikwad also related the story of Khalsa College to me in 1964.

to Buddhism. The Siddharth College of Arts was started in 1946 and housed in the hutments along Queens Road in Churchgate and the old military barracks on Marine Lines in south Bombay. In 1949, the Albert Building was renamed Anand Bhavan. And in 1951, the Menkwa Building (I have been told this was the old Japanese Bank building confiscated during the war.) was renamed Buddha Bhavan. At first, Siddharth College was a morning college which began at 11 a.m., allowing the students to hold down their jobs. Its first principal was Lt. Col. A. B. Gajendragadkar, a Brahman and a Sanskritist, who died a year and a half later. He was succeeded by the vice-principal, Dr V. S. Patankar, then by H. R. Karnik, and in 1964 by J. V. Deshpande, all of them high-caste.

Within five years of its founding, Siddharth College had 3,000 students on its rolls. Within twenty years, there were 7,000 students—3,000 of them from the 'Backward Classes'—enrolled in the seven colleges and three high schools of the Society. The nature of the colleges and their locations by 1965 is important: Siddharth College of Arts and Sciences; Siddharth College of Commerce and Economics; Siddharth College of Law, and Siddharth College of Mass Communications and Media were located in Bombay, as well as Siddharth Night High School. The Siddharth Vihar (in this context, a hostel) at Wadala was begun in 1964 with 300 students, making it easier for students from outside Bombay to attend the various institutions of the People's Education Society in the city. The reputation of the original college has varied from year to year, but some of its achievements are truly noteworthy. In 1950, the first graduating class of Siddharth College started the Siddharth Sahitya Sangh (Siddharth Literary Club), and the Dalit literary movement owes its origin to Siddharth and other colleges. Gokhale notes that the 'new graduates of Siddharth College had received an education which was different from that of the earlier Mahar elite ... they saw themselves as new men, inferior to none, and harbingers of a new era... They did not wish to use traditional culture but instead they sought to create a new one through their words.'[29]

29. Jayashree Gokhale, *From Concessions to Confrontation: The Politics of an Indian Untouchable Community*, Bombay: Popular Prakashan, 1993, pp. 308–09.

In Aurangabad, Milind Mahavidhyalaya, Milind College of Science, Dr. Ambedkar College of Commerce, and Milind Multipurpose High School were all functioning within a twenty-year period. Here the Buddhist influence seemed strongest, and later the college complex was called Nagsena Vana Party, in reference to Nagasena, and the Nag people, a tribal group whom Ambedkar felt were Buddhists in the ancient period. The colleges are at the foot of the Aurangabad Buddhist caves, and a small Buddhist structure near the caves' entrance provides shelter to *bhikshus* (Buddhist monks). The famous cave temples of Ajanta and Ellora are nearby. However, the city was also the site of one of the most devastating caste riots in recent history. Since Ambedkar had begun higher education in Marathwada, his followers wanted the university, which was founded in Aurangabad after Ambedkar's death, to be renamed in his honour. After much violence in the 1980s, a 'Long March' to the city, and the passage of several years, the university was renamed Dr. Babasaheb Ambedkar Marathwada University in 1994.

In Mahad, the site of the 1927 satyagraha, the Dr. Babasaheb Ambedkar College of Arts, Science and Commerce was founded in 1961. So important is the Mahad event that a gathering to commemorate the satyagraha was held in December 1998. In Dalit poetry, the single word 'Mahad' stands for protest against inequality and injustice. The Subhedar Savadkar Vidhyarthi Ashram—named after one of the participants in the satyagraha—is another school in Mahad which provides elementary education along with boarding facilities for its students. Also in Ratnagiri district, near Ambedkar's ancestral home, the Matashri Ramabai Vidyarthi Ashram—named after Ambedkar's first wife—assists girls in an area where they find it difficult to receive a good education. In Pandharpur, the heart of the Maharashtrian Bhakti movement, Ambedkar aided in the establishment of the Shri Gadge Maharaj Backward Class Hostel, named after the most radical of Maharashtra's many religious figures of the twentieth century, and to this was added the Gautam Vidyalaya, an institution of the People's Education Society.[30]

30. From K. B. Talwatkar's report as secretary in the initial issue of *Boddhisattva* (1965), noted in Adele Fiske,'Scheduled Caste Buddhist

By the mid-sixties, there were caste Hindus on the People's Education Society board, and a good many Dalits in positions of administration and teaching. There were also efforts to broaden the base of the leadership to include non-Maharashtrians. In 1988, the chairman of People's Education Society was B. Basavalingappa, a former minister and Congress party Member of the Legislative Assembly of Karnataka. The Society has continued to open colleges, and the most recent is the Dr. Ambedkar College of Arts and Commerce in Pune which was inaugurated in 1992. In Aurangabad, the Ambedkar Physical Education College and the colleges of science, arts, commerce, and law were added. Kshirsagar lists the People's Education Society's institutions as twelve colleges (in Bombay, Aurangabad, Mahad and Pune); two diploma institutes in Bombay; nine high schools in Bombay, Aurangabad, Pandharpur, New Bombay, Nanded and Bangalore, and four hostels in Pandharpur, Mahad, Dapoli and Bombay.[31]

This list of names and places conveys the impression that there is a vast commitment to education among the various Dalit communities across India. Although, this may not be entirely true, I have seen impressive institutions that really met a felt need; and I have seen badly furnished rooms that barely sheltered the students from the rain. What cannot be denied, however, is that Ambedkar's commitment to education and message of pride and self-respect was shared widely and has resulted in a better India.

Organizations,' in *The Untouchables in Contemporary India*, ed. J. Michael Mahar, Tucson: University of Arizona Press, 1972, pp. 113–42. Gadge Maharaj is the only Hindu religious figure associated with Ambedkar. For his message, see 'The Last Kirtan of Gadge Baba' in *The Experience of Hinduism*, ed. Eleanor Zelliot and Maxine Berntsen, Albany: SUNY Press, 1988.

31. Kshirsagar, *Dalit Movement in India*, pp. 98–99.

2

A College of One's Own

An International Perspective on the Value of Historically Dalit Colleges

LAURA DUDLEY JENKINS

As an American scholar I am aware of the difficult debates over the closure of historically black colleges and universities (HBCUs) or their consolidation with neighbouring universities. While a Fulbright scholar in South Africa and India in 2007–08, I followed the effort to combine historically black, 'coloured' and white institutions of higher education in South Africa as part of an ongoing commitment to de-segregate higher education. Although partly motivated by economic pressures, these efforts are also laudable attempts to create multiracial institutions. At the same time, they raise dilemmas for those seeking social justice. Even if separate institutions are, in part, a remnant of the ugly, racist past of the Jim Crow era in the United States and apartheid in South Africa, many became political, cultural and social bastions for oppressed groups. Some were equally a legacy of the anti-racist ideals of their founders. What is lost when these colleges disappear?

These can be difficult questions to discuss; but often, considering a similar issue in another context can be revealing and move the conversation forward. As a scholar of Indian politics, I have always found that the study of India sheds new light on policy dilemmas in other contexts.[1] Thus, in this essay, I will draw on the

1. Laura Dudley Jenkins, 'Race, Caste and Justice: Social Science Categories and Antidiscrimination Politics in India and the United States', *Connecticut Law Review*, vol. 36, no. 3, 2004, pp. 747–85; see

example of colleges founded by and for Dalits—formerly known as 'untouchables'—to highlight the value of institutions serving marginalised populations. While not arguing that all such institutions in all contexts should be preserved, I point out that they do serve important purposes for oppressed communities. Inspired by Virginia Woolf's famous argument that women need money and a room of their own in order to write, I argue that historically oppressed groups can benefit from resources and learning environments of their own.[2] Dalit colleges offer both a distinct educational space and significant resources and opportunities that can facilitate the advancement of marginalised communities. If such institutions are disbanded or absorbed, policymakers must consider how such functions can be realised in more integrated institutions. In this regard, other Dalit-led initiatives, particularly study centres, offer possibilities that may be useful models elsewhere.

In the United States, there has been an ongoing debate over separate schools, colleges and universities for African Americans. The notorious 'separate but equal' doctrine of the Supreme Court in the 1896 case *Plessy v. Ferguson* was a low point for racial justice, allowing white racists to deny educational opportunities and integration to African American students. Efforts from within the African American community to provide the option of separate schools, even in contexts of limited integration, constitute another aspect of the separation debate.

For example, in Cincinnati, in 1921, at a time when public schools were somewhat integrated for students (although no black faculty were allowed to teach in them), the Harriet Beecher Stowe School was founded by some local African American leaders and the Board of Education as 'a "separate" school' with all-black students, faculty and staff; the school was a 'source of intense disagreement and debate among black Cincinnatians'.[3] Opponents viewed it 'as a blow

---

also Laura Dudley Jenkins, *Identity and Identification in India: Defining the Disadvantaged*, London and New York: Routledge, 2009.

2. Virginia Woolf, *A Room of One's Own*, New York: Harcourt, 1989.
3. David Sandor, 'Black is as Good a Color as White: The Harriet Beecher Stowe School and the Debate Over Separate Schools in Cincinnati', *Ohio Valley History*, vol. 9, no. 2, 2009, p. 27.

to racial equality'; but proponents argued that '[a] separate school could preserve a degree of black independence in education, instil racial pride, and help foster equal opportunities for black children'.[4] Similar dilemmas and arguments have emerged more recently in debates over the advisability of racially- or culturally-based charter schools[5] and the sustainability of historically black colleges and universities.[6]

Due to the different demographic landscape, South African colleges for black students under apartheid did not constitute 'minority' institutions in the numerical sense, but as institutions for an oppressed racial group they had some similar dynamics. Compared to the United States, fewer were founded on the basis of anti-racist ideals: 'With the exception of Fort Hare, which predated apartheid and assumed university status in 1959, all were set up after 1960 to train African workers, especially as teachers and civil servants. These institutions were managed by Afrikaners loyal to the Nationalist government'.[7] Nevertheless, black universities became centres of resistance to racial domination, and University College of

4. Ibid., pp. 28–29.
5. Chris Levister, 'A Case for Segregation: Charter Schools Catering to Black Students Wildly Popular', *Black Voice News Online*, 23 August 2007, http://www.blackvoicenews.com/content/view/41191/4/, viewed 19 November 2009; James R Riffel, 'Mostly Somali Charter School Allowed to Open High School', *San Diego News Network* (*SDNN.com*), 5 August 2009, retrieved from http://www.sdnn.com/sandiego/2009-08-05/local-county-news/mostly-somali-charter-school-allowed-to-open-high-school, viewed 19 November 2009.
6. Marybeth Gasman, 'Views: Obama's Agenda for Black Colleges', *Inside Higher Education*, 25 August 2009, retrieved from http://www.insidehighereducation.com/views/2009/08/25/gasman, viewed 19 November 2009; Scott Jaschick, 'Threat to Black Colleges', *Inside Higher Education*, 17 November 2009, http://www.insidehighered.com/news/2009/11/17/hbcu, viewed 19 November 2009.
7. Edward B. Fiske and Helen F. Ladd, *Elusive Equity: Educational Reform in Post-Apartheid South Africa*, Washington, D.C.: Brookings Institution Press, 2004.

Fort Hare (established in 1916 by Scottish missionaries) stood out for its role as an incubator of black leadership.

Like the illustrious list of prominent African Americans who graduated from HBCUs in the United States, the alumni roll of Fort Hare 'reads like a Who's Who of southern African leaders'.[8] Thus, democratic South African leaders faced a dilemma: Should they invest in colleges like Fort Hare to make up for years of unequal resources or close or merge them as 'vestiges of the hated apartheid system'?[9] Although at one point it was threatened with absorption by the historically white Rhodes University, the University of Fort Hare continues to exist and has itself absorbed one campus of Rhodes University.[10] This is one of the many post-apartheid mergers of previously segregated colleges. The University of Kwazulu Natal (UKZN) in Durban, for example, includes formerly white, black and Indian institutions, and is the result of a government-led reorganisation to both racially integrate higher education and to facilitate economies of scale.[11]

In India, Dr B. R. Ambedkar (1891–1956) was the remarkable man who both fought for equality of opportunity in education as independent India's first law minister and founded distinct colleges for the Dalit community. Born into a caste considered untouchable, he was eventually educated at Columbia University and the London School of Economics. In the years leading up to India's Independence, he advocated the rights of the castes traditionally considered low in the Hindu caste hierarchy, and was the architect of India's democratic constitution. In addition to ensuring legal protection and programmes for the lower-caste citizens, he was mindful of the need for empowerment from within for these weaker communities

8. Ibid., p. 201.
9. Ibid., p. 202.
10. David Jobbins, 'Fort Hare Fights Back from Brink', *Times Higher Education*, 29 November 2002, http://www.timeshighereducation.co.uk/story.asp?storyCode=173301&sectioncode=26, viewed 20 November 2009.
11. Roshen Kishun, Dean UKZN International, interview by author, 4 March 2008.

in the areas of education and religion. In this regard, he led a mass conversion of roughly half a million Dalits to Buddhism in 1956. Buddhist converts report that education became a central focus of their post-conversion lives, and the colleges founded by Ambedkar have been influenced by Buddhist ideals.[12] Ambedkar remains the inspiration for the contemporary Dalit (literally 'oppressed' or 'crushed') movement in India.

To serve students who did not have access to higher education, Ambedkar, through his People's Education Society, founded several colleges, including Siddharth College in Bombay (now Mumbai) in 1946 and Milind College in Aurangabad in 1950. 'It was his dream to found an ideal educational institution with modern scientific apparatus and with a staff of proved merit, with a view to promoting higher education among the lower middle classes and especially among the Scheduled Castes.'[13] These institutions continue today; and although they are not exclusively for Dalit students, historically disadvantaged students predominate in them. Institutions such as Milind College and Siddharth College provide Dalit and other disadvantaged students a distinct educational space and significant resources and opportunities to pursue their studies.

The contexts and histories of education in the United States, South Africa and India vary tremendously. The legal landscapes, the histories and forms of discrimination, the demographic contexts, the motivations of the founders of separate colleges, and the terms of historical and current debates are all different. Thus, the rather rosy view of Indian Dalit colleges that follows should not be taken as a blanket defence of distinct educational systems for minorities

12. Laura Dudley Jenkins, 'Women's Empowerment through Religious Conversion: Voices of Buddhists in Nagpur, India' in *'Speaking Truth to Power': Religion, Caste and the Subaltern Question in India*, ed. Manu Bhagavan and Anne Feldhaus, New Delhi: Oxford University Press, 2008.
13. Scheduled Castes is a government administrative term for Dalits, formerly known as 'untouchables'. See Dhananjay Keer, *Dr. Ambedkar, Life and Mission*, (originally published in 1954; 1971 edition, reprinted in 2002), Bombay: Popular Prakashan, 1971, p. 380.

and other marginalised groups—certainly not of those systems motivated by racism or even of institutions established with the best of intentions. Rather, I point out some of the aspects of Dalit colleges that have been empowering students and their communities to highlight what could be lost if such institutions disappear, and then consider another Dalit educational initiative—a study centre—that serves some of the same purposes and might provide useful ideas for those societies, like the United States and South Africa, considering or experiencing the closure or absorption of colleges for historically oppressed groups.

Distinct Educational Space

Caste discrimination continues to prevent many Indian citizens from achieving their potential. Although many students from lower-caste backgrounds—aided by a longstanding policy of affirmative action (known as 'reservations') in education (and employment)—have navigated their way through mainstream education to higher levels, caste discrimination can still be a roadblock to success.[14] A recent human rights report documented casteism in some Indian schools, resulting in 'discrimination, discouragement, exclusion, alienation, physical and psychological abuse, and even segregation, from both their teachers and their fellow students'.[15] Discrimination at educational institutions persists even in urban areas and at the highest levels of higher education. In 2006, Dalit medical students at India's premier medical school, the All India Institute of Medical Sciences (AIIMS), filed a complaint about intimidation and discrimination, accompanied by a memorandum from forty other students reporting similar incidents. One student wrote: 'I have been subjected to mental and physical torture from my very first day at this institute ... I was abused on my caste and, in the last few days my room had

14. Jenkins, *Identity and Identification in India*.
15. Quoted in Human Rights Watch and Centre for Human Rights and Global Justice, *Hidden Apartheid: Caste Discrimination Against India's Untouchables*, 2007, p. 92, http://www.hrw.org/en/reports/2007/02/12/hidden-apartheid-0, viewed 1 June 2013.

been locked from outside because of which I was unable to attend classes.'[16]

The chairman of the Union government's University Grants Commission (UGC), which oversees higher education in India, Sukhadeo Thorat, took a particular interest in such caste-based abuse and hazing (also known as 'ragging') activities more generally. The UGC's 24-hour anti-ragging helpline may have been motivated in part by such caste-based bullying. Thorat also headed a government committee set up to investigate the incidents at AIIMS in the wake of protests against an expansion of the ambit of reservations. The committee reported on the experiences of lower caste students:

> In practical examinations and viva voce, these students said, the treatment meted out to them was 'not fair'. Worse, 76 per cent said higher-caste faculty members enquired about the castes of their students while 84 per cent said they were asked, directly or indirectly, about their caste backgrounds. An equal percentage of students alleged that their grading was adversely affected due to their background. The reserved category students also alleged 'social isolation' at various levels, including even from faculty members, with 84 per cent students saying they faced violence and segregation in the hostel that often forced them to shift to hostels No. 4 and 5 where there was a concentration of SC/ST students.[17]

Notably the chair of the committee that produced this report, Thorat, is a graduate of Milind College, where he received his BA degree. After higher studies at other universities, he has gone on to be a leading figure through his work as chairman of the UGC, professor at Jawaharlal Nehru University (JNU), Delhi, and director of the Indian Institute of Dalit Studies (IIDS), Delhi which publishes a wide range of research on Dalit issues.[18] Thorat's success and continuing advocacy on behalf of Dalits is a testament to the important role

16. Ibid.
17. Aarti Dhar, 'AIIMS Director Venugopal played provocative role in anti-quota stir', *The Hindu*, 6 May 2007, http://www.hinduonnet.com/2007/05/06/stories/2007050609700100.htm, viewed 22 November 2009.
18. See http://www.ugc.ac.in, http://www.dalitstudies.org.in/.

institutions such as Milind College continue to play in the education of community leaders.

Many leaders and activists of the contemporary Dalit movement in Maharashtra attended Milind or Siddharth Colleges. The confidence that current students and alumni exude is compelling. Walking around the campus, I heard students and teachers at these colleges loudly greet each other and me with the salutation, 'Jai Bhim!' This is an alternative to the distinctly caste—Hindu greetings 'Namaste' or 'Namaskar', commonly used in India. 'Jai Bhim' means victory to Ambedkar, or, as one faculty member put it, victory to Ambedkar's thought.[19] Rather than trying to blend in or risk facing the hostility discussed above, students walking around these campuses are free to signal their identities. As the principal of Milind College emphasised, 'They are free to express' themselves and 'to greet freely Jai Bhim'.[20]

Instead of being forcibly locked into their hostels, or facing de facto segregation into certain hostels, many poor students are empowered through free hostels and books;[21] the Siddharth College mission-statement and 'declaration' make the commitment to underprivileged students clear.[22] Other aspects of the campus structures and spaces are empowering as well. In front of the main building of Milind College, there is a large peepul tree which, the faculty members noted, was a descendent of the tree under which the Buddha received enlightenment—the historic Bodhi Tree at Bodh Gaya. Ambedkar, they stated, brought the cutting from another descendent of the Bodhi Tree in Sri Lanka. The symbolic significance of this tree is not just religious. Although Buddhism started in what

19. J. S. Sardar, director of Dr. Babasaheb Ambedkar Research Centre, Milind College of Science, Aurangabad, interview by author, 12 February 2008.
20. L. B. Waghmare, principal of Milind College of the Arts, interview by author, 12 February 2008.
21. J. S. Sardar, director of Dr. Babasaheb Ambedkar Research Centre, Milind College of Science, Aurangabad, interview by author, 12 February 2008.
22. http://siddharthcollegeofasc.com/, viewed 1 June 2013. See 'Profile' and 'Vision and Mission' under 'About Us' tab.

is now India, today Buddhists comprise only 0.8 per cent of the population.[23] Many of these Buddhists, particularly in Maharashtra, are descended from the former untouchables. Although they feel they have transcended caste barriers by embracing Buddhism, others remember their origins. For example, whereas they see themselves as Buddhists, the government, the press, and society at large often refer to them with a distinct label: 'neo-Buddhists'. The 'Bodhi Tree' on the Milind College campus provides a living 'link' to the broader global Buddhist community in Sri Lanka and around the world, which helps to inspire confidence in the Buddhist students who see it every day. My faculty guides also pointed out that the architecture of Milind College is partly inspired by Buddhist architecture, and noted the college's proximity to the magnificent Buddhist caves of Ajanta and Ellora.

Thus, even the geographic location of these colleges is significant and strategically empowering. The principal of Milind College of Arts, Dr L. B. Waghmare, commented that the Marathwada region, where this college is situated, is a 'very backward region even today'.[24] When Milind College was founded in 1950, there was only one government college in the region, and in order to get a degree students had to travel to Osmania University in Hyderabad; thus, 'in spite of the talents, Buddhist students had no chance for higher education'.[25] Ambedkar founded the college in this region 'for all people, not only for Buddhists', recognising the general need for local higher education, although the college remains uniquely focused on Buddhist and lower-caste students.[26] There are now many colleges in Aurangabad, and all have some Buddhist students; but they are a minority in these other colleges, reported Waghmare. What is different for students at Milind College? 'The feeling of equality is imbibed ... They don't have a chance to feel inferior to anybody.'[27]

23. http://censusindia.gov.in/Census_Data_2001/India_at_glance/religion.aspx, viewed 22 November 2009.
24. L. B. Waghmare, interview by author, 12 February 2008.
25. Ibid.
26. Ibid.
27. Ibid.

Siddharth College is located in the Fort area of Mumbai, which is the administrative and business hub of this huge city. Headquartered in an imposing colonial-era building, this, the first college established by Ambedkar's People's Education Society, was designed and destined 'to promote intellectual, moral and social democracy' during a time of rapid political change, just one year before Independence. Although the plight of lower-caste families in rural areas is severe, many that have migrated to cities such as Mumbai face challenges as well; and Siddharth College continues to honour the People's Education Society's original objective 'to cater to the educational needs of the ever-growing population of this cosmopolitan city in general and to promote higher education among the Scheduled Castes in particular'.[28]

The Hobson's choice between rural immiserisation and urban alienation is compellingly brought out in Dr Narendra Jadhav's biography of his father, which is also in part a memoir of his own youth as a member of a Dalit family that migrated from a village to Mumbai.[29] Notably, Jadhav's brother was initially able to receive education by attending Siddharth College, and he himself went on to become chief economist of the Reserve Bank of India and vice chancellor of the University of Pune.[30] Recalling how important 'learn and earn' or work/study opportunities were for his elder brother's college education at Siddharth College, Jadhav prioritised the expansion of 'learn and earn' programmes at the University of Pune. Moreover, his goal was to make these programmes 'skill building' (rather than manual labour) and available 'on demand' (for students who need or desire work) to avoid categorising or stigmatising disadvantaged students.[31] In this case, possibilities and ideas from a college with historically Dalit roots now contribute to the enhancement of opportunities at other colleges and universities.

28. http://siddharthcollegeasc.com/, viewed, 22 November 2009.
29. Narendra Jadhav, *Untouchables: My Family's Triumphant Escape from India's Caste System*, Berkeley: University of California Press, 2005.
30. Narendra Jadhav, interview by author, 8 February 2009.
31. Ibid.

The names of the colleges also reflect their distinct goals and character. Siddharth College is named after the Buddha, and Milind College is named after a Greek king, Menander, who converted to Buddhism. According to Waghmare, Milind (or Menander) became king 'not by virtue of birth' but after engaging in debates and acquiring knowledge. King Milind declared that he would become the disciple of the learned person who defeated him in debate; and after philosophical disputations with the learned Buddhist *bhikkhu* (monk), Nagasena, Milind embraced Buddhism—an event recorded in the Buddhist canonical text *Milindpanho* (Questions of King Milind). Waghmare told the story to emphasise that King Milind exemplified 'intellectual honesty' as opposed to 'slavery', and that this intellectual honesty is the 'ideal' of the college.[32] The space provided by colleges such as Milind and Siddharth offers a safe zone, a place to live, study, work and express oneself, and a sense of pride and connection with the broader Buddhist community. The geographic locations, campus structures, and even the landscape of these colleges serve to empower their students.

Significant Resources and Opportunities

The colleges with historically Dalit roots offer resources and opportunities in the form of community mentors, a community archive and curriculum, an alumni network, and an incubator for community leaders. The significance of access to resources is clear from the early days of these colleges. When Ambedkar, through his People's Education Society, was building Milind College, his correspondence was filled with inquiries and concerns about resources—from the mundane (bricks needed for construction and negotiations for hiring trucks) to scholarships and other needs of the students.[33] Ambedkar's frustration over resources is clear when he lamented in an essay on

32. L. B. Waghmare, interview by author, 12 February 2008.
33. 'Telegram about scholarship meeting', p. 341; 'Correspondence about bricks and trucks', pp. 371, 375–76, in B. R. Ambedkar, *Dr. Babasaheb Ambedkar, Writings and Speeches; Vol. 21: Correspondence* vol. 21, Government of Maharashtra: Mumbai, 2006.

'Hindus and their want of social conscience' that Americans spent far more on 'Negro education' than Hindus spent on any funds for untouchables. He included tables of American bequests, educational funds, and religious organisations' donations and estimated that American whites spent $85,000,000 between 1865 and 1930 'on the advancement of the Negroes', whereas the 'only organization the Hindus can boast of is the Harijan Sevak Sangh ... Its annual expenditure does not go beyond a few thousand rupees on petty and insignificant and insubstantial purposes'.[34] Thus the concentration of resources involved in setting up these colleges was a remarkable achievement.

Although the Indian government has made far-reaching efforts to provide scholarships and housing for lower-caste students in higher education, resources and opportunities can be scarce for them in mainstream colleges. At a national seminar on Dalit postgraduate and research students, Lakshmi et al. critiqued, in their paper, the way Scheduled Caste (SC) or Scheduled Tribe (ST) students in mainstream colleges may be placed in separate dormitories and face discrimination in the classroom, denying them both material resources and academic support and mentoring:

> The Dalits are again forced by the state machinery to remain isolated and at the same time under-nourished in the SC/ST Hostels. In Colleges and Universities, they are normally under rated; described as inferior not only by the fellow students but also by the teaching community, which is highly dominated by Brahminic elements. Even the brilliant Dalit students are looked down and discriminated on the basis of caste. They are not even recognized by their teachers.[35]

34. B. R. Ambedkar, *Dr. Babasaheb Ambedkar: Writings and Speeches, Vol. 5: Unpublished Writings*, Government of Maharashtra: Education Department, 1989, pp. 97–99.
35. K. Vijaya Lakshmi, Y. Srilatha and T. Rajani, 'Dalit Mobilization through Education,' in *Dalits: Assertion for Identity*, ed. Ambrose Pinto (Proceedings of the National Seminar of Dalit Postgraduate and Research Students held from 23–25 January 1999 at the Indian Social Institute), New Delhi: Indian Social Institute, 1999, pp. 153–54.

Although some Dalit students are mentored by upper-caste teachers and professors, most have had some experience of discrimination in their school or college days. Kumud Pawde, a Dalit woman who became a professor of Sanskrit (a subject traditionally forbidden to women and Dalits) writes compellingly about two upper-caste men who taught her Sanskrit—her supportive and inspirational Sanskrit teacher in school[36] and her Sanskrit professor at college, whose 'taunts left my mind wounded and bleeding'.[37] Although Milind and Siddharth Colleges have professors from all caste backgrounds, the histories and ideals of these colleges make it more likely that students will find mentors among the faculty.

Across the world, historical archives of minority or marginalised communities are sometimes missing or face the risk of destruction. The Siddharth College library, however, is a valuable repository of many of Ambedkar's writings, his reports of many conferences in pursuit of the empowerment of lower castes and women, his personal notebooks, as well as books from his personal library. An interested student can turn to the *Report of the Depressed Classes Conference Nagpur Sessions* of 1942 and read Ambedkar's speech to the assembled women, including his exhortation: 'Give education to your children. Instil ambition in them. Remove from them all inferiority complex'.[38] A Siddharth College student can browse through Ambedkar's handwritten notes on political, religious and legal topics as varied as the life of the Buddha, ancestral property, the French Revolution, the undue influence of money in politics, maternity benefits, or his thoughts on the question, 'Why are untouchables untouchables?'.[39] Several previously unpublished

36. Kumud Pawde, 'The Story of My Sanskrit', in *Poisoned Bread: Translations from Modern Marathi Dalit Literature*, ed. Arjun Dangle, Bombay: Orient Longman, 1994, pp. 101–03.
37. Ibid., p. 104.
38. *Report of Depressed Classes Conference Nagpur Sessions*, Nagpur: G. T. Meshram, 1942, p. 66. ('Depressed Classes' was the official term for the Dalits or Scheduled Castes prior to Independence).
39. 'Dr. Ambedkar's notebooks', viewed in Siddharth College Library, Mumbai on 20 October 2006.

essays by Ambedkar were provided by a former librarian of Siddharth College for inclusion in a series of books published by the Government of Maharastra's Department of Education, and they are now more widely available.[40] The library provides an intellectual space for students and researchers, and is headed by a librarian who received his degree at the college itself, as did his father and daughter.

In India, education is tightly controlled by the state, but Siddharth College includes special subjects in its curriculum to reflect the priorities of the institution. For example, one can receive a degree in Pali, the ancient language of the majority of the key Buddhist texts that is close to the language that the Buddha himself spoke.[41] Siddharth College also attaches much importance to the sciences, reflecting Ambedkar's emphasis on both religion and rationality that foreshadowed current efforts to encourage scientific education among the lesser-educated communities. Thus, the curriculum both looks back to the community's linguistic and religious heritage as well as embraces opportunities of the future in science.

Alumni networks are another important resource. Intel (USA) donated computers to the Siddharth College physics laboratory because a Siddharth graduate worked there.[42] This is just one example of the importance of alumni networks for a community. Networking for political empowerment and economic opportunities through the alumni networks of Dalit colleges helps the colleges and the students. When I spoke with Dalit activists in Maharashtra and mentioned that I had visited Siddharth and Milind Colleges, their eyes invariably lit up because they or someone close to them is an alumnus. The role of these colleges as fulcrums for community networking is an important function.

One possible argument against distinct institutions for minority or marginalised communities is that their separation from mainstream colleges limits networking opportunities. Yet in contexts

40. Ambedkar, *Dr. Babasaheb Ambedkar, Writings and Speeches; Vol. 5: Unpublished Writings* vol. 5, p. xiii.
41. Karen Armstrong, *Buddha*, New York: Penguin, 2001, p. xiii.
42. Nagnath Sao, retired professor of physics of Siddharth College, in conversation with the author, 12 October 2006.

of continuing discrimination in social circles and job markets, networking *within* communities may be particularly crucial for the students' future employability. In a study replicating, in India, the methods used in the American study, 'Are Emily and Greg More Employable than Lakisha and Jamal?',[43] Sukhadeo Thorat and Paul Attewell found that qualified Dalit graduates are less likely to be called in for interviews than their non-Dalit counterparts.[44] After sending over 4,000 résumés (from fictional, equally qualified male graduates) to over 500 private sector employers who had advertised jobs, the researchers found that résumés with names associated with the Dalit community were only two-thirds as likely as those featuring higher-caste names to progress to the next stage in the hiring process.[45]

Not only are job markets impacted by caste distinctions; investors considering entrepreneurs and innovations can be quite insular as well. Many wealthy Indians prefer to invest in 'family members or close friends', making it difficult for entrepreneurs without these wealthy family connections to get companies off the ground.[46] Narendra Jadhav argues that both contemporary and historical barriers to economic opportunity play a role because past exclusion and discrimination have 'impacted Dalit access to capital assets and employment opportunities. This has meant a greater incidence of poverty and deprivation among Dalits'.[47]

Dalit or Buddhist students choosing a college face a Catch-22 situation. Having a Dalit institution one's résumé may mark someone

43. Marianne Bertrand and Sendhil Mullainathan, 'Are Emily and Greg More Employable than Lakisha and Jamal? A Field Experiment on Labor Market Discrimination', *National Bureau of Economic Research Working Paper Series*, 2003, http://www.nber.org/papers/w9873, viewed 1 June 2013.
44. See Sukhadeo Thorat and Paul Attewell, 'The Legacy of Social Exclusion: A Correspondence Study of Job Discrimination in India', *Economic and Political Weekly*, vol. 42, no. 21, 13 October 2007, pp. 4141–45, http://www.epw.org.in/uploads/articles/11135.pdf.
45. Ibid.
46. Vikas Bajaj, 'In India, a Developing Case of Innovation Envy,' *New York Times*, 9 December 2009, p. B7.
47. Jadhav, *Untouchables*, p. 9.

off as low-caste and thus make her/him vulnerable to discrimination; yet being an alumnus of such an institution can open up networks within one's community. Such dilemmas are also faced by minorities in the United States. Citing racial disparities in hiring, some African Americans have decided not only to use less racially marked names, but also to delete from their résumés references to African American organisations or even a degree from a historically black college.[48] Many Dalit students continue to enrol in historically Dalit colleges, perhaps in part because the in-community networking opportunities of these colleges is seen as crucial in a society in which they may be denied jobs or investment opportunities by those outside their own community.

Another Dalit Educational Initiative: Study Centres

In India, there are other distinctly Dalit initiatives that strive for access to and equity in higher education for Dalits and other oppressed and marginalised groups. These also serve or complement some of the goals of the Dalit colleges. They are not attempts to replace them; as Dalit colleges are not currently at risk of being closed or absorbed like the historically black colleges in the United States or South Africa. One study centre initiative in India provides an example of ways that countries consolidating distinct colleges for minorities or marginalised groups can try to perpetuate some of their positive aspects. By providing a distinct learning space and educational resources, these centres can both better equip students for college and supplement their college education in mainstream institutions.

The educational divide in Mumbai is stark. Some students dream of entering the renowned Indian Institute of Technology (IIT). (The entrance examination to the several IITs across India is so competitive that candidates apply to Harvard University or Massachusetts Institute of Technology as a backup plan.) Many

48. 'In Job Hunt, College Degree Can't Close Racial Gap', *New York Times*, 1 December 2009, '"Whitening" the Résumé', *New York Times*, 5 December 2009.

students in Mumbai, however, do not have access to computers or even to a quiet place with electricity, lights, desks, and space free from siblings and other distractions to do their homework after school. The Lumbini Cultural Centre provides these students a room of their own. Although it is just a small upper-storey room in a crowded neighbourhood, it provides a space conducive to completing current lessons and planning for the future. The Centre started with the goal of not only keeping the students in school, but also encouraging them to pursue higher education. Currently only 11 per cent of people in the age group 18–24 in India pursue higher education.

The Lumbini Cultural Centre helps students in standards nine through twelve in a poor Mumbai neighbourhood to realise their dreams. During my conversation with some of these students, I was told that they consider 'computers and English' to be the keys to their upward and geographic mobility in a highly stratified society. The Centre offers tutoring, career counselling, peer support, and a place to study and work toward a better future. Many of the students take classes at a nearby, storefront computer training centre. Students I spoke with were upbeat and enthusiastic, and they planned to go into accounting, insurance, software engineering or commerce. One planned to attend Siddharth College to get a Bachelor of Commerce degree. When I asked why, the student referred to the college's reputation rather than its historical association with the Dalit community, saying that it is a 'reputed institution for the commerce stream'.[49] This student was planning to start taking a computer course in addition to commerce studies, after completing the twelfth standard.

Lumbini Cultural Centre was started in January 2006 by a non-governmental organisation for Dalit empowerment, the National Institute for Studies in Social, Economic and Cultural Transformation (NISSECT). This organisation conducts workshops in various locations in India on study skills and provides academic and career guidance for disadvantaged populations. Leaders of these sessions, who also act as mentors for the students at Lumbini Cultural

49. Comments by students at the Lumbini Cultural Centre, Mumbai, 20 January 2008.

Centre, include Prof. Nagnath Sao, a retired physics professor from Siddharth College, and Mr Shuddhodhan Aher, a civil servant in the Government of Maharashtra. Sao advises those students interested in the sciences, while Aher guides students preparing for the competitive civil services examinations. Those students particularly interested in computers are mentored by a former assistant professor in computer sciences who now works in the private sector. He offers advice on computer courses and the skills that are currently in demand in the IT job market.

Aher describes the neighbourhood as mostly 'Buddhist, Muslim, lower-caste, and a few upper castes ... Most of the residents are daily wage earners. There is no conducive atmosphere for study, so NISSECT decided to run a study centre where students would get study material and guidance paving the way for their development'.[50] Sao notes, 'Experts visit the centre and motivate and teach them different skills like public speaking, group discussion, etc. In an environment that is hostile to the development of children, the centre has succeeded in forming regular study habits and given them the opportunity to interact with resource persons.'[51]

The gap between elite and non-elite schools is universal. Sociologist Satish Deshpande of the University of Delhi points out that there is a 'parallel system' right from primary school whereby wealthier students have private 'coaching' throughout their school-going years.[52] This entrenches inequity and deepens the inequality between the different strata of schools. To compete with students from more privileged backgrounds (who have access to higher quality, often private, schools, and routinely hire tutors to prepare for examinations), some poorer students in India can turn to free after-school programmes and tutoring—but only if these are available. The Lumbini Cultural Centre is just one such free programme.

50. Shuddhodhan Aher, in conversation with and email to the author, January 2008.
51. Nagnath Sao, in conversation with and email to the author, January 2008.
52. Satish Deshpande, interview by author, 7 January 2008.

If they go to collage, Dalit students who attend mainstream universities can benefit from other initiatives, such as student organisations or online networks. For example, the United Dalit Student's Forum (UDSF) at JNU provides students at this university with a support group and critical mass to advocate on behalf of Dalit students.[53] Such organisations can provide, for students at mainstream colleges, some of the functions historically Dalit colleges have provided for students, including a safe haven, mentors, community networks, and leadership opportunities. The UDSF contributes in additional ways, by censuring the university administration when Dalit student interests are ignored or harmed, and by educating other, non-Dalit students and raising broader social awareness about Dalit identity and issues.

Various online discussion lists and networks organised by Dalit activists can provide some of the networking functions of historically Dalit colleges, irrespective of whether one attended such a college or not. Internet discussion lists, for example, spread the word about opportunities ranging from jobs to educational seminars, scholarships, further studies abroad, petitions, and more, as well as provide a forum for publicising and protesting against atrocities. Online discussions contribute to international networking as well, with Dalits in the diaspora, other Buddhists, interested scholars, and human rights activists. Although they do not provide the in-person exchanges of a historically Dalit college campus, online networks or

53. C. Lakshmanan, 'Activating Social Capital for Dalit Identity', in *Dalits: Assertion for Identity*, ed. Ambrose Pinto (Proceedings of the National Seminar of Dalit Postgraduate and Research Students held from 23–25 January 1999 in the Indian Social Institute), New Delhi: Indian Social Institute, 1999, pp. 160–71; Anoop Kumar, 'Quest for a Strong Dalit Student Politics.' *Indian Dalit Muslims' Voice* (*IDMV*), 5 July 2009, retrieved from http://www.dalitmuslims.com/2009/07/jnu-quest-for-strong-dalit-student.html, viewed 17 December 2009; Narendra Kumar, 'Dalit Identity and Student Politics at JNU', in *Dalits: Assertion for Identity*, ed. Ambrose Pinto (Proceedings of the National Seminar of Dalit Postgraduate and Research Students held from 23–25 January 1999 in the Indian Social Institute), New Delhi: Indian Social Institute, 1999, pp. 40–47.

organisational web pages can provide a relatively safe place to express one's Dalit identity, a network, and a community organising tool.[54]

These are just a few examples of the plethora of Dalit initiatives to empower and educate more and more students. Although community-based study centres, student organisations or online networks are not new ideas, these examples of success in a highly stratified society may be instructive or inspiring for those working towards expanding access to and equity in higher education in other contexts.

Conclusion: Lessons for South Africa and the United States

Before closing or combining historically black colleges or universities, the important functions they serve should be thoroughly considered. At their best, historically black colleges, like historically Dalit colleges can provide a distinct educational space in which students may gain confidence, feel connected to a broader community, and develop a set of skills and ideals that can benefit them long after graduation. These colleges may offer significant resources and opportunities in the form of material assets such as housing and books, mentors, community archives, a distinctive curriculum, and an alumni network, often leading to the education of the next generation of leaders. The examples of two historically Dalit colleges, Siddharth College in Mumbai and Milind College in Aurangabad, illustrate all of these important contributions. For students who do not have the opportunity to attend such a college, a community-based study centre, such as the Lumbini Study Centre in Mumbai, or a Dalit student organisation or online discussion group can fill some, if not all, of the functions of a historically Dalit college, while also providing

54. Eva-Maria Hardtmann, *The Dalit Movement in India: Local Practices, Global Connections*, New Delhi: Oxford University Press, 2009, pp. 119–20; Clifford Bob, 'Dalit Rights are Human Rights: Untouchables, NGOs, and the Indian State', in *The International Struggle for New Human Rights*, ed. Clifford Bob, Philadelphia: University of Pennsylvania Press, 2009, p. 47.

additional benefits, such as speedy international networking, consciousness-raising in the broader society, or collaboration with the non-Dalit community.

There are important limits to the abilities of distinct colleges for minorities or marginalised groups to address issues of educational access and equity. First, inequity and inadequacy in primary and secondary educational institutions make an uneven playing field that colleges cannot fix. The uneven state of Indian primary education has been amply documented, and children in South Africa and the United States also face staggering inequities in access to good education.[55] Second, the unique historical origins or character of colleges alone is not enough to truly empower minority or marginalised students if the curriculum is not relevant and teaching is not first-rate. HBCUs or historically Dalit colleges cannot empower students if they are not attuned to trends in job markets. In her study of Scheduled Caste college students in Mumbai, Marika Vicziany found that many lower-caste students were not studying subjects that would prepare them for the latest opportunities; thus the boom in IT was not upsetting social hierarchies by providing upward mobility for many lower-caste students.[56] Although her study did not focus on historically Dalit institutions, certainly the common problem of educational tracks not matching job opportunities is one that unfortunately has hurt marginalised students' prospects, not just in India, but also in South Africa and the United States; thus this is an issue that colleges dedicated to reducing inequities should address.

55. Kin Bing Wu, Pete Goldschmidt, Christy Kim Boscardin and Mehtabul Azam, 'Girls in India: Poverty, Location and Social Disparities', in *Exclusion, Gender and Education: Case Studies from the Developing World*, ed. Maureen A. Lewis and Marlaine E. Lockheed, Washington, D.C.: Center for Global Development, 2007, pp. 120–25; Fiske and Ladd, *Elusive Equity*, pp. 55–59; Jonathan Kozol, *Savage Inequalities: Children in America's Schools*, New York: Harper Perennial, 1992.
56. Marika Vicziany, 'The New Indian IT Industry in the Late 1990s: Rapid Economic Growth and Social Revolution?' in *South Asia in the Era of Globalization: Trade, Industrialization and Welfare*, ed. Mita Bhattacharya, Russel Mythe and Marika Vicziany, New York: Nova Science, 2004, pp. 128–29.

A final important lesson from India's historically Dalit colleges is that these were not conceived to be separate institutions (implying exclusion), but rather, distinct institutions, which any student is welcome to attend. Today, these colleges educate students from a variety of social backgrounds, while continuing to promote their original goal of educating those with little access to higher education. This goal is important both for the students themselves and for the greater good of their families and society. The ripple effect of this educational effort for the broader community is a key contribution of distinctive institutions for marginalised students. Ambedkar, the founder of many historically Dalit colleges, made this point in a message he sent to be delivered to the All India Scheduled Castes Students Federation Conference, held in 1946. His hope was that these students should learn two things: 'Firstly, to prove that given the opportunities, they are inferior to none in intelligence and capacity. Secondly, to prove that they are not merely to tread the path of personal happiness, but to lead their Community to be free, to be strong and to be respected.'[57] Siddharth College, which opened that same year, as well as the other colleges Ambedkar went on to found, continue to strive towards the realisation of both these goals.

57. Message sent by Ambedkar to be read to students at the All India Scheduled Castes Students Federation Conference, held in Nagpur on 25–26 December 1946, quoted in Nanak Chand Rattu, *Dr. Ambedkar Important Messages, Sayings, Wit and Wisdom*, New Delhi: Rajgriha, 2001, p. 52.

3

Silent Voices

Women's Perceptions about Self and Education in Late Nineteenth-century India

Radha Gayathri

> The solution to a problem lies in the knowledge of that problem. And the knowledge expects a seeker. It follows therefore that one desirous of attaining rights should also possess them. Generally it is this particular characteristic that will be found lacking in the Indian woman.[1]

As per the 2011 census, female literacy rate in India is only 65.46 per cent (male literacy is 82.14 per cent), which is one of the lowest in the world. Today, female education may be widely advocated as a fundamental right and matter of social justice and equality, but it is still regarded as 'consumption' and welfare expenditure, if not as a burden.[2] However, female education occupies a special place in the history of modern India, and its development is marked with controversies, debates and immense struggles as it involved breaking down the barriers of social customs and deep-rooted prejudices. This essay attempts to understand the social context of and educational opportunities in the late-nineteenth century as perceived by women, through some of the works of women writers of this period. The above quotation of the famous Hindi poet, Mahadevi Varma from her work, *Shrinkhala Ki Kadiyan* encapsulates the situation of Indian

1. Mahadevi Varma, *Links in the Chain*, trans. Neera Kuckrcja Sohoni, Delhi: Katha, 2005, pp. xv–xvi.
2. Jandhyala B. G. Tilak, *Women's Education and Development*, New Delhi: Gyan Publishing House, 2007, p. 22.

women of the period who were so subjugated and marginalised that they were actually ignorant of what they needed.

Unlike writings by men, women's writings of the period do not reflect their social and individual perceptions. The closing years of the nineteenth century saw for the first time educated women voicing their views through their writings. These writers—educated in the most adverse of times—had a heightened awareness of their own situation. There were other works of the period which only echoed men's views. However, the writers discussed in the present essay—Pandita Ramabai, Tarabai Shinde, Rukhmabai, Anandibai Joshi, Cornelia Sorabji, Rokeya Sakhawat Hossein, Haimabati Sen and Mahadevi Varma[3]—trenchantly critiqued their contemporary social milieu. Their writings not only provide a sharper evaluation of the condition of women of that period, but also the reasons for their degraded position in society. They analytically showed the double standards of morality operating on men and women in the socio-cultural practices of the period, and how women's consent for oppression by men was produced through them.[4] These writers articulated many issues that were ignored and discounted by men, and in process they provided many counterpoints and challenges to the prevalent social discourse. Most of these works were autobiographical in nature and faithful reflections of their times.

Another important reason for studying these early women writers is the fact that they were different from the writers of the later period who not only voiced their opinions but also fought for their rights. The women of the twentieth century were indeed the 'daughters of reform' who benefited from the nineteenth-century reforms and

3. The present study focuses on Tarabai Shinde's *Stri Purusha Tulana* (1882); Pandita Ramabai's *The High Caste Hindu Woman* (1882); Rukhmabai's letters to *The Times of India* in 1885; Anandibai Joshi's letters to B. F. Carpenter; the autobiography of Haimabati Sen; Rokeya Sakhawat Hossein's *Sultana's Dream* (n.d.); Cornelia Sorabji's *India Calling* (1934) and *The Purdanashins* (1917), and Mahadevi Varma's *Ateet Ke Chalchitra* (1941) and *Shrinkhala Ki Kadiyan* (1942).
4. Susie Tharu and K. Lalita (eds.), *Women Writing in India: 600 B.C. to the Present*, vol. 1, New Delhi: Oxford University Press, 1991.

were thus able to voice their rights and privileges through organising exclusive women's forums—something which was not possible for their predecessors.

Social Reforms in the Nineteenth Century

Before trying to analyse the works of the period, it is imperative first to have a brief glimpse at the working of the other major agencies involved, i.e., the colonial state and the nationalist reformers, as this would enable one to understand how the whole question of educating women came about. The post-Enlightenment state in general—and the colonial state in particular—exercised power through hegemony; it exercised power not through instilling fear of punishment, but by nurturing the body and inculcating loyalty in the minds of the subjects through Western education, public health and law.[5] In the Indian context, British colonialism sought to legitimise itself through self-characterisation as rule of law and social reform, leading to much significant legislation which sought to penetrate deeply into the everyday life and culture of Indians. 'Through the reforming gesture the colonizing country posed as the universal standard of perfection, as a prescribed social model, upon which to base the moral improvement of the colony.'[6] In this discourse, the condition of women was used as an index of both societies—of the perfection of one, and the baseness of the other.[7] This strategy was carried out by singling out the most extraordinary of cultural practices, especially those like *sati*, *purdah*, enforced widowhood, child marriages, female infanticide, etc., and then making them emblematic of the culture

5. Dagmar Engels and Shula Marks, *Contesting Colonial Hegemony: State and Society in Africa and India,* London: British Academic Press, 1994, p. 7.
6. Himani Bannerji, 'Age of Consent and the Hegemonic Social Reforms', in *Gender and Imperialism*, ed. Clare Midgely, Manchester: Manchester University Press, 1998, p. 27.
7. Janaki Nair, *Women and Law in Colonial India: A Social History,* Delhi: Kali for Women, 1996, p. 51.

as a whole.[8] This provided a basis not only for arguments about the backwardness of Indian culture but also for the ideological justification of the 'civilizing mission' of British imperialism in India. Subsequently, many laws were enacted to redeem Indian women from these degrading conditions.[9] This criticism of the condition of women in India and the related 'social evils' was echoed not only in the writings of colonial administrators but also of the Christian missionaries, historians, and even travellers from the West of that period.

The socio-religious reform movements of the nineteenth century emerged mainly in response to the above criticism. The educated urban middle classes sought to reform some of the denigrating socio-religious practices of their time rather than face the criticism of the colonisers.[10] With the exception, perhaps, of the issue of caste and untouchability, all major questions of reform of Hindu society taken up in this period concerned women: sati, female infanticide, child marriage, the remarriage of widows, the seclusion and education of women, prostitution, and bride price and dowry. The improvement in the social position of women and a redefinition of their role in society came to occupy the central place in all schemes of socio-religious reform. Secondly, it was a distinctly patriarchal form of social reform, with women being the beneficiaries of male concerns and actions.[11]

8. The concept of analysing the status women to gauge the progress of a nation was used for first time by James Mill in his *History of British India* (first published in 1826) in the Indian context. See James Mill, *History of British India*, London: Baldwin, Cradock, and Joy, 1826.
9. Some of the major reform legislations pertaining to women are the Bengal Sati Regulation Act, 1829; The Hindu Widow's Remarriage Act, 1856; The Age of Consent Act, 1860 (amended 1891); The Prohibition of Female Infanticide Act, 1872, and The Child Marriage Restraint Act, 1929.
10. For better insights into analysis of the social reform debates refer to Sumit Sarkar and Tanika Sarkar (eds.), *Women and Social Reform in Modern India*, 2 vol., New Delhi: Permanent Black, 2007.
11. Kumkum Sangari and Sudesh Vaid (eds.), *Recasting Women: Essays in Colonial History*, Delhi: Kali for Women, 1990 and Lata Mani,

The model of new womanhood invented in the nineteenth century was of enlightened mothers and companions to men in their own 'separate sphere' of the home. 'Reaction to the attacks by colonial writers ensured that Indian women were almost built up as superwomen: a combination of the spiritual Maitreyi, the learned Gargi, the suffering Sita, the faithful Savitri and the heroic Lakshmibai ... In this model of womanhood there was no difference between the perceptions of progressives and of conservatives.'[12] Education was the tool of grooming the new ideal woman; but this education did not serve as a means for external advancement, because there was no place for them in the public domain as such.

Women's Education

The traditional patriarchal definition of women solely as housewives or mothers meant an early pre-pubertal marriage for girls, an immediate post-pubertal consummation of marriage, early and frequent childbearing, and finally, secluded widowhood. In this definition there was no space for education; and even if it was imparted for a few years in childhood, it was only rudimentary—informal, religious and practical—so as to enable them to fulfil their domestic roles. But in the social reform discourse, the importance of education in order to train women for their new roles as companionable wives, good mothers, and socialisers was recognised and became a key theme.

Ironically, education was also the anchor by which women were tied more securely to the home and to domestic tasks by realigning patriarchal domesticity. For the kind of education imparted to women of this period shows that the purpose of that education

---

Contentious Traditions: The Debate on Sati in Colonial India, Berkeley: University of California Press, 1998 provide excellent historiographical insights.

12. Uma Charavarti, 'Whatever Happened to the Vedic Dasi?' in *Recasting Women: Essays in Colonial History*, eds. Kumkum Sangari and Sudesh Vaid, New Delhi: Kali for Women, 1990, p. 70.

was merely better management of the household.[13] 'They wanted to unveil women's minds, in other words, without unveiling their faces.'[14] No major structural changes in patriarchy occurred through this type of education, and thus 'female education' proved to be the least difficult segment of social reform. Thus, despite many reservations, women's education became a prominent axis of the social reform discourse, and the reforms concerning women came to be concentrated on their education. 'Even the social conservatives were compelled to reconsider their position and evolve a new agenda supporting women's education selectively where it directly benefited men and the family, while discursively undercutting it in trope of domesticity.'[15] It is important to note here that on the issue of the significance of women's proper sphere and the duties concerning them, colonial officials and key groups of elite Indian men shared very similar ideas and preconceptions. For both, debates about the moral worth of cultures and traditions were most appropriately conducted by objectifying the figure of the woman with no voice in these debates. Both agreed that women's space was in the domain of the family, custom and religion, and thus, outside the realm of politics and the state.

13. How the curriculum was differentiated for boys and girls socialising them for their gendered roles can be understood from: Madhu Kishwar, 'Arya Samaj and Women's Education: Kanya Mahavidyalaya, Jalandhar', *Economic and Political Weekly*, vol. 21, no. 17, April 1986, pp. 9–24; Indu Banga, 'Socio-Religious Reform and Patriarchy', in *Women in Indian History*, ed. Kiran Pawar, New Delhi: Vision and Venture, 1996; Nita Kumar, 'Oranges for the Girls; or the Half-known Story of the Education of Girls in Twentieth Century Benaras', in *Women as Subjects: South Asian Histories*, ed. Nita Kumar, New Delhi: Stree, 1994, pp. 211–31; Geraldine Forbes, 'No "Science" for Lady Doctors', in *Women and Science in India: A Reader*, ed. Neelam Kumar, New Delhi: Oxford University Press, 2009, pp. 3–20.
14. Gail Minault, 'Other Voices, Other Rooms: The View from the Zenana', in *Women as Subjects: South Asian Histories*, ed. Nita Kumar, New Delhi: Stree, 1994, p. 119.
15. Meera Kosambi, 'A Window in The Prison House: Women's Education and the Politics of Social Reform in Nineteenth Century Western India', *History of Education*, vol. 29, no. 5, 2000, p. 433.

Profile, Context and Significance

The profile of seven writers selected for this study shows three doctors, a lawyer, a writer, a social reformer and a housewife. They fought against many odds to be educated and their works reflect their personal hardships. Of the many issues addressed by these writers, the present essay focuses only on those associated with education and the social factors which hindered it. Thus, from the larger analyses of the subjugation of women in society, only certain issues like the questions of identity, seclusion, female infanticide, early marriage, widowhood and denial of education have been studied.

Tarabai Shinde (1850–1910) belonged to Buldhana, a small town in Berar. She was the only daughter of Bapuji Hari Shinde, an early member of the Satyashodhak Samaj who not only taught her how to read and write in Marathi, but also to some extent, English and Sanskrit. *Stri Purusha Tulana* (1881) us the only work written by Tarabai. This is one of the most polemical works ever written by a woman and intends to express the anger that many women felt at their ill-treatment by menfolk. In the introduction to her work, Tarabai clearly explains her reason of writing as 'I am doing it out in the hope that you might stop treating all women as though they have committed a crime and making their lives a hell for it'.[16]

She exposed the hypocrisies embedded in the Hindu patriarchal system by analysing social issues concerning women like marriage, widowhood and *purdah*, women's education and personal mobility, domestic politics, and the problems associated with everyday marital and family relationships. Parts of her essay clearly suggest that she is speaking of her own experiences. She spoke of herself as '[a] powerless, dull woman, prisoner within a Maratha household.'[17] In her work, Tarabai raised many historical and political questions and asserted that there has been a long-term loss in women's access to power, compounded by the emergence of a new and exclusively masculine sphere of public life.

16. Rosalind O' Hanlon, *A Comparison Between Women and Men: Tarabai Shinde and the Critique of Gender Relations in Colonial India*, New Delhi: Oxford University Press, 1994, p. 76.
17. Tharu and Lalita, *Women Writing in India*, p. 222.

Pandita Ramabai (1858–1922) was born into a Chitpavan Brahman family and her father Anant Shastri Dongre was a Sanskrit scholar. She received her training in Sanskrit from both her parents. She lost both her parents and her elder sister when she was sixteen, and then visited Calcutta—where she studied the Vedas and the Shastras—with her brother. Later, she came to be called 'Pandita' for her Sanskrit scholarship. At twenty-two, she married Bipin Bihari Madhavi, a Bengali Shudra of the Brahmo Samaj, but was widowed after two years. Ramabai returned to Poona in 1882 and worked with reformers like Mahadev Govind Ranade and Ramakrishna Gopal Bhandarkar. She set up a chain of Arya Mahila Sabhas all over Maharashtra.[18] Disappointed with her countrymen she decided to build up her own skills and develop contacts with people outside India. Ramabai wanted to be trained as a doctor but could not. In 1889, she set up Sharada Sadan, a house of learning for widows, in Bombay. For conservatives, Pandita Ramabai was a startling and uncomfortable figure: a widow at twenty-four, an excellent Sanskrit scholar, a woman with pronounced views on the position of women in Hindu society, and finally, in 1883, a highly publicised convert to Christianity, on the grounds that it made no distinction on the basis of spiritual worth between men and women in the way that Hinduism did.[19]

Pandita Ramabai's work, *The High Caste Hindu Woman*, published in 1888 in Philadelphia, was basically meant for foreign readers who wanted to know about social customs of the Hindus. In this work, she describes the condition of women in India by analysing their childhood, married life and widowhood, and shows how they were marginalised by men. Like Tarabai's work, it too reflects its author's own experiences, especially her widowhood.[20]

18. Meera Kosambi, 'Indian Response to Christianity, Church and Colonialsim: Case of Pandita Ramabai', *Economic and Political Weekly*, vol. XXVII, nos. 43–44, 24–31 October 1992, p. WS-62.
19. Ibid., p. 17.
20. Uma Chakravarti, *Rewriting History: The Life and Times of Pandita Ramabai,* New Delhi: Zubaan, 1998, pp. 281–82.

Rukhmabai (1860–1950), belonging to an affluent family, lost her father when she was just two-and-a-half years old. Six years after her father's death, her mother Jayantibai broke the custom that widows should not remarry by marrying Dr Sakharam Arjun of the Grant Medical College. Rukhmabai was married off at the age of eleven to Dadaji Bhikaji who was nineteen, but continued to stay at her paternal home and pursue her studies. It was Dr Edith Pechey who constantly encouraged her to go to England and pursue medicine.[21] In 1884, when she was twenty-two, she refused to live with her husband and went to court for 'restitution of conjugal rights'. Though she won in the lower court, she lost in the high court, where she was asked to live with her husband or go to prison. It was only when Queen Victoria reacted to a special appeal in this case and issued a royal decree dissolving the marriage that Rukhmabai was saved from serving the sentence. During the trial, Rukhmabai faced public ridicule for her refusal to live with her husband. She wrote letters to *The Times of India* in May and September 1885, under the pseudonym, 'A Hindu Lady'. She not only discussed the evils of child marriage and widowhood, but also tried to analyse the reasons behind them and suggested steps to redeem the situation.

Rukhmabai later went to England and did an intensive English-language course, passed the Society of Apothecaries examination, and graduated from the London School of Medicine. She also obtained qualifications in Edinburgh, Glasgow and Brussels, and returned to India in 1894. Rukhmabai was appointed as the first doctor in charge of a dispensary established at Surat under the Dufferin scheme. Because of her dedication to her work, and the popularity she won, the dispensary—named after Seth Morarbhai Vijbhukhandas, the donor who provided money for its establishment—continues to be popularly known as the 'Rukhmabai Hospital' even today, more than a hundred years after she joined it.[22]

21. Kumari Jayawardena, *The White Woman's Other Burden: Western Women and South Asia during British Rule*, New York and London: Routledge, 1995, p. 87.
22. Sudhir Chandra, *Enslaved Daughters: Colonialism, Law and Women's Right*, New Delhi: Oxford University Press, 1998, p. 211.

Anandibai Joshi (1865–87), born in a Chitpavan Brahman family of Poona, was named Yamuna Ganapatrao Joshi. She was married off at the age of nine to Gopalrao Joshi, who was an avowed reformist aimed at educating his wife despite all the odds. Anandibai became a mother at fourteen, but the child did not survive. This, however, led to the deterioration of her health leading to the inability to bear children. She endured a difficult life, often filled with privations, abuse, and social ostracism; yet, with sheer will, she became the first foreign-trained woman doctor from India. At age of eighteen, she went to the United States to study medicine at the Women's Medical College of Pennsylvania in Philadelphia where she graduated in 1886. Although she broke the caste taboos by crossing the seas and took the bold step of studying medicine, the fact that she remained a Hindu made her a heroine among orthodox circles.[23] In 1886, she was appointed physician-in-charge of the women's ward of Albert Edward Hospital in Kolhapur; but she died tragically young due to consumption soon after, in 1887. She became an icon of the virtues of ideal Hindu womanhood as she proved that well-educated Hindu wives were in no danger of losing their religion or their values.[24] Anandibai was just fifteen when she started corresponding with B. F. Carpenter of Roselle, New Jersey whom she affectionately called 'aunt'. Her correspondence reveals the kind of hardships she faced while pursuing her studies.

Haimabati Sen, née Ghosh (1866–1932), was the daughter of a wealthy *zamindar* of Khulna district in eastern Bengal (now in Bangladesh). Married at the age of ten, she was widowed within a year, and struggled for the next eight years as a child widow to just survive. After the death of her parents and her mother-in-law, her brother appropriated what was rightfully her share of ancestral property and drove her away from home. Even her brothers-in-law refused to provide shelter to her, thus forcing her to go to Benaras and live in utter poverty. Despite all her hardships, she continued to study whenever she could and learned enough to become a teacher in a girls' school in Benaras. Haimabati's quest for education led her to

23. Jayawardena, *The White Woman's Other Burden*, p. 81.
24. Chakravarti, *Rewriting History*, p. 255.

Calcutta where she married Kunjabehari Sen, a Brahmo missionary who never cared for responsibilities as a husband or father. Haimabati joined the Campbell Medical College programme that trained women hospital assistants in the vernacular. As the programme offered a scholarship she was able to fend for herself. Having joined the programme in 1891 as a twenty-six-year-old remarried widow, she graduated in 1894, and became the 'lady doctor' of the Hooghly Dufferin Hospital for Women in Chinsurah. Haimabati's memoirs provide a vivid insight into the problems faced by a child widow and the oppressions faced by a wife, even though she was an educated professional.

Cornelia Sorabji (1866–1954) was India's first woman barrister. Her parents Sorabji Kharsedji and Francina who moved to Poona from Nasik came to be known for their missionary work, social service and educational reforms. Cornelia was brought up in English tradition. Despite many odds she went on to became the first woman to graduate from the University of Bombay as well as receive the Bachelor of Civil Law degree from the University of Oxford. And although she was denied admission to the Bar, she was made a representative of the Hindu *purdahnashin*s who were wards of the British Indian government. This gave her the opportunity to travel across the country and see the condition of women, especially the high-caste women, who were secluded in the *zenana*s. Her writings thus afford insights into an area, which was accessible neither to men nor Western women.

Cornelia was a prolific writer and authored several works of fictional and non-fictional prose. Her concern and commitment to contemporary women's issues is reflected in *The Purdahnashin* (1917), *India Calling* (1934) and *India Recalled* (1936). *Love and Life Behind the Purdah* (1901) contains short stories about Hindu women and children, interwoven with her concern for them and her frustrated ambitions to liberate them from their enforced and often self-willed femininity. Her analysis of the customs, practices, and conditions of life 'inside' helps us to understand the socio-economic conditions of zenana life at the turn of the century.[25]

25. Antoinette Burton, 'The Purdanashin in Her Setting', *Feminist Review*, no. 65, Summer 2000, pp. 145–58.

Rokeya Sakhawat Hossein (1880–1932) was born in Payraband in Rangpur district (now in Bangladesh) into a rigidly conservative zamindari family. Though her two brothers were educated at St. Xavier's College, Calcutta, she and her two sisters received traditional education and were never allowed to attend formal school. She learnt Bengali and English with the help of her elder brother; and later in life, she improved her English with her husband's help. Widowed at an early age, Rokeya left her husband's home in Bihar and settled in Calcutta where she founded the Sakhawat Memorial Girls' School for Muslim girls in 1911. At the same time, Rokeya pursued her writing career, producing pieces of social criticism aimed at exposing patriarchal subjugation which left many conservatives unhappy. Rokeya was in fact the first Muslim woman to launch a systematic and uncompromising campaign for women's education as she considered it to be the first prerequisite for emancipation. Many of her essays were written in Bengali and reflect her vision of women's emancipation. Some of her works are *Stree Jatir Abanati*, *Ardhangi*, *Griha*, *Aborodhbashini* and *Narir Adhikar*. In her various essays where she propounds her theory of feminism, Rokeya forcefully demonstrated how women have been disempowered throughout history within the home and outside it, till they were reduced to the status of domestic slaves.

It was during the early years of her marriage that she wrote an outstanding—almost revolutionary—piece, *Sultana's Dream*, in English, which made its first appearance in *Indian Ladies' Magazine* in 1905. It is a feminist utopian fantasy, and describes a society in an imaginary land, 'Ladyland', where women rule and men stay at home.[26] In this land of role reversals, men did the menial work and stayed in the *mardana* (men's quarters) as opposed to zenanas. Women were intelligent, free, independent, and issued orders to men. With truth, love, compassion and welfare as the guiding principles, women governed Ladyland. This remarkable piece, though written in the form of a satirical fantasy, gives a clear indication of Rokeya's

26. Bharati Ray, *Early Feminists of Colonial India: Sarala Devi Chaudhurani and Rokeya Sahawat Hossain*, New Delhi: Oxford University Press, 2002, p. 23.

attitude towards patriarchy, her resentment against the many unfair restrictions on women, and her dream of transforming society into a more egalitarian order.

Mahadevi Varma (1907–87) was a distinguished poet, essayist and critic of her time. Though strictly speaking she belonged to the twentieth century, women's issues were publicly debated in the United Provinces much later than in other parts of the country. She was born into an educated middle-class family in Farukhabad and was raised under the cultural tutelage of her mother and Westernised and reformist father. And although she was married off at nine, she was yet fortunate enough to continue her studies.[27] She completed her MA in Sanskrit from Allahabad University in 1933, and was one of the two girls in that class. From her daily encounters with women and girls, she understood the basis of gender prejudice and socio-cultural suffocation of women; and her works hold up a mirror to the condition of women all around her. She narrated real-life stories of oppressed women in her *Ateet Ke Chalchitra*. Mahadevi wrote many articles between 1931 and 1937, which appeared in contemporary women's magazines and journals like *Chand* and *Stri Darpan*. These were compiled into a volume titled *Shrinkhala Ki Kadiyan* (1931). Mahadevi was not just a writer but a social worker too. She became principal of the Prayag Mahila Vidyapeeth in the 1932. Throughout her years in Allahabad, she spent her weekends in the villages of Jhusi and Arail, teaching rural children elementary lessons and basic hygiene.[28]

Seclusion, Ignorance and Loss of Identity

Most of the women in nineteenth-century India were so secluded that they were totally ignorant of their own needs, so much so that they did not even have an identity and remained mere shadows of

27. Visalakshi Menon, 'Women's Education in North India in Colonial Period: A Survey', *Samyukta*, vol. 3, no.1, January 2003, p. 47.
28. Visalakshi Menon, *Indian Women and Nationalism: The UP Story*, New Delhi: Shakti Books, 2003, p. 37.

their menfolk. While men gained access to a new range of powers structures under colonial rule and used them for their own vanity and self-aggrandisement, women were denied the same benefits and locked in ossified religious cultures. The following words of Tarabai show how this isolation of women led to ignorance and how they never got opportunities for education.

> You shut women endlessly in the prison of the home, while you go about building up your own importance, becoming Mr, Sir, so on ... Right from your childhood you collect all rights in your own hands and womankind you just push in a dark corner, shut up in purdah, frightened, sat on, dominated as if she was a female slave. And all the while you go about dazzling us all with the light of your own virtue. Learning isn't for women, nor can they come and go as they please. Even if [a] woman is allowed to go outside, the women she meets are all ignorant like her, they're all just the same. So how's she to get any greater understanding and intelligence?[29]

Ramabai also talked about how seclusion of women had not only led to their loss of identity but also to total ignorance. She said that women had become slavery-loving creatures due to complete submission under the Hindu law for millennia, and this had taken a toll on their mental and physical health, which was now telling on the nation. Rukhmabai wrote in angst: 'Men cannot, in the least, understand the wretchedness which we Hindu women have to endure, but this did not belie women's desires: because you cannot enter our feelings, do not think that we are satisfied with the life of drudgery that we live, and that we have no taste for and aspiration after a higher life.'[30]

In her book *The Purdanashins*, Cornelia described in detail life in the zenana; and the most important thing which she noticed was the ignorance among the women in the zenanas. 'What is the zenana attitude towards domestic sanitation, towards the care of children, towards education? The answer is simple. There is no knowledge at

29. O'Hanlon, *A Comparison Between Women and Men*, p. 87.
30. Chandra, *Enslaved Daughters*, p. 30.

all in zenana of these subjects, *as such*.'[31] Rokeya first discussed the issue of purdah and seclusion, and saw it as a construct of patriarchy. She also showed how women had simply ignored these realities and were living without any rights or freedom. Thereby, she implied that it is women who need to fight for their own freedom. 'In India, man is lord and master. He has taken to himself all powers and privileges and shut up the women in the zenana ... You have neglected the duty you owe to yourselves, and you have lost your natural rights by shutting your eyes to your own interests.'[32]

Similary, Mahadevi in her book *Shrinkhala Ki Kadiyan*, says that women have lost their individual existence and have turned into mere shadows of men. Instead of looking within women sought the reflection of their success and failure in a man's approval or disapproval.[33] '[H]er condition is similar to that of a mute animal who is crippled with burden, has tears streaming from its woeful eyes but is totally oblivious of the reason for its suffering or the means to overcome it. She neither has knowledge of the sources of her affliction nor is aquainted with the feeling of avenging her unbearable agony ... [O]ur society has ordained the woman to live a uniform and unchanging life like a statue, devoid of all pulsation, vibrancy and human failings.'[34] All these writers pointed out that only in a free and conducive environment was the overall mental and physical development of women possible.

Preference for Male Children and Female Infanticide

Women in the nineteenth century were not only secluded but often eliminated too. During this period, female infaniticide cases were very much prevalent in Rajputana, North-Western Provinces and Punjab. Thus, in a way women, were denied identity not only literally but also

31 Cornelia Sorabji, *The Purdanashins,* London: Nisbet & Co., 1934, p. 5.

32. Tharu and Lalita, *Women Writing in India*, pp. 344–45.

33. Mahadevi Varma, *Links in the Chain*, p. 9.

34. Ibid., p. 31.

physically.[35] In 1868, Hobart, the joint magistrate of Basti district in the North-Western Provinces, reported about the large number of female infanticide cases amongst the Surajbansis, Gautams and other Rajput clans. The following table provides interesting data on the sex ratio in Basti district in 1868:

TABLE 3.1: Village-wise Sex Ratio among the Rajput Clans of Basti District

Name of Village	No. of Married Male Rajputs	No. of Unmarried Male Rajputs	Boys under the Age of 10	Girls under the Age of 10
Kaour Pakera	446	303	284	23
Nagpore	280	202	210	43
Sohangia	186	177	100	52
Luchmipura	64	57	47	26
Babu Ranghar Khas	123	68	71	7
Pratapgarh	39	20	31	1
Bhudawar	199	108	104	1
Asoypur	22	9	20	0
Deokuli	6	8	7	1
Kudurhi	29	18	14	10
Dhirouli	46	35	18	9
Khunrea	57	32	34	1
Kaisalla	31	14	19	5
Mahuwapur	54	42	35	9
Poora Marna	303	263	173	54

Source: As cited in Lalita Panigrahi, *British Social Policy and Female Infanticide in India*, New Delhi: Munshiram Manoharlal, 1972, p. 139.

35. Barbara D. Miller who has worked on female infanticide in North-West Provinces before 1900 writes that it was one of the most infanticide-endemic areas and that one-fourth of the population of the North-West Provinces murdered one-half of their female offspring. Barbara. D. Miller, *The Endangered Sex*, London: Cornell University Press, 1981.

Hobart inspected and collected statistics of ninety-nine villages in which there were 1,204 boys as against 259 girls under the age of ten. The clan-wise statement on the same subject as investigated by Hobart in the Basti district was as follows:

TABLE 3.2: Clan-wise Sex Ratio among the Rajput Clans of Basti District

No. of Villages Investigated	Name of Clan	No. of Married Adult Males	No. of Unmarried Adult Males	Boys under the Age of 10	Girls under the Age of 10
88	Surajbansi	1,756	1,224	1,109	170
19	Bais	119	76	97	31
10	Burwar	105	145	76	28
7	Chowhan	116	70	83	15
22	Gautam	461	252	354	47
10	Kalhans	232	148	177	65
156		2,789	1,915	1,896	356

Source: As cited in Panigrahi, *British Social Policy and Female Infanticide in India*, p. 140.

The above two tables clearly show the preference for male children in Indian society and the consequent problem of female infanticide which was taken up by these writers. Ramabai tells us how expectant mothers could hope to win their husbands' loyalty only by bearing sons. Similarly, in her letter dated 15 November 1880, Anandibai makes a somewhat sarcastic reference to the universal preference for male children in Indian families. 'We have no polygamy to speak of ... our people, if they at all take more than one wife, marry for the sake of sons if they do not have any by first or second wife. So you see how fond we are of sons socially and religiously. The Heavens are open to the man who has a son, but not otherwise.'[36]

36. Meera Kosambi, 'Anandibai Joshee: Retrieving a Fragmented Feminist Image', *Economic and Political Weekly*, vol. 31, no. 49, December 1996, p. 3193.

Ramabai also discussed the reasons for the inhuman and irreligious practice of female infanticide among certain Rajput clans of north, north-western and central India, who belong to the Kshatriya or warrior caste. 'This cruel act was performed by the fathers themselves, or even by mothers, at the command of the husband whom they are bound to obey in *all* things.'[37] She writes how a girl was considered as 'nothing' and often killed as easily as a mosquito or any other annoying insect. Ramabai wrote of the commonly-used excuse of the theft of baby girls by wolves. 'Then there are not a few child-thieves who generally steal girls: even the wild animals are so intelligent and of such refined taste that they mock at British law, and always steal girls to satisfy their hunger.'[38]

In a typical north-Indian family, the very birth of a daughter was greeted with dismay. Mahadevi Varma wrote about the preference for a son to a daughter in the following words: 'The moment the arrival of the Goddess Lakshmi in the form of a daughter was announced in a subdued voice, a wretched despair would pervade the house from one end to the other. The elder ladies would silently gesture to the women singers to leave, and the elder men would quietly bid farewell to the soundless drummers.'[39]

Early Marriage and Widowhood

In Indian tradition, it was imperative for all girls to be married early. This being the case, parents were obliged to marry off girls usually before the onset of puberty, and within the limits of caste endogamy, irrespective of whether it was a suitable match or not. The custom of child marriage exposed the girl-bride to emotional harassment and physical violence, while simultaneously depriving her of the opportunity of education and the chance of personality development. Early motherhood, maternal mortality and widowhood

37. Ramabai, *The High Caste Hindu Woman*, p. 52.
38. Ibid., p. 53.
39. Mahadevi Varma, *Sketches from My Past*, tr. Neera Kuckreja Sohoni, New Delhi: Kali for Women, 1994, p. xiii.

(as husbands were usually much elder to the child bride) were the other consequences of early marriages.

Rukhmabai described in detail the evils of early marriage. She said that early marriages spelt doom for the education of girls. 'If a girl is married at eight and if she has enlightened parents her education continues till she is ten. Later it depends on the permission of mother-in-law. Even those given an exceptional reprieve did not enjoy it long. Early maternity obliged them to give up their education. Higher female education was not possible while early marriage persisted.'[40]

Anandibai Joshi in a letter to her husband written in 1884, expressed the unkind treatment and harassment that she had faced in his hands. She recollected how he hit her with broken pieces of wood at the tender age of ten. When she was but twelve he flung chairs and books at her and often threatened to leave her. Such brutal treatment not only caused physical, but also psychological, harm.[41] By voicing her struggle through her writings, Anandibai, therefore, brought out the asymmetrical gender relations of her society. Admitting the rigidity of customs, Anandibai pragmatically said that it was better for women to live in subordination if they lack any other option. She, however, hoped that through the spread of Western education, and its liberal ideas and institutions, women would be emancipated from their sufferings. Talking about the evils of early marriage, Anandibai said that women were unwell most of the time due to the early and repeated pregnancies. Though she initially sought to defend child marriage as 'national custom' she later on went to say that there was something wrong in the system of marriage itself.[42] She believed that the problem of early marriage could be solved only through legislation for social reform.

In the nineteenth century, widowhood was considered a curse on women and was often enforced by their own family members. The presence of a widow was shunned, and she was destined to spend the rest of her life in seclusion. If a widow unwittingly chanced upon any joyous or festive gathering, her presence was cursed and regarded

40. Chandra, *Enslaved Daughters*, p. 29.
41. Kosambi, 'Anandibai Joshee', p. 3192.
42. Ibid., p. 3193.

as an evil omen, sure to be followed by some great calamity. The fact that young girls of even five or six years were forced to live like widows for the rest of their lives, while elderly men could remarry as many times as they wished, reflects the social hypocrisy of the times.

Tarabai Shinde strongly addressed the problems faced by widows and the hardships they had to endure all their lives. 'Once a woman's husband has died not even a dog would swallow what she's got to. What's in store for her? The barber comes to shave all the curls and hair just to cool your eyes. All her ornaments are taken away ... She's stripped and exposed in all sorts of ways as if she belonged to no one; she becomes a widow-pot hidden in the corner.'[43] She questioned why men were never subjected to enforced widowhood like women, and why men, unlike women, did not hide their faces, shave off their beards and moustaches, and go off to live in the wilderness for the rest of your lives when their wives died. Tarabai also criticised the hypocrisy of repeated marriages by males, even when one had grown old. As mentioned earlier, many young girls were married off to men who were much older to them, often leading to enforced widowhood. 'The old corpse pays out a couple of thousand rupees and gets a pretty doe-eyed girl for himself, just like you buy a goat from the butcher and tie up as bait to catch a tiger. Then out he goes one day and falls down dead, and it's all over. His worldly life is all finished and its her again who's left to suffer.'[44]

Ramabai said that widowhood was a living hell for women as they were devoid of all pleasure, hope and social advantage. According to the census of 1881, there were 20,930,626 widows, of all age and castes.[45] Among them were 286,364 widows who were below fifteen years, i.e., what is today considered as the school-going age.

In a letter dated 19 September 1885, Rukhmabai wrote very critically about the practise of enforced widowhood and the condition of a Hindu widow in her times. 'Our shastris ... have invented a mode of torture for the special benefit of Hindu widows

43. Hanlon, *A Comparison Between Women and Men*, p. 89.
44. Ibid., p. 92.
45. Ramabai, *The High Caste Hindu Woman*, p. 133.

by the side of which the torture practised by the followers of Ignatius Loyola pales. This is no exaggeration, for the torture inflicted by the Inquisition, horrible as they were could last only for few hours, and whatever physical agony they occasioned was at worst but temporary. But our throes are mental as well as physical, and they end only with our wretched lives.'[46] She also tells us how the same men who were so solicitous as to gratify their vanity even at the ripe age of sixty became philosophically rigid in the case of their own widowed daughters or granddaughters who were still children. Rukhmabai concluded by saying that the problem of enforced widowhood could be removed only by legislation. '[T]he Hindu widow—unbeloved of God and despised of man—a social paraiah and domestic drudge, must continue for centuries together to bear her hard portion and pine in solitude till pressure of legislation or the influence of foreign civilization comes to her help and restore her the place which God seems to have assigned her in the scale of humanity.'[47]

Mahadevi Varma talked about widowhood in her works and she said that if a girl is widowed then her entire world is destroyed as she must spend the rest of her life in utter misery with each moment stretching into eternity. Widowhood is a crime for which she has to bear a punishment graver than the death sentence.[48] The story 'Bhabhi' (sister-in-law) written on 11 October 1933[49] was the recollection of one of the momentous events of her life, and in it she shows the miserable life that a widow is destined to lead. Mahadevi was just eight years old when she befriended a Marwari child widow who was always starving and often whipped soundly, without any provocation whatsoever. The innocent act of wrapping her in a colourful *dupatta* invited such rage that the *bhabhi* was beaten till she fell unconscious.

46. *The Times of India*, 19 September 1885, reprinted in *Shadow Lives: Writings on Widowhood*, eds. Uma Chakravarti and Preeti Gill, New Delhi: Kali for Women, 2000, p. 82.
47. Ibid., p. 88.
48. Varma, *Links in The Chain*, p. 31.
49. Mahadevi Varma, *Atith Ke Chalchitra*, Allahabad: Bandhar Leader Press, 1970, pp. 24–32.

Mahadevi was sick for many days after this brutal incident which left a deep impression on her on her mind.[50]

In her story 'Squirrel Lady', Cornelia shows how the elderly Hindu widows were often abused by their sons for the want of wealth. Sometimes it went to the extent of killing them by poisoning or burning them alive.[51] Haimabati was married off at the age of ten and was widowed within a year of her marriage. Her first husband was a forty-five-year-old, twice-widowed man with two daughters only slightly younger than her. Talking of widowhood and its misery she writes, 'I was but a mere child and I had already relieved my parents of all responsibilities for me and become a slave dependent for sustenance on my husband's elder brothers. I had to learn to accept the fact that at this tender age I would be a slave to other people's whims for a handful of rice.'[52] Her own experiences and those of the innumerable widows she came across throughout her life, testify to the miserable life of widows. During her later years at Chinsura as a doctor, many other child widows who were pregnant, were sent to her. She took care of many orphans who were left behind by these young widows.

Education for Girls

Every society considers knowledge as power and education as the most important tool of empowerment. As education was denied to women in nineteenth-century India they remained greatly ignorant of the world around them and their own place in it. Educational opportunities for girls were very rare and the practise of child marriage, often followed soon by widowhood, further ended any scope for a proper education. Girls who were married off by the age of nine or ten were cut off from acquiring any skills in reading or writing because it was considered shameful to read in the presence of others

50. Varma, *Sketches From My Past*, p. 33.
51. Sorabji, *India Calling*.
52. Geraldine Forbes and Tapan Raychaudhuri (eds.), *The Memoirs of Dr. Haimabati Sen: From Child Widow to Lady Doctor*, New Delhi: Roli Books, 2000, p. 98.

in her husband's house. The fear of widowhood overwhelmed the desire for knowledge. Ramabai wrote in her book that 'Shut in from the world and destitute of the ability to engage in newspaper and useful book-reading, they have little or no knowledge of common things around them, and of the most important events that are daily occurring in their own or foreign lands; ignorant, unpatriotic, selfish and uncultivated, they drag the men down with them into [a] dark abyss where they dwell together without hope, without ambition to be something or to do something in the world.'[53] She emphasised the immediate need for educating women, and that the need to improve their condition should come from within and not from outside. 'We, the women of India, are hungering and thirsting for knowledge; only education under God's grace, can give us the needful strength to rise up from our degraded condition.'[54] Ramabai also said that for the general diffusion of education among women in India, a large number of Indian women must teach their fellow countrywomen by precept and example. She pleaded before the Hunter Commission on education in 1882 for the great need of women teachers and women inspectresses for girls' schools. One reason for the insistence was that 'in ninety-nine cases out of a hundred, the educated men of this country are opposed to Female Education and the proper position of woman. If they observe the slightest fault, they magnify the grain of mustard seed into a mountain, and try to ruin the character of the woman.'[55]

To educate the women enclosed in the zenana, according to Cornelia, was a very daunting task. '[The] first step in the education of the Purdanashin women and girls is to inspire a desire to be taught; the next, to give them confidence, to make them realize that education need not outcaste them, or outrage Hindu custom.' She went on to give some practical suggestions on how to educate the

53. Ramabai, *The High Caste Hindu Woman*, pp. 128–29.
54. Ibid., p. 131.
55. Kosambi, 'A Window in the Prison House', *History of Education*, p. 438.

purdanashins and bring them healthcare without outraging their custom of zenana.[56]

Anandibai's description of her experiences of going to school at about the age of fifteen provide first-hand accounts of the ridicule and opposition faced by women while pursuing education. She narrated in the following words the immense public scorn she faced even in the supposedly progressive city of Bombay in the late 1870s:

> To continue to live as a Hindu and go to school in any part of India is very difficult ... [W]hen people saw me going with books in my hands, they had the goodness to put their heads out of the windows just to have a look at me. Some stopped their carriages for the purpose. Others walking in the streets stood laughing and crying out [derisive remarks] so that I could hear [them] ... Passers-by, whenever they saw me going, gathered round me. Some of them made fun and were convulsed with laughter. Others, sitting respectably in their verandahs, made ridiculous remarks and did not feel ashamed to throw pebbles at me. The shopkeepers and vendors spat at the sight of me, and made gestures too indecent to describe. I leave it to you to imagine what was my condition at such time, and how I could gladly have burst through the crowd to make my home nearer![57]

Women's education was one of the many controversial issues that Rokeya Hossein addressed in *Sultana's Dream*. The tasks that education had to equip women for were the tasks of rebuilding the entire world. She believed that women needed modern scientific knowledge and training in the fearless use of reason. To Rokeya, household duties were secondary and education for self-development was an end in itself. 'Like our bedrooms which shut out sunlight, our intellect is denied the fruits of enlightenment because there are no adequate schools and institutions of learning available to women.'[58] Through education, she aimed at the attainment of economic independence, which was a very radical idea for that period. She went further to claim women's equality which was possible only through education.

56. Sorabji, *India Calling*, p. 73.
57. Kosambi, 'Anandibai Joshee', p. 3194.
58. As quoted in Bharati Ray, *Early Feminists of Colonial India*, p. 69.

> Our good Queen liked science very much. She circulated an order that all the women in her country should be educated. Accordingly, a number of girls' schools were founded and supported by the Government. Education was spread far and wide among women. And early marriage also was stopped. No woman was to be allowed to marry before she was twenty-one. I must tell you that, before this change, we had been kept in strict purdah.[59]

Haimabati recollects how education was denied to girls, and the problems she faced while learning to read and write. It was considered evil to read and write as it would make a girl a child widow; and when Haimabati returned to her paternal home, her husband's death was attributed to her ability to read and write. The fact that she won many prizes for her proficiency in reading was a source of misfortune for her; she was considered a 'hussy' given to masculine ways.

In the essay, *Our Problems*, written in 1936, Mahadevi addresses the problem of education for girls. She says that when the structure of intermediary education is erected on the feeble, unsteady foundation of primary education, then it is bound to be devoid of durability and utility. 'By the time Indian women reach the intermediary level of education, the special qualities that distinguish them tend to fade away like morning stars or become rare. What is defined as higher education either ends up as a source of ultimate dissatisfaction towards life or as the means to procure necessary amenities. The bitter truth is that only two kinds of women head for higher education. Those who aspire to have a degree that can enable them to live an independent life like men or the others whose goal it is to use education to increase their value in the marriage market.'[60]

Anandibai Joshi and Haimabati Sen, who were both trained medical practitioners, also spoke of the professional discrimination they faced in medical colleges due to their gender. Anandibai wrote that 'the education imparted is defective and not sufficient, as the instructors who teach the classes are conservative, and to some extent jealous. I do not find fault with them. That is the characteristic of the male sex. We must put up with this inconvenience until we have a

59. Tharu and Lalita, *Women Writing in India*, p. 346.
60. Varma, *Links in the Chain*, pp. 108–09.

class of educated ladies to relieve these men.'[61] Similarly, Haimabati wrote about the discrimination faced by the women doctors at the hands of their male counterparts. 'Lady doctors and midwives were but pawns in the hands of the male doctors ... I lamented the fact that we were born as women.'[62]

Reformers and British Administrators

The efforts made by the reformers and British administrators for ameliorating women's conditions did not go unnoticed by these women writers. Tarabai Shinde was very cynical of them and wrote that the social reformers of the period were people of little consequence. 'This is so true: your mouths are full of talk about reform, but who actually does anything? You hold these great meetings, you turn up at them in your fancy shawl and embroidered turbans, you hand out all sorts of garlands, you use up a tank full of rose water, then you come home. And that's it. That's all you do. These phoney reform societies of yours have been around for thirty, thirty-five years. What's the use of them? You're all there patting yourselves on the back, but if we look closely; they're about as much use as a spare tit on a goat.'[63]

Ramabai felt that the reform activities taken up were not enough to bring about improvement in the condition of women in society. During Rukhmabai's trial, Ramabai commented sharply about the same, and used the occasion to condemn Hindu law. She showed how all men—be they Indian or British—shared the same view about the position to be assigned to women. 'Our only wonder is that a defenceless woman like Rukhmabai dared to raise her voice in the face of the powerful Hindu law, the mighty British government, the one hundred and twenty-nine million men and the three hundred and thirty million gods of Hindus, all these having conspired together to crush her into nothingness. We cannot blame the English

61. Kosambi, 'A Window in The Prison House', *History of Education*, p. 438.
62. Forbes and Raychaudhuri, *The Memoirs of Dr. Haimabati Sen*, p. 317.
63. Hanlon, *A Comparison Between Women and Men*, p. 84.

government for not defending a helpless woman; it is only fulfilling its agreement made with the male population of India.'[64]

Rukhmabai also spoke of the unadaptability of the Hindu laws in the changing circumstances and the immediate need to reform them. 'Everywhere a law needs revision in at least a few centuries, to suit the prevailing ages; and how is it possible that our Hindoo matrimonial laws, formed about thousands of years ago, suit the present age (an age half-Europeanized)? The only way to face the difficulties is the law reform.'[65] She said that although social reformers like Behramji Malabari had been trying for many years to eradicate pernicious customs like child marriages and enforced widowhood, the efforts had been of little consequence. 'But alas! What can one person do without unity and support? By their continuous perseverance and requests the Indian Government was kind enough to make inquiries into the matter, asking the opinions of many influential Hindoo gentlemen: but to the greatest dissatisfaction of every reformer, the numbers of the opponents to the intended reform surpassed that of advocates, and all the aspirations of the anxious reformers were thus at an end.'[66]

Some of these writers, besides speaking about the various problems faced by women, suggested ways to improve their condition. While Rukhmabai believed in legal reforms for women's betterment, Cornelia Sorabji believed that this alone would not solve the problem. Given the fact that throughout the Age of Consent debate, 'the Indian woman' was invoked as a mute and monolithic character, Sorabji wanted to demonstrate that not all women fulfilled that kind of colonial cultural expectation. She believed that through proper education the problem would be solved by itself, and she differed from others by saying that even men needed to be educated on these issues. 'We have yet to learn in India how to supplement, without appropriating and imitating; and those who would help India have yet to learn in India how to expand what is best and noblest in her without reproducing a faded and monotonous copy

64. Jayawardena, *The White Woman's Other Burden*, p. 85.
65. Rukhmabai's letter to *The Times of India*, dated 9 April 1887.
66. Ibid.

of themselves. Marriage reform must begin not in legislation but in education.'[67] She realised that it would take time for society to accept widow remarriage and knew that the pioneers would suffer. Rokeya also believed that education alone could change the existing social conditions and believed that the government should encourage girls' education by establishing more schools.

Ramabai not only pointed out the problems of Indian women, but also highlighted the chief needs of high-caste Hindu women: firstly, self-reliance; secondly, education, and thirdly, native women teachers. Working-class women were better off than high-caste women as they were not economically dependent on their menfolk. The higher-caste women were not self-reliant.[68] Mahadevi Varma felt that women could find help from other women in improving their lot. According to her, the educated women needed to come forward in helping the uneducated women. She, however, goes on to say that 'the enlightened women from the fields of education and medicine have formed a separate social class of their own which has made them indifferent towards the housewife, and has in turn made the housewives suspicious of them ... If they fail to emerge as representatives of their less fortunate sisters and continue to view their sacrifice-filled lives with contempt despite their education, wisdom, resources, leisure and self-reliance then the fear of the entire society coming to harm is sure to come true.'[69]

Conclusion

Though these writers were often very radical in their views, they often tried to live and work within the existing ideology. The power of organised social authority to command obedience through the sheer pressure of implicit expectations was so high that even these stringent critics of social customs were muted out. Despite all her radical views

67. Antoinette Burton, 'Stray Thoughts of an Indian Girl by Cornelia Sorabji', in *Feminisim in India*, ed. Maitrayee Chaudhuri, New Delhi: Kali for Women and Women Unlimited, p. 100.
68. Ramabai, *The High Caste Hindu Woman*, pp. 125–26.
69. Varma, *Sketches from My Past*, p. 14.

and activities, throughout her career, Rokeya wore the *burqa* and never appeared in public without this outer covering. She even wrote a piece in defence of the burqa and hence purdah, which she was always careful to distinguish from *abarodh* or strict seclusion.

Similarly, an interesting point to be noted about Rukhmabai's life is that after the death of Dadaji—whom she refused to accept as a husband—in 1904, she decided to don the Hindu widow's garb. And at that time she was not even under any perceptible social pressure, as she had been during her trial. Rukhmabai's 'conformist' gesture was not to champion the cause of either reform or orthodoxy. At that time, she was a doctor in Surat, who was combating the resistance of its small-town conservative population to sending their pregnant women to her hospital. She had struggled for eight years to establish herself, and now had her image and reputation to worry about. Her refusal to accept her widowed status would have put an end to her career. 'Having chosen to fade out of limelight, and do quiet medical work in a local arena, so important in the context of her times, Rukhmabai could not have neglected the pressure to be "correct" in terms that made sense to the beneficiaries of her efforts.'[70] Rukhmabai spent thirty-five years as chief medical officer in Surat and Rajkot hospitals; and after retirement in 1930, went to Bombay, where she supported movements of social reform and wrote on the harmful effects of women's seclusion.

Much of the work written by men during this period, often glorify women of the ancient Indian past. On the other hand, the women's works bring out the first-hand accounts of the miserable lives they were leading and try to analyse the reasons that were responsible for it. If the works of Cornelia describe women in the upper-class and higher-caste families, Mahadevi's works speak about women from the lowest strata of society, and the works of Rokeya bring out the problems faced by Muslim women. The works of Anandibai, Rukhmabai and Haimabati speak volumes about the immense hardships faced by the first women who ventured into the male bastion of medicine. The problems of enforced widowhood, early marriages, denial of education, female infanticide, purdah,

70. Chandra, *Enslaved Daughters*, p. 203.

widow remarriage, etc., were addressed by all these women. They believed that inadequate opportunities and the lack of knowledge had perpetuated women's sufferings for centuries. Most of these writers agreed that education alone could ameliorate the condition of Indian women. They were most definitely among the first women to give voice to the needs and aspirations of the modern Indian woman, and draw a clear analytical picture of the true condition of women in Indian society; and their's were also the voices least heard and heeded. Their outreach was limited and restricted; and thus their's remained the 'silent voices' of late nineteenth-century India.

4

Contested Domains

Reconstructing Education and Religious Identity in Sikh and Arya Samaj Schools in Punjab

MAHIMA MANCHANDA

INTRODUCTION

Late nineteenth-century Punjab witnessed the emergence of the need for women's education, as reformers grappled with the kind of education that was to be imparted to girls to counter the onslaught of missionary education and government schools. This essay seeks to explore two pioneering schools that were established by indigenous reformers to meet the demand for female education. For the reformers, the question of women's education, which included the need to equip girls with Western education while preventing them from being transformed into *memsahibs* (foreigners), was of crucial import. The Sikh Kanya Mahavidyalaya, Ferozepur (1892) and the Kanya Mahavidyalaya, Jullundur (1896) were set up with these ideals in mind.

The Sikh Kanya Mahavidyalaya was set up under the guidance of Bhai Takht Singh and his wife, Harnam Kaur. After the latter's death, Bhai Takht Singh's second wife, Agya Kaur, became the lady superintendent of the school. Bhai Takht Singh had started this school single-handedly with only three students under a thatched roof. He was later lionized for this effort and was hailed as a *zinda shahid* (living martyr). This institution was hailed as one of the pioneering institutions imparting quality education to girls.[1] The inculcation of religious instruction to Sikh girls was a special agenda of this school. Bhai Takht Singh was a Sikh preacher associated with the local Singh Sabha. However, not only Sikhs, but students from other religious communities too studied in this school, since the goal of female education was the same across communities. At the same time, this school also became an arena where larger questions of religiosity and identity formation came to the fore. In this sense, the school was trying to cope with the religious and the secular, the traditional and the modern, at the same time. These may appear as opposing binaries, yet, at the Sikh Kanya Mahavidyalaya, an attempt was made to blur the boundaries between them, in an effort to make them co-exist.

The Kanya Mahavidyalaya, an Arya Samaji school was established by Lala Dev Raj in 1896. (The Arya Samaj was founded by Swami Dayanand Saraswati and its motto was to 'go back to the Vedas' as forming the basis for a reformed Hinduism.) The purpose behind the inception of this school was to impart physical, mental and religious instruction; to develop skills in the making of handicrafts and household cooking, and to produce literature in Hindi and Sanskrit for females. The identity that was sought to be created was that of an 'Arya' woman, with the medium of instruction being 'Arya Bhasha', a purified version of Hindi. The school opened its own *sahitya bhandar* (bookstore), and Lala Devraj himself wrote many of the books that formed a part of the school curriculum. Some of these books were taught in government schools as well, and translated into other languages.[2]

At the Sikh Kanya Mahavidyalaya, books written by the Singh Sabha stalwarts, Bhai Vir Singh and Bhai Mohan Singh Vaid were taught. However, in an article in *Punjabi Bhain*, the journal of the

1. Sardul Singh Caveeshar, 'The Sikh Kanya Mahavidyalaya', in *The Singh Sabha and other Socio-Religious Movements in the Punjab*, ed. Ganda Singh, Patiala: Publication Bureau, 1997, p. 111.
2. Madhu Kishwar, 'Arya Samaj and Women's Education: Kanya Mahavidyalaya, Jalandhar', *Economic and Political Weekly*, vol. 21, no. 17, April 1986, p. 11.

school, the progress achieved by the Kanya Mahavidyalaya and other Arya Samaji schools in translating and writing books for girls was noted, and the comparatively slow growth in this direction by the Sikh community was lamented.[3] In the *Khalsa Samachar*, a mouthpiece of the Singh Sabha, articles appeared that warned the Sikhs not to fall for the Arya Samaji propaganda that Sikhs were Hindu, and discouraged them from sending their children to the Arya Samaji schools.[4]

It is this twin objective of education and religious identity that I want to explore. As a case study of these two schools demonstrates, female education became a contested terrain where larger questions of religious identity came to the forefront. The question of female education brought into the arena of public debate the contesting claims of religious identity, as indigenous reformers sought the right kind of education for girls. As the Sikh Kanya Mahavidyalaya struggled to compete with the Kanya Mahavidyalaya, certain questions assumed importance—What would be the agenda for reformers regarding education of women in their respective schools? How would they attempt to create a distinctive religious identity amongst women, and what role would education provided at the two schools play in it? The question of proselytisation also needs to be explored in the background of the specific religious identity being propounded by the two schools. Regarding the issue of language, the attempt of the Singh Sabha to make Punjabi the language of the Sikhs alone, as against the broader connotation of Punjabi representing a distinct regional identity irrespective of religion, needs to be looked at in the context of the two schools. This essay seeks to look at the course structure, ambience, and aims and ideals of these institutions, as well to understand the reasons why they came to acquire a prestigious position not just in Punjab, but outside the province as well. These, in short, are the broad themes explored in this essay.

3. 'Hamari Padhai Ki Zaroorat', *Punjabi Bhain*, January 1909.
4. 'Arya Samaj di navichaal', *Khalsa Samachar*, January 1911.

The Condition of Women's Education on the Eve of the Establishment of the Sikh Kanya Mahavidyalaya and the Kanya Mahavidyalaya

As far as female education is concerned, H. R. Mehta, in a 1929 thesis based on Punjab administrative and education reports and government resolutions, traced the history of the growth and development of Western education in Punjab from 1846 to 1884. Looking at the history of female education prior to the intervention of the British Raj, he stated in his introduction that the education imparted to girls was of a religious or semi-religious character that regarded the home to be the proper sphere for women. The ability to read and recite a religious text was considered enough: Muslim girls read the Quran at the mosque along with their brothers; Sikh girls attended *dharmashalas*, while Hindu girls were taught to read at home. The teacher was generally the *mullah*, the *bhai* or the family priest, although there were instances of female teachers—usually widows.[5]

G. W. Lietner, a British Orientalist who was appointed the first principal of Government College, Lahore in 1864 and was the founder of a society called Anjuman-i-Punjab, also prepared a report on the condition of indigenous education in Punjab. In his *A History of Indigenous Education in Punjab*, he stressed how indigenous female education in Punjab required less development than revival, as a girl was taught to read Nagri or Gurmukhi or Arabic at her home or a friend's home. Knowledge of the scriptures, along with instruction in sewing, cooking, embroidery and elementary account-keeping was deemed sufficient for a girl. Among the Muslims and the Sikhs, emphasis on the reading of religious texts made literacy socially acceptable. To the question, 'What is the character of indigenous instruction for girls in the province?', he stressed that the wives of maulvis and bhais were taught by their husbands and instructed their children up to a certain age, in scriptural reading and religious

5. H. R. Mehta, *A History of the Growth and Development of Western Education in Punjab 1846–1884*, Lahore: Language Department, Punjab, 1929, p. 18.

duties. The Hindu girls of the upper castes were taught in the privacy of their homes. Lietner went on to add that even when women from respectable families knew how to write, they dared not mention this fact as it was considered an accomplishment of only the superior class of courtesans![6]

With annexation of Punjab, initially, it was the missionary societies that played an active role in the promotion of female education. The first elementary school for girls was established by the American Presbyterian Mission, Ludhiana in 1836.[7] In Lahore, by 1883–84, eighteen schools existed for non-Christian girls under the charge of European ladies like Mrs Anderson, Jane Harris and Ms Rose, with 205 Hindus, 175 Muslims, forty-four Sikhs, and fifty-six children belonging to the families of sweepers. Urdu, Persian, Gurmukhi and Hindi were taught, along with lessons in arithmetic, history, geography, and sewing and knitting. These ladies also visited the *zenanas* (women's section of the households). Most significantly, teaching of the Bible was an essential part of the curriculum of these schools.[8] However, Lala Munshi Ram (later called Swami Shraddhanand), a famous Arya Samaji leader, decided to take up the education of Hindu girls when his young daughter, studying at a missionary school, recited the following couplet to him: *Ek bar Isa Isa bol, tera kya lagega mol? Isa mera Ram Ramayya, Isa mera Krishna Kanhayya* (Take the name of Jesus just once, what will it cost you? Jesus is my Lord Rama, Jesus is my Lord Krishna).[9] These activities were regarded as proselytising and gave an impetus to the establishment of indigenous schools like the Sikh Kanya Mahavidyalaya and the Kanya Mahavidyalaya to educate women while ensuring the preservation of the communities' religion and culture.

6. G. W. Leitner, *A History of Indigenous Education in the Punjab: Since Annexation and in 1882*, Calcutta,1882, pp. 97–98, 104.
7. Mehta, *A History of the Growth and Development of Western Education in Punjab*, p. 27.
8. *Gazetteer of the Lahore District, 1883–4*, Lahore: Sang-e-Meel Publishers, p. 62.
9. Madhu Kishwar, 'Arya Samaj and Women's Education', p. 10.

This is not to suggest that it was merely the threat of proselytising activities of the missionary schools that led to establishment of indigenous schools for girls. Reforms for women were seen as essential to the agenda being put forward by the religious reformers. For the Lahore Singh Sabha, female education was tied to the creation of a homogenous Tat Khalsa identity for the Sikhs. It was stressed that without educated mothers, the Sikhs would continue to be mired in superstition and immoral practices.[10] Similarly, the Arya Samaj aimed at creating a reformed Hinduism and a true Arya woman. Gail Minault's excellent study on Muslim socio-religious reforms has shown similar concerns as far as Muslim women are concerned—wives who were better companions to their husbands and better managers of the household in the face of uncertain economic forces, better mothers who would raise their children to be healthy and disciplined, and Muslims who knew the tenets of their faith as contained in the scriptures, rather than in customary rituals.[11]

As far as government schools were concerned, female education received due attention in Wood's Despatch of 1854. Seventeen female schools were opened during 1856–57, but most of these had to be closed down soon for want of teachers and poor attendance. An important contribution in this direction was made by Sir Robert Montgomery who held a grand 'Educational Durbar' in Lahore in February 1862. He impressed upon the European officers and the native gentlemen present the importance which he attached to the education of women, and invited their cooperation in the promotion of women's education. After this, renewed efforts were made in this direction by the government, with an important role being played by Baba Khem Singh. By 1865–66, the number of government schools had risen to 333. However, these schools, too, suffered from a lack

10 Doris R. Jakobsh, *Relocating Gender in Sikh History: Transformation, Meaning and Identity*, New Delhi: Oxford University Press, 2003, p. 132.

11. Gail Minault, *Secluded Scholars: Women's Education and Muslim Social Reform in Colonial India*, New Delhi: Oxford University Press, 1998, p. 215.

of teachers, poor attendance and insufficient instruction.[12] In fact, both Mehta and Lietner highlight that female education in Punjab suffered a decline with the British annexation of the province.

A number of factors were held responsible for this phenomenon. Firstly, the inspection of schools by male government officials was looked upon with disfavour by the indigenous population. Lietner spoke against this when he stated, 'Keeping the female schools in public places, and ... always attempting in spite of any pledges that may have been given at the commencement of the female education movement, to inspect them, prevent[s] the very patrons of the schools from sending their own daughters to them.'[13] And Mehta said that the kind of education imparted to girls in government schools being very similar to the one being imparted to boys, was looked upon with uneasiness.[14] The teaching of Urdu in the government girls' schools was frowned upon, and it was asked why girls needed to taught Urdu—the language of administration, and one that was alien to the native population—when they did not have to find jobs. Hence, Lietner advocated the teaching of Gurmukhi first and lessons in sewing, knitting, spinning and embroidery to cater to the needs of female education.[15]

Another important reason for the unpopularity of government schools (and to some extent, missionary schools) was the perception of caste status amongst the Punjabi reformers. The Lahore Singh Sabha claimed that all Sikhs were equal, and the question of caste did not hold any significance for them. Yet, the refusal of the local Singh Sabha members of Ferozepur to dine with Ditt Singh, an influential Singh Sabha member who was an 'untouchable' by caste, questions the above claim.[16] Bhai Takht Singh's own position was ambivalent

12. Mehta, *A History of the Growth and Development of Western Education in Punjab*, p. 27.
13. Lietner, *A History of Indigenous Education*, p. 109.
14. Mehta, *A History of the Growth and Development of Western Education in Punjab*, p. 72.
15. Lietner, *A History of Indigenous Education in the Punjab*, p. 110.
16. S. S. Amol, *Bhai Sahib Takht Singh Da Jiwan te Panth Seva*, 1938, p. 15.

with regard to caste. He refused to refer to the castes of the girls who studied in his school. Yet, in an interview, when he was asked (by Sardul Singh Caveeshar) about the complaint that educated girls shirk ordinary duties, Bhai Takht Singh replied:

> The complaint is due to some misunderstanding. A well-educated girl who could become useful in other spheres of life should not be expected to do the work which could be safely entrusted to menials.[17]

The use of the term 'menial' needs to be noted in its Indian context. It clearly refers to the untouchable castes who were employed in occupations that were considered degrading by upper-caste Hindus. Thus, Bhai Takht Singh's reference to the menials shows how embedded the idea of caste status was in his consciousness.

The position of the Arya Samaj with regard to caste was also quite ambivalent. Both Anshu Malhotra and Kenneth W. Jones have highlighted in their works that the Arya Samaj drew its followers from among the higher-caste, literate Hindus. Some historians have stressed on Dayanand's rejection of the caste system based on birth in his influential work *Satyarth Prakash* to account for the attraction for the movement in Punjab. Yet, his desire to create a race of pure and healthy Aryas led him to lay down a variety of rules and regulations for ideal conception of the twice-born. Similar concerns led him to advocate *niyog* (levirate) for widows from the twice-born castes. What is significant is his advocacy for the appointment of a wet nurse for the child. This was to enable women to conceive two months after childbirth, a practice which was central to his desire to create a pure Aryan race.[18] However, who was the wet nurse? Which caste did the non-Aryas belong to? Clearly, not to the twice-born; and hence, to the castes referred to as menials by Bhai Takht Singh—the Shudras and the untouchables. In Lietner's report as well, a concern is voiced over the fact that upper-caste families

17. Caveeshar, 'The Sikh Kanya Mahavidyalaya', p. 107.
18. Uma Chakravarty, 'Whatever Happened to the Vedic Dasi', in *Recasting Women: Essays in Colonial History*, eds. Kumkum Sangari and Sudesh Vaid, New Delhi: Kali for Women, 1989, pp. 55–57.

did not send their daughters to government schools, and emphasis is placed on the appointment of wives of priests or of teachers of higher castes to teach in these schools.[19] Thus, there was clearly a lack of teachers from upper-caste families. The few female teachers who were available were looked upon with disfavour because of the view that no 'respectable' native woman had as yet taken to teaching as a means of obtaining a livelihood. The word, respectable, here refers to upper-caste families.[20]

The picture that emerges thus, as far as government intervention in female education is concerned, is one of continuous decline. The number of government schools for females decreased continuously, and by 1878–79, stood at only 195 schools.[21] At the same time, with Western education for boys becoming essential for government jobs, the ideal of companionable wives dedicated to their household, but not steeped in superstition, became an aspiration. Different communities, while acknowledging the need for female education, grappled with the question of the kind of education to be provided to girls. Thus, it was with the introduction of modern Western education under colonial rule that the question—What should girls be taught?—came to be asked. The proselytising activities of the missionary schools and the appointment of male inspectors in government schools, along with reformist agendas regarding the education of girls led to the Indian reformers taking over the task of setting up schools for girls. The Sikh Kanya Mahavidyalaya under Bhai Takht Singh and the Kanya Mahavidyalaya under Lala Devraj were instances of this effort. Hence, the next question that arose—What should girls be taught?—will be discussed through an analysis of the course curricula and textbooks introduced in the two schools.

19. Lietner, *History of Indigenous Education in the Punjab*, p. 105.
20. Madhu Kishwar, 'The Daughters of Aryavarta', *Indian Economic and Social History Review*, 1986, p. 165.
21. Ibid., p. 109.

Course Structures at the Sikh Kanya Mahavidyalaya and the Kanya Mahavidyalaya: New Curricula and Books

Reformers like Bhai Takht Singh and Lala Devraj who took an active part in establishing schools for girls also grappled with the kind of education that was to be provided to girls. They had to deal with the opponents of female education, as well as orthodox sections that favoured a special curriculum for girls with emphasis on sewing, knitting, and managing the household economy as against the teaching of English, mathematics and science. For example, nationalists like Tilak, while supporting female education, declared that subjects like English, arithmetic, science and music were useless to girls, while advocating the teaching of the vernaculars, moral science and needlework. He stressed that the object of female education was not to make the woman equal to man. Women, who had to perform the wifely and maternal duties, required 'a fund of energy to perform them satisfactorily ... education should be so planned as to give to their minds a minimum amount of useful culture and information with minimum expenditure of energy.'[22] A practical consideration of satisfying the parents of the students had also to be kept in mind.

In the Sikh Kanya Mahavidyalaya, thus, Bhai Takht Singh tried to cater to both the conservative demand as well as the modernist approach with regard to education of girls. An analysis of the scheme of studies followed in the Sikh Kanya Mahavidyalaya between 1916 and 1929 reflects this. Arithmetic was introduced in the school right from first standard upwards, and the syllabus comprised figures and notations up to twenty, multiplication tables up to five, and addition and subtraction with concrete illustrations up to twenty.[23] As the

22. Parimala V. Rao, 'Women in the Nationalist Discourse: A Case Study of Tilak's Approach to Women's Education and Emancipation', in *Development of Modern Indian Thought and the Social Science*, ed. Sabyasachi Bhattacharya, New Delhi: Oxford University Press, 2007, pp. 247, 259.
23. *Scheme of Studies current in the Sikh Kanya Mahavidyalaya, Ferozepur*, Amritsar: Coronation Printing Works, 1916, p. 1.

students progressed through the standards, they were introduced to higher multiplication tables, fractions, LCM and GCM, averages, simple interest, percentage, profit and loss, etc., with the syllabus for eighth standard comprising problems on volume, area, compound interest, calendars, trains and mixtures.[24] This was done to equip the students to handle the ninth and tenth standard courses prescribed by the Punjab University. Thus, the syllabus had to cater to students who wished to study at the intermediate and higher stages, and the subjects taught to them had to meet the government standards.

Students were introduced to science in the form of object lessons from the first standard onwards; and from the sixth standard onwards it was taught as a separate subject. The attempt to teach science through practical methods in the form of object lessons was an innovative step taken by this school. For example, in the fourth standard, object lessons were divided into two parts—on animals and on plants. Animals were divided into three different categories, namely, (a) carnivores, (b) hoofed ruminants and (c) rodents, with stress on their habitats and comparison between the different categories. With regard to plants, they were divided into (a) leguminous plants, (b) parts of a flower as illustrated by the rose or jasmine, (c) cucurbitaceous plants such as cucumber, (d) lilia such as tulips and (e) grains such as rice and maize, with emphasis on characteristics and comparisons between the different categories. In these lessons, pictures of the animals and samples of the plants were provided to make them more meaningful. In the Kanya Mahavidyalaya, Jullundur, gardening and botany were combined to provide a contrast to textbook reading alone. For example, the course structure comprised naming trees on the campus, making bouquets and garlands, sowing and harvesting grain, etc. In short, emphasis was laid on practical knowledge, and not simply book learning.[25]

In the botany lessons, parts of a flower were referred to, while physiology lessons described the skin and perspiration. The prescribed course at the Sikh Kanya Mahavidyalaya comprised

24. *Scheme of Studies Current in the Sikh Kanya Mahavidyalaya, Ferozepur*, p. 8.
25. Kishwar, 'Arya Samaj and Women's Education', p. 13.

botany and physiology, in 1918. In 1929, the course was revised to comprise *Qudrat ke Khel*, parts I and II for the seventh and eighth standards. The introduction of this book reflected the availability of new books in vernacular languages. This was considered important as schools set up for girls—like the Kanya Mahavidyalaya, the Sikh Kanya Mahavidyalaya, and the Muslim Girls' School (Madrasat-ul-Banat), Jullundur (set up by Abdul Haq Abbas)[26]—had to make available books in the vernacular languages which were the medium of instruction in these schools. Related to this was the question of identity formation in Punjab in which language played an important part. The founder of the Kanya Mahavidyalaya, Lala Devraj, for example, himself wrote books in Hindi such as *Pahli Pathawali* (First Primer), *Doosri Pathawali* (Second Primer) and *Balodyan Sangit* (Kindergarten Songs), and these books were sold from the school's own bookshop.[27] An article published in *Punjabi Bhain* in 1909 referred to the lack of Punjabi readers for students of the Sikh Kanya Mahavidyalaya after the third standard and referred to the progress made in this direction by the Arya Samaji schools. It was stressed that the Arya Samajis were promoting education through a new language, i.e., Hindi, while the Sikh Kanya Mahavidyalaya was providing instruction in Punjabi, the language of the province. Yet, they were progressing at a faster pace than Sikh Kanya Mahavidyalaya. The article ended with an appeal for funds to change the dismal situation, and write and publish more books in Punjabi for girls.[28]

Thus, as far as language is concerned, Punjabi was the medium of instruction in the Sikh Kanya Mahavidyalaya, and it was introduced at the primary level. Emphasis was laid on both reading and writing. In writing, special emphasis was laid on letter-writing. This was a big step forward considering the fact that the opponents of girls' education had claimed that girls who were educated would write love letters! Inherent in this was the fear for women's sexuality, and also the notion of *izzat* (honour, prestige and reputation), of

26. For a detailed discussion on this school, refer to Gail Minault's work mentioned in footnote no. 11.
27. Kishwar, 'Arya Samaj and Women's Education', p. 12.
28. 'Hamari Padhaiki Zaroorat', *Punjabi Bhain*, January 1909.

which women were regarded as the sole repositories.[29] In the Kanya Mahavidyalaya as well, *Patra Kamudi* was a prescribed textbook in Hindi that comprised sample letters for different occasions—from letters ordering books to sick-leave applications to letters to doctors describing a patients symptoms.[30] In the Sikh Kanya Mahavidyalaya, the syllabus also comprised essay-writing and grammar and composition in Punjabi. As far as reading was concerned, it comprised books written by important Singh Sabha leaders like Bhai Vir Singh (*Sundri*), Bhai Mohan Singh (*Bal Bodh* and *Punjabi Grammar*) as well as specially designed course books like *Vidya Ratnakar,* Middle Course I and II, and a Punjabi reader. It is also important to note that while the school was set up with the objective of creation of a Tat Khalsa identity amongst the Sikh girls, the course books did not comprise works written by Singh Sabha leaders alone; the works of other socio-religious reformers were also included as part of a programme to inculcate in girls right values that would help them to lead happily married lives. This can be seen from the inclusion of *Dulhan Darpan* (Brides Mirror), a prescribed text for students of the fourth standard. This book—originally written in Urdu by Moulvi Nazir Ahmad, and translated into Gurmukhi—was a didactic guide for young wives, praising the virtues of education, astute household management, pious living, and skilful diplomacy in inter-personal relationships.[31] Written on the lines of an English novel, an important purpose of this book was encouraging female education.[32]

Apart from this, a Gurmukhi magazine called *Punjabi Bhain* was published every month by the Sikh Kanya Mahavidyalaya. In an advertisement that appeared on the pages of this magazine, it was described as:

> A Punjabi monthly in Gurmukhi especially suited for our women folk. It contains articles on domestic economy, hygiene, cooking,

29. Doris Jakobsh (ed.), *Sikhism and Women; History, Texts and Experience*, New Delhi: Oxford University Press, p. 8.
30. Kishwar, 'Arya Samaj and Women's Education', p. 12.
31. Gail Minault, 'Sayyid Ahmad Dehlavi and the Delhi Renaissance', *The Delhi Omnibus*, New Delhi: Oxford University Press, 2007.
32. Lietner, *A History of Indigenous Education in the Punjab*, p. 107.

training of children, series of great women of all ages and other kindred subjects. Very useful for ladies. Annual subscription: Indian Rs 1, Foreign Rs 14.[33]

The special charges for overseas subscription show the reach of this magazine, which was supposed to cater to women not just in Punjab and India, but also to the Sikh diaspora across the world. The influence of this school amongst the Sikh diaspora can be seen from the presence of its former students in Sikh families settled in China, Malaya, Singapore and Burma. The Kanya Mahavidyalaya also brought out its own magazine in Hindi called the *Panchal Pandita*. It was also a monthly magazine which was described as a handy periodical for educated ladies and young students. It contained information on the activities of the institution and emerged as its mouthpiece.[34] The publication of magazines by the two schools is symbolic of how the print media emerged as an important tool for the dissemination of knowledge and the popularisation of female education at that time.

Interestingly, Hindi was also taught at the Sikh Kanya Mahavidyalaya and was introduced from the third standard onwards. We may note that Punjabi had special relevance in the Sikh Kanya Mahavidyalaya because of the assertion of Lahore Singh Sabha that Punjabi in Gurmukhi script was the language of the Sikhs. As against this, a Sanskritised Hindi called Arya Bhasha was imbibed by the Arya Samajis and was the medium of instruction at the Kanya Mahavidyalaya. Urdu, on the other hand, was the medium of instruction in government schools (especially for boys) as it was the language of administration. What then led to the introduction of Hindi in the Sikh Kanya Mahavidyalaya? One reason may have been the sense of competition with the Kanya Mahavidyalaya and a desire to attract girls from the Hindu families as well. It may also be noted that girls who attended the Sikh Kanya Mahavidyalaya belonged not only to Punjab, but from across north India and even Burma.[35]

33. *Punjabi Bhain*, November 1917.
34. Kishwar, 'Arya Samaj and Women's Education', p. 12.
35. 'Sikh Kanya Mahavidyalaya sambandhi ek sajjan de 40 prashnan de uttar', *Punjabi Bhain*, April 1909.

Another significant step taken by both the Sikh Kanya Mahavidyalaya and the Kanya Mahavidyalaya was the introduction of English in their respective syllabi. It was introduced in the Sikh Kanya Mahavidyalaya from the fourth standard onwards and consisted of reading, writing (with stress on letter-writing), grammar, composition, conversation and recitation of poems. Special emphasis was placed on recitation of poems, letter-writing and conversation to develop skills that companionable wives (of men with newly acquired Western education) should possess. This was a reflection of the views of Bhai Takht Singh who insisted that girls should be taught English; he felt that boys who knew English would only want to marry girls who did so as well, and if they could not find Indian girls who knew English, they would marry foreigners and become *meman*.[36] However, it is important to note that while Bhai Takht Singh was influenced by a desire to teach the girls of his school to be good wives in a rapidly changing society where men were acquiring English education, he also wanted girls to know English so that they could pursue higher education and even study abroad. The Sikh Kanya Mahavidyalaya regularly appealed for setting up a college for girls, and Harnam Kaur, too, at a Sikh educational conference, urged for the establishment of a girls' college by the Sikh community. In the Kanya Mahavidyalaya as well, English was introduced from 1907 onwards, and stress was laid on developing skills that women required in their daily lives. Moreover, doing *prachar* (spreading the message of the Arya Samaj) and translating English texts into Arya Bhasha for the progress of the community required proficiency in English.[37] Thus, in the Kanya Mahavidyalaya, English was not only essential for the making of companionable wives and higher studies; it was also necessary for spreading the message of the Arya Samaj. In this sense, the Kanya Mahavidyalaya envisaged a special role for women within the Arya Samaj movement.

History and geography were also taught in both the schools. Geography was introduced from the second standard in the Sikh Kanya Mahavidyalaya with stress on distance and direction, followed

36. Bhai Sahib Bhai Takht Singh, *Khalsa Samachar*, January 1938.
37. Kishwar, 'Arya Samaj and Women's Education', pp. 16–17.

by teaching the meaning and the use of the map of Ferozepur district in the third standard, and the geography of Punjab, India and the world in higher standards.[38] History lessons were introduced in the sixth standard and commenced with the history of India till the reign of Babur; in the seventh standard, the history of India till the Battle of Plassey was taught, while in the eighth standard, modern Indian history—with special reference to developments since 1857—was taught.[39] A similar course structure was followed in the Kanya Mahavidyalaya.

Physical exercise was also given due importance at the Sikh Kanya Mahavidyalaya and was begun right from first standard. It consisted of activities like *chakkar*, breathing exercises, skipping, countryside games, etc. Interestingly, in the syllabus of 1918, 'dumble' (dumb-bell) and tug of war were also included. These games are associated with masculinity, and also reflect the Punjabi culture that viewed women as hardy and strong. This was also the opinion of Prem Chaudhry who felt that hard work was a general feature of the life of rural Punjab where Jat women were engaged in agricultural operations with their husbands.[40] The inclusion of physical training as a part of school education also reflected the views of Bhai Takht Singh:

> Indian girls can work as hard as any man. In Malwa I have seen Sikh ladies doing everything except ploughing. In weight-lifting they are hardly surpassed by their brothers. Generally our women do not get sufficient opportunity for work; this disuse of their limbs greatly weakens them. Sedentary habits also have a degenerating effect upon their physique.[41]

38. *Scheme of Studies Current the Sikh Kanya Mahavidyalaya, Ferozepur*, pp. 1–11.
39. Ibid., p. 10.
40. Prem Chaudhry, 'Customs in a Peasant Economy: Women in Colonial Haryana,' in *Recasting Women: Essays in Colonial History*, ed. Kumkum Sangari and Sudesh Vaid, New Delhi: Kali for Women, 1989, pp. 301–04.
41. Caveeshar, 'The Sikh Kanya Mahavidyalaya', pp. 106–07.

However, in the scheme of studies issued in 1929, both dumb-bell and tug of war were dropped the syllabus. This should be seen in the context of the ideal of a Victorian housewife which became something to be aspired for. Women were meant to make the home the sanctum for a husband, and serve him with her prowess in cooking, household management and conversation skills; her participation in agricultural work along with her husband came to be looked upon with disfavour. It was also based on the aspiration for a higher-caste status under the colonial gaze, which came to be based upon imposing greater control over women and confining them to the home. Chastity and domestic work within the home as opposed to work outside came to be regarded as the epitome of good training of women which reformers like Bhai Takht Singh aspired for.[42] Physical training was imparted in the Kanya Mahavidyalaya through games that combined physical exercise with mental concentration. The magazine *Panchal Pandita* provided a list of some of the games including *rang pehchan* (colour recognition) and *chun chunav* (choices). The focus of the school, as far as physical exercise and outdoor games was concerned, was to provide *hansi khel mein shiksha*.[43] Thus, through an innovative step taken by the school, games became a means of education.

Domestic economy and needlework were part of the course at both the Sikh Kanya Mahavidyalaya and the Kanya Mahavidyalaya. In the Kanya Mahavidyalaya, an attempt was made to impart all the skills needed to make a girl a successful housewife. Cooking, sewing, domestic economy, hygiene, etc., were part of the curriculum. Needlework was introduced from the second standard, and by the tenth standard, girls were taught to make shirts and petticoats, do fancy embroidery, as well as knit sweaters and blouses.[44] In the Sikh Kanya Mahavidyalaya, while practical skills for the home were provided in the form of object lessons (which combined knowledge of physical science and home science) till the fifth standard, domestic

42. Anshu Malhotra, *Gender, Caste and Religious Identity: Restructuring Class in Colonial Punjab*, New Delhi: Oxford University Press, 2002, p. 43.
43. Kishwar, 'Arya Samaj and Women's Education', p. 13.
44. Ibid., p. 13.

economy as a separate subject was introduced from sixth standard. The prescribed books included of *Sughar Bibi*,[45] *Swastha Vidhi*,[46] and *Arogta Marag*,[47] which provided information on household management, hygiene, good health practices, prevention of diseases, etc. *Punjabi Bhain* also contained articles on these topics. As far as needlework is concerned, it was introduced right from the first standard, and the syllabus for first standard consisted of twisting threads and threading the needle. Cross-stitching and hemming was introduced in the second standard. In the higher standards, knitting of crochet handkerchiefs and embroidery were included the syllabus. By the eighth standard, students were equipped to handle sewing and cutting of all garments by hand and machine, knit comforters and ties, and do embroidery work on fancy Indian waistcoats, cushions and handkerchiefs.[48] However, this training was not just meant to contribute to a woman's skill as a housewife. Mrs Francis, Inspectress, Eastern Circle, while commending the contribution made by Bhai Takht Singh towards female education, spoke about needlework, firstly, as a useful domestic handicraft, and secondly, as an art or remunerative industry under which she included lace, embroidery and other works which could be a means of livelihood.[49] Bhai Takht Singh, too, saw needlework not just as a domestic art, but as a means of remuneration as well. An article in *Punjabi Bhain* encouraged women to develop the traditional arts of embroidery and knitting, a task which could be accomplished at home.[50] Thus, Bhai Takht Singh not only wanted his students to acquire the skills and

45. *Sughar Bibi* was a prescribed reading in domestic economy for students of sixth standard.
46. *Swastha Vidhi* was a prescribed reading in domestic economy for students of seventh standard.
47. *Arogta Marag* was a prescribed reading in domestic economy for students of sixth standard.
48. *Scheme of Studies Current the Sikh Kanya Mahavidyalaya, Ferozepur*, pp. 1–11.
49. *Report on the Public Instruction in the Punjab and its Dependencies for 1905–6*, Lahore: Civil and Military Press, 1906, p. 43.
50. 'Hindi Striliyekaam', *Punjabi Bhain*, April 1931.

values considered essential for a married life, but also to equip them with a means of livelihood. Yet, the skills that were imparted were ones that did not require women to leave the house. Clearly then, the purpose of this education was to make girls good helpmates who would serve their families and communities.

What is significant is that in both the Sikh Kanya Mahavidyalaya and Kanya Mahavidyalaya, the goal of education was also intertwined with the larger objective of creation of a religious identity. Bhai Takht Singh wanted his school to become a model institution of the Sikh community. As a result, religious instruction was accorded special importance. A gurdwara was constructed within the school premises, which the girls visited every morning and evening. Religious instruction was part of the syllabus, and began right from the first standard. The religious instruction for the first standard, for example, comprised

> How to respect and bow to Sri Guru Granth Sahib, to keep quiet and stand with clasped hands when praying or reciting shabads, to sit by squatting in congregation, to take the prashad with both hands open and to say fateh with both hands clasped.[51]

Gurbaksh Kaur, the daughter of Bhai Takht Singh pointed out how the daily life of the boarders was centred around religion. She recalls that on getting up at 6 a.m., the boarders used to begin their day with a *kirtan* of *Assa di var*. Bhai Takht Singh was of the view that the *bhog* of Assa di var should be offered before the sunrise. After this, the girls studied the Guru Granth Sahib; and only then did they go to their classes. The girls also took turns in preparing the *langar* themselves.[52] As the students moved up through the standards, the *Japji Sahib*, the *Gurbani*, the lives of the Sikh gurus, etc., were taught. Practical lessons on how to close the Guru Granth Sahib and make *karahprashad*[53] was also provided. This school, in fact,

51. *Scheme of Studies Current in the Sikh Kanya Mahavidyalaya, Ferozepur*, p. 43.
52. Dalwinder Singh, *Bhai Sahib Bhai Takht Singh Zinda Shahid*, Ludhiana: Ludhiana Sikh Missionary College, p. 188.
53. *Karahprashad* is a sweet pudding offered as a blessing from the guru to all the visitors of the gurdwara.

came to represent and idealise the Tat Khalsa image of the Sikhs made popular by the Lahore Singh Sabha. The girls were also taught the rites to be performed at the time of birth and death, as well as the *Amritchakhna* ceremony[54] and the *Anandkaraj* rite. Before this, Sikhs and Hindus shared common rites during birth and death, and not every Sikh underwent *khande da pahul.*[55] However, under the initiative of the Singh Sabhas, notably the Lahore Singh Sabha, a massive campaign was started to replace the Hindu rites with new Sikh rites. Between 1884 and 1915, at least twenty-four manuals were written to determine what sort of life-cycle rituals should be performed by the Sikhs. For example, when a child was born, Hindu rites were no longer performed. A set of five verses on birth were to be recited from the Adi Granth. A child was to be named by a *granthi* by consulting the Adi Granth. Consultation of *purohits*, making of horoscopes and the use of amulets was forbidden.[56] As far as marriage was concerned, the Sikh ceremony initially involved *pheras* around a fire. However, under the influence of the Singh Sabha initiative, this was replaced by pheras around the Adi Granth. This came to be known as the Anandkaraj rite and became the standard form of Sikh marriage with the passing of the Anand Karaj Act in 1909. The reformers claimed that this was an early Sikh practice and not the result of the campaign of the Singh Sabha.[57] This can be questioned on the basis of an incident mentioned in Bhai Takht Singh's biography, which refers to a debate on *anandkaraj* ceremony about whether the *parikrama* should start from the left or the right. Bhai Takht

54. It refers to initiation by the sword.
55. The process of initiation into the Khalsa was begun by Guru Gobind Singh in 1699. This includes maintenance of the five 'K's and the observance of the injunctions laid down in *rahit-namas* or code of conduct manuals.
56. Harjot S. Oberoi, 'From Ritual to Counter Ritual: Rethinking the Hindu-Sikh Question, 1884–1915 in *Sikh History and Religion in the Twentieth Century*, ed. Joseph T. O Connell, New Delhi: Manohar, 1990, pp. 150–51.
57. W. H. McLeod, *Who is a Sikh? The Problem of Sikh Identity*, New Delhi: Oxford University Press, 1989, pp. 80–81.

Singh was in favour of parikrama from the left, as the Guru Granth Sahib would be on the right and the *kripan* on the left. This shows that there were no early scriptures in which the rite of *Anandkaraj* was explicitly stated; and its overwhelming acceptance by the Sikh community was a result of Singh Sabha efforts.[58] The death ceremony was also not left untouched. The transferring of the dead body from the bed to the ground, placing a lamp in its hand, and *siyapa* or the mourning ritual by women came under attack—it came to be seen as anti-Sikh and was forbidden.[59] The five 'K's of Sikh faith were to be left on the dead body after washing, and the *Kirtan Sohila* was to be recited at the cremation ground. The *shraddh* ceremony was also forbidden and replaced by an uninterrupted forty-eight-hour recitation of the Adi Granth. Interestingly, the custom of siyapa was forbidden not just by the Sikh reformers but by the Arya Samajis as well. This was because it involved a fear for women's sexuality with women, indecently dressed, exposing themselves to the gaze of men other than their husbands.[60]

The identity that the Kanya Mahavidyalaya sought to create was an 'Arya' identity. Religious education in the form of a reformed Hinduism was an essential part of the curriculum of the Kanya Mahavidyalaya. Hymns and *bhajan*s were taught, and the girls were to be well trained in the principles of the Arya Samaj. *Sandhya ucharan* (utterance of evening prayers), the *Ramayana* and the *Satyarth Prakash* were part of the curriculum. By the tenth standard, the Vedas, the *Manusmriti*, and the Bhagavadgita, too, formed a part of the syllabus. Performance of the *havan* (purification ritual) was also taught along with a thorough training in *vedprachar* (preaching of the Vedas) and *aryadharma* (way of life of the Aryas).[61]

Thus, the Sikh Kanya Mahavidyalaya tried to cater to the specific demand of education of girls as envisaged by the Lahore Singh Sabha—to make the girls true Sikhs who would inculcate the

58. S. S. Amol, *Bhai Sahib Bhai Takht Singh da Jivante Panth Seva*, 1938, p. 27.
59. Oberoi, 'From Ritual to Counter Ritual', pp. 151–52.
60. Malhotra, *Gender, Caste and Religious Identity*, pp. 196–97.
61. Kishwar, 'Arya Samaj and Women's Education', p. 15.

Tat Khalsa ideology and pass it on to their families and children. The Kanya Mahavidyalaya, on the other hand, tried to espouse the identity of an 'Arya' woman well-versed in vedprachar, who would prove to be an enlightened wife and mother and train her children in the principles of the Arya Samaj. The two schools attracted students from across Punjab as well as outside. Again, these schools taught subjects and developed curricula that were similar to those for boys. Girls were encouraged to appear for examinations and pursue higher education. This provided them with similar opportunities as men. Yet, as a survey of curricula and textbooks has shown, the reformist agenda did not contain the idea of gender equality and women's independence. Women were taught to serve their men folk better, and not to compete with them. Yet, did this agenda go on smoothly, or did it develop cracks that worked in favour of women?

Breaking New Grounds or Reinforcing Traditional Roles?

In this essay, I have tried to explore the complexities and contradictions that arose when reformers asked the question, 'What should women be taught?' On the one hand, there was emphasis on a curriculum that would teach girls how to manage the household economy and provide religious instruction, with emphasis on the vernaculars. At the same time, certain subjects like mathematics and science had to be taught to meet official standards and prepare girls for higher studies. What was the purpose of this education? It was to help women to fulfil their traditional roles in a more fruitful way—to be good wives and mothers. It was also meant to internalise the Tat Khalsa ideology as envisaged by the Singh Sabha reformers, or alternately provide a thorough grounding in the Arya Samaj ideology. But did this education open up a few careers for women, and if so, which careers? Also, while women were expected to fulfil their traditional roles, did this education provide a sense of individual self-worth, identity and agency?

The Sikh Kanya Mahavidyalaya, while stressing the need to create ideal wives and mothers, did not want to restrict women to their homes. Bhai Takht Singh bemoaned the fact that men did not allow women to work outside their homes even as teachers. He was also of the opinion that girls could be as successful as their brothers in examinations.[62] Numerous articles published in *Punjabi Bhain* stressed the need for higher education and colleges for girls. The school also conducted teachers' training classes which were open to students who had cleared middle school.[63] The girls were also encouraged to return to the institution as teachers. An article titled 'Sikh Ladies and Higher Education' stressed on the need to provide scholarships to girls from poor families. The achievements of three students—Bibi Sharan Kaur, who studied medicine in Ludhiana, Bibi Balwant Kaur, who studied in Punjab University, and Bibi Raminder Kaur, who studied medicine in Agra—was highlighted. Emphasis was laid on the fact that financial stringency and lack of parental support had prevented these girls from studying further, until Bhai Takht Singh lent a helping hand. The need for more help for such students was stressed.[64] Pamphlets published by the school also point out how its students had gone on to become doctors, school inspectors and teachers.[65] Students of the Sikh Kanya Mahavidyalaya also participated in Sikh educational conferences and took an active part in raising funds for setting up a boarding house. In this sense, the students of the Sikh Kanya Mahavidyalaya did break new ground.

In the Kanya Mahavidyalaya as well, girls were encouraged to pursue higher education, and the *Panchal Pandita* published articles on the achievements of women from around the world. This school, too, conducted training classes for teachers, and by 1910, fifty female teachers had been trained by the school. The girls were also encouraged to take up voluntary teaching assignments in the school. They also took an active part in the fundraising campaign of the school, accompanying Lala Devraj to different countries and

62. Caveeshar, 'The Sikh Kanya Mahavidyalaya,' pp. 105, 107.
63. *Sikh Kanya Mayavidyalaya Ferozepur De School Te Boarding House De Niyam-Upniyam Ate Dakhala Faram*, Ferozepur, 1917.
64. 'Sikh Ladies and Higher Education', *Punjabi Bhain*, November 1932.
65. Sukhdev Singh, *Bhai Sahib Bhai Takht Singhji Zinda Shahid ate Sikh Kanya Mahavidyalaya*, Ludhiana: Ludhiana Printing Service, 2006, p. 8.

organising campaigns themselves.[66] Yet, the school and its founder laid great emphasis on the religiosity and chastity of the girls, teaching them to be ideal homemakers who were wholly and solely devoted to their husbands and catered to the wishes of their mothers-in-law. The Sikh Kanya Mahavidyalaya, too, while highlighting the achievements of its successful students, maintained that they were totally devoted to the Sikh *panth* and had firm faith in the tenets of Sikhism. While highlighting the achievements of Dr Raminder Kaur, a former student who became a doctor, stress was laid on the fact that despite her professional success, her foremost identity remained that of a Sikh woman devoted to her faith.[67] Consequently, articles teaching women to emerge as ideal wives and daughters-in-laws were frequently published in *Punjabi Bhain*. An article written by a lady named Roop Kaur stressed on the ways to make one's husband and mother-in-law happy. A woman was taught that in order to win over her husband, she should devote herself totally to him, shower him with love, obey his every command, treat him with respect, and never question or criticise him.[68] Thus, women were taught that the best way of controlling their husbands was by serving them. If women were willing to accept their subordination, then they could be invested with an artificial power and a moral authority.[69] As far as the mother-in-law was concerned, the best way to keep her happy was by showing more love than necessary towards other members of her family, showing utmost obedience, keeping utensils in their proper places, not hiding anything, and always asking for forgiveness for wrong deeds. Most importantly, a girl was to refrain from visiting her parents as much as possible and praise her mother-in-law in front of her parents.[70] Bibi Harnam Kaur, the co-founder of the school, was eulogised for emerging as an ideal *pativrata* and imbibing the qualities mentioned above.

66. Kishwar, 'Arya Samaj and Women's Education', p. 20.
67. 'Shrimati Raminder Kaurji', *Punjabi Bhain*, April 1931.
68. 'Ek Prem Patra', *Punjabi Bhain*, November 1931, p. 28, 'Pati Vas Karne Da Jadu', *Punjabi Bhain*, February 1918, pp. 6–7.
69. Malhotra, *Gender, Caste and Religious Identity*, pp. 166–67.
70. 'Ek Prem Patra', *Punjabi Bhain*, November 1931.

Thus, the emphasis remained on providing women with an education that would enable them to fulfil their traditional roles as wives, daughters-in-law and mothers. Along with this came a thorough grounding in the ideals of their religion that would free them from superstition. Thus, the reformist zeal was for women's education that would help them play their traditional roles better, rather than undertake new ones.[71] Nonetheless, education did open up certain avenues for women, though they were limited in character. Teaching and medicine became careers acceptable to women. Debates arose in favour of higher education for women: they had to be well-educated, as university-educated men could expect only well-educated women to be companionable wives. The careers that opened up for women—notably teaching and medicine—were those that were considered 'feminine' and enhanced the role of a woman as a nurturer. Furthermore, doing *naukri* was frowned upon, and we find that many women who taught at the Sikh Kanya Mahavidyalaya and the Kanya Mahavidyalaya did so on a voluntary basis and not for a living. Education, thus, was not meant to free women from their domestic obligations, but to reinforce them.

It is true that women's education with an emphasis on a reformed religion eroded the autonomous domain for women, the attack on popular cultural practices being one example. Yet, education also opened up an arena that provided women a sense of individual self-worth and agency—the world of letters as women sought to express themselves in print—through diaries, letters and autobiographies. The two school magazines *Panchal Pandita* and *Punjabi Bhain* emerged as mouthpieces for the women associated with the schools as teachers, students and administrators. Lala Devraj wrote extensively for *Panchal Pandita*; and the students and teachers were actively involved in writing and editing the magazine that created a space for these women to reflect their thoughts. *Punjabi Bhain* as a mouthpiece for the present and former students of the Sikh Kanya Mahavidyalaya highlighted the achievements of the students. A former student, Dr Raminder Kaur, wrote regular columns in

71. Minault, *Secluded Scholars*, pp. 156–57.

Punjabi Bhain titled 'Child Psychology and Child Care'.[72] Many of the letters written by the girls during the fund-raising campaigns were also printed in the magazine. The students also wrote articles, short stories and poems. A former student, Bayant Kaur, wrote a poem titled 'Do Koylan Punjab Diyan'. Ultimately, to borrow from Judith Walsh, what women learned when men gave them advice was that they learned to read. This opened up for them a world hitherto unknown—the world of print culture that provided them a medium for agency and self-discovery.[73]

Conclusion

To conclude, as a survey of the courses of the Sikh Kanya Mahavidalaya and the Kanya Mahavidyalaya has shown, the purpose behind education for girls was to create western-educated women who would emerge as good companions for their husbands and assets to their community. Emphasis was placed on domestic affairs; and official standards ensured that girls were taught the same subjects as boys. These opened up new opportunities for women, though limited in character, as education was to serve different purposes as far as men and women were concerned. Hence, a separate curriculum was developed for women with emphasis on domestic economy, cooking, child-care, sewing and knitting, etc. Women were not expected to do naukri, but education was meant to equip them with the skills required for married life.

At the same time, women's education had to serve a special purpose apart from creation of companionable wives and ideal mothers. Schools like the Sikh Kanya Mahavidyalaya and Kanya Mahavidyalaya had a special goal in terms of identity formation and tried to cater to the specific demands of their own communities. In the Sikh Kanya Mahavidyalaya, education had to facilitate the complete separation of Sikhism from Hinduism. This was significant, as unlike the five external symbols or the five 'K's (*panchkakkas*),

72. 'Shrimati Doctor Raminder Kaurji, *Punjabi Bhain*', April 1931.
73. Judith Walsh, *What Women Learned When Men Gave Them Advice*, New Delhi: Oxford University Press, 2004, pp. 3–4.

the markers of external identity are not so rigid for women. The Sikh Kanya Mahavidyalaya became an embodiment of this process and the women who passed out of this school were expected to be stamped with a distinctive Tat Khalsa image.

Within this reformist agenda undertaken by schools, education emerged as a contested domain for the Singh Sabha reformers on the one hand and the Arya Samajis on the other. For the latter who wished to define and mould a true Arya woman, Sikhs and Hindus were not separate, and Sikhs did not represent a distinct religious identity. In fact, many of the leading Singh Sabha reformers like Bhai Ditt Singh were initially drawn towards Arya Samaj before Dayanand's critique of Sikhism drew them away.[74] For these Singh Sabha reformers, the eulogisation of the ideal Sikh wife and the notion of social service became the two-pronged ideal of Sikh educational initiatives for women.[75] On the other hand, the Arya Samaj movement aimed at creating a true Arya woman, well-versed in Sanskrit along with a thorough grounding in Vedic knowledge. At the same time, the need for companionable wives led to girl's introduction to modern Western education. Madhu Kishwar in her study of the Kanya Mahavidyalaya, has summed it up well by saying that 'Arya institutions were geared towards producing a modernized, educated woman striding forward into the Vedic past'.[76]

However, it is important to note that though the Sikh Kanya Mahavidyalaya aimed at establishing a homogenous Tat Khalsa identity among Sikh girls, the reality was different as shared cultural practices between the Sikhs and Hindus continued to exist. Both the schools attracted students not just from the adherents of their own faith (Tat Khalsa Sikhs in case of the Sikh Kanya Mahavidyalaya and Arya Samajis in case of the Kanya Mahavidyalaya) but others

74. See, Kenneth W. Jones, *Arya Dharma: Hindu Consciousness in the 19th Century Punjab*, New Delhi: Oxford University Press, 1976, 'Hum Hindu Nahin Hain: Arya-Sikh Relations (1877–1905)', *Punjab Past and Present*, vol. 11, no. 2, 1977 and Malhotra, *Gender, Caste and Religious Identity*.
75. Jakobsh, *Relocating Gender in Sikh History*, p. 5.
76. Kishwar, 'Arya Samaj and Women's Education', p. 1.

as well. In the Sikh Kanya Mahavidyalaya, not just Sikhs, but Muslim and Hindu girls studied as well. How did they take to this religious instruction? In 1909, for example, out of 170 students, only twenty-four were Sikh girls. Pritam Kaur Bhatia, a former student and principal of the school between 1978 and 1994, recalls her friendship with Hindu and Muslim girls.[77] She also refers to the shared practices between Hindus and Sikhs when she talks of daily visits to the gurdwara by Hindu and Sikh girls, the taking of karahprashad, and the marriage of one of her Hindu friends to a Sikh. My own grandmother, for example, a Punjabi Hindu, read the Guru Granth Sahib along with the *Ramayana*, and there are plenty of such examples. Nonica Dutta, in an article, also highlighted that her grandmother, a Sikh and a student of the Sikh Kanya Mahavidyalaya, though married into an Arya Samaji family, considered herself a Sikh first and followed the tenets of Sikhism all her life.[78] Yet, her marriage into an Arya Samaji family shows that the ambiguous relation between Sikhism and Hinduism had by no means been resolved. In this situation, female education itself became a contested site as far as the two schools are concerned.

Yet, to regard women as mere passive recipients of this ideology would be misleading. The students and teachers of both the schools emerged as active agents of their school's ideology and undertook *sikhiprachar* (in the Sikh Kanya Mahavidyalaya) and vedprachar (in the Kanya Mahavidyalaya). This gave them an arena for participation outside their homes. Bibi Harnam Kaur, the co-founder of the Sikh Kanya Mahavidyalaya came to be admired as she had imbibed the qualities expected of a true Sikh woman—the active propagation of the tenets of her faith and her being an ideal pativrata, totally devoted to her husband's cause. This ideal enabled her to receive an education and be a companionable wife. Most importantly, it accorded her a place of respect and adulation in society, and made it an ideal worth striving for.

77. Pritam Kaur Bhatia, interview with author, August 2009.
78. Nonica Datta, 'Are the Sikhs Hindus?', *The Hindu*, 4 March 2003.

Part II

Political Context of Education

5

Compulsory Education and the Political Leadership in Colonial India, 1840–1947

PARIMALA V. RAO

The sphere of school education in colonial India presents a fascinating picture that transcends the principal contradiction of the coloniser and the colonised, and brings forth the internal contradictions of class, caste and patriarchal concerns. In England, exponents of compulsory education considered it as a sure means of 'protecting the children from the oppressive factory system'.[1] In India, the justification for the same was not a similar child-centric notion. In an agrarian economy like India, working children below the age of ten or eleven were rare; and when they did work in poor families, it was mainly to assist parents (who were artisans and agricultural labourers) by running errands or taking care of younger siblings. They were not sent out to work as their labour was not measured in terms of wages. Hence, there was little pressure to employ them in a formal way. The early reports on the state of education prepared by Thomas Munro, T. B. Jervis, William Adam and others record that boys were admitted to the indigenous schools at the age of seven

An earlier version of this essay was presented at the conference on 'New Histories of Education' held on 24 June 2011 at the Institute of Education, London. I am thankful to Prof. Gary McCulloch and Dr Peter Cunningham for their suggestions.

1. R. Szreter, 'The Origins of Full-Time Compulsory Education at Five', *British Journal of Educational Studies*, vol. 13, no. 1, November 1964, pp. 16–28.

or eight, and do not mention incidents of children below the age of eleven working for a wage. In fact, William Adam suggested the introduction of modern schools to give these unsupervised children 'enlarged views of moral and social obligation'.[2] The British officials who advocated the introduction of modern education argued that in an agrarian economy, the prevention of abuse of the adult rural population—particularly the peasantry—from the oppressive landlords, grain merchants and moneylenders was vital.

Between 1815 to the 1840s, several British officials like William Fraser in north India (1816), Thomas Munro in Madras Presidency (1826), and Robert Shortrede in Bombay Presidency (1839), established schools for the masses in rural areas to prevent the peasants from becoming 'easy prey to the land lords and moneylenders'.[3] In Bengal, in 1840, after observing the oppressive treatment meted out to the peasantry by the *zamindar*s, the judge of Jessore, W. Seton-Karr suggested a system of village schools which would

> [E]nable a peasant to write a letter of business, to draw out a bond, to understand the terms of a mortgage, to cast up his accounts to know if his receipts for rent are correctly signed.[4]

Indians, too, recognised the importance of modern education. There were continuous demands for the establishment of schools in remote villages and small towns.[5] Governor-General Bentinck supported the expansion of educational infrastructure in rural areas. However, before the Indian demand and the British official support could gain momentum and turn into a powerful movement towards the introduction of a regular rural school system across British India, Bentinck's successor Auckland (1836–42) opposed 'the education

2. William Adam, *Reports on the State of Education in Bengal, 1835 and 1838* (Reprint edition), Calcutta: University of Calcutta, 1941, p. 147. (Henceforth cited as Adam's *Report*.)
3. General Department 10 of 1836, Maharashtra State Archives, p. 110.
4. Adam's *Report*, pp. 59–60.
5. See Adam's *Report* and R. V. Parulekar and C. L. Bakshi, *Selections from Educational Records: Bombay, 1815–1840*, part 2, Bombay: Asia Publishing House, 1955, p. 232.

of the children of the peasants as it would make them unhappy with their cottage', and declared that the government policy was to educate the 'respectable natives'.[6] Encouraged by this, the Indian landed interests mounted an aggressive attack on the establishment of schools in the villages and the admission of peasant children into the existing schools. Radha Kanta Deb, an important leader of the day, a staunch defender of *sati*,[7] and a founder of the Dharma Sabha, the first aggressive Hindu organisation, argued that

> Nothing should be guarded more carefully than the insensible introduction of education ... Education would wean the youth from the plough, the axe, and the loom to render them ambitious only for the clerkship for which hosts would besiege the government and mercantile offices, and majority being disappointed would be unable to return to their trade and would necessarily turn vagabonds.[8]

Under the administration of Auckland and his successors, Ellenborough (1842–44) and Hardinge (1844–48), the schools established by Munro and Shortrede were closed down.[9] These measures were strongly protested by many Indians. A petition signed by 70,000 persons protesting against the closing down of 81 schools established by Munro was completely ignored by the Madras government.[10]

6. Minute by Auckland dated 24 November 1839, Report of the GCPI, 1841, pp. i–xxxvii, India Office Records, London.
7. Sati was a funeral practice in which the widow 'voluntarily' mounted the funeral pyre of her husband. The scriptural religious sanction for it was vague. In most cases it was a combination of force and coercion and social sanction with a definite motive to appropriate the property by the family of the husband. This was banned by Governor-General William Bentinck with support from Indian reformers like Rammohan Roy.
8. Adam's *Report*, pp. 494–95.
9. Report of the Board of Education, 1847, India Office Records, pp. 10–11.
10. Public address to the Governor of Madras, 1839, Appendix 1, P. K. P. Pillay, *History of Higher Education in South India*, Madras: University of Madras, 1957, pp. 220–22.

The next attempt to introduce compulsory and free education was made during the 1870s. These efforts were influenced by developments in England like the Elementary Education Act of 1870. During the same decade, Governors-General Mayo, Northbrook, Lytton and Ripon and the Lt.-Governor of Bengal, George Campbell attempted to introduce compulsory education in India. They were supported by Indian social reformers and Sanskrit scholars like Mahadev Govind Ranade, Jotirao Phule, Kashinath Trimbak Telang, Ramakrishna Gopal Bhandarkar and Ishwarchandra Vidyasagar. At this stage, the discussions were limited to the five years of compulsory elementary education of boys between the age of five and ten. This education was to be free for the children of the peasants, and others were to pay a nominal fee of 4 annas (one-fourth of a rupee) a month.[11]

These initiatives provoked strong opposition from the Indian landlords and political leaders. The landlords organised thirty-nine public meetings to protest against the introduction of compulsory and free education in Bengal Presidency.[12] Rajendra Lal Mitra, an Indologist, organised these public meetings and drafted memorandums opposing the expansion of educational infrastructure. Mitra's agitation was ably supported by the members of the Governor-General's Executive Council (the most powerful body in British India) like Vishwanath Narayan Mandalik, Peary Mohan Mukerjee and Syed Amir Ali. Mukerjee, opposing the introduction of compulsory education, argued that

> Even in England a copy of Shakespeare or Milton is not placed in the hands of all boys ... In England the system of education recognizes the actual wants of society and does not disturb its harmony. They alone receive a liberal education who intends to take part in the administration of the country or to enter the ranks of her civil or military service, or to become member of one of the

11. Home/Education, 25 April 1868, A, nos. 15–17, National Archives of India (henceforth NAI).
12. 'A Full Report of the Public Meetings on Education and Road Cess Question', 2 September 1868, Home/Education, 1 January 1870, 1–10A, NAI.

> learned profession[s].... In this country, however, the condition of no boy is deemed too low, or his natural parts too unpromising, but that he is expected some day to adorn the Bench of the High Court, or to assist the Viceroy in the deliberation of His Excellency's Council.[13]

He further argued that the government should aim to make the masses into useful members of the society like 'servants, shepherds, apprentices and not scholars' as 'the educated mock at all distinctions of caste, wealth and lineage which had enthralled them for centuries'. So the fear of the educated competing for jobs as well as challenging the feudal order was evident in the opposition to the introduction of mass education. In the face of such decided opposition, Governor-General Ripon did not attempt to introduce compulsory and free education in 1880. Instead, in an attempt to evaluate the wider public opinion on the state of education, he appointed an Education Commission headed by W. W. Hunter in 1881. As the commission travelled across India, the supporters and the opponents of compulsory education began to organise themselves. The supporters argued that 'the chief requirement of the country was the establishment of a school in every village which had more than two hundred inhabitants and insisted on the continuation of secular education imparted in the government schools'.[14] Dadabhai Naoroji, testifying before the Education Commission, pleaded for the extension of free education for the entire population.[15] Phule and Bhandarkar pointed out that the children from the lower castes—and particularly from the untouchable communities—could have access to schools by compulsory education alone.[16]

13. T. N. Mukerjee, *Selections from the Writings and Speeches of the Late Raja Peary Mohan Mukerjee,* Calcutta: Tarak Nath Mukerjee, 1914, pp. 30–34.
14. S. Bhattacharya et al. (eds.), *Educating the Nation: Documents on the Discourse of National Education in India,* 1880–1920, New Delhi: Kanishka, 2003, pp. 103–07.
15. Ibid., pp. 56–58.
16. Ibid., pp. 125–27; G. P. Deshpande (ed.), *Selected Works of Jotirao Phule,* New Delhi: Left World, 2002, pp. 102–12.

The opponents of free education like Mitra argued that

> [A] fisherman's son who keeps himself all day in a school-room instead of wallowing in water, does not get the best training for the amphibious character of his family calling.[17]

Mitra asked the British to take 'Indians into confidence, and give them perfect freedom to mould the schools in the way they think best'. In order to make the schools efficient he asked for 'disbanding the department of education and handing over the schools in rural areas to the village councils (or *panchayats*)'. Since the village councils were actually controlled by affluent landed communities, restricting the access of the children from lower-caste and poor families to education would be easy. Mitra opposed fee concessions given to poor students by the government:

> It should be borne in mind, that the contributions made to the revenue by the rich are much more substantial than those drawn from the poor, and therefore the rich have stronger claim on the consideration of Government ... [T]he imperative duty of the Government leaves no room for unequal charges for the same commodity. As trustee of the revenue contributed by the people, the Government is bound to disburse the same in all fairness with reference to the requirement of the State. I cannot conceive how it can say, with any show of justice, that the son of a rich man shall pay double or treble the amount paid by a poor student in the same class. Wealth is no crime, and there should be no penalty or fine attached to the condition of being wealthy.[18]

The leaders representing feudal interests opposed the introduction of compulsory education. They supported the expansion of higher education and asked for limiting the number of primary schools. Syed Ahmad Khan testifying before the Hunter Commission argued that 'the Muslims had kept aloof from English education as the government schools admitted students from lower classes'. He opposed the fee exemption given to poor Muslim students.[19] Many

17. Bhattacharya et al., *Educating the Nation*, pp. 103–07.
18. Ibid.
19. Shan Mohamad, *Writings and Speeches of Sir Syed Ahmad Khan*, Bombay: Nachiketa, 1972, pp. 83–98.

influential leaders who claimed to speak on behalf of the Hindu community exhibited equal vehemence towards the introduction of mass education. Bal Gangadhar Tilak argued

> You take away a farmer's boy from the plough, the blacksmith's boy from the bellows and the cobbler's boy from his awl with the object of giving him liberal education ... and the boy learns to condemn the profession of his father, not to speak of the loss to which the latter is put by being deprived of the son's assistance at the old trade. Having done this the boy looks up to the government for employment: you remove him from a sphere where he would have been contented and happy and useful to those who depend upon him, and teach him to be discontented with his lot and with the government.[20]

Tilak said that the introduction of compulsory education was 'irrational, and would have a de-nationalising effect on the society'. When Ranade defended compulsory education by arguing that the municipal schools are supported by public funds, and hence schools should be open to all, Tilak countered by insisting that 'public money means tax payers' money and only the tax payers have the right to decide how the money is spent and spending it on the education of Kunbi's (peasant) children is a sheer waste of money'.[21] He also argued that the admission of untouchable children into the government schools was against the spirit of the Queen's Proclamation which guaranteed that the government would 'abstain from all interference with religious beliefs'.[22] Tilak and his supporters regarded their opinion as 'the Nationalist opinion' and labelled the supporters of compulsory education as 'the denationalised persons' bent upon 'injuring the social fabric of the Indian nation'.[23]

With such formidable opposition from influential Indian leaders, the Hunter Commission did not recommend the introduction of

20. 'Our System of Education—A Defect and a Cure', *The Mahratta*, 15 May 1881, pp. 3–4.
21. 'The Educational Policy of Government', *The Mahratta*, 24 September 1882, p. 8.
22. 'Admission of Mahar Boys into Government Schools', *The Mahratta*, 26 March 1882, pp. 5–6.
23. *The Mahratta*, 21 August 1881, p. 3.

compulsory education, but took an ambiguous stand. It declared that 'the educational department throughout India was in favour of admitting lower caste children to government schools as a matter of right ... hence no boy should be refused admission merely on the grounds of caste'. It also tried to pacify the upper-caste interests by suggesting that those who objected to this had the 'liberty to withhold their contributions' and advised the teachers and inspectors 'not to urge the low castes to claim the rights about which they are themselves indifferent'.[24] This infuriated the supporters of compulsory education. One of the members of the commission, K. T. Telang, in his fourteen-page note of dissent argued that 'you must bestow brains on those who have only hands ... without mass education the country will never be able to enjoy to the full the fruits which it has a right to expect from higher education'.[25]

With the establishment of the Indian National Congress in 1885, the supporters of compulsory education began to use the Congress platform to advocate the same. Syed Ahmad Khan and Syed Ameer Ali, supported by both the Muslim and the Hindu landlords, voiced 'the resentment of the Indian upper classes'. They opposed the Congress demand for holding of simultaneous examinations for the Indian Civil Service in India and England and elections to the Viceroy's Executive Council because 'it would open the door to low-class men to achieve high positions'. They argued that 'men of good families would never like to trust their lives and property to people of low rank'.[26] Syed Ahmad Khan, opposing Muslim participation in the Congress, argued:

> I ask you, would our aristocracy like a man of low caste or insignificant origin, though he may be a B.A. or M.A., and have the requisite ability, should be in a position of authority above them and have power in making the laws that affect their lives and property? Never![27]

24. *The Report of the Indian Education Commission*, Calcutta: Superintendent of Government Printing, 1883, pp. 514–17.
25. Ibid., pp. 606–19.
26. Mohamad, *Writings and Speeches of Sir Syed Ahmad Khan*, p. 208.
27. Ibid., p. 204.

Badruddin Tyabji countered Syed Ahmad Khan's 'aristocracy of birth and wealth' by the superiority of 'the aristocracy of intellect, education and position which the Congress represented'.[28] During the 1888 and 1891 Congress sessions, two important resolutions were adopted which urged the government to introduce compulsory education.[29] In the 1891 session at Nagpur, Gopal Krishna Gokhale argued that in the countries of Europe, 90 per cent of the school-going population were in schools while in India it was only 11 per cent.[30] Tilak refuted Gokhale's contention that 'knowledge of English was essential for the lower classes to convey their grievances to the officials and manage their court cases' by arguing that 'the only grievances that exist are national grievances'.[31] Surendranath Banerjee, in his presidential address in 1895, demonstrated that the per capita expenditure by the government on education in India was 7½ paise which was lower than most colonies, including Ceylon, which spent 2 annas per head.[32] However, a formidable opposition built up by Mitra, Motilal Ghosh and Tilak undermined the power of the reform-minded leadership to effectively urge for the introduction of compulsory education.

The Indian independence movement from its very inception represented two distinct and diverse ideologies. They essentially concerned the nature of the economy and society in building the Indian nation. The Congressmen, that is those who were founders of the Congress like Dadabhai Naoroji, Surendranath Banerjee, Pherozeshah Mehta, Gopal Krishna Gokhale, Badruddin Tyabji, Rahmatullah Sayani, G. Subramanya Iyer, etc., advocated a liberal egalitarian society, free from caste and religious prejudices, and a single Indian nationality based on citizenship. They wanted to bring about simultaneously social and economic transformation along

28. *The Proceedings of the Indian National Congress*, 1887, pp. 25–26, NAI.
29. *The Proceedings of the Indian National Congress*, 1888, pp. 70–72, NAI.
30. *The Proceedings of the Indian National Congress*, 1891, pp. 58–60, NAI.
31. 'Babu Surendranath', *Kesari,* 6 October 1891, p. 1.
32. *Speeches and Writings of Babu Surendranath Banerjea,* Madras: G. A. Natesan and Co., 1940, p. 87.

with freedom from British rule, because they were not only moved by economic, caste and gender inequalities, but also knew that if these inequalities persisted for long, the young nation would be torn apart by these very negative forces. This group supported compulsory and free education. They were humanists and universalists like Rabindranath Tagore and opposed every form of tyranny across the boundaries. This group has been described as 'Moderates'. The second group that came to dominate the public sphere in opposing economic and social reforms and the introduction of compulsory and free education consisted of Bal Gangadhar Tilak, Bipin Chandra Pal, Lala Lajpat Rai and others. This group has been considered as the 'Extremists'. They were not the founders of the Indian National Congress, and did not share its liberal and egalitarian basis of constructing the Indian nation. They were against every form of economic and social reform and defended the economic, caste and gender inequalities in society. They believed in the motto 'my country right or wrong, my religion right or wrong'. They were 'nationalists' in the true sense.[33] This essay uses the categories of the Congressmen and the nationalists and not the traditional categories of Moderates and Extremists.

The Two-Tier System

The criticism of the introduction of compulsory education by a section of the Indian leadership was not located in the political and ideological opposition to Western education. Mitra believed that 'to give up English was to commit intellectual suicide'.[34] Tilak was of the view that 'before the English education was introduced into the country, we were as ignorant a mass of people as could

33. For a detailed discussion on this issue see, Parimala V. Rao, *Foundations of Tilak's Nationalism: Discrimination, Education and Hindutva*, Hyderabad: Orient BlackSwan, 2010.
34. Poromesh Acharya, 'Bengali Bhadralok and Educational Development in Nineteenth Century Bengal', in *Education, Development and Underdevelopment*, eds. Sureshchandra Shukla and Rekha Kaul, New Delhi: Sage Publications, 1998, pp. 28–35.

exist in the nineteenth century'. Tilak eloquently defended 'the elevating influences of English education provided by the British', and explained that he was only against the 'indiscriminate spread of education which is unsuited, useless and positively injurious to children of the peasants'.[35]

The Indian leaders who were opposed to compulsory education also opposed a common curriculum for the elites and the masses. Mitra declared that 'if the government wants to introduce the universal compulsory education then it should provide for all classes of its subjects, according to their respective wants just as the father of a family provides milk for infants and solid meat for grown-up boys'.[36] Tilak, supporting Mitra, emphasised that 'the curriculum taught to upper caste children was unsuitable to peasant children' and 'rational system of education meant teaching of only those subjects which would be necessary for their living'. He suggested that if the government was bent upon providing education for all, then only 'the education befitting their rank and station in life' should be provided to the peasant children while the upper-caste children who had 'natural inclination' should be taught the existing curriculum. Tilak insisted that the lower classes should be trained as 'carpenters, black smiths, masons and tailors'.[37]

Syed Ameer Ali acknowledged that there was no demand for Arabic and Persian education among the Muslims, but a strong desire to acquire English education. However, Ali emphasised that 'the Arabic teaching schools called the *Muktab*s and *Madrasa*s attached to the mosques were sufficient for imparting education to the lower classes'.[38] Syed Ahmad Khan's suggestion of raising the standard of education, and his opposition to an increase in the number of primary schools for the education of Muslim masses (*Ajlaf*s) and

35. 'The Functions of our Universities', *The Mahratta*, 15 February 1885, p. 2.
36. Bhattacharya et al., *Educating the Nation*, p. 107.
37. 'Our System of Education—A Defect and a Cure', *The Mahratta*, 15 May 1881, pp. 3–4.
38. Bhattacharya et al., *Educating the Nation*, pp. 227–30.

insistence on *Madrasa* education for poor Muslims, [39] points to the same direction. In Bombay Presidency, the opponents of compulsory education formed an organisation called the Hindu Union Club in 1885, which held public meetings to oppose uniform curriculum and pressurise the government to establish a two-tier system of education. The members of the club questioned:

> What does our cultivator's son care whether Peshwa reigned in Poona and Aurangzeb had his court in Delhi? Of course a knowledge of the history and geography of one's own and foreign countries has its advantages for advanced students, but to an agriculturist there are none. The Educational Department ought to remodel the courses prescribed for village schools for rayat's children and introduce in them agricultural subjects such as preparing of soil, the tending of bullocks, the implements of husbandry etc.[40]

Tilak supported the stand taken by the members of the club and prominently printed their speeches, some of which ran into several pages. By advocating a two-tier system, higher English education for the upper castes and vocational education for the masses, the Indian leaders attempted to perpetuate social and economic inequalities within society. The government on its part ignored the plea to introduce the two-tier school system, but handed over primary schools to the elected municipalities. This measure strengthened the hands of the Indian political leadership.

The Indian nationalist leaders controlled the various municipalities, and hence were successful in enforcing their agenda in many areas where schools already existed. The working of the Dapoli municipality in Bombay Presidency can be cited as an example of the power of the municipalities to prevent children from the lower classes from entering the schools. In 1892, the Dapoli municipal president, Vishnu Hari Barve, a supporter of Tilak, refused to allow untouchable children to enter the classrooms of the Municipal Board School and made them sit on the veranda of the school. The Mahar and Chambhar retired army officers took up the matter with the Director of Public Instruction, who directed Barve to allow the untouchable

39. Mohamad, *Writings and Speeches of Sir Syed Ahmad Khan,* pp. 83–98.
40. 'Hindu Union Club', *The Mahratta*, 21 February 1886, p. 5.

children inside the classroom in accordance with the grants-in-aid rules. The municipality avoided the issue by stating that it would have to expand the classroom first, in order to accommodate more children. It conveniently stated at a later date that such expansions could not be made due to a lack of funds, and untouchable children remained outside the classrooms during the next two decades.[41] Similarly, the nationalists who controlled the Poona municipality successfully defeated for thirty years (1890–1920) the resolutions on compulsory education on the pretext that 'the tax payers have already been heavily taxed'.[42]

National Education

While opposing compulsory education proposed by the British and Indian reformers, some political leaders developed the alternative model called 'National Education'. They asserted that the national identity of Indians was their religious identity and attacked the secular education imparted in schools. Tilak argued that secular education had a 'de-nationalising effect on the society; hence it should be substituted by religious education'.[43] Syed Husain Bilgrami argued that 'the public education divorced from religion' had produced 'arrogance and want of manners among the Muslim children'; hence, 'teaching religion is a national need'.[44] Another important leader, Bishan Narain Dhar, compared the English-educated Indians to the Russian nihilists and argued that they both had 'high intellectual education but had no grounding in their respective religions'. Just as 'mystic reverence for the Czar appears absurd to the young philosopher and the church itself is despised, the Indian counterpart

41. Philip Constable, 'Sitting on the School Verandah: The Ideology and Practice of "Untouchable" Educational Protest in Late Nineteenth-century Western India', *Indian Economic and Social History Review*, vol. 37, no. 4, 2000, pp. 404–06.
42. 'Nationalists and Compulsory Education', *The Mahratta*, 29 February 1920, p. 103.
43. *The Mahratta*, 21 August 1881.
44. Bhattacharya et al., *Educating the Nation*, pp. 348–56.

had dispensed with reverence to religion and customs ... secular education has placed the destiny of the nation at stake'.[45]

Tilak defined national education as 'that which gives us knowledge of the experience of our ancestors' and argued that the secular education of the government schools had created 'a race of agnostics, sceptics, atheists and religious nihilism in the country'.[46] He argued that 'the education system based on religious dogma alone promoted nationality' and that 'what is not familiar through the family cannot serve as a pedagogical tool'.[47] He demanded that the government should replace the existing syllabi—that included Hindu philosophy and Sanskrit poetry—with religious texts like the Smritis, Shastras and Puranas'[48]

> [M]uch of the religious instruction should consist of dogma pure and simple. The schoolboys will have to be told dogmatically that there is God ... of course, the schoolboy who wants an ocular proof of the existence of God will have to be caned into silence.[49]

The leaders of the Swadeshi Movement (1903–08) like Aurobindo Ghosh and Bipin Chandra Pal also supported 'denominational religious education' along with secular subjects.[50] Lala Lajpat Rai was the first to introduce religion along with secular subjects in the Arya

45. H. L. Chatterji, *Pt. Bishan Narain Dhar: Speeches and Writings,* Lucknow: Anglo-Oriental Press, 1921, pp. 25–30.
46. 'Moral and Religious Instructions in Schools', *The Mahratta*, 17 March 1901, pp. 4–5.
47. *Kesari*, 3 November 1903, p. 2.
48. 'Religious Education in Schools and Colleges', *The Mahratta*, 5 July 1903, pp. 3–18, Smritis, Shastras and Puranas refer to those Hindu religious texts which validate a hierarchical society while Hindu philosophical texts like the *Upanishad*s uphold equality of all human beings.
49. 'Religious Education Suggestion Towards a Practical Scheme' (Editorial), *The Mahratta*, 3 July 1904, p. 313.
50. Haridas and Uma Mukerjee, *The Origins of the National Education Movement, 1905–1910*, Calcutta: Jadavpur University, 1957, pp. 50–56.

Samaj schools in the 1880s.[51] Tilak and his supporters completely did away with secular subjects by insisting that national education should consist of some technical subjects and the Bhagavadgita.[52] Vishnu Govind Vijapurkar who established National Schools in several places across Bombay Presidency explained that national education had its roots in two fundamental principles, namely, the caste system (*Chaturvarna*) and the theory of rebirth.[53]

The desire of the Indian leaders to acquire only technical knowledge from the West and adopt it to suit their caste-class interests would have made India at best an importer of technical knowhow and not an equal participant in knowledge creation. By not locating the technical achievement of the West in its scientific temperament and rationality, Indian leaders were committing grave errors.

The Opposition in Perspective

The opposition to compulsory education was also linked to the larger issue of child labour. By the middle of the nineteenth century, cotton mills came to be established in Bombay Presidency. These mills employed children. The supporters of compulsory education opposed child labour and worked hard to get legislations passed to improve the condition of children. Tilak condemned the Factory Act of 1881 which prohibited the employment of children below the age of seven and opined that children between seven and fourteen could be employed for only nine hours per day with an hour of rest with one holiday per week.[54] The Factory (Amendment) Act of 1891 reduced the number of working hours for women to eleven and children to seven, and the minimum age for employment of children

51. B. R. Nanda (ed.), *The Collected Works of Lala Lajpat Rai*, vol. 2, New Delhi: Manohar, 2003, pp. 226, 257.
52. 'Moral and Religious Education', *The Mahratta*, 10 April 1910, p. 173.
53. Dhananjay Keer, *Shahu Chatrapati, A Royal Revolutionary*, Bombay: Popular Prakashan, 1976, pp. 148–49.
54. *The Mahratta*, 13 March 1881, p. 2.

was raised to nine.[55] Tilak did not agree that long hours of work for young children and women meant exploitation. He argued that 'the children are taken to the factories by their own parents and are not likely to be overworked'.[56]

The opposition to compulsory education was also intrinsically linked to feudal interests. Vishwanath Narayan Mandalik, Peary Mohan Mukerjee, Syed Amir Ali and Rajendra Lal Mitra opposed the Bengal Rent Bill of 1884, which attempted to protect the peasants from arbitrary eviction. Similarly, Syed Ahmad Khan and Tilak opposed the Deccan Agriculturists Relief Act of 1879, which attempted to free the peasants from the clutches of moneylenders.[57] They viewed society in terms of master and servant, and were categorical in denouncing the role of education in reversing what they called 'the natural order of things'.[58]

The opponents of compulsory education were driven by patriarchal concerns too. They were also defenders of child marriage. Tilak, Mitra and Motilal Ghosh fought against the Age of Consent Act of 1891, which raised the marriageable age of girls to twelve.[59] They also vehemently opposed women's education. Lajpat Rai opposed the establishment of a girls' school at Jullundur and Tilak virulently attacked the first girls' high school in Poona established by

55. *The Mahratta*, 20 September 1890, p. 3; 'Factories Act Amendment Bill', *The Mahratta*, 5 October 1890, p. 3.
56. 'The Indian Factories Bill', *The Mahratta*, 16 August 1891, p. 3.
57. K. K. Sengupta, 'Agrarian Disturbances in the Nineteenth Century Bengal', in *Peasent Struggle in India*, ed. A. R. Desai, Bombay: Oxford University Press, 1979, p. 190; Parimala V. Rao, 'New Insights into the Debates on Rural Indebtedness in the Nineteenth-century Deccan', *Economic and Political Weekly*, vol. 44, no. 4, 24–30 January 2009, pp. 55–61.
58. David Lelyveld, *Aligarh's First Generation: Muslim Solidarity in British India*, Princeton: Princeton University Press, 1978, pp. 265–66. *The Mahratta* (Editorial), 8 November 1903, p. 521
59. Parimala V. Rao, 'Nationalism and the Visibility of Women in Public Space: Tilak's Criticism of Rakhmabai and Ramabai', *Indian Historical Review*, vol. 35, no. 2, July 2008, pp. 166–73.

Ranade. Mitra and Ghosh opposed women's education in Bengal.[60] Tilak insisted that 'the brain of a woman on an average weighed less by five ounces than that of a man', and 'English education had a dewomanising impact on women, mugging western knowledge without performing household duties denied women a happy worldly life'.[61] By providing for women's education, Tilak argued, 'India would lose its nationality and its individuality as a separate nation'.[62] Tilak also opposed Ranade for admitting girls from lower castes into the Poona Girls' High School.[63] Similarly, Syed Ahmad Khan held 'the enthusiastic implementation of girls' education by officials in certain districts' as one of the causes responsible for the revolt of 1857.[64] Testifying before the Hunter Commission, he argued that 'the informal literacy received by Muslim girls in Urdu and Persian by their father or brothers is enough for domestic happiness'.[65] He opposed Sayyid Mumtaz Ali's efforts to improve the education of Muslim women.[66]

The opponents of compulsory education not only had social and economic capital, but had also had acquired enormous political capital. Some of them were the outspoken critics of British rule and were regarded as leaders of their respective communities and nationalists in general. By 1910, the supporters of compulsory

60. Nanda, *The Collected Works of Lala Lajpat Rai,* vol. I, pp. 82–83; 'High School for Native Girls', *The Mahratta,* 17 August 1884, p. 1.
61. *Kesari,* 11 October 1887.
62. 'Higher Female Education', *The Mahratta,* 24 August 1884, p. 2.
63. 'Maharashtra Female Education Society', *The Mahratta,* 7 October 1900, p. 5.
64. Mohammad (ed.), *Writings and Speeches of Sir Syed Ahmad Khan,* p. 24.
65. Bhattacharya et al. (eds.), *The Development of Women's Education,* pp. 101–02.
66. Gail Minault, 'Sayyid Mumtaz Ali and Tahzib un-Niswan: Women's Rights in Islam and Women's Journalism in Urdu', in *Religious Controversy in British India: Dialogues in South Asian Languages,* ed. Kenneth W. Jones, New York: State University of New York Press, 1992, pp. 180–83.

education were labelled as 'denationalised collaborators of the British rule', while the opponents of compulsory education were called 'the uncompromising champions of India's freedom'. Gokhale refuted Tilak's argument of achieving political freedom before social and educational reform by asking, 'Will a shoemaker ever be able to rise in India no matter how gifted he might be?'[67] In 1908, Gokhale urged the government to abolish school fees.[68] For these and similar such efforts, the nationalists called Gokhale 'the spokesman of the British'.[69] This, coupled with political violence following the Swadeshi Movement, made the situation extremely precarious for the introduction of compulsory education.

Elementary Education Bill of 1910

It was in this atmosphere of intense antagonism and hostility that Gokhale introduced his Elementary Education Bill in 1910. He called it 'a small humble attempt to suggest the first steps of a journey, which is bound to prove long and tedious, but which must be performed, if the mass of our people are to emerge from their present condition'.[70] Gokhale argued

> [F]ree and compulsory education is the first remedy of all the remedies to be applied ... without compulsion the educational developments in the last 60 years have been hopelessly slow. The only way that the world has discovered to secure universal education in a country has been by making it compulsory and free. Compulsion would operate harshly on the poorer classes of the community if it is not made free.[71]

67. *Speeches of Gopal Krishna Gokhale,* Madras: G. A. Natesan and Co., 1920, p. 898.
68. Ibid., p. 627.
69. *The Mahratta,* 30 August 1908, p. 415; *The Mahratta* (Editorial), 17 February 1907, pp. 77–79, *The Mahratta* (Editorial Notes), 17 May 1908, p. 231.
70. *Speeches of Gopal Krishna Gokhale,* p. 610.
71. Ibid., pp. 640, 598.

He suggested that only those students whose family income was 25 rupees and above per month should pay fees; for the rest, education was to be free. Out of the total expenditure required for it, two-thirds should be borne by the state and one-third by the local bodies.[72] He suggested imposing an additional 8-anna tax on salt on the grounds that 'my countrymen should eat less salt than that their children should continue to grow up in ignorance and darkness'.[73]

Gokhale accepted that 'the girls' education is more important than boys' but advocated 'compulsion only for boys'. Gokhale had witnessed a strong nationalist opposition particularly in his hometown, Poona, where the attacks on Ranade's girls' high school were particularly uncivil. The Poona municipality controlled by the supporters of Tilak had violently opposed girls' education and repeatedly defeated a bill that sought to introduce compulsory education for girls during 1890 and 1910[74] had made him cautious. He also preferred the Japanese system of four years of compulsory education from the age of six to ten to the European model of seven years.[75] This bill did not plead for immediate implementation of compulsory and free education, but made the provincial and local bodies accept the responsibility of gradually implementing the same. He considered that the material condition of the masses could be improved only with the universalisation of elementary education.

> If you want to increase the wage earning capacity of the workmen, if you want the peasant to grow stronger and healthier and take better care of himself and understand his dealings with the money lender and understand better the benefits of sanitation and agriculture,

72. 'Gokhale's Note dated Feb 28, 1911' in *The Servants of India Society Papers*, p. 8, Nehru Memorial Museum and Library (henceforth NMML)
73. *Speeches of Gopal Krishna Gokhale*, p. 604.
74. Parimala V. Rao, 'Women in the Nationalist Discourse: A Case Study of Tilak's Approach to Women's Education and Emancipation', in *Development of Modern Indian Thought and the Social Sciences*, ed. S. Bhattacharya, New Delhi: Oxford University Press, 2007, pp. 241–64.
75. *Speeches of Gopal Krishna Gokhale*, p. 599.

> then compulsion alone had been proved effective in spreading education.[76]

The reaction within the bureaucracy consisting of both Indian and British officials was divided. The supporters of the bill were predominantly judges, magistrates, district collectors, deputy commissioners and members of the department of public instruction, while the secretaries, officials of the finance department and non-official members of the provincial legislative councils opposed the bill. The Lt.-Governor of Punjab stated that 'people are strongly opposed not merely to compulsion, but to any education whatsoever', while twenty out of thirty-eight British officials from the same province supported the bill. The British officials opposed the bill on the grounds of financial constraints. They also cited the countrywide Swadeshi Movement that had just subsided, and argued that new taxes would lead to further 'discontent and danger'.[77] Some of them also expressed scepticism of its success in the absence of the availability of sufficient classrooms and trained teachers.[78]

Formidable opposition to Gokhale's bill also came from the Indian leaders. The nationalists argued that what the masses needed was information and not literacy; hence, the ignorance of the masses could be tackled by providing information and not by opening schools. They suggested that graduates attached to government schools at the district and sub-district level should travel from village to village and impart religious education to the masses aiming towards 'imposing the uniformity of religious beliefs. Since everybody loves to write his name, he should be taught to do so.'[79] Beyond this, the nationalists argued, the people did not require education.

Within the legislatures, Congressmen like R. N. Mudholkar and Mazhar-ul-Haq supported Gokhale, while the nationalist and Muslim League members opposed him. The Muslim League members

76. 'Elementary Education Bill Objections Answered, Hon. Mr. Gokhale's Speech', *The Mahratta*, 30 July 1911, pp. 367–69.
77. Ibid., p. 640.
78. Ibid., p. 675.
79. 'A Supplement to Primary Education', *The Mahratta*, 14 May 1911, pp. 234–36.

argued that the introduction of compulsory education may be used to compel Muslim children to learn non-Muslim languages.[80] Gangadhar Chitnavis, a leading landlord and moneylender and a supporter of Tilak through his Berar Provincial Association, and the aristocratic Nawab Abdul Majid opposed compulsion on the grounds that 'if all children were sent to school it would be difficult to get labour'.[81] The nationalists joined hands with the Muslim League in opposing the bill with the argument that they were 'speaking on behalf of the very poor masses and defending the means of livelihood of such a population'.[82] Another member, M. B. Dadabhai, a staunch supporter of child labour in the Bombay textile industry, opposed an additional tax 'to educate poor children'. In a rare display of solidarity, the state, the nationalists and the Muslim League joined hands to defeat the bill. An exasperated Gokhale exclaimed that the opponents of the bill were concerned only about 'providing better dividends for the capitalists'.[83]

'Basic Education' of Gandhi

By the time Mohandas Karamchand Gandhi emerged as a formidable political leader, the attempts to introduce compulsory education had been defeated twice and the nationalists had declared that technical skills and religion alone formed the basis of national education. Though Gandhi claimed that Gokhale was his political guru, he undermined Gokhale in every aspect as far as education was concerned. Gandhi opposed compulsory education advocated by Gokhale.[84] Gokhale had advocated an 8-anna tax on salt to fund primary education; but by making opposition to the salt tax the cornerstone of his campaign against the government, Gandhi

80. *Speeches of Gopal Krishna Gokhale*, p. 649.
81. Ibid., p. 630.
82. Mian Mohamed Shafi's speech in *The Servants of India Society Papers*, p. 11, NMML.
83. *Speeches of Gopal Krishna Gokhale*, p. 623.
84. *Young India*, 14 August 1924.

undermined Gokhale's original intentions. Gandhi opposed modern education. As early as 1908, Gandhi wrote in the *Hind Swaraj*

> [A]study of geography, astronomy, algebra, geometry is false education and it is not for the millions. To give millions knowledge of English is to enslave them. Our ancient school system is enough. Character building has the first place in it and that is primary education.[85]

Though Gandhi upheld the secularism of Gokhale, Tilak's views were constantly reflected in the Gandhian scheme of education. When the Maharaja of Baroda began to implement compulsory mass education in his princely state, he drew criticism not only from Tilak but also from Gandhi. Like Tilak, Gandhi too asked, 'Do you wish to make a peasant discontented with his cottage or his lot?' Gandhi criticised the supporters of compulsory mass education as 'those carried away by the flood of western thought'.[86] Like Tilak, Gandhi too argued that modern education is 'calculated to wean the masses from their traditional culture. They are never taught to have any pride in their surroundings and the government schools had entirely denationalized the masses.'[87]

Gandhi took an ambiguous stand on the question of compulsory mass education. He declared that 'mass illiteracy is India's sin and shame and must be liquidated'.[88] Yet, he also stated that 'I am not quite sure that I would not oppose compulsory education at all times. All compulsion is hateful to me. Only a despotic Government passes laws in the teeth of the opposition from a majority.'[89] This moralistic stand against 'compulsion' contradicts his stand on forcing a particular kind of pedagogy on the children.

> If I had the powers of a despot, I would today stop the tuition of our boys and girls through a foreign medium. If I had my way, I would certainly destroy the majority of the present text-books and cause to be written text-books which have a bearing on and correspondence

85. M. K. Gandhi, *Hind Swaraj*, Ahmedabad: Navajivan Publishing House, 1946, pp. 63–67.
86. Ibid., pp. 63–64
87. *Young India*, 1 June 1921.
88. *Harijan*, 18 February 1939.
89. *Young India*, 14 August 1924.

with the home life, so that a boy as he learns may react upon his immediate surroundings.[90]

Gandhi argued that 'the curriculum and pedagogic ideas which form the fabric of modern education are foreign, and till they are repudiated there never can be national education. The force that maintains society together is a series of high loyalties, loyalty to faith, calling, parents, family, *dharma*. The ancient educational system in India certainly maintained the long tradition of pride and service.'[91] Elaborating on this, Gandhi explained that 'when our children are admitted to schools, they do not need slate and pencil and books, but simple village tools which they can handle freely and remuneratively. This means a revolution in educational methods. Only, reading and writing would come during the last year when really the boy or girl is ready for learning the alphabet correctly.'[92] Textbooks, especially for children, 'are for the most part useless, when they are not harmful'.[93] These were exactly the issues that the nationalists, particularly Tilak, had campaigned for four decades. The only difference was that while Tilak campaigned against the education of the lower castes and classes, Gandhi extended this opposition to the entire population.

Gandhi justified his educational ideas on the basis of 'securing to the students economic, social and spiritual freedom'.[94] To secure these three freedoms, he advocated 'the self supporting school system'. He did not see 'anything wrong in the children as young as 7–12 paying for their education through work from the very threshold of their education'.[95] The self-supporting schools were partially self-supporting, as the cost of buildings, equipment as well as numerous recurring items of expenditure were born by the state.[96]

90. *Young India*, 1 September 1921.
91. *Young India*, 20 March 1924.
92. *Young India*, 1 July 1929.
93. *Harijan*, 1 December 1933.
94. M. K. Gandhi, *The Problem of Education*, Ahmedabad: Navajivan Publishing House, 1962, p. 77.
95. *Young India*, 2 February and 15 June 1921.
96. C. J. Verkey, *The Wardha Scheme of Education: An Exposition and Examination*, London: Oxford University Press, 1940, p. 79.

So, Gandhi's 'Basic Education' did not liberate education from the clutches of the state. What it actually did was to place the body and mind of a child under the control of the teacher. The schools were to work for six hours a day, out of which the child would work for four hours, and the remaining two hours would be utilised for learning. Within these two hours, music, drawing and arithmetic were to be taught within a period of forty minutes which allotted thirteen minutes for each subject, while both social studies and general science were to be taught within a period of thirty minutes, thereby devoting fifteen minutes for each subject.[97] Since the salary of the teacher was derived from the labour of the child, there was a greater tendency to concentrate on the labour than acquisition of knowledge. These schools worked for 288 days a year, i.e., twenty-four days a month, without summer or winter breaks. So, Gandhian 'Basic Education' left little scope for an ideal situation.

Gandhi was equally ambiguous about women's education. The schools under *Nai Talim* did not make any distinction between boys and girls as far as curriculum was concerned, and he brought women into the public arena. However, like Tilak, he regarded 'man as supreme in the outward activities while home life is entirely the sphere of woman'. He was also opposed to 'women working for a living or undertaking commercial enterprise'.[98] So, Gandhi virtually sanctified the educational ideas of Tilak.

Though Gandhi claimed that his 'Basic Education' was rooted in Indian tradition, forcing a seven-year-old child to earn by working was certainly against the Indian tradition. It was not rooted in the traditional agrarian economy but was located in the modern industrial economy. In the Indian *gurukul* tradition, the students lived with the guru who not only taught, but also fed them and took care of them. The students, alongside learning, assisted the guru in running errands, but did not carry the burden of running the household of the guru. In the traditional Arabic schools, the master took care of the food and shelter of the students. Gandhi reversed it

97. Ibid., p. 85
98. Bharatan Kumarappa (ed.), *Towards New Education*, Ahmedabad: Navajivan Publishing House, 1963, pp. 85–86.

and made young seven-year-olds responsible for the food and shelter of the grown-up teachers.

In the past 140 years there have been only two major attempts to introduce compulsory and free education, both of which failed miserably. The Indian political leadership often claimed to represent and defend Indian interests from colonial oppression in every field, particularly in education. The introduction of compulsory education which aimed to empower children—who as adults would be in a position to defend their interests and fight against oppression—was vehemently opposed in the name of defending religion by leaders like Syed Ahmad Khan and Tilak, or defending Indian spiritual tradition by a leader like Gandhi. The failure to introduce compulsory and free education in India was not due to poverty or colonial rule, but the refusal of the political leadership to place the nation's interest above the interests of caste and class.

6

Education, Missionaries and the Indian Nation, c. 1880–1920

HAYDEN BELLENOIT

The aim of this essay is to examine some of the overlooked, yet crucial, interactions between north Indian students and Christian mission schools between 1880 and 1920. This was a period which saw a budding articulation of anti-colonial sentiments that after 1920 erupted into an all-India movement against British rule. This essay is less concerned with the 'technologies of education' as a bureaucratic process and system, and more with education as a site of interaction wherein ideas of patriotism were articulated and contested. By 1920, missionary schools bore witness to a vibrant interaction between teachers and increasingly patriotic Indian students, an atmosphere which permeated classrooms, corridors and courtyards. It is the aim of this essay to demonstrate how missionary schools, rather than being a distant footnote in the emergence of Indian nationalism, was in fact an important factor which helped facilitate its emergence. Here, within the educational sphere, Christian missionary teachers were not so much an arm of colonial rule, as they were often a thorn in its more prickly side.

MISSIONARIES AND EDUCATION IN COLONIAL INDIA

Before delving into the role that missionary schools played in the emergence of Indian nationalism, it is necessary to understand the broader context in which Christian missionaries had been religious actors in the Indian subcontinent since the 1700s. With the rise of British power under the East India Company, and later the crown, missionaries of various denominations made India one of their largest areas of activity. This was especially true after the amendment of the company's charter in 1813, which allowed missionaries unhindered access to the company's domains. But it was through their involvement in new forms of education that the missionaries made a significant—and perhaps the most lasting—impact.

Many 'educational missionaries' initially saw Western learning and knowledge as a stepping stone to spreading Christianity. By the 1870s, however, this approach to the conversion of India's Brahmans and other high castes had largely fallen out of favour. By then, the most active Anglican missionary societies—the Church Missionary Society (CMS), the London Missionary Society (LMS), the Society for the Propagation of the Gospel (SPG), and the Cambridge Mission to Delhi (CMD)—were mostly involved in teaching in high schools and colleges across north India. In the United Provinces, India's most populous province, these societies ran over half of the high schools and colleges.[1] American missionary societies, by contrast, worked overwhelmingly with the lower-caste communities and were far less involved in higher levels of education. Anglican mission schools, therefore, interacted with the very groups and communities who would go on to lead the Indian nationalist movement. An analysis of these Anglican mission schools in north India, therefore, offers a new and refreshing way of viewing the interconnectedness between pedagogy, institutions and nationalism.

Education, Human Interaction and 'Colonial Knowledge'

Before we examine how mission schools connected with Indian nationalism, it is important to delineate the relationship between the colonial state, education and 'colonial knowledge'. Education in colonial India was more than just about policy, structures and institutions. By 1900, Indian students at the high school and university levels had begun to increasingly question British colonial

1. *General Report on Public Instruction in the United Provinces of Agra and Oudh*, Allahabad: Government Press, 1912, pp. 4a–8a.

policies. Indeed, it was largely the 'student movement' which British officialdom feared the most. But it was also a demographic block and an upcoming generation about whom the colonial state knew very little. The British had a fairly good sense of the sentiments of college and university students in Bengal; but often, this was clouded by a more poignant racism. Denzil Ibbetson,[2] Robert Needham Cust,[3] and William Miller[4] all admitted that in spite of Britain's statistical mastery over India, colonial officialdom lacked a deep understanding of the very students who conceivably posed the greatest threat to colonial rule. A genuine network of spies and informants in colleges was also lacking until after the partition of Bengal and the Swadeshi Movement (1903–08). The Intelligence Departments also had difficulty in placing informants in schools and hostels, particularly in the United Provinces.[5] This was hampered by the sheer vastness of the UP Department of Public Instruction, the perennial focus on 'Bengali radicalism', and as we will see, the resistant attitudes of many missionary teachers themselves.

British policy had undoubtedly become markedly disparaging towards the students' political sentiments and expressions of patriotism. This was a reflection of not simply white racism, but also an absence of close interactions with the students that the missionaries undertook. Robert Needham Cust, for example, claimed that Indian

2. D. Ibbetson, *Outlines of Panjab Ethnography: Being Extracts from the Panjab Census Report of 1881, Treating Religion, Language and Caste*, Calcutta: Superintendent of Government Printing, 1883, p. 2.
3. R. N. Cust, *Linguistic and Oriental Essays: Written from the Year 1847 to 1887*, London: Trubner & Co, 1887, p. 152; also see a mid-twentieth century critic, B. K. Boman-Behram, *Educational Controversies of India: The Cultural Conquest of India under British Imperialism*, Bombay: D. B. Taraporevala, 1943, p. viii.
4. W. Miller, *Unrest and Education in India*, Edinburgh: Edinburgh & Co., 1911, p. 47.
5. R. J. Popplewell, *Intelligence and Imperial Defence: British Intelligence and the Defence of the Indian Empire, 1904–1924*, London: Frank Cass, 1995, pp. 8–124, especially pp. 75–77. The British seem to have been slightly more successful in Bengal compared to other parts of India.

demands for increased participation in government were from mere 'state-quack'[6] graduates who lacked real patriotism. Thomas Lewis, the UP Director of Public Instruction, dismissed Indian patriotism as a 'poor copy taken from English history and literature'.[7] These attitudes were also visible in contestations between missionary teachers and the colonial officialdom. Rev. Charles Tyndale-Biscoe of the CMS High School in Srinagar was regularly questioned by educational officials who told him that teaching Indians anything useful was 'fatal' to British rule. Citing numerous instances of student 'disloyalty' and 'sedition', they called his work a waste of time.[8] During Tyndale-Biscoe's years in India, he never met a high-ranking British official who was sympathetic to the cause of educating Indians. One official even advised him to pack his bags and go back to help Britain's working classes.[9]

This is where mission schools enter the equation. Teachers in schools run by the CMS, LMS and the CMD, in contrast to colonial officialdom, knew much more about Indian students and those who led agitations against British rule. This was due to their religious aims (conversion and a loose degree of influence) which ensured that they knew students at a personal level—and not at the removed, aloof and statistical level of knowledge which characterised the Raj by 1900. But this was also because they interacted with students in classrooms and villages, and established relationships which were sustained over the years. Missionary teachers were also religious actors inasmuch as

6. Cust, *Linguistic and Oriental Essays*, pp. 151, 163.
7. Education Files, nos. 39–55-, 1901, T. C. Lewis, 12 September 1898, Home Department, National Archives of India, New Delhi.
8. C. Tyndale-Biscoe, 'Seeing is Believing: A Scene in Kashmir', *The East and the West*, 1915, pp. 275–76. These attitudes were increasingly punctuated with racism after the mutiny of 1857. One army officer scolded a missionary teacher: '[W]hat ... is the good of teaching the niggers, Sir? You taught Nana Sahib ... and he learned to read French novels and cut our throats.' See E. Arnold, *Education in India: A Letter from the Ex-Principal of an Indian Government College to His Appointed Successor*, London: Bell & Daldy, 1860, p. 8.
9. Tyndale-Biscoe, 'Seeing is Believing: A Scene in Kashmir', pp. 275–76.

they regularly tapped into information gleaned from communities of piety, faith and pilgrimage. They roamed the bazaars after the class hours, preached in urban locales, and conversed with *pundits* at the local *mandir* (Hindu temple), though less frequently at the *masjid* (mosque). William Miller, principal of the Madras Christian College, argued that teachers of Hindu and Muslim students possessed the best possible feeling for a rising, politically conscious generation.[10] Indian newspapers confirmed this. The *Advocate* of Allahabad remarked that if British officials treated Indians the way missionaries did, then there would be less European racism towards Indians.[11] When the editor of *The Englishman*, Fraser Blair, called for greater interaction between Englishmen and Indians, he pointedly excluded missionaries, whom Blair called the most engaged social actors in India.[12] Missionary teachers and headmasters also regularly played cricket and other games (including even *gilli-danda*) with their students.[13] E. M. Forster was not simply conjuring up tales when he noted that the missionaries, Mr Grayford and Mr Sorley, never entered the Anglo-Indian club of Chandrapur and always travelled third class in the railways.[14] There was, therefore, a significant disjuncture between the Raj's knowledge of students and the deep, engaging interactions by missionary teachers in corridors and classrooms. Missionary teachers had their finger on the pulse of Indian society more than any other European group in India. Education was therefore a vital channel through which Indian national and political sentiments were moulded, expressed and contested.

'Pedagogical Patriotism' in Schools and Colleges

As we have seen, missionary teachers and British officialdom differed (though it was less obvious to contemporaries) over how far a reach

10. Miller, *Unrest and Education in India*, pp. 4–5.
11. *Advocate*, Lucknow, 17 July 1910, Selections from Vernacular Newspapers, Uttar Pradesh State Archives, Lucknow.
12. *CMS Intelligencer*, 1905, p. 546.
13. *CMS Intelligencer*, 1883, p. 496.
14. E. M. Forster, *A Passage to India*, New York: Harcourt, Brace and Company, 1924, p. 58.

education should have in India. This resembled Ernest Gellner's concept of the inherent tension between state and religious authority, i.e., between individual salvation (religion) and that of the common good (civil society).[15] This does seem to have spilled over into colonial India. Expatriate missionary teachers found themselves in some degree of tension with their ruling, racial kin, albeit in a form which contemporaries (and for a long time historians) saw overshadowed by 'imperial Christianity'.[16] Yet, both Gellner's dichotomy and the concept of an imperial Christianity are far more complex when viewed against the historical evidence. Missionary teachers were certainly somewhat cautious when it came to Indian nationalism. But this did not preclude them from contributing to its development. They had a qualified interest in empire: British rule allowed them to maximise their own influence upon an upcoming Indian generation. The missionaries needed British rule, but at the same time were critical of many of its policies, trappings and tendencies. This was nowhere better seen than in the interaction between missionary education and Indian nationalism. A good number of mission schools in northern India positioned themselves against the very worldly interests of empire in the decades before Gandhi's arrival on the national scene around 1920. Charlie Andrews' 1906 letter to the *Civil and Military Gazette*,[17] which lent support to Indian nationalism, was indeed the tip of a much larger iceberg overlooked by colonial officialdom, and until more recently, historians of South Asia.

This essay employs a concept known as 'pedagogical patriotism'. It is defined here as lukewarm support for Indian political consciousness which was forged in the experiences of school, examination and association. It was not the result of the missionary teachers' desire to

15. E. Gellner, *Conditions of Liberty: Civil Society and its Rivals*, London: Hamish Hamilton, 1994, pp. 44–49.
16. See G. Studdert-Kennedy, *Providence and the Raj: Imperial Mission and Missionary Imperialism*, New Delhi: Sage Publications, 1998 for an overview of how some missionaries saw a connection between British rule and the expansion of Christianity.
17. *Civil and Military Gazette*, Lahore: Civil and Military Gazette Press, 1906.

see immediate Indian *swaraj/azadi* (self-rule/freedom), but because of a wish to exercise a long-term influence upon Indian society. Pedagogical patriotism included, but was not limited to, service societies, social programmes and defending Indian students and patriotism against what they were not.

After the 1870s, north Indian mission schools were increasingly infused with discussions about the Indian nation and a love for *desh* (country). Missionary teachers interpreted this as an opportunity. They understood that their students were in their formative years, and that an Indian patriotic movement was beyond its embryonic stage. When the LMS Parent Committee in London considered withdrawing from work in north India due the society's financial difficulties in the early 1900s, their teachers thought it 'unthinkable' since the next few decades would see the emergence of an organised nationalist movement and a challenge to British rule.[18] This suggested a remarkable degree of foresight. The English-educated classes were a group who would pass through mission classrooms, courtyards and corridors. Teachers were almost compelled to show sympathy towards Indian political sentiments; but many of them also genuinely felt it. Rev. William Holland was one who was acutely aware of his lodgers' political aspirations during his management of the Oxford and Cambridge Hostel in Allahabad after 1898. He reported that 'the formative and defining [sic] lines of Indian history in the next twenty years will very largely depend on the men who are in college today'.[19] George Westcott of the SPG clearly had India's future in mind when he stated that 'what you want to put into the life of a nation, put into its schools'.[20] Andrew Fraser was another teacher who argued that missionaries 'must aim in education as

18. North India, Incoming Correspondence, 1910–12, Box 21, Ashton to Thompson, 5 March 1910, School of Oriental and African Studies Archives, London.
19. 'Oxford and Cambridge Hostel Magazine', 1905–6, G2/I7/O, Birmingham University Library Archives, Birmingham.
20. J. Haythornwaite, Annual Letters, 1908, pp. 279–80, Birmingham University Library Archives, Birmingham.

creating national leaders',[21] whilst Rev. Partiger at St. John's College in Agra noted that the college was 'building up a new type of man ... [and] this new Indian will play a very important part in the future history of India'.[22] Partiger could not have anything else in mind but a political future of India that would eventually be free from colonial rule. These were all examples of how mission schools, rather than being marginal to processes of large patriotic changes, were firmly anchored within emergent debates regarding the Indian nation.

'Sedition' and the School

The relationship between students, schools and nationalism was seen in the ways in which the question of 'sedition' was addressed within corridors and classrooms. One of the best examples was seen in the aftermath of the 1905 partition of Bengal and the ensuing Swadeshi Movement. The call, *bande mataram* (I bow to you mother), shook British officialdom to its core, and it was swiftly branded as seditious. This anxiety was used to justify heavy-handed repression, press censorship and imprisonment. It also spawned an embryonic intelligence department which focused primarily on schools and hostels—often the loci of nationalist activities. Missionary teachers, however, interpreted these events differently from a now paranoid and reactionary officialdom. Because they had a better sense of student sensibilities and aspirations, they saw the 1905 disturbances as manifestations of patriotism—not simply anti-foreign nationalism. One British writer in the *Daily Telegraph* clearly had mission schools in mind when he called schools and hostels 'nurseries of sedition'. But he was quickly rebuked by a missionary teacher, who said that schools were not breeding sedition, and that *bande mataram*, infused with an understandable sense of anger, was not simply anti-British. This teacher remarked that *bande mataram* technically referred to

21. A. G. Fraser, 'The Place and Policy of Educational Missions', 1907, H/H5/E2, pp. 5–6, Birmingham University Library Archives, Birmingham.
22. *Proceedings of the CMS*, 1886–87, p. 97, Birmingham University Library Archives, Birmingham.

Kali, the mother goddess, a point which he noted was probably lost on most Europeans.[23] This might have been a moot point. So, many missionary teachers viewed the Swadeshi Movement as an exercise in patriotism rather than a purely bellicose, anti-foreign movement.

The Swadeshi Movement ignited a wider debate about patriotism and the Indian nation amongst teachers and students. Andrew Fraser of the CMS, a former bishop of Bombay, maintained that increasing student political activism and awareness should not be feared. Fraser was greatly involved with, and knowledgeable of, the wider all-India field of education, and was an authoritative commentator. He interpreted the agitations firstly by distinguishing between patriotism and anti-foreign nationalism, something which the British clearly refused to do. Fraser wrote that the Indians' love for their country 'is not primarily political nor does it involve any necessary hostility to British rule'.[24] In doing so, he ascribed a good deal of official ignorance to the manner in which the colonial state reacted to student activism. The more well-known Charlie Andrews was another example. He thought that 'it would be a grave calamity if this true love of country were misunderstood by Government in the sphere of politics'.[25] Such sentiments demonstrate how those most involved with educating Indian students did not see a zero-sum relationship between 'love of *desh*' and the Raj. John Ellwood of the CMS broadened the vocabulary of patriotism by insisting that *mulk* (sovereignty, control), *qaum* (nation), and *deshi* (countryman) should be used when conversing in Hindi and Urdu, for they denoted the English equivalents of 'country' and 'nation'.[26] This was telling, for it suggested that missionary teachers challenged the condescending lexicon which punctuated the Raj.

23. *Proceedings of the CMS*, 1908–09, pp. 100–01, Birmingham University Library Archives, Birmingham.
24. A. G. Fraser, 'Education in India and Ceylon in View of the National Movement', *The East and the West*, 1908, p. 29.
25. C. F. Andrews, 'The Effect of the Japanese Victories upon India', *The East and the West*, 1905, p. 371.
26. J. Ellwood, Notes, February 1901, G2/I6/O, Birmingham University Library Archives, Birmingham.

The nexus of education and nationalism was also seen in cases where particular students were accused of 'sedition'. Missionary teachers knew that they could never overtly criticise colonial policies, but this did not prevent them from defending their pupils. One former mission school student, A. K. Chatterjee, was appointed to teach at the government-run Jubilee High School in Benares. Charles de la Fosse, the Director of Public Instruction, was furious that he would inflame political agitation amongst the large number of Benares students. De la Fosse was convinced that this English-educated Bengali was innately sympathetic towards the Swadeshi Movement and would encourage his students to boycott British goods and institutions. He demanded that Chatterjee respond to a few questions and be reconsidered for a desk job. Yet the first person to defend Chatterjee was Patrick Davis, the principal of St. Andrew's College in Gorakhpur, who vouched for him.[27] More famously, when Amir Chand had to testify in a magistrate's court in the case of the bomb attack on Hardinge in Delhi in 1912, he was defended by Rev. Samuel Scott Allnutt, his teacher at St. Stephen's College in Delhi.[28] One LMS teacher's pupil, an Arya Samajist, caught the attention of local government officials in the lower Doab town of Dudhi. They were afraid he would encourage 'sedition' in the LMS's high school. The teacher, however, refused to have him silenced. He retorted that such discussions were good for the health of his institution.[29] This support sometimes pierced the higher echelons of colonial administration. After the Morley-Minto constitutional reforms (Indian Councils Act, 1909), missionaries pushed to have

27. 'Restricting Numbers of Admissions', No. 320, 1908, North-West Provinces & Oudh Educational Proceedings, Uttar Pradesh State Archives, Lucknow.
28. D. Baker, 'St. Stephen's College, Delhi, 1881–1997: An "Alexandria on the Banks of the Jamuna"'? in *Knowledge, Power and Politics: Educational Institutions in India*, ed. M. Hasan, New Delhi: Lotus Collection, 1998, p. 74.
29. J. C. Jackson, North India Report 1912, School of Oriental and African Studies Archives, London.

the condescending and diminutive term 'native' replaced by 'Indian' in government proceedings and communications.[30]

Emergent Patriotism in Halls and Corridors

The Swadeshi Movement electrified mission schools all the way from Bengal to the upcountry townships between the upper and lower Doab. Places with a large mission school presence, such as Allahabad, Kanpur, Benares and Lucknow, felt these reverberations within classrooms. The attitudes of missionary teachers thus far suggest that they welcomed this emergent Indian patriotism. They offered a generally positive reaction to this emergent consciousness and activism. And the evidence suggests that this was an identifiable trend, rather than an exception. Bishop Montgomery, for example, called the recent Indian stirrings 'beautiful',[31] whilst the *CMS Intelligencer* called the critiques of British colonial policies 'admirable'.[32] Another missionary teacher called the Swadeshi Movement 'a healthy sign'.[33] John Haythornwaite, the headmaster at St. John's College, never believed that India should be denied political independence (even though it would have to come after some degree of social reform). He felt that the mission school had an obligation to shape 'a generation which will not be less distinguished for its love of freedom ... independence, and a desire for self-government'.[34] Henry Packenham-Walsh similarly thought that missionaries 'should rejoice ... and should guide [and] direct ... this new spirit of patriotism'.[35] Another teacher, F. J. Watson, wanted teachers to embrace their students' political yearnings and consciousness, rather than turn

30. C. F. Andrews, 'The King's Announcement at Delhi: Its Missionary Bearing', *The East and the West*, 1912, p. 341n.
31. Bishop Montgomery, 'India', *The East and the West*, 1914, p. 288.
32. *CMS Intelligencer*, 1897, p. 45.
33. *Annual Report of the London Missionary Society*, 1909, p. 15.
34. St. John's College Prospectus and Report, 1908, G2/I7/O, Birmingham University Library Archives, Birmingham.
35. H. Pakenham-Walsh, 'The Attitude of Educated Hindus towards Christianity', *The East and the West*, 1906, pp. 396–97.

adverse to any nationalistic sentiments. He tellingly reported that it was best 'not to stand aloof from the students' political hopes and beliefs, but to show all possible sympathy'.[36] It was perhaps sentiments like these from their ethnic kin which frightened colonial officials the most.

Missionary teachers, it must be stressed, largely accepted Indian nationalism as inevitable and natural. This was in contrast to the views of officialdom, which saw it as either an aberration or a phenomenon unrepresentative of the Indian people. Of course, this was a pragmatic approach: missionaries wanted to maximise their influence amongst a rising generation that they knew would produce India's future leaders. Most Indian students formed warm, close relationships with these teachers, so long as they did not dabble in anything resembling 'communalism' or violence. Yet, instead of just dismissing students' personal grievances as a result of their 'inability to secure employment'—which British officialdom repeatedly emphasised—missionary teachers universalised the concepts of patriotism and love for the country. They argued that these were not unique, exclusive inventions of the West, and questioned the prevailing colonial assumption that Indians could not feel a larger national sentiment beyond community and caste. John Haythornwaite, for example, reported in the *St. John's College Prospectus and Report* that 'the rising tide of patriotism and national aspiration cannot be checked ... it is a natural outcome'.[37] He spoke frequently of a 'New Spirit', and stressed that Indian patriotism should be 'encouraged ... sympathetically, by College professors ... [and] not repressed and banned as a thing of evil'.[38] This was significant, and was clearly a

36. *The Guardian*, 26 May 1911, no. 31, Cambridge Mission to Delhi, Rhodes House Library, Oxford. Rev. James Carter prophesied that if colleges such as St. Stephen's kept bringing up this rising Indian generation, the West would inevitably come to submit itself to the East. See *Church Times*, 21 May 1909, no. 31, Cambridge Mission to Delhi, Rhodes House Library, Oxford.
37. *St. John's College Prospectus and Report*, 1908, G2/I7/O, Birmingham University Library Archives, Birmingham.
38. J. Haythornwaite, Annual Letters, 1908, p. 279, Birmingham University Library Archives, Birmingham.

rebuttal of official colonial policy. One of Haythornwaite's colleagues lauded his stirring activism: '[T]he [Indian] reaction is thus a very real force, moved by reasons we cannot but respect. Patriotism lives behind and within it; in it the Orient stands up against the Occident, defies it, challenges its right to come to the East and impose itself.'[39] Another LMS mission teacher argued that further steps towards Indian self-government would be 'the merest justice' to a natural, organic and inevitable outcome.[40] Here, mission schools were clearly pitting themselves against the predominant colonial view of Indian agitators as mere 'rebels' and 'seditionists'.

Controversies over educational legislation also saw examples of this pedagogical patriotism. British officialdom constantly sought to check the ballooning numbers of Indian students, either by bringing universities under greater state control, or by cutting back the number of seats in universities (and by extension, channelising more resources towards primary vernacular education). Missionary teachers and headmasters, by contrast, regularly pushed for the expansion of educational access. The 1882 Education Commission proceedings offer a case in point. British officials were worried that students were acquiring 'seditious' sentiments, sharing them through reform societies such as the Brahmo Samaj, and disseminating them through the Hindi and Urdu press. Rev. John Hewlett was asked by the commission if the large number of English-educated graduates was a political problem. He simply replied 'no'.[41]

Two decades later, Curzon's controversial and divisive educational reforms, culminating in the Universities Act of 1904,[42] drew an unfavourable response. Missionary teachers across a wide spectrum were against cutting back the number of Indian university students. Rev. Henry Durrant of the CMS argued that the educational system

39. H. E. P., 'Indian Notes', *CMS Intelligencer*, April 1899, p. 786.
40. *Annual Report of the LMS*, 1915, p. 16.
41. North India, Incoming Correspondence, 1881–82, 'Education Commission of 1882: Evidence of Rev. John Hewlett', School of Oriental and African Studies Archives, London.
42. See the essay in this volume by Suresh Chandra Ghosh which examines the origins of Curzon's educational reforms.

was in fact not overproducing graduates, which clearly agitated the viceroy. Durrant criticised the government, pointing out that officials had created the problem of 'sedition' themselves. He argued that it boiled down to racism, which exacerbated Indian reactions against the minutiae of educational legislation. Education, he argued, hardly produced 'seditious rebels'.[43] Durrant approached the question of enrolments morally, arguing that sympathy should be shown towards the students' aspirations rather than either condemning them or denying them the means to realise them.[44] Anticipating what was to come, the Calcutta Missionary Conference in 1903 sent a petition to the viceroy contending that if university senates comprised mostly government appointments, it would further radicalise students.[45] The petition also claimed that the combination of a minimum set rate fees (which ensured that mainly the scions of the elite landed and banking families could afford it), and the disaffiliation of FA (First Arts) degrees from universities, would keep large numbers of students away from the Allahabad, Punjab and Calcutta Universities. Missionaries from the CMS, LMS and CMD were all united in their opposition.[46] Whilst official policy sought to roll back overall numbers, Edward Oakley of the LMS[47] and other mission teachers,[48] with decades of experience in India, were talking about expanding access in order to accommodate Indian demand.

Race, Religious Community and the Nation

There were other ways in which this pedagogical patriotism was engendered within mission schools. These had to do with questions of

43. *CMS Intelligencer*, 1903, p. 649.
44. Ibid., p. 46; W. Gray, 'Mission Societies and Higher Education in India', *CMS Intelligencer*, January 1889, p. 217.
45. Education Files, nos. 66–67, 1903, Home Department, National Archives of India, New Delhi.
46. Ibid.
47. E. S. Oakley, North India Report, 1903, School of Oriental and African Studies Archives, London.
48. B. Wilton and G. M. Bulloch, North India Report, 1903, School of Oriental and African Studies Archives, London.

race and religious community. When it comes to race, the hardened attitudes of the late-colonial officialdom and Anglo-India have been well documented by historians.[49] Yet, when viewed through the prism of missionary education, an alternative perspective on race emerges. Missionary teachers were substantially less inflected with race consciousness than their ruling kin.[50] The newspaper *Christian Patriot*, for example, chided British administrators for maintaining strict racial divisions which hindered students from getting their deserved share in the management of their own country.[51] Rev. William 'Pundit' Hooper, who spent years conversing with Benares' pandits, observed with satisfaction that mission schools proved that 'race and religion have no necessary connection',[52] whilst the *Annual Report of the LMS* argued that mission schools were the 'most effective solvents of race hatred'.[53] The Hindi and Urdu press consistently noted this. *The Advocate* of Lucknow lauded missionaries who, despite their religious differences with Hindus and Muslims, were generally popular and well-respected. The editor tellingly reported that missionaries

49. C. Bates, *Race, Caste and Tribe in Central India: The Early Origins of Anthropometry*, Edinburgh: Centre for South Asian Studies, 1995; R. G. Gregory, *India and East Africa: A History of Race Relations within the British Empire*, Oxford: Clarendon Press, 1971; P. Robb (ed.), *The Concept of Race in South Asia*, New Delhi: Oxford University Press, 1995, and K. Ballhatchet, *Race, Sex and Class under the Raj: Imperial Attitudes and Policies and Their Critics*, London: Weidenfeld and Nicolson, 1980.
50. Here I disagree slightly with Nandini Chatterjee, who argues that colonial racial understandings still imbibed the administrative structure of the Indian church. Whist this may be true, this essay argues that an understanding of racism cannot be gleaned solely from an understanding of institutional organisation and employment. See Nandini Chatterjee, *The Making of Indian Secularism: Empire, Law and Christianity, 1830–1960*, Basingstoke: Palgrave Macmillan, 2011.
51. *CMS Intelligencer*, 1902, p. 771.
52. *Proceedings of the CMS*, 1903–04, pp. 197–98. Hooper had his stipend cut because he spent too much time conversing in Sanskrit rather than attempting conversion.
53 *Annual Report of the LMS*, 1910, p. 63.

'were free from [that] race pride and are desirous of removing the obstacles which stand in the way of a better understanding between the East and the West'.[54] One St. Stephen's College teacher wrote to *The Guardian* that the most urgent Indian social problem was neither caste nor Hindu-Muslim 'communalism', but the growing racial divide between Europeans and Indians.[55] Even though Sushil Rudra's appointment as principal of St. Stephen's College in 1906 came amidst a racial debate that broke out in wider missionary circles,[56] a good number of missionary teachers still supported the Indian Christian's candidacy. Mission schools were also far more progressive when compared to government-run schools, nearly all of which had European headmasters. Perhaps Rev. Charles Crosthwaite of St. John's College refuted colonial racism most pointedly when he told a group of his students that he wanted Kipling, with his 'East is East and West is West, and never the 'twain shall meet' dictum, to see mission schools for himself 'for it might strike him that he was wrong after all'.[57]

Pedagogical patriotism was also engendered when it came to more contested points of colonial policy and administration. Missionary teachers were sometimes unusually blunt in their criticism of the colonial state's policies and tendencies. They argued that colonial polices were heavy-handed and unmindful of their contradiction to Christian morality. Charlie Andrews has always been seen as an exception in terms of the extent to which he went in supporting

54. *Advocate*, Lucknow, 17 July 1910, Selections form Vernacular Newspapers, Uttar Pradesh State Archives, Lucknow.
55. *The Guardian*, 26 May 1909, p. 11, no. 31, Cambridge Mission to Delhi, Rhodes House Library, Oxford.
56. Ibid., Dr Stanton to Bishop Allnutt, 19 September 1905, No. 31, Cambridge Mission to Delhi, Rhodes House Library, Oxford. Also see *The Guardian*, 13 October 1911, no. 31, Cambridge Mission to Delhi, Rhodes House Library, Oxford and D. O'Conner et al., *Three Centuries of Mission: The United Society for the Propagation of the Gospel, 1701–2000*, London: Continuum, 2000, pp. 104–05.
57. Ibid. Also see D. E. Evans, North India Report, Council for World Missions, School of Oriental and African Studies Library Archives, London.

the nationalist movement, and to a degree, in how he sometimes chided British officialdom. Yet, beneath the surface, numerous other missionaries fired salvos against colonial officialdom. Rev. John Maconachie of the CMS derided the Raj for its 'selfish greed, cupidity, petty intrigue and reckless want of principle' in dealing with university graduates.[58] This was the language normally reserved for *The Englishman*'s most reactionary descriptions of 'uncivilised' and 'effeminate' Indians. As early as 1905, George Hibbert-Ware of St. Stephen's College joined the nascent nationalist movement with unbridled enthusiasm, throwing himself into student activism and encouraging political societies and debate.[59] He was unusually critical of the move to partition Bengal, and called Curzon's decision reckless.[60] William Holland declared in the contentious decade of the 1920s that British rule in India 'must be service, not rule or exploitation',[61] and noted the colonial government's 'pitiful' hypocrisy.[62] Charlie Andrews perhaps also exposed this hypocrisy when he stated that 'England and the English Church owe too much to the struggle for national liberty in the past to grudge that liberty to India'.[63] Perhaps, the most poignant example was Rev. Bernard Lucas' rebuke of one English commentator in *The Englishman* who referred to Indians as 'subject peoples'.

> The time has gone by for speaking of the people of India as a subject people ... the one inalienable right of a subject people is to throw off foreign yoke ... this desire to emancipate themselves is perfectly natural, whether it be regarded as seditious or not.[64]

58. *CMS Intelligencer*, 1903, p. 91.
59. S. S. Allnutt to Stanton, 16 March 1906, no. 31, Cambridge Mission to Delhi, Rhodes House Library, Oxford.
60. Ibid.
61. W. Holland, *The Indian Outlook*, London: Edinburgh House Press, 1926, p. 238.
62. W. Holland, *The Goal of India*, London: United Council for Missionary Education, 1917, pp. 195–96.
63. Andrews, 'The Effect of the Japanese Victories upon India', p. 371.
64. *Chronicle of the LMS*, 1909, p. 154.

Again, even though these did not equal to unwavering missionary support for *purna swaraj* (complete self-rule), it demonstrated, more importantly, that education was a site where questions of patriotism and the nation were vibrantly discussed, and indeed, interconnected.

Mission schools also built upon these critiques by arguing that India's religious and spiritual diversity was an asset, and not, as understood and practiced by the Raj, an impediment to nationhood. To missionary teachers, India's various castes, tribes and religions were individual patchworks in the stitched quilt of the nation. William Holland admitted that the diversity of India's numerous kingdoms, communities and castes was greatly (and unfairly) overemphasised by British officialdom and Orientalist scholars.[65] Holland found from his experience that Indian students possessed a palpable patriotism and a general love for their country, which transcended caste and community.[66] Matthew Sherring's 1872 anthropological taxonomy, *Hindu Tribes and Castes as Represented in Benares*, did indeed argue that social reform needed to precede formal political independence. But he still noted that India possessed a noted civilisation-based cohesiveness: '[M]ust we on these grounds separate them from one another, and regard them as so many distinct nationalities and races? Obviously not.'[67] This was another example of how missionary interpretations of Indian society, as experienced through their interactions and associations with students, differed from the dominant 'ideologies of the Raj'[68] which saw India along the lines of irreconcilably opposed castes and religions.

There were also more direct political connections between mission schools and the emergent nation. Numerous students of

65. Holland, *The Indian Outlook*, p. 23.
66. Ibid., p. 23. Of course, this might be expected from many mission teachers, for their students had yet to enter the harsh realities of political patronage and identity politics.
67. M. Sherring, *Hindu Tribes and Castes as Represented in Benares*, Vol. II, Calcutta: Thacker Spink, 1872, p. 272.
68. Thomas R. Metcalf, *Ideologies of the Raj*, Cambridge: Cambridge University Press, 1995.

mission schools ended up entering the world of public service and politics. Even though they rarely ended up becoming all-India level leaders in the nationalist movement, they were often seen at the provincial and local levels as translators, educational inspectors and assistants to agricultural surveys. They would become, in a way, the mortar of India's subordinate tiers of bureaucratic authority, and were celebrated examples as contributors to India's political future. Many of Rev. Henry Tubb's former students went on to serve as barristers and educational inspectors in the UP judiciary and Department of Public Instruction.[69] The editor of the *Hindustan*, an influential north Indian newspaper, was himself the product of a mission school.[70] Another student of St. John's College in Agra went on to become a member of the UP Legislative Council. He successfully petitioned the Department of Public Instruction to increase the department's annual grant to the college, citing it as an institution that was beneficial to India's civic life.[71] Many students who passed through the corridors of St. Stephen's College went on to join both the Arya Samaj, and later on, the Non-Cooperation Movement (1920–22).[72] And perhaps most tellingly, the manifesto for the Non-Cooperation Movement was written in Sushil Rudra's residence. Indeed, before the launching of countrywide mobilisation by Gandhi, there were already direct connections between the actual products of mission schools and the activities which would go on to influence civic life and the course of the nationalist movement.

Conclusion

This essay has argued that the nexus of Christian missionary schools and nationalism offers an alternative way of viewing education in

69. *Proceedings of the CMS*, 1912–13, p. 129.
70. H. Nevison, *The New Spirit in India*, London: Harper & Brothers, 1908, p. 303.
71. *Proceedings of the CMS*, 1912 13, p. 129.
72. N. Gupta, *Delhi Between Two Empires 1803–1931: Society, Government and Urban Growth*, New Delhi: Oxford University Press, 1981, pp. 111–12.

colonial India. Missionary teachers by 1920 possessed a deeper and more intimate knowledge of Indian culture and religion compared to the colonial state and its officials. This came from teaching, mentoring and sustaining relationships between teachers and pupils that often went beyond their enrolment. A part of this invariably revolved around their students' sense of patriotism and reaction to colonial policies. These all became increasingly palpable particularly after the Swadeshi Movement and its reverberations in north India. These mission schools helped engender a 'pedagogical patriotism' which not only defended students against charges of 'sedition', but also fashioned comparatively positive ideas about the Indians' love for their country and its religious and social diversity. This countenanced the Raj's idea of an India endlessly divided by caste, region and religion. Of course, a lot of this was due to the missionaries' own selfish interests. But this does not make the fashioning of patriotism in schools, classrooms and corridors less of a contribution to the wider trajectory of Indian nationalism than Dadabhai Naoroji's 'Drain of Wealth' theory or Gandhi's *Hind Swaraj*. It is hoped that this essay, by examining the interaction between missionary schools and Indian students in the decades before 1920, will further contribute to our understanding of the antecedents of the organised, all-India-level nationalism that would eventually emerge under the Congress led by Gandhi.

7

Re-defining Work and Education as a Means to National Self-determination

A Comparative Study of Gandhian India and Peronist Argentina

SIMONE HOLZWARTH
AND
VERÓNICA OELSNER

On the surface, Argentina and India share little with regard to their colonial history: by the early twentieth century, Argentina was an independent country, whilst any form of self-government in India was still decades away. Yet, a comparative analysis of Gandhi's strategies regarding vocational education and work, and those of the Argentinian president, Juan Domingo Perón, reveal that the two leaders, in fact, had much in common. Both fashioned similar approaches in making, and indeed re-defining, education into a means by which to bolster the nation. For sure, Gandhi's strategies, symbolism and achievements served as an inspirational model for a wider group of anti-colonial nationalists and proponents of civil rights the world over. But this essay does not aim to look so much at these casuistic connections, as it aims to shed new light upon parallel developments: how both Perón and Gandhi envisioned educational strategies which served to make their nations self-sufficient. Perón's aim was to minimise dependence on British economic forces, while Gandhi's was to eliminate British rule. This essay, therefore, serves to offer an international and comparative perspective on Indian education.

Introduction

Between the 1920s and 1940s and in the 1940s respectively, both the icon of the Indian independence movement, Mohandas Karamchand Gandhi (1869–1948) and the Argentinian, President Juan Domingo Perón (1895–1974) aimed at creating in their respective countries a new social order enabling national self-determination. In this framework they advocated far-reaching social, economic and political reforms. They also sought to introduce extensive reforms of vocational education structures. Conjointly with these reforms, both the Peronist government and Gandhi and his followers re-defined hitherto dominant representations (concepts, values, convictions) of work, workers and education. They both presented manual work as respectable and dignifying instead of degrading, and enacted this radical change of representations by portraying themselves as 'the first worker' (in the case of Perón) and the rural manual worker at the spinning wheel (in the case of Gandhi).

Our comparative research takes these parallel phenomena as a starting point and concentrates on the structural and semantic reforms related to work and education. Following a theoretical perspective that emphasises the interdependency of semantics and structures, it analyses how representations related to work and education supported, hindered, or even impeded the establishment of specific models of education and vocational training.

In this essay, we focus especially on the axes of comparison that we elaborated during the process of collecting and analysing sources. In the first part of the essay, we describe the theoretical framework and assumptions of the project and explain in more detail why we chose Peronist Argentina and the Indian independence movement as units of comparison. In the second part, we present the axes of comparison we are working with, including preliminary findings. Since the project is still going on as of 2012, the findings summarised are more advanced for some axes than for others. These axes are: (1) political upheavals and new social orders; (2) the role of vocational training; (3) intentionally constructed representations of work and education; (4) sources of inspiration for the institutional and symbolic constructions, and (5) sustainability of symbolic and institutional constructions.

FIGURE 7.1: Perón as the 'First Worker'

Source: Archivo General de la Nación, Argentina, 1953

THEORETICAL PERSPECTIVE AND RESEARCH DESIGN

Internationally, research on vocational education has been done mostly from a functionalist perspective. In this perspective, vocational education is analysed in its relationship with economic demands or technological development.[1] As Georg criticises, vocational education is usually either seen as a response to requirements of technological progress and the labour market, or as a factor that influences economic achievement or failure of a country.[2] However, there has

1. See discussion line from Gary S. Becker, *Human Capital: A Theoretical and Empirical Analysis, with Special Reference to Education*, New York: Columbia University Press, 1964, to Alison Wolf, *Does Education Matter? Myths about Education and Economic Growth*, London: Penguin Books, 2002.
2. Walter Georg, 'Zwischen Tradition und Moderne: Berufsbildung im internationalen Vergleich', in *Weiterungen der Berufspädagogik. Von der Berufsbildungstheorie zur internationalen Berufsbildung. Festschrift*

also been research that postulates that types of vocational education have 'social, historical, institutional and political roots'.[3] Especially, a group of German researchers emphasises that vocational education is not simply determined by 'external' factors like the economy. In their perspective, context-dependent representations (values, convictions, concepts) related to work and education that are dominant in a given time in a given society act as 'structural and mental premises'[4] or as a 'powerful basis'[5] for thinking and designing vocational education.[6]

---

für Antonius Lipsmeier zum 60. Geburtstag, eds. Rolf Arnold, Rolf Dobischat and Bernd Ott, Stuttgart: Franz Steiner Verlag, 1997, p. 153.

3. Linda Clarke and Christopher Winch, *Vocational Education: International Approaches, Developments and Systems*, London, New York: Routledge, 2007, p. 8.
4. Klaus Harney and Heinz-Elmar Tenorth, *Berufsbildung und industrielles Ausbildungsverhältnis. Zur Genese, Formalisierung und Pädagogisierung beruflicher Ausbildung in Preussen bis 1914*, Zeitschrift für Pädagogik, vol. 32, no. 1, 1986, pp. 9–14.
5. Georg, *Zwischen Tradition und Moderne: Berufsbildung im internationalen Vergleich*, p. 160.
6. See also Ute Clement, Vom Sinn beruflicher Bildung. Zur Modellbildung in der vergleichenden Berufsbildungsforschung, Zeitschrift für Berufs- und Wirtschaftspädagogik, vol. 92, no. 6, 1996, pp. 617–26; Thomas Deißinger, *Beruflichkeit als „organisierendes Prinzip" der deutschen Berufsbildung*, Marktschwaben: Eusl, 1998; Walter Georg, *Zwischen Tradition und Moderne: Berufsbildung im internationalen Vergleich*, 1997; Philipp Gonon, *Ende oder Wandel der Beruflichkeit?—Beruf und Berufspädagogik im Wandel*, Zeitschrift für Berufs- und Wirtschaftspädagogik, vol. 97, no. 3, 2001, pp. 404–14; Klaus Harney, *Der Beruf als Umwelt des Betriebs. Vergleichende, historische und systematische Aspekte einer Differenz, Die Relevanz neuer Technologien für die Berufsausbildung*; Verband der Lehrer an berufsbildenden Schulen und Kollegschulen (Teachers' association which edited the book): Krefeld, 1985, pp. 118–30; Klaus Harney, Zum Beginn von Anfang und Ende: Tradition und Kontingenz der Berufsausbildung am Beispiel schwerindustrieller Betriebsformen in *Zwischen Anfang und Ende. Fragen an die Pädagogik*, ed. Niklas Luhmann Karl Eberhard Schorr, Frankfurt am Main, Suhrkamp,

These assumptions have already proven valuable for the investigation of countries like Germany, France and England.[7] In the German case for instance, researchers agree that the tradition of a powerful artisanry and their representation of the *beruf* (profession/vocation)—with its implicit meaning of qualification, specialised activity, personal identification, social status and career possibilities—facilitated the design of a system based on the traditional apprenticeship that combines qualification in the workplace and in vocational schools.[8] This fruitful research perspective has so far not been practically utilised for contexts outside Western Europe.

1990, pp. 206–27; Harney, 'Berufsbildung' in *Historisches Wörterbuch der Pädagogik*, ed. Dietrich Benner and Jürgen Oelkers, Weinheim, Basel: Juventa, 2004, pp. 153–73, Jürgen Schriewer, 'Alternativen in Europa: Frankreich. Lehrlingsausbildung unter dem Anspruch von Theorie und Systematik', in *Sekundarstufe II—Jugendbildung zwischen Schule und Beruf (Enzyklopädie Erziehungswissenschaft* (vol. 9), ed. Herwig Blankertz et al., Stuttgart, Dresden: Ernst Klett Verlag, 1995, pp. 250–85; Barbara Schulte, *Zur Rettung des Landes: Bildung und Beruf im China der Republikzeit*, Frankfurt am Main and New York: Campus, 2008.

7. See in particular Jürgen Schriewer and Klaus Harney, 'Beruflichkeit versus *culture technique*. Zu einer Soziogenese arbeitsbezogener Semantik', in *Arbeit und Nationalstaat. Frankreich und Deutschland in europäischer Perspektive*, ed. Peter Wagner, Claude Didry and Bénédicte Zimmermann, Frankfurt am Main and New York: Campus, 2000, pp. 128–168; Thomas Deißinger, *Beruflichkeit als Zusammenhang. Ein Vergleich mit England*, Zeitschrift für Pädagogik (Beiheft 40, 1999: *Beruf und Berufsbildung. Situation, Reformperspektiven, Gestaltungsmöglichkeiten*, pp. 189–207.
8. See Clement, *Vom Sinn beruflicher Bildung*; Deißinger, *Beruflichkeit als „organisierendes Prinzip" der deutschen Berufsbildung*; Georg, *Zwischen Tradition und Moderne: Berufsbildung im internationalen Vergleich*; Wolf-Dietrich Greinert, 'Geschichte der Berufsausbildung in Deutschland', in *Handbuch der Berufsbildung*, ed. Rolf Arnold and Antonius Lipsmeier, Wiesbaden: VS Verlag für Sozialwissenschaften, 2006, pp. 500–08; Klaus Harney and Peter Storz, 'Strukturwandel beruflicher Bildung', in *Pädagogik, Erziehungswissenschaft, Bildung*, Köln, Weimar, Wien, Böhlau, 1994, pp. 353–81; Katrin Kraus,

For that reason, following this theoretical framework, we have chosen to study and compare two non-European contexts: Argentina and India around the middle of the twentieth century. On the one hand, these countries had a socio-historical development very different from Europe as well as from each other. On the other hand, between the 1930s and the 1950s, they show remarkable similarities. Firstly, between the 1920s and 1940s and in the 1940s respectively, India and Argentina experienced analogous political upheavals. In both cases, the emerging political movements intended a clear rupture with the previous social orders; they strove for national self-determination and radical social and economic change. Secondly, against this background, both movements paid special attention to vocational education. The Peronist government built up a large system of vocational education, and Gandhi proposed educational reforms in which manual work played a central role. Thirdly, the political leaders of both countries deliberately disseminated a new complex of representations related to work and education. These representations were meant, as we assume, to dignify manual work and workers, and by doing so, to support the intended structural reforms, including vocational education.

The comparison of these events against the background of great socio-cultural differences is especially appropriate for proving our leading hypothesis. We concentrate on representations related to work and education and the emerging models of vocational education, assuming that the constructed representations played an important role in shaping vocational education. These representations may have adopted a very different content in each country, and in that way may have enabled different models of vocational education.

Our data sources are legal documents, government publications, curricula, schoolbooks, public speeches and festivities, and visual material (like pictures, posters, monuments and architecture). For the analysis we consider arguments and concepts, as well as

---

Die ‚berufliche Ordnung' im Spannungsfeld von nationaler Tradition und europäischer Integration, Zeitschrift für Pädagogik, vol. 53, no. 3, 2007, pp. 382–98; Jürgen Schriewer and Klaus Harney, 'Beruflichkeit versus *culture technique*'.

categorisations and value hierarchies that are contained in these written and visual documents.

Axes of Comparison

Political Upheavals and New Social Orders

The emerging political movements led by Perón in Argentina in the 1940s and by Gandhi in India in the 1930s aimed at achieving national self-determination. Therefore, they envisioned new social orders which presupposed massive political, economic and social reforms. These upheavals built the context in which both movements designed important educational reforms and constructed new representations related to work and education. For that reason, they constitute our first axis of study and comparison.

As National Secretary of Labour from 1943 onwards, Perón wielded remarkable power and became one of the most popular men of the military regime he was part of. From this position he initiated a work policy without precedent in Argentina. This led him to presidency in 1946.[9] During his national-populist governments (1946–52 and 1952–55), Perón presented himself as the leader of a revolution and defined his political party named Justicialismo (derived from the word 'justice') not just as a political party, but as a national movement.[10] Thereby, Perón frequently stressed that this movement and its programme responded neither to capitalism nor to communism: it represented the 'Third Position'—a position that was defined as succeeding and being superior to capitalism and communism.[11]

9. See Robert A. Potash, *El ejército y la política en la Argentina, 1928–1945*, Buenos Aires: Sudamericana, 1981.
10. See Raúl A. Mende, *Der Justizialismus: Peronistische Doktrin und Tatsache*, Buenos Aires: Imprenta López, 1952. See also Cristian Buchrucker, *Nationalismus, Faschismus und Peronismus (1927–1955): Ein Beitrag zur Geschichte der politischen Ideen in Argentinien*, Ph.D. dissertation, Freie Universität Berlin, 1982, p. 444.
11. See Pablo Gerchunoff and Lucas Llach, *El ciclo de la ilusión y el desencanto. Un siglo de políticas económicas argentinas*, Buenos Aires: Ariel, 1998, p. 170.

The proclaimed aim was to create a 'new Argentina' and a 'new citizen'.[12] The guiding principles for that were 'economic independence' from abroad, 'political sovereignty', and 'social justice'. In his speeches, Perón defined 'economic independence' from abroad (especially from Great Britain, which owned important companies in Argentina like railways and granaries) as a second independence after political independence from Spain in 1816. This 'argentinisation of economy', as it was also labelled, demanded the nationalisation of existing industries, and the consolidation of the industrialisation that had begun in the 1930s as an alternative to the collapsed agrarian-export model after the world economic crisis.[13] 'Political sovereignty' was characterised both as self-determination of the country and as strengthening of the citizens, who would find in the new government their 'real representation'.[14] 'Social justice' was meant to protect the weakest sections of society from the exploitation by the strongest, and improve the living and working conditions of the working classes.[15]

The Peronist government not only declared, but also implemented, much of its intended aims. Amongst others, it implemented many measures like accessible credit for national industries, hike in salaries, freezing of rental fees, and subsidy for products of mass consumption, as well as increased expenditure in education, health and housing for the benefit of the working classes. It also passed comprehensive work legislation (responding to old claims of workers and socialists), organised (and that way controlled) labour unions, and created a vocational education commission under the umbrella

12. Mónica E. Rein, *Politics and Education in Argentina (1946–1962)*, Armonk: New York, London: M. E. Sharpe, 1998, p. 19.
13. Gerchunoff and Llach, *El ciclo de la ilusión y el desencanto*, p. 185. See also Miguel Somoza Rodríguez, *Educación y política en Argentina (1946–1955)*, Buenos Aires: Miño y Dávila, 2006, p. 15; Buchrucker, *Nationalismus, Faschismus und Peronismus*, p. 441.
14. See Buchrucker, *Nationalismus, Faschismus und Peronismus*, pp. 441–42.
15. Ibid., p. 439.

of the State Secretary of Labour that would provide education and training exclusively for workers.[16]

In the case of India, Gandhi proposed a vision of a new social order with the aim of 'reconstructing' India and achieving *swaraj* (self-rule). Inspired by critics of industrialisation and early socialist thinkers like John Ruskin—whose *Unto This Last* (1860), with its main idea that a life of manual labour and of artisans is worth living, remained one of his favourite texts[17]—Gandhi emphasised the idea of the 'dignity of manual work' and developed his concept of *sarvodaya*,[18] a society based on the principles of equality and 'upliftment of the masses', communal self-sufficiency and the equitable distribution of wealth. Similar to the Argentinian case, a 'social revolution' was at the heart of Gandhi's visions for a 'Young India',[19] meaning an improvement of the lives of the rural masses ('village *swaraj*', self-rule of the villages). The goal thereby was to overcome the hierarchical caste system and to integrate the so-called 'untouchables' into society.[20] He describes his vision for a new social order thus:

16. See Horacio Gaggero, 'La etapa populista (1943–1955)', in *Argentina en busca de una nueva estabilidad (1930–1966)*, ed. Horacio Gaggero, Buenos Aires: Proyecto Editorial, 2005, pp. 60–61; María Seoane, *Argentina. El siglo del progreso y la oscuridad (1900–2003)*, Buenos Aires: Crítica, 2004, p. 74; Horacio Chitarroni Maceyra, *El ciclo peronista: apogeo y crisis*, Buenos Aires: Grupo Editor Universitario, 1997, pp. 38–39. See also Pablo Pineau, Peronism, Secondary Schooling and Work (Argentina, 1944–1955): An Approach through Cultural Hierarchies, *Paedagogica Historica*, vol. 40, nos. 1–2, 2004, pp. 183–91.
17. John Ruskin, *Unto This Last*, Lincoln: University of Nebraska Press, 1967.
18. Title of Gandhi's translation of Ruskin's *Unto This Last* into Gujarati.
19. Title of Gandhi's journal. He used the term *Young India* as the title of his envisioned post-colonial social order.
20. Gandhi called them *harijans* ('children of God'), a term rejected widely within untouchable communities. Today these communities prefer the term *Dalit* as an emancipatory term, meaning 'downtrodden, oppressed'. Gandhi's approach towards overcoming the caste system

> In this structure composed of innumerable villages, there will be ever widening, never-ascending circles. Life will not be a pyramid with the apex sustained by the bottom. But it will be an oceanic circle whose centre will be the individual always ready to perish for the village, the latter ready to perish for the circle of villages, till at last the whole becomes one life composed of individuals, never aggressive in their arrogance, but ever humble, sharing the majesty of the oceanic circle of which they are integral units.[21]

Gandhi strongly emphasised the importance of not just copying 'the West' in the search for a post-colonial model of society, but to create an 'Indian' alternative to 'Western' ideas of development. His idea was to create a 'modernity' that would be morally superior to 'the West', and therefore be a model not only for India but also for other countries in the world.[22]

The Role of Vocational Training

In both contexts, education related to work was presented as a key instrument to achieve the proclaimed revolutions. However, both movements realised the scarce existence of such kind of education in their countries. Accordingly, they emphasised the importance of it and designed extensive educational reforms. In this second axis, we examine how vocational education was conceived by both movements, as well as how it was planned and implemented.

---

was heavily criticised by B. R. Ambedkar, the leader of the Dalit movement. In his view, Gandhi was not really against the caste system (see also M. K. Gandhi, *Varnashramadharma*, Ahmedabad: Navajivan Publishing House, 1962) and his appeals towards the dominant castes to end untouchability were not enough to overcome the social, political and economic exclusion of Dalits.

21. Gandhi wrote this in his newspaper *Harijan* on 28 July 1946. See M. K. Gandhi, *The Collected Works of Mahatma Gandhi* (98 vols.), vol. 91, New Delhi: Publications Division, Ministry of Information and Broadcasting, Government of India, 1999, p. 236.
22. Chapter VI in M. K. Gandhi, *Hind Swaraj or Indian Home Rule*, Madras: G. A. Natesan and Co., 1922.

In Peronist Argentina, vocational education was proclaimed to be as important as earlier alphabetisation—as the slogan said: 'Alphabetisation in the past century; vocational education in the present'.[23] It was also designed as one of the tools 'to create the new Argentina'.[24] At the same time, it was presented as an instrument for the implementation of the idea of 'social justice', since it would improve the material, cultural, moral, and social situation of individuals. It was thereby represented as a direct way of benefiting the working classes through securing their support and consolidating their political hegemony. Vocational education was also portrayed as a way to achieve 'economic independence' from abroad, since it would prepare the labour force necessary for industrialisation, and in that way strengthen the national economy.[25]

By the mid-1940s, the Peronist government had created a concrete centralised system of vocational education exclusively for the working classes that was independent of the formal education system. This gradually-growing, large-scale system was run by a state agency for vocational education (Comisión Nacional de Aprendizaje y Orientación Profesional, CNAOP), which at first functioned under the Ministry of Labour, and was later transferred to the Ministry of Education. It had three levels, multiple professional orientations (including mechanics, carpentry, turnery, foundry, electro-techniques, motors, bricklaying, and radio and telecommunication), and different institutional arrangements (evening courses, factory-schools, professional schools, culminating in a workers' university) (see Table 7.1).

23. Comisión Nacional de Aprendizaje y Orientación Profesional, *Aprendizaje*, no. 3, 1952, p. 8.
24. Comisión Nacional de Aprendizaje y Orientación Profesional, *Universidad Obrera Nacional*, 1948.
25. See Juan Balduzzi, 'Peronismo, saber y poder', in *Hacia una pedagogía de la imaginación para América Latina* Adriana Puiggrós, eds. Susana José and Juan Balduzzi, Buenos Aires: Editorial Contrapunto, 1988, pp. 175–91; David L. Wiñar, *Poder político y educación. El peronismo y la Comisión Nacional de Aprendizaje y Orientación Profesional*, Buenos Aires: Instituto Torcuato Di Tella, 1970, pp. 32–36. See also Miguel Somoza Rodríguez, *Educación y política en Argentina*, pp. 37–38.

Table 7.1: Peronist System of Vocational Education

Education Level and Duration	Institutional Arrangement	Degree
First level (3 years) prerequisite for admission in the following level	factory-schools, vocational schools, half-day schools	expert in the trade
Second level (4 years) prerequisite for admission in the following level	evening courses for workers	factory technician
Third level (5 years)	workers' university	factory engineer

While during the 1930s, before the Peronist government, the state ran thirty-five vocational schools with approximately 2,800 students, by the beginning of the 1950s the Peronist vocational education system had 130 educational institutions with approximately 40,000 students (see Figure 7.2).

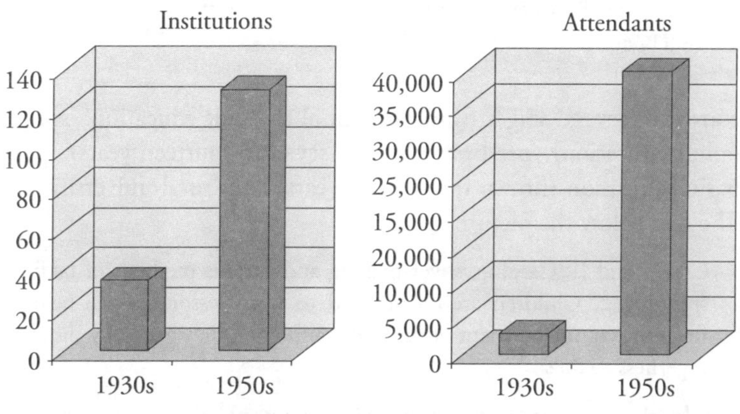

Figure 7.2: Vocational Education Institutions and their Attendants in the 1930s and in the 1950s

Connecting education with manual work was also central to Gandhi's visions of economy and society.

Figure 7.3 shows children sitting on the floor in a rural setting, spinning with hand-spinning devices (*takli*). It was printed in a book advertising the educational concept, *Nai Talim* (literally meaning 'new education', also called 'rural national education through village handicrafts') put forward by Gandhi. He envisioned Nai Talim to

FIGURE 7.3: Standards I and II students spinning with the *takli* at the Basic School in Sevagram in 1948

Source: Hindustani Talimi Sangh, India, 1948

consist of several stages from pre-school to adult education: 'social' (adult education), 'pre-basic', 'basic' (seven to fourteen years), 'post basic' education (fifteen to eighteen years) and 'rural universities'.[26] The text below the picture says:

> Class I and II. Carding, sliver-making and various methods of takli spinning ... Children are encouraged to learn lessons of self-help from the commencement of their education and they generally show eagerness to do so.[27]

In the context of the national movement, there was a heated debate about a national education model. As many others, Gandhi criticised the colonial legacy in education: rote learning, education geared towards an elite, neglect of mass education and the

26. Hindustani Talimi Sangh, *Basic National Education: Syllabus for a Complete Basic School Grades I to VIII*, Sevagram (Wardha): Hindustani Talimi Sangh, 1950, pp. 11–13.
27. Hindustani Talimi Sangh, *Nai Talim Sevagram*, Sevagram (Wardha): Hindustani Talimi Sangh, 1948, p. 3.

underdevelopment of practical education. In his view, the premium on 'literary' knowledge had led to a situation in which manual work was devalued and seen as something that did not need special training. This pattern of thinking is also called the 'Brahmanical-cum-Colonial Paradigm'.[28] It developed through the connection between high-caste ideas (the valuing of Brahmanical book knowledge) and colonial education (the training of elites as mediators between the colonisers and the colonised population).

In Gandhi's view, education was of vital importance for the realisation of his vision of a self-sufficient, self-organising rural economy as the basis of a society based on selflessness and the dignity of manual work. Instead of concentrating on an urban colonial bureaucracy and economy, teaching and learning should be practical and based on a 'productive trade'—a village craft or trade such as spinning, weaving or agriculture—in order to overcome the 'bookish' character of colonial education. The pedagogical idea behind Nai Talim was to teach through the method of 'correlation'. This means that while busy in their craftwork, children should listen to and discuss with the teacher topics related to the craft.[29] One example of this method is the teaching of spinning in relation to lessons on Indian economic history. While spinning yarn to produce handmade cotton clothing (*khadi*), the children should learn about the economic history of textile production in India and the problems caused by colonial trade relations (India had to buy industrially manufactured textiles from English textile mills, causing unemployment in the Indian textile sector).[30]

The Wardha conference in 1937 was the starting point for the central ideas of Nai Talim to come to the centre stage of educational debates on a national level. Gandhi presented his educational ideas at

28. See Anil Sadgopal, *Position Paper of the National Focus Group on Work and Education*, New Delhi: NCERT, 2007.
29. See also A. B. Solanki, *The Technique of Correlation in Basic Education*, Ahmedabad: Navajivan Publishing House, 1958.
30. See Gandhi's speech at the Wardha conference in 1937, quoted in *Position Paper of the National Focus Group on Work and Education*, Delhi: NCERT, 2007, p. 4.

this conference and initiated a debate about the feasibility of his ideas. In the end, the conference passed a resolution of four demands for national education that were very close to Gandhi's suggestions:[31]

1. That in the opinion of the conference, free and compulsory education be provided for seven years on a nation-wide scale.
2. That the medium of instruction be the mother tongue.
3. That the conference endorses the proposal made by Mahatma Gandhi that the process of education throughout this period should centre round some form of manual and productive work, and all the abilities to be developed or training to be given should, as far as possible, be integrally related to the central handicraft chosen with due regard to the environment of the child.
4. That the conference expects that this system of education will be gradually able to cover the remuneration of teachers.

Zakir Husain, the president of the 'national university', Jamia Millia Islamia (founded in the context of the Non-Cooperation Movement), was appointed to chair a committee and write a report to summarise the discussions of the Wardha conference. This report became the most influential document for the further implementation of the Gandhian educational reforms. It also included a syllabus for standards 1–7, the stage of Nai Talim called 'basic' education.[32] As the sources about the implementation of the ideas of Nai Talim reveal, this 'new education' was thought to contribute to Gandhi's social revolution. On the one hand, it was expected to form the new (democratic, cooperative and manually skilled) citizen for the

31. See the full resolution in Hindustani Talimi Sangh, *Basic National Education. Report of the Zakir Husain Committee and Detailed Syllabus with a Foreword by Mahatma Gandhi*, Segaon (Wardha): Hindustani Talimi Sangh, 1939.
32. The syllabus lists three crafts that should be taught in basic schools: 1. agriculture, 2. spinning and weaving and 3. cardboard, wood and metal work. In 'correlation' to these crafts, the following subjects were to be taught: mother tongue and Hindustani, mathematics, social studies, general science and drawing.

intended new social order by transmitting a particular discipline and work ethic and valuing manual work. On the other hand, it would foster rural development, enabling the 'self-sufficiency' of people and villages.

The Indian National Congress adopted the outcome of the Wardha conference as its programme of national education in 1938, and 'basic' education was implemented on an experimental basis in United Provinces, Bihar, Orissa, Central Provinces, Bombay Presidency, Madras Presidency and the princely states of Kashmir and Mysore. The Congress mandate also provided for the creation of the Hindustani Talimi Sangh—also called the 'All India Education Board'—'to work out in a consolidated manner a programme of Basic national education and to recommend it for acceptance to those who are in control of State or private education'.[33] By October 1939, there were 247 'basic' schools and fourteen teacher training schools.[34] After 1940, however, the experiments received a major setback due to political developments. In 1939, Congress ministries in the provinces resigned in order to protest against India's involvement in the Second World War. The Individual Satyagraha (1940) and Quit India (1942) campaigns led by Gandhi resulted in large-scale arrests of participants and the closure of institutions inspired by his ideas. The government became suspicious of the educational experiments and feared that the new institutions provided the inspiration for anti-British activities. Especially, the Hindustani Talimi Sangh was under suspicion; and by 1942, fifteen of its members were imprisoned.[35] The experiments were interrupted in most places, teachers arrested and schools closed down. After 1946, when the Congress governments resumed their work, a second phase of expansion of 'basic' education and other institutions of Nai Talim followed.

33. Hindustani Talimi Sangh, *Sixth Annual Report (1938–1944)*, Sevagram (Wardha), 1944, p. 1.
34. E. W. Aryanayakam, *The Story of Twelve Years*, Sevagram (Wardha): Hindustani Talimi Sangh, 1950.
35. Marjorie Sykes, *The Story of Nai Talim: Fifty Years of Education at Sevagram (1937–1987)*, Sevagram (Wardha): Nai Talim Samiti, 1988.

Intentionally Constructed Representations of Work and Education

In the context of broader reforms, both the Argentinian Peronist government and the Indian independence movement promoted not only new designs of education related to work. In both cases, these designs went hand in hand with the construction and dissemination of new representations (concepts, values, convictions) related to work that aimed at replacing hitherto dominant representations. These constructed and disseminated representations constitute a third axis of our comparative study, since, as already presented at the beginning of this essay, its leading hypothesis is that these representations supported the implementation of the new education models.

In the case of Argentina, before the Peronist era, the execution of manual work was not lucrative and was associated with servitude and even impurity of blood. For a long time, apprenticeship did not mean learning and ascending in a trade or craft. Apprentices were more often slaves, women and children, who served primarily as cheap workforce.[36] The Peronist government tried to substitute these meanings and values related to manual work, workers and their training by disseminating new ones through massive propaganda.

The Peronist government presented the worker as the leading actor of the new social and political order through monuments (see Figure 7.4) and festivals, as well as official magazines, schoolbooks, posters (see Figures 7.5 and 7.6) and speeches. As the following images suggest, it shaped the worker as a national hero and as the constructor of the fatherland. In the words of Perón, the workers were 'the ones who construct the greatness of Argentina'.[37]

36. José M. Mariluz Urquijo, *La industria sombrerera porteña (1780–1835): Derecho, sociedad, economía*, Buenos Aires: Editorial Dunken, 2002; See Hilda Sábato and Luis A. Romero, *Los trabajadores de Buenos Aires: La experiencia del mercado (1850–1880)*, Buenos Aires: Editorial Sudamericana, 1992.
37. From one speech of Perón in 1953, Juan D. Perón, *Obras Completas*, Band XVII, vol. 1, 1997, p. 334.

FIGURE 7.4: Monumento al descamisado ('Monument to the Shirtless One')

Source: Archivo General de la Nación, Argentina, 1953

FIGURE 7.5: 'Forging the Fatherland'

Source: María A. de Silveira, *Forjando la patria: libro de lectura para tercer grado*, 1953, cover of school text book for Standard 3

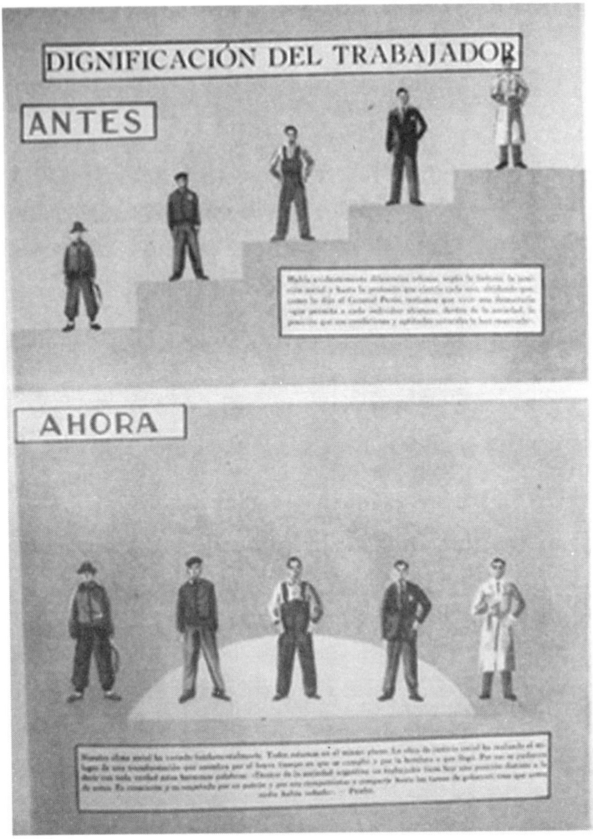

FIGURE 7.6: 'Dignification of the Worker'—Abolition of professional hierarchies in the Peronist complex of representations

Source: *La Nación Argentina: justa, libre y soberana*, 1950, p. 154

Thereby, manual work should no longer be considered as degrading. As a Peronist slogan said, 'work dignifies'. Accordingly, the Peronist discourse emphasised the abolition of professional hierarchies. Some posters from that time stressed that while 'in the past' the physician constituted the highest and the rural labourer the lowest grade of this hierarchy, 'in the present' the physician, the public officer, the industrial worker and the rural worker had the same professional value.

In the same vein, the importance of apprentices and their vocational training, too, was upgraded. Perón started, for instance, the 'Apprentice Day', which was celebrated on a large scale with apprentices' processions, ceremonial acts and awards ceremonies across the country every year. In speeches and official publications, the apprentice was portrayed as 'the definitive hope of the fatherland',[38] 'vital phalanx of the national society',[39] and 'the spring of the fatherland', as well as 'boosting force' that contributed to 'the greatness and progress of the Nation'.[40]

A radical shift of the hitherto dominant representations towards the 'dignity of manual labour' is also visible in the Indian case. Gandhi himself and his followers constructed and advertised a new set of representations opposed to the old representations of work and education as exemplified in the Brahmanical-cum-colonial paradigm (e.g., teaching and learning based on books for an elite group of society). In order to deconstruct the historically deeply embedded representations of work and education (e.g., the disregard of manual work) and to lend credibility to his political programmes aiming at transforming the society, Gandhi presented himself as the rural manual worker and created an iconic image: Gandhi sitting at the spinning wheel, dressed in the hand spun khadi dress of villagers. He thereby developed a rhetoric of hailing the spinning wheel:

> The message of the spinning-wheel is much wider than its circumference. Its message is one of simplicity, service of mankind, living so as not to hurt others, creating an indissoluble bond between the rich and the poor, capital and labour, the prince and the peasant.[41]

38. Comisión Nacional de Aprendizaje y Orientación Profesional, *Aprendizaje*, no. 3, 1952, p. 1.
39. Comisión Nacional de Aprendizaje y Orientación Profesional, *Aprendizaje*, no. 8, 1953, p. 3.
40. Comisión Nacional de Aprendizaje y Orientación Profesional, *Aprendizaje*, no. 11, 1953, p. 3.
41. Gandhi wrote this on 17 September 1925. See M. K. Gandhi, *The Collected Works of Mahatma Gandhi*, vol. 32.

The khadi dress, the spinning wheel, rural life in *ashrams* and Gandhi's ascetic-like body symbolising voluntary poverty, discipline and the suffering for the nation were central symbols of the Gandhian movement. Especially, the practice of spinning and the wearing of a unifying dress were used by Gandhi to create a collective identity of a mass movement.[42]

These symbols are also visible in the images on the implementation of Nai Talim with its central idea to connect education to everyday life in the villages and to organise learning processes in such a way that children would learn to support themselves with basic necessities such as food and clothing. The images depict scenes of happy communal rural life with children involved in production processes, as Figure 7.1 shows. Furthermore, the idea of creating a new social order through the connection between intellectual and manual work is dominant in the literature on Nai Talim, as this quotation from the Zakir Husain report shows:

> The introduction of such practical productive work in education to be participated in by all children of the nation will tend to break down the existing barriers of prejudice between manual and intellectual workers, harmful alike for both. It will also cultivate in the only possible way a true sense of the dignity of labour and of human solidarity—an ethical and moral gain of incalculable significance.[43]

Sources of Inspiration for the Institutional and Symbolic Constructions

In both cases the institutional and symbolic constructions were not completely new. On the contrary, some sources support our assumption that for their construction both the Peronist government and the Indian independence movement adopted ideas and models that already existed in their local contexts or abroad. Therefore, an additional focus of the research project is the examination of sources

42. See also Lisa Trivedi, *Clothing Gandhi's Nation: Homespun and Modern India*, Bloomington: Indiana University Press, 2007.
43. Hindustani Talimi Sangh, *Basic National Education. Report of the Zakir Husain Committee and Detailed Syllabus with a Foreword by Mahatma Gandhi*, Segaon (Wardha): Hindustani Talimi Sangh, 1939.

of inspiration and transfer processes for the vocational education designs as well as for the complex of representations. In this axis, we pay attention to similarities with local and foreign precedents, personal contacts, experiences and writings of key persons, and transformations of borrowed models and ideas by both movements. In the next few paragraphs we outline some of the paths we are following.

For the Argentinian case, we concentrate mainly on three dimensions: first, socio-economic and labour policies; second, visual and discursive representation of the worker, and third, design of vocational educational structures. In the first dimension we found out, for example, that a Spanish immigrant, José Figuerola, who had served as a functionary in the Spanish dictatorship of Primo de Rivera (1923–30), played a central role by defining Peronist socio-economic and labour policies.[44] In this first dimension, we also see that many of the Peronist social and labour policies seem to be actually the implementation of earlier projects designed mostly by socialist representatives, as well as of old, until-then unattended claims of the labour movement.[45]

European fascisms were certainly an important source of inspiration for the Peronist government. The literature on this topic mentions as some of the borrowed elements the *Führer*-principle, propaganda, and the use of the mass media.[46] Also, the construction

44. Raanan Rein, *The Second Line of Peronist Leadership: A Revised Conceptualization of Populism*, College Park: University of Maryland Press, 2000. Before migrating to Argentina, Figuerola served as a functionary in the Spanish dictatorship of Primo de Rivera. From 1930, he worked in the Argentinian Labour Department, dependent on the Ministry of the Interior. When Perón became Secretary of Labour in 1943, he entrusted Figuerola more responsibilities and made him one of his closest political advisors. Figuerola, who had a deep knowledge of the workers' situation, had a great influence in the socio-economic programme of the Peronist government.
45. See Carlos S. Fayt, *Naturaleza del peronismo*, Buenos Aires: Viracocha, 1967.
46. See Alberto Ciria, 'La doctrina peronista y sus Fuentes', *Mundo Nuevo*, no. 47, 1970, pp. 16–29.

and glorification of a 'new man'—in the Peronist case, mostly represented as a worker—has parallels with European regimes. But this aesthetic, more precisely, seems to have similarities with American and Soviet portrayals of Roosevelt and Stalin respectively, as a recent art history study highlights.[47]

In the case of vocational education, there are virtually no studies examining its local precedents or entanglements with experiences abroad. Nevertheless, the sources we collected suggest commonalities between Peronist structures and earlier ideas circulating at the local as well as at the international level. At the local level, firstly, we find significant commonalities with the ideas that a Catholic organisation (Círculo de Obreros Católicos) had been propagating and defending for many years; and secondly, with a bill drafted by a socialist representative, Américo Ghioldi, in 1942. Internationally, the ideas from the Catholics, Américo Ghioldi, and Peronist functionaries may have been influenced by the models of vocational education promoted by the International Labour Organization, especially in 1938 and 1939, as some references suggest. The Peronist structures show similarities to Spanish structures too; and this is probably to trace back to the horizon of reference of some Peronist functionaries.

All these (in part, cross-linked) connections support the idea that the Peronist regime was original not because of its postulations and policies, which at least partially circulated before the existence of the government. Rather, it was original due to its capacity of adopting, integrating and implementing them. In this sense, Perón and his government were able assimilators of existing, still-unattended claims.

Similar observations can be made in the Indian case. The available literature and our sources suggest that Gandhi's conceptions of a new social order (including education) were premised on the ideas of intellectuals and organisations both in India and abroad. Gandhi's comprehensive ideas about society and economy borrowed and

47. See Marcela Gené, *Un mundo feliz. Imágenes de los trabajadores en el primer peronismo (1946–1955)*, Buenos Aires: Fondo de Cultura Económica, 2005.

integrated demands, proposals, and concepts like, amongst others, the boycott of imported goods and the revival of traditional handicrafts from the Swadeshi Movement; representations of justice from John Ruskin;[48] representations of the Indian village before colonisation in European writings,[49] and the ideas of non-violent resistance from Leo Tolstoy.[50] With regard to education, Nai Talim also took on and combined ideas that had been circulating locally and internationally well before his concept was discussed at a national level. For example, the idea to establish indigenous educational institutions teaching practical skills had already been developed during the Swadeshi Movement (1903–08). In the context of the boycott of British and other foreign goods as a means to protest against the partition of Bengal, the debate about how to overcome economic dependence led to experimentation with vocational education.[51]

For the examination of Gandhi's ideas of education in the context of village development and 'rural reconstruction', an important connection is that between Gandhi and Rabindranath Tagore. There already existed a concrete programme of rural development connected to educational institutions that Gandhi must have been aware of by the time he proposed his ideas on education. Tagore had established a school (that later expanded into a national university)

48. In his autobiography, he writes about how he was inspired by the ideas of John Ruskin. He summarises Ruskin's main ideas like this: '1. That the good of the individual is contained the good of all.; 2. That a lawyer's work has the same value as the barber's inasmuch as all have the same right of earning their livelihood from their work.; 3. That a life of labour, i.e., the life of the tiller of the soil and the handicraftsman is the life worth living.' See M. K. Gandhi, *The Collected Works of Mahatma Gandhi*, vol. 44, p. 313.
49. See Surinder S. Jodhka, 'Nation and Village: Images of Rural India in Gandhi, Nehru and Ambedkar', *Economic and Political Weekly*, vol. 37, no. 32, 2002, pp. 3343–53.
50. B. Srinivasa Murthy, *Mahatma Gandhi and Leo Tolstoy Letters*, Long Beach: Long Beach Publications, 1987.
51. See also Haridas Mukherjee, *The Origins of the National Education Movement*, Calcutta: National Council of Education, 2000.

in the rural setting of Shantiniketan in Bengal in 1905. In 1923, Leonard Elmhirst, an agricultural scientist from New York, opened the Sriniketan Institute for Rural Reconstruction under Tagore's supervision. There was a close relationship between Gandhi and Tagore even at the institutional level. After 1938, teachers from Shantiniketan came to Gandhi's Sevagram in Wardha to impart 'basic' education and to establish a teacher training centre.[52]

Gandhi's educational ideas also reveal commonalities with the ideas of educational thinkers and the movements and institutions outside India. In particular, the idea of a 'holistic' education (the education of 'head, heart and hands'), in which manual education played an important role, is reminiscent of the ideas of the progressive education movement that gained considerable influence throughout Europe and the United States in the early-twentieth century.[53] There is evidence that Christian missionary societies active in India channelised progressive educational ideas from Europe and the United States to their educational institutions in India.[54] There may also have been other networks through which these ideas filtered into India. Progressive educators were active in the New

52. E. W. Aryanayakam, the founder secretary of the Hindustani Talimi Sangh, had worked with Tagore before. He and his wife, Asha Devi Aryanayakam, were the main force behind the institutionalisation of Nai Talim in Sevagram and other parts of India. See E. W. Aryanayakam, *The Story of Twelve Years*, Sevagram (Wardha): Hindustani Talimi Sangh, 1950.
53. Hermann Röhrs writes about the movement: 'Something approximating what might be termed a global education conscience took shape, with figures such as Tolstoi, Blonski no less operative than John Dewey, William H. Kilpatrick, Helen Parkhurst, Alexander Neill, Maria Montessori, Paul Geheeb and Georg Kerschensteiner.' See p. 183 in Hermann Röhrs, 'The New Education Fellowship: An International Forum for Progressive Education', in *Progressive Education Across the Continents: A Handbook*, eds. Hermann Röhrs and Volker Lenhart, Frankfurt: Peter Lang, 1995, pp. 179–91.
54. Joseph Bara, 'Christian Missionaries and Popular Education in India, 1910–40', *Indian Social Science Review: A Multidisciplinary Journal*, vol. 2, no. 2, 2000, pp. 301–33.

Education Fellowship, a network that aimed to spread the new ideas on education.[55] This network was active mainly (but not only) in Europe and the United States. So far, no research has taken place on the activities of the New Education Fellowship in India. We have found, however, a speech by Tagore on the occasion of a meeting of the fellowship in Calcutta in 1936, in which he invited the participants to come and visit his institution after the conference.[56] An important personal connection with ideas of progressive education existed through Zakir Husain, Gandhi's close companion in the implementation of Nai Talim. Husain had studied in Berlin in the 1920s, and was highly impressed by German progressive experiments such as the Odenwaldschule and the German reformer of vocational education, Georg Kerschensteiner.[57] Gandhi also met Maria Montessori in London in 1931, while he was there for the second Round Table Conference. Montessori was in India between 1939 and 1945; however, there is no evidence that Gandhi and Montessori met while she was in India.[58]

55. Kevin J. Brehony, 'A New Education for a New Era: The Contribution of the Conferences of the New Education Fellowship to the Disciplinary Field of Education, (1921–1938)', *Paedagogica Historica*, vol. 40, no. 5, 2004, pp. 733–55.
56. Rabindranath Tagore, *The English Writings of Rabindranath Tagore*, New Delhi: Sahitya Akademi, 1996, p. 814.
57. See for example Ziaul Hasan Faruqui, *Dr. Zakir Hussain: Quest for Truth*, New Delhi: APH Publishing Corporation, 1999; Joachim Oesterheld, 'Zakir Husain: Begegnungen und Erfahrungen bei der Suche nach moderner Bildung für ein freies Indien', in *Abgrenzung und Aneignung in der Globalisierung: Asien, Afrika und Europa seit dem 18. Jahrhundert. Ein Arbeitsbericht*, Berlin: Das Arabische Buch, 2001.
58. Gerald Lee Gutek, *The Montessori Method, The Origins of an Educational Innovation: Including an Abridged and Annotated Version of Maria Montessori's 'The Montessori Method'*, Oxford: Rowman & Littlefield, 2004, p. 39.

Sustainability of the Symbolic and Institutional Constructions

In both contexts, the disseminated representations were intentionally constructed to support the radical shifts that the Peronist government and the Indian independence movement projected in their respective countries. In that sense, the new representations that opposed historically grown and hitherto dominant social representations, were artificial and strongly connected to particular political programmes. Consequently, with the decline of the leaderships of Perón and Gandhi, their constructed complex of representations, too, were dissolved. At the same time, the created vocational educational structures were disregarded or were gradually dismantled. In this fifth axis, we trace these developments after the decline of both movements, in order to further prove our hypothesis about the linkage between *representations related to work* and *structures of education for work*.

In Argentina, after the overthrow of Perón's government in 1955, the succeeding governments suppressed its complex of ideas and symbols and reformed Peronist vocational education. They not only prohibited the use of Peronist terms, but also pulled down monuments and destroyed a large number of publications and visual material. Thereby, they especially suppressed the political centrality of the worker-figure and the discourse and festivities related to it. According to our hypothesis, we maintain that with the suppression of the glorifying representations of work and workers, the vocational education system lost its semantic basis. In fact, the post-Peronist governments shifted the focus from vocational education for factory-workers to polytechnic education for technicians. In doing so, the vocational education system that had been created for factory workers was gradually dissolved, and elementary vocational education became once again marginal and informal.

Nai Talim, with its idea of education through rural crafts was envisioned to be a radical break with the legacy of the Brahmanical-cum-colonial paradigm that had dominated representations of education and work in early-twentieth-century India. In the decades between 1937 and 1964, 'basic' education as part of Nai Talim was implemented on an experimental basis parallel to the existing education system. Between 1949 and 1956, the number of 'basic' schools increased from 32,182 to 47,814, while the number of students in these schools nearly doubled (from 2,535,710 to 5,060,207).[59] However, its implementation always paralleled the 'old' (colonial) education system. The net addition to primary schools following the old system outnumbered the new and converted 'basic' schools.[60] Nai Talim was never extended beyond this experimental basis, and totally disappeared from official educational policy documents after 1964. The concept had been heavily criticised from the beginning of the debates about it, and it gradually lost its public and political support. The loss of Gandhi's charismatic leadership was probably the most serious problem for the implementation of his ideas of a new social order. After Gandhi's assassination in 1948, his ideas slowly lost political support. The development model followed by the Jawaharlal Nehru-led Congress governments after Independence was based on socialist ideas of centralised planning and import-substituting industrialisation, which had very limited potential for the incorporation of Gandhi's ideas of a self-sufficient village society. However, the break with the representations of work in the Indian case is not as radical as in the Argentinian case. Even though Gandhi's ideas lost their basis of a charismatic leadership, they continued to function as an important pattern for legitimising concepts of village welfare schemes such as adult education programmes ('social' education) in the decades following independence. Remnants of the vision of Nai Talim are still present today, and appear as a recurring pattern to criticise problems in education.[61]

59. National Institute of Basic Education, *Progress of Basic Education (1949–50–1955–56)*, New Delhi: Government of India, 1958.
60. M. E. Sinclair and Kevin Lillis, *School and Community in the Third World*, London: Croom Helm in association with the Institute of Development Studies, Sussex, 1980, p. 54.
61. Krishna Kumar, *Crafts at School*, *India Seminar*, no. 570, February 2007.

8

The Genesis of Curzon's University Reforms, 1899–1905

Suresh Chandra Ghosh

Curzon's viceroyalty of India is noted not only for the successful creation of a North-West Frontier Province under tribal administration; restoration of Afghan confidence by a wise restraint based on the concentration of power; countering of Russian penetration of northern Persia by strengthening British influence in the south and warding off any attack from the Persian Gulf by a display of British naval power, and his failed dealings with Tibet which became the swansong of British imperialism in Central Asia, but also for many internal reforms which have left a lasting impact on us. While the partition of Bengal was a bitter pill for our ancestors to swallow, there are other areas where his internal reforms acted as beacon for our future development. For example, Curzon added 6,000 miles to the existing 27,000 miles of railways introduced by Dalhousie, and created a new railway board to operate the railways and plan future development. He created a new department of commerce and industry headed by a sixth member of the viceroy's council. As a sequel to the ravages of the famine of 1899, in the first year of his administration he not only developed an elastic system of land assessment and passed the Punjab Land Alienation Act to stop the eviction of cultivators from their lands for debt, but also established co-operative credit societies to liberate the peasants from the moneylenders. He further expanded the works of the department of irrigation to cover nearly 6.5 million acres of the land for cultivation, and worked for the scientific development of agriculture by creating an agricultural department with laboratories and experimental farms and a research institute at Pusa in Bihar. In his great concern and love for Indian art and architecture, he not only patronised the Asiatic Society of Bengal, but also created the department of archaeology to serve the twin purposes of conservation of the artistic heritage as well as carrying out fresh excavations. He conceived and carried out the project of the stately Victoria Memorial Hall at Calcutta as a monument of British rule. He founded the Imperial Library which he wanted to see as a future Bodleian Library or a British Museum of the East.

However, it was Curzon's attempt at the reform of university education which kept him busy for the entire period of his viceroyalty; and unlike his other reforms, formed a bridge between his administrative and political work. For education was rapidly becoming, since 1835, an important aspect in the lives of many Westernised Indians. The non-Muslims generally did not participate in educational activities sponsored by the state during the period of Muslim rule, except during the reign of Akbar. In the nineteenth century, however, their descendants saw in the Western education and ideas imparted by the British rulers an opportunity for liberation through the realisation of their aspirations for immediate employment and a gradual move towards self-government. And this dream of the Western-educated youth directly threatened the very existence and interests of the British Raj in India. So a dexterous jugglery and a shrewd manoeuvring of policies vis-à-vis higher education to control its further expansion was the need of the hour; and Curzon came forward, immediately after his arrival as viceroy, to meet the growing challenge with his projected reform of university education in the country.

The Indian Universities Act of 1904

In 1904, Curzon was the moving force behind the enactment of the Indian Universities Act. The Act was intended to introduce radical changes into the five existing universities of Calcutta, Bombay, Madras, Punjab (in Lahore) and Allahabad. These changes included: (a) an enlargement of the functions of the university; (b) a reduction in the size of the university senates; (c) the introduction of the new principle of election to the senate; (d) statutory recognition of the syndicates where university teachers were to be more adequately represented; (e) stricter conditions for the affiliation of colleges to a university, and (f) a definition of the territorial limits of the universities. The Act provided for a grant of Rs. 5 lakh each year for five years in order to carry out these changes in the five universities, and conferred powers on the government to make additions and alterations while approving the regulations passed by the university senates.[1]

The new law, which had not found favour with educated Indians, faced difficulties almost as soon as the government began to implement it. Very soon after the selection of the provisional syndicate, the validity of the directions issued by the chancellor of the University of Bombay for the holding of elections by the faculty of that university was challenged in the Bombay High Court.[2] There was evidence that similar action would be taken at Calcutta, and that the controversy would soon 'extend to Madras, Allahabad, and Lahore and that litigation may become general'.[3] Curzon wanted, by legislation suggested by the governor of Bombay,[4] to put a speedy end to the doubts raised about the interpretation of the Indian Universities Act and the validity of some of the directions issued under it by the chancellors; he wished to do so by introducing a bill in his legislative council validating the action of the chancellors and the constitution of the senates and the syndicates.[5] The Validating Bill was passed on 10 February 1905. It stated that all directives

1. See Papers Relating to the Act VIII of 1904, Calcutta, 1904.
2. Telegram from the Governor of Bombay to the Viceroy, 24 January 1905, Curzon Papers, Microfilm Reel no. 11 (Hereafter cited as 'Reel'.), Curzon Papers on microfilm in the National Archives of India, New Delhi
3. Proceedings of the Legislative Council, 3 February 1905, nos. 20–29, p. 36.
4. Lamington to Curzon, 28 January 1905, Letter 77, Curzon Papers, Reel 11.
5. Curzon to Brodrick, 3 February 1905, Letter 92, Curzon Papers, Reel 6.

issued under the authority of the Indian Universities Act of 1904 had been duly issued and constituted.[6]

Curzon was preoccupied with the question of university reform from the very beginning of his term as the viceroy of India in January 1899, and he continued to be so until the end of his term in 1905. On the eve of the enactment of the Act of 1904, while addressing the convocation of the University of Calcutta, Curzon observed that he 'now' occupied the unusual position of the last chancellor of an old regime, addressing the last senate and the last syndicate of an era that was about to disappear:

> There may be some who think that they see in the Vice-Chancellor and myself the two chief executioners, about to admonish their victims before leading them to the scaffold, and who may think that the position is one of some painfulness and restraint. But I can assure this convocation on behalf of my honourable colleagues as well as for myself that we entertain no such feelings. For the patient in our view is in no wise doomed to extinction, but is about to reappear with a fresh lease of life; and the instruments of the sentence held in their hand, [are] not the executioner's axe, but the phial that contains the elixir of a new and happy resurrection.[7]

The Acts of Incorporation and the Establishment of Universities in Calcutta, Bombay and Madras

According to Curzon's declaration at the convocation, the object of the Indian Universities Act was to cure the universities of the various ills which had plagued them since their birth. The majority of these ills could be traced to the Acts of Incorporation passed by the governor-general and viceroy, Lord Canning, in January 1857, which provided for the establishment of universities in Calcutta, Bombay and Madras. The direction to set up universities on the model of the University of London was provided by the Education

6. Act No. 11 of 1905. See Appendix in Legislative Assembly Proceedings, February 1905, nos. 20–29, p. 63.
7. *University of Calcutta Convocation Addresses*, 3 vols., Calcutta, 1915, vol. III, p. 955.

Despatch of 1854 (popularly known as Wood's Despatch after its author, Charles Wood, president of the Board of Control between 1853 and 1855 and secretary of state for India between 1859 and 1866) which was received by Canning's predecessor, Lord Dalhousie. Dalhousie himself would have taken immediate steps to establish the universities but for an ambiguity in the wording of the paragraph relating to their establishment, which asked him to report to London about procedures to be adopted.[8] Accordingly, Dalhousie set up a committee, and it was on the recommendations of this committee that the Acts of Incorporation of the universities were passed.

The preambles in the Acts of Incorporation establishing the three universities were identical. They defined the objects of the universities to be 'ascertaining by means of examination the persons who have acquired proficiency in different branches of Literatures, Science and Art and of rewarding them by Academic Degrees as evidence of their respective attainments'. There was to be a chancellor, a vice-chancellor and fellows, both ex-officio and ordinary, who together would constitute the 'Body Politic and Corporate' for each of the three universities. The number of fellows excluding the chancellor and vice-chancellor was to be not less than thirty. While the fellows ex-officio were to hold their fellowships during their official tenure only, the ordinary fellows were to be appointed by the government for life—vacancies in their ranks could arise only by death, resignation or permanent retirement from India in the case of European officials, or by cancellation of the appointment by the government.[9]

In 1882, the University of the Punjab was established by a special Act of Incorporation. In 1887, another special Act of Incorporation established the fifth Indian university at Allahabad. The general framework of these two special Acts of Incorporation was similar to the Acts of 1857, though power was given to the senates of the Punjab and Allahabad Universities 'to appoint or provide for the

8. S. C. Ghosh, *Dalhousie in India, 1848–56*, Delhi: Munshiram Manoharlal, 1975, pp. 28–29.
9. See *Papers Connected with the Establishment of Universities in India*, Calcutta, 1857 and J. A. Richey (ed.), *Selections from Educational Records, Part II: 1840–59*, Calcutta, 1922, pp. 408 ff.

appointment of Professor and Lecturers'[10]—a privilege which was denied by the Acts of Incorporation of the first three universities. The first three universities were deliberately intended to be examining bodies only, in the same sense and on the same model as the then University of London.

These three Acts of Incorporation ignored an important passage in the Education Despatch of 1854 which suggested the possibility of 'professorships for the purpose of the delivery of lectures in various branches of learning for the acquisition of which, at any rate in an advanced degree, facilities do not now exist in other institutions in India'.[11] When the Universities of Punjab and Allahabad were accorded this privilege in 1882 and 1887 respectively, some Indians asked for its extension to the Universities of Calcutta, Bombay and Madras, but European officials closely connected with the universities refused it on two grounds. They said that the need for a teaching university had in reality been satisfied by the collegiate system which had sprung into existence since 1857. They also said that it would be vain and foolish to constitute professorships or lectureships for students more advanced than those who attended the college lectures, because there were insufficient students and courses, and no funds for the purpose.[12] Only in the case of the Punjab University, funds would come from an annual grant of Rs. 12,000 from the Government of India to maintain the Oriental Department and the classes on Oriental subjects.[13]

However, one major difficulty arising from the Acts of Incorporation of the five universities was the appointment of fellows to their senates. These unofficial fellows were appointed for life; there was no upper limit to the number of fellows to be appointed, though the minimum was fixed at thirty.[14] At Allahabad, the number of

10. J. P. Naik (ed.), *Selections from Educational Records*, Delhi: Manager of Publication, 1963, vol. II, pp. 319, 467.
11. Richey, *Selections from Educational Records*, pp. 372–73.
12. Home Education, A Progs., December 1901, nos. 122–29, p. 20.
13. Ibid., November 1899, nos. 25–27, para. 39, p. 74.
14. See *Papers Connected with the Establishment of Universities in India.*

fellows was indeed thirty,[15] but at Lahore the minimum was raised to fifty.[16] The number of fellows at Calcutta steadily rose from forty in 1857 to 220 in 1890. Lord Lansdowne, in his convocation address on 18 January 1890, recognised the anomaly and proposed to bring about its reduction gradually. How small an advance had been made could be seen from the fact that when Curzon came to India in the last week of December 1898, the number still stood at 200; helped by 'natural causes' and by his refusal to exercise the right of nomination, he was able to reduce it to a little over 180 in 1901.[17]

As regards the composition and qualifications of the 180 fellows, apart from those who had been elected, the practice had been for the chancellor to invite recommendations from the lieutenant-governor of Bengal (representing the provincial government), the vice-chancellor (who knew the working of the senate), and public figures he might care to consult. As a result, the fellowship had come to be regarded as a titular award, conferred without much reference to academic qualifications, but rather as a stage of promotion in one's career. Prominent British officials and Indians had been thus honoured. Although a good many drifted away from Calcutta into other provinces, their names continued on the list. Of those who continued to dwell in Bengal, many never attended the meetings of the senate. The list actually included the name of the lieutenant-governors of the North-Western Provinces and Punjab, although they were chancellors of the Universities of Allahabad and Punjab respectively. From time to time, names had been recommended by the provincial government and accepted by the chancellor with the purpose of recognising special interests such as medicine and engineering. The list of nominated fellows was on the whole a list of distinguished persons, but as Curzon later pointed out, 'it is largely an absentee list: and the distinction that it reflects is official or professional rather than academic'.[18]

15. Naik, *Selections from Educational Records*, p. 463.
16. Ibid., p. 317.
17. Home Education, A Progs., December 1901, nos. 122–29, p. 29.
18. Ibid., p. 21

In 1891, the privilege of voting in the election on a limited scale was conceded by Lansdowne to graduates of the university. This was done as an experiment, and there was no assurance of its continuation. The qualifications laid down, both for the electoral body and the elected, were the possession of an MA degree (BA before 1867) and holding a higher degree in any other faculty. In other words, the electorate could choose from among persons who shared their own qualifications.[19] This restriction was imposed on a reluctant senate to prevent election of political agitators from outside. However, the low standard of qualification formulated in 1891 had resulted in the creation of a large and heterogeneous electorate scattered throughout Burma, Assam, Bengal, the Central Provinces and Ceylon, a cleverly organised system of canvassing, and a thoroughly undistinguished list of fellows. Of the twenty-four fellows elected since 1891, two had died. Of the twenty-four, four had been chosen in 1892 on the basis of the right of the government to reserve occasional vacancies for the faculties of medicine and engineering or for eminent persons in education and literature. Of the remainder, sixteen were practicing lawyers and none was qualified for election by his degree in the faculty of law; none was a doctor of law. All were nominally elected on the grounds of their attainments in the faculty of arts; but only three had obtained a first class in their examinations in the faculty of arts, several a second class, and some had achieved only a third class. All the lawyers came from 'unaided colleges' where there had been no government supervision. Of the twenty-two living members, only two or three were engaged in genuine educational work and these were elected in the reserved categories.

Election was only achieved by systematic and elaborate canvassing. Lists were kept by 'the vakils of the elections' who having taken their degrees, had dispersed throughout India. Agents were employed to hunt them and canvass for them, and very considerable expense was incurred. No candidate had a chance of being returned without resort to these methods and the support of 'the vakils' party'. The system, whether looked at from the point of view of methods or of the quality of the elected, seemed to stand equally condemned. It was

19. *University of Calcutta Convocation Address*, pp. 633 ff.

felt that any chancellor who 'acquiesces in its continuance is shutting his eyes while a weapon is being forged which will ultimately extrude European standards and influence from the Senate altogether, and will hand over its government to a clique of political *frondeurs* who have no interest in education'.[20]

The syndicate of the University of Calcutta—the real governing body of the senate, which was the nominal and statutory governing body of the university—was in the anomalous position of lacking recognition in any statutes. No mention was made of any syndicate in the Act of 1857, but its origin could be traced to an interpretation of clause VIII of the Act of Incorporation which gave to the chancellor, vice-chancellor and fellows, powers to control university affairs, as well as to make and alter by-laws and regulations in general, touching on all matters regarding the university.[21] The senate had not only almost completely abdicated its functions to the syndicate, but its own annual meeting for purposes of business was held during the most inconvenient season of the year: on the third Saturday in April, when the majority of the Europeans were absent from Calcutta, as Maclean, the vice-chancellor later reported to Curzon.[22]

The Affiliated Colleges

The universities established in 1857 by the Acts of Incorporation were affiliating bodies, and no geographical limits to the areas of affiliation were indicated. The University of Calcutta, for example, functioned not merely for Bengal, but for Burma, Assam, the Central Provinces and Ceylon, and the affiliated colleges were dispersed from Simla and Mussorie to Indore and Jaipur, and from Jaffna and Batticaloa to Sylhet and Chittagong. Managed by their own governing bodies, the affiliated colleges were not part of the university. By no means were all of them residential institutions with a long history and tradition. They were created mostly through the

20. Home Education , A Progs., December 1901, nos. 122–29, p. 21.
21. Ibid., p. 21.
22. Maclean to Curzon, 23 April 1900, Letter 182, Curzon Papers, Reel 8.

generosity of philanthropic societies, missionary bodies, or wealthy Indians, interested in spreading education. For the most part, they were collections of lecture rooms, classrooms and laboratories. They had no control over their required courses of study which were laid out by the university. Their only function was to prepare students for examinations, which were set and conducted by the university. A large number of colleges—government, aided and unaided—were affiliated with each of the three universities, but the rules for affiliation framed by the university were not very strict. Indeed, the first rules for affiliation prepared by the University of Calcutta in February 1857 demanded, for example, only that the college seeking affiliation submit a declaration, countersigned by at least two members of the university senate, enumerating the staff and courses of study for the previous two years and of the institution's ability to impart education up to the standard of a BA degree.[23] Despite the Hunter Commission's attempt in 1882 to enforce a stricter application of the rules regarding affiliation, the growth in the number of affiliated colleges continued unabated. When Curzon came to India, the total number of affiliated colleges in the whole of British India was 191, of which 145 were arts colleges and the rest professional colleges, including thirty in law, five in teaching, three in agriculture, four in medicine, and four in engineering.[24]

Thus, the universities were not merely examining bodies—their influence extended far beyond examinations in consequence of their practical power to refuse or permit the affiliation of colleges. They were independent of the provincial education departments in British India; the Education Despatch of 1854 had required such power for the provincial education departments. While a provincial education department could exercise control over the government and aided colleges, it had no control over the private colleges which had 'the chief part in the education of undergraduates' of the universities. The education departments were unable to banish politics from

23. University of Calcutta, *Hundred Years of the University of Calcutta 1857–1956*, Calcutta, 1957, p. 82.
24. R. Nathan, *Quinquennial Review of the Progress of Education*, 1897–98 to 1901–02, Calcutta, 1902.

the unaided colleges where the managers and professors were likely to educate their pupils 'in all the political and financial fallacies' antagonistic to the British connection. The number of such unaided colleges providing legal education was particularly high in Bengal where the students of law, perhaps more than any other class of students, were exposed to political ideas. It was feared that the government had made a mistake in letting 'the control of legal education go entirely out of its hands', by not providing a properly instituted government law college in Calcutta as it had done in Madras and Bombay.[25]

The affiliated colleges in different parts of British India could not have been expected to maintain a high and uniform academic standard; there was no separate education department in the Government of India, as there was in England, with an organisation for the whole of British India. Madras normally produced considerably more graduates than Calcutta and many more than Bombay, Allahabad and Punjab taken together; this aroused doubts about the standards adhered to by the affiliated colleges of the University of Madras.[26] Many of the affiliated colleges that came into existence as a result of the local and private efforts before Curzon's viceroyalty were 'weak, understaffed and incapable of affording the individual attention either to the needs of the student or of providing the varied courses of study, practical as well as literary'.[27] This was still the case in 1917 when the Calcutta University Commission reported on the state of higher education in Calcutta.

The Confrontation with the University of Calcutta

Within three months of his arrival in India, Curzon's confrontation with the University of Calcutta began. In March 1899, he learned that the university had frustrated the attempt of the government

25. Home Education, November 1899, nos. 25–27, paras. 41–45, pp. 80–85.
26. Ibid., pp. 74–75.
27. *Report of the Calcutta University Commission*, 1917–19, 13 vols., Calcutta, 1919–20, vol. 1, pp. 59–60.

of Bengal to introduce William Lee-Warner's *Citizen of India* as a textbook. According to a clause in the Acts of Incorporation, the senates alone enjoyed the power to prescribe textbooks in affiliated colleges. Since they were independent of governmental control, they enjoyed and often took delight in slighting and thwarting proposals put to them by the provincial governments. Curzon was astonished that Lee-Warner's 'excellent manual' could not be introduced into any government school or college in India because the committee on which there was a majority of 'Babus and only one government representative, had declined to admit it'.[28] He informed Hamilton, the secretary of state for India, that he was going to Simla to think how 'the management of our educational system' could be brought under 'central authority and government control'.[29] Curzon wrote to Arthur Godley, permanent under-secretary of state:

> I have seen enough to know that in its desire to decentralize, government has surrendered its control to a very dangerous degree, and that the Local Governments, inspired by their attractive example, have also forfeited a good deal of their necessary authority. In fact, the management of Education has gradually drifted into the hands of Committees or bodies upon which Englishmen are often in a numerical minority, who exercise their power in mischievous independence of Government.[30]

It was because of this that Burke's *Reflections on the French Revolution*, which was 'certainly dangerous food for Indian students', could be selected as a textbook.[31] While in Simla, Curzon gave much thought to the subject of education. Godley told him that if Woodburn's observation that the University of Calcutta 'alone in India, is independent of the Local Government and its delight is to slight and thwart it' were correct, 'it would seem to be in need

28. Curzon to Hamilton, 23 March 1899, Letter 12, Curzon Papers, Reel 1.
29. Ibid.
30. Curzon to Godley, 18 October 1899, Letter 48, Curzon Papers, Reel 1.
31. Curzon to Maclean, 14 February 1900, Letter 44, Curzon Papers, Reel 8.

of your reforming hand'.[32] However, more information was needed before the idea of reform could be mooted. Curzon, in addition to consulting Woodburn, consulted Sir Stafford Northcote and Lord Northbrook, both of whom were then in England. The consultation with Northbrook was particularly useful because he had, as Charles Wood's secretary, drafted the Education Despatch of 1854.[33] Curzon also asked his secretary, Luson, as well as Fraser, a member of his council, to prepare elaborate comments on Cotton's *Quinquennial Review of the Progress of Education from 1882–3 to 1896–7*. When these were ready, his observations on their comments provided the basis for the issue, on 28 October 1899, of the resolution on education by the Government of India, which specified the areas where governmental control was necessary.[34] However, Curzon did not follow it up by other administrative orders and actions since he did not consider the moment opportune. Preoccupied with the famine and the frontier problem, he had no alternative but to move slowly in the field of education. He had always been a firm believer in the maxim about going slowly. He knew that the 'prudent' general reconnoitred his country before he delivered the final assault.[35]

Much of Curzon's time was taken up by his thorough and absorbing investigation into the subject of higher education since 1857, as well as in the selection of a successor to Maclean whose term as the vice-chancellor of the University of Calcutta was coming to an end. Curzon's first choice was one of his personal friends, the bishop of Calcutta, who 'would assist me in the schemes which I have in view for co-ordinating and controlling the higher education

32. Godley to Curzon, 15 December 1899, letter 74, Curzon Papers, Reel 1.
33. 'It is 47 years ago since I wrote for C. Wood the Education Despatch of 1854', Northbrook to Curzon, 12 December 1901, Letter 44, Curzon Papers, Reel 6, See also S. C. Ghosh, 'Dalhousie, Charles Wood and Education Despatch of 1854', *History of Education*, vol. 4, Summer 1975, p. 38.
34. Home Education, November 1899, pp. 133–36.
35. C. S. Raghunatha Rao (ed.), *Notable Speeches of Lord Curzon,* Madras: Arya Press, 1905, p. 240.

of this country'.[36] However, Woodburn pointed out that at least one reason why the office was so frequently given to judges of the high court was that the lawyers who preponderated in the senate were amenable to no one but a judge.[37] Woodburn anticipated 'stormy times' in the senate during the next two years in view of Curzon's scheme of reorganising higher education; there would, therefore, it would be advantageous to have as influential a head of the senate as could be found for the period.[38] 'And the only person I can think of as an alternative to the Bishop', he wrote, 'is Mr. Raleigh.' Raleigh was a member of Curzon's legislative council, since there was at that moment no judge on the bench who would fit the post.[39] Curzon agreed,[40] and towards the end of August 1900, appointed Raleigh as the vice-chancellor of the University of Calcutta. Raleigh, like Curzon, had been an undergraduate and a graduate of Balliol College, Oxford, under Benjamin Jowett; he later became a fellow of All Souls when Sir William Anson was warden. While Curzon had been 'swept off his feet in the mill-race of English politics', Raleigh became an Oxford don.[41] Curzon hoped that Raleigh's abilities and academic knowledge would now find fuller scope in this new assignment.[42]

Deliberations on Reform Begin

Aided by Raleigh who 'had the leisure, as well as the inclination to devote himself more exclusively to university affairs',[43] Curzon

36. Curzon to Woodburn, 13 July 1900, Letter 10, Curzon Papers, Reel 8.
37. Woodburn to Curzon, 24 July 1900, Letter 30, Curzon Papers, Reel 8.
38. Ibid.
39. Ibid.
40. Curzon to Woodburn, 29 July 1900, Letter 43, Curzon Papers, Reel 8.
41. Home Education, December 1901, nos. 122–29. p. 17.
42. Curzon to Godley, 29 August 1900, Letter 56, Curzon Papers, Reel 2.
43. Home Education, December 1901, nos. 122–29, p. 17.

prepared to deal with 'the most difficult perhaps and certainly most delicate' of all his tasks, as Dawkins wrote to him.[44] Until the arrival of the rains in Simla, Curzon suffered from 'a good deal more of personal weakness and back pain than last year', but once the rains arrived he felt much better and was able to devote full attention to his scheme.[45]

By 23 February 1901, his scheme was ready. He recorded an extremely long minute on the subject, revealing the tremendous capacity for hard work, for which he had a great reputation at Oxford, and for which he almost impaired his health in India. His main arguments in the minute were that legislation was necessary to enlarge the functions of the Indian universities from examining to teaching; to regulate the number, tenure and qualifications of the fellows, as well as to maintain a proper balance between Europeans and Indians, officials and non-officials, and between the various faculties or professions, and to reconstitute the electorate of graduates by adding residential qualifications (just as the convocation of Oxford now consisted of resident MAs) or rather such graduates as were capable of coming to the senate meetings to vote. He also wished to lay down some academic or educational criteria which would have to be met for election to the senate. He desired that the syndicate, which was the real executive body of the university, should have a statutory position. The objective was to narrow the geophysical areas of each university. Other aims were the strengthening of the law; the recognition, affiliation and withdrawal of affiliation (in cases where discipline had become lax and the standard had fallen too low); the curtailment of the power of the boards of studies which prescribed textbooks for the colleges, and the regulation of the courses of study of candidates preparing for university examinations. Finally, he wanted a resolution of the question of revocation of university degrees in cases where the holder had been convicted by a criminal

44. Dawkins to Curzon, 5 October 1900, Letter 187a, Curzon papers, Reel 6.
45. Curzon to Dawkins, 29 August 1900, Letter 143, Curzon Papers, Reel 6.

court.[46] After listing the legislative action needed to tighten control over universities, Curzon still felt that his plate was not full:

> There are doubtless other subjects affecting the case for or against legislation which have not occurred to me, or of which I am ignorant.... There also remains the question as to the competence of the Government of India to reform (either by legislative or by executive action) the University of Calcutta without reference to the case of the universities of Madras and Bombay; and even if the competence be indisputable, the expedience or desirability of the same.[47]

It was, therefore, necessary to consult a body of experts. Six months after he had drafted the proposals for the reform of the universities, he summoned a conference at Simla to examine his proposals.[48]

The first educational conference met at Simla on 2 September 1901. It was attended by Curzon and members of his council, the vice-chancellors of the Universities of Calcutta, Bombay and Madras, the directors of public instruction in Bengal, Bombay, Madras, the North-Western Provinces and Punjab, the inspector-general of education in the Central Provinces and Punjab, the principal of the Deccan College at Poona, the principal of the School of Arts in Madras, the reporter on economic products to the Government of India, and finally, Curzon's secretary, Risley.[49] No Indian expert was invited, though the conference was going to discuss 'confidentially'[50] a subject which concerned the Indians most. 'The private ... hole-and-corner character of the Conference' had become a subject of much discussion among the Indians—hence Curzon thought of opening the conference with a statement which could be communicated to the press. In it, he intended to outline all the features in which 'our

46. Home Education, December 1901, nos. 122–29, pp. 19–27.
47. Ibid., p. 28.
48. Curzon to Godley, 1 May 1901, Letter 32, Curzon Papers, Reel 2, Curzon to Woodburn, 28 May 1901, Telegram 160, Curzon Papers, Reel 2.
49. Home Education, December 1901, nos. 47–71, p. 9.
50. Curzon to MacDonnell, 3 August 1901, Letter 34, Curzon Papers, Reel 9.

system' was deficient and to indicate the lines on which reform ought to proceed.[51] Curzon wrote to Hamilton:

> India is a country where you can do almost everything provided that you allow your critics and opponents to have their say. I shall, therefore, invite the fullest discussion on all the points to be mentioned by me.... I think it very likely that in the case of universities for the reform of which we shall almost inevitably be compelled to resort to legislation, I shall have to appoint a small preliminary commission to go around and take evidence at Calcutta, Madras, and Bombay, and allow the instructed M.A.s and B.A.s who swarm at these capitals to have their say in advance.[52]

Curzon himself meticulously planned and drafted the strictly confidential agenda papers. The first subject to be taken up for discussion by the conference was university education. In his strictly confidential agenda papers, he listed thirteen items on the subject. These included, among others, the scope and character of Indian universities, the administration of Indian universities, academic standards, the affiliation of colleges and the recognition of schools, the selection of textbooks and courses of instruction, and finally, the question: 'Is a commission desirable?'[53] Curzon divided the item on the administration of Indian universities into three parts. The first part bore on the reform of the senates, the second on the election of the fellows, and the third on the composition and function of the syndicates.[54]

As the discussion on university education advanced, it became more and more apparent to the participants that there had been 'a total lack of system, an ignorance of principles, and a want of uniformity in practice, that have reduced education in India to a state almost of chaos'.[55] By 10 September, the deliberations on university

51. Curzon to Hamilton, 28 August, 1901, Letter 59, Curzon Papers, Reel 2.
52. Ibid.
53. Home Education, November 1901, nos. 47–61, pp. 167–68.
54. Ibid.
55. Curzon to Hamilton, 11 September, 1901, Letter 62, Curzon Papers, Reel 2.

education were over, the delegates having passed unanimously no fewer than forty-five 'strictly confidential' resolutions,[56] each drafted by Curzon himself.[57] The delegates emphatically declared in favour of a thorough reform of the Indian universities. They also recommended that the powers of affiliation, recognition and prescribing textbooks should be strengthened; a director-general of Indian education should be appointed; the rules for examination and degrees should be co-ordinated and improved; the institution of hostels should be encouraged, and a minimum scale of fees should be fixed.[58] The conference also supported Curzon's decision to appoint a commission to examine university education in all its aspects.[59]

The Indian Universities Commission

In a telegram to Hamilton on 13 January 1902, Curzon proposed to appoint six persons as permanent members of the commission, including Raleigh who was to be the chairman.[60] The other five were Hewett, Pedler, Bourne, Mackichan and Syed H. Bilgrami.[61] Bilgrami was the only Indian representative, and when the appointment of the commission was made public after obtaining Hamilton's approval, the absence of a Hindu among the six permanent commissioners created a great stir since the Hindus had 'the largest interest in the educational problems that were to be considered'. Surendranath Banerjee, who had been dismissed on flimsy grounds from the Indian

56. Home Education, October, 1901, no. 19, pp. 25–28.
57. Curzon to Dawkins, 16 November, 1901, Letter 33, Curzon Papers, Reel 7.
58. Home Education, October 1901, no. 19, pp. 25–28.
59. Curzon to Dawkins, 16 November, 190, Letter 33, Curzon Papers, Reel 7.
60. Home Education, January 1902, no. 139, p. 15.
61. J. P. Hewett was Curzon's home secretary; A. Pedler was Director of Public Instruction for Bengal; A. G. Bourne was acting principal of the Madras Presidency College, the Rev. D. Mackichan was Principal of the Bombay Wilson College, and Syed H. Bilgrami, better known as Nawab Imad-ul-Mulk , was graduate of a British university.

Civil Service (ICS), and had earlier led the agitation in the civil service in 1876–77, raised 'a vigorous protest' in the columns of the *Bengalee*, which he himself edited, against 'this ostracism of the Hindu element'.[62] Indian public opinion supported Banerjee's view, and Curzon decided to send a private telegram to Hamilton seeking his approval for the nomination of Gooroodas Banerjee, a former vice-chancellor of the University of Calcutta, and now a prominent judge of the Calcutta High Court.[63]

In their collection of evidence from 'the disgruntled M.A.s and B.A.s', the permanent members of the commission were to be assisted by five local commissioners—Ashutosh Mukherjee for Bengal, Sankaran Nair for Madras, Chandavarkar for Bombay, and Lewis and Bell for North-Western Provinces and Punjab respectively.[64] While announcing the appointment of the Indian Universities Commission, Curzon also made an appointment to the newly created post of director-general of education, which had been discussed at the conference at Simla and later approved by Hamilton. Orange, who was a graduate of Oxford and was then working in the department of education as an examiner in Whitehall, was appointed to the post on the recommendation of Sadler,[65] who had been offered the post but had declined it.[66]

The Indian Universities Commission began its work in Madras on 18 February. After examining 156 witnesses, including

62. Surendranath Banerjee, *A Nation in the Making*, New York: Oxford University Press, 1925, p. 162.
63. Curzon to Hamilton, 7 February 1902, Telegram 91, Curzon Papers, Reel 5.
64. Home Education, January 1902, no. 139, p. 15. Mukherjee was the member of the Bengal Legislative Council; Nair a practicing lawyer at the Madras High Court; Chandrashekhar a judge at Bombay High Court, and Lewis and Bell were both directors of public instruction for the provinces they represented.
65. Hamilton to Curzon, 6 January 1902, Telegram 27, Curzon Papers, Reel 5.
66. Hamilton to Curzon, 11 November 1901, Telegram 378, Curzon Papers, Reel 5.

sixty-three Indians at different places, the commission submitted its recommendations on 9 June to Curzon, who was very pleased.[67] The commission's recommendations faithfully reflected Curzon's views on the reform of the Indian universities first elaborately delineated and endorsed at the conference at Simla; Gooroodas Banerjee disagreed with them in a note of dissent. On legislation to realise its recommendations, the commission felt—since the changes did not 'involve repeal of the existing Acts of Incorporation'—the legislature could 'give effect to our proposal by passing a General Indian University Act, which would be construed as supplementing and amending the Acts of Incorporation'.[68]

Curzon did not want to make public the recommendations of the commission, just as he had earlier prevented the proceedings of the conference at Simla from becoming public. A local newspaper obtained a copy of the report 'probably through the agency of some clerk', and began 'publishing a series of daily denunciations of the Government or rather of myself, for having rung the death-knell of higher education in India'.[69] Hamilton wrote:

> You are certain to be attacked if you attempt to in any way purify university Education and to free it from its existing excrescences. The Babu believes that one of the main objects for which British Rule was established in India was to enable him to get [a] university degree; and any attempt to heighten the standard is sure to meet with violent abuse. But I have been so long the subject of almost universal abuse and misrepresentation by the Indian Press, that I am compelled to attach little importance to what they say.[70]

A fortnight after Hamilton had despatched his letter to Curzon from London, Curzon wrote to Sir Henry Cotton on 31 August:

67. Curzon to Northbrook, 21 July 1902, Letter 102, Curzon Papers, Reel 7.
68. *Report of the Indian Universities Commission*, Simla, 1902, vol. 1, pp. 55ff.
69. Curzon to Hamilton, 23 July 1902, Letter 57, Curzon Papers, Reel 3.
70. Hamilton to Curzon, 13 August, 1902, Letter 57, Curzon Papers, Reel 3.

'The Bengalis are denouncing me like fury because the University Commission has reported in a sense that they dislike. They seem to think that I both dominated the enquiry and wrote the Report. What a strange people! They take the heart [out] of one.'[71] Ten days later he wrote to Hamilton: 'The Town Hall and the senate Hall of the university have been packed with shouting and perspiring graduates, and my name has been loudly hissed as the author of the doom of higher education.'[72]

The Reform Becomes Law

Curzon reacted to the 'fierce agitation'—as he described it in one of his letters to Hamilton—conducted by Indians not only in Bengal, but also in Bombay and Madras. He decided to consult the provincial governments before drafting the Indian Universities Bill which was drawn up on the basis of the recommendations of the commission. As there were few differences in the views offered in these deliberations, he went ahead with the drafting of the Indian Universities Bill.[73] At the same time, he asked Ibbetson, Risley and Orange to help him prepare a White Paper on education 'to assuage the ill-feeling that may be aroused in some quarters by the Universities Bill, and [so] that the public may be more inclined to accept reforms which are shown to be part of a great scheme, conceived on liberal principles and directed towards raising the standard, of every aspect of education'.[74] In the same vein and acting on the same principle, Curzon added a clause to the bill to provide financial assistance to the Indian universities for a period of five years 'to gild as much as we can, that somewhat unpalatable pill that we are offering to the native patient, and the greater the generosity that we can show at

71. Curzon to Cotton, 31 August 1902, Letter 124, Curzon Papers, Reel 7.
72. Curzon to Hamilton, 10 August 1902, Curzon Papers, Reel 3.
73. Home Education, December 1903, nos. 67–74, 77–80.
74. Curzon to Brodrick, 4 November 1903, Letter 83, Curzon Papers, Reel 4.

the present juncture, the more likely we are to disarm antagonism, and to succeed'.[75]

The White Paper on Indian education was issued on 11 March 1904, and the Indian Universities Bill was passed and became law on 21 March 1904. There was stiff resistance on every stage of its passage by G. K. Gokhale and Ashutosh Mukherjee. It marked the end of 'a long and arduous struggle conducted for five years in the face of every discouragement and of bitter opposition'.[76] Two days after the bill had been passed, Curzon privately sent an identical letter to the governors of Bombay and Madras and the lieutenant-governors of the North-Western Provinces and Bengal: 'The Universities Bill is now passed into Law; and the various Chancellors of the universities will before long be called upon to take action under it.'[77] Next day, he wrote to Godley: 'Here I have had the stiffest session on record, and have carried the Universities Bill, which was my child.'[78]

The Effects of the Spread of Higher Education from the mid-1850s

Curzon's university reforms were a high point in the development of the official attitude towards the spread of higher education which had been developing since the mid-1850s. It took place against the historical backdrop of the efforts made by English officials to spread Western higher education in the first half of the nineteenth century. The attempts were part of the wider programme of reforming Indian society and purging it of evils such as *sati*, infanticide, *purdah* and polygamy, and of bringing Indians and English officials closer together. These efforts had been strongly resisted in 1793 by the East India Company, partly because of its reluctance to interfere with Indian

75. Curzon to Godley, 23 September, 1903, Letter 69, Curzon Papers, Reel 4.
76. Curzon to Brodrick, 5 April, 1904, Letter 18, Curzon Papers, Reel 4.
77. Curzon Papers, Letter 15, Reel 11.
78. Curzon to Godley, 24 March, 1904, Letter 16, Curzon Papers, Reel.

society, and partly because of apprehensions about social disorder. The same efforts were revived later by Macaulay. This culminated in the governmental order that followed Macaulay's minute of February 1835, which made English the official language of British India, replacing Persian, and which forbade further expenditure on Oriental education. The changes were the fruits of the utilitarian ideas of young British officials in India, together with the enlightened ideas of a body of Indians headed by Raja Rammohan Roy.[79]

These Indians saw in the introduction of English education, among other benefits, an opportunity for employment in various British establishments, official as well as non-official, that were being set up in British India—in the metropolitan centres of Calcutta, Bombay and Madras and 'up-country'. They met the demand for local staff-members who assisted the officials of the East India Company—the writers and cadets—in the administration of these establishments. The East India Company authorised its Indian representatives to make local appointments for very poorly paid posts; Indians whom they appointed knew the English language, but they did not necessarily know English literature.[80] A modicum of higher education helped the Indians towards the attainments needed for these appointments. A number of colleges imparted Western education in the main urban centres of British India. Many of them, like the Hindu College established in 1817 (which became Presidency College in 1853 when Dalhousie reformed it), grew out of schools teaching the alphabet along with 'Shakespeare, the Calculus, Smith's *Wealth of Nations*, and the *Ramanyana*'. The number of students attending these colleges was not large; they could easily be absorbed in the service of the East India Company and other British institutions. They were active and eager participants in the British administration, and they stimulated the demand for higher education in Bombay, Calcutta and Madras. This led F. J. Mouat, secretary of the council

79. S. C. Ghosh, 'Formation of an Education Policy of the British Raj between 1757 and 1857' in *The Supply of Schooling*, ed. William Frijhoff, Paris: Pulications de la Sorbonne, 1983, pp. 43–56.
80. *Papers of the Indian Education Commission, 1881–82*, Calcutta, 1883, p. 18.

of education in Bengal, to submit a plan for university education in India in 1845. The Indians who demanded the provision of such education the most formed the nucleus of the Indian middle classes. They were admirers, not critics, of British administration because of the benefits they derived from it. When the revolt of 1857 broke out, they remained silent spectators. They had actually become the class envisaged by Macaulay in 1835: 'a class of persons Indian in blood and colour, but English in taste, in opinions, in morals and intellect.'

This situation changed in the second half of the mid-1850s. The starting point of the change may be regarded as the establishment of the three universities in Calcutta, Bombay and Madras in 1857. Henceforth, colleges became an integral part of the higher educational system of India. They admitted students who had passed the entrance or matriculation examinations conducted by the universities to which the colleges were affiliated, and they offered instruction only in such courses as had been prescribed by the universities. Contrary to Canning's expectation in 1857—that the universities in India would become 'an aristocratic institution' which could be mainly attended by the children of 'the nobility and upper classes of India'—they became 'popular institutions', attended largely by the children of the new middle classes that had emerged since the beginning of the nineteenth century.[81] Because of the pecuniary advantages of the possession of university degrees, a very large number of those who passed the matriculation sought admission to the universities. The number of colleges rose from twenty-seven in 1857 to fifty-five in 1873; the number of students rose from 219 in 1857 to 4,499 in 1873.[82] In 1881, the corresponding figures were eighty-five colleges and 7,582 students.[83] Between 1857 and 1873, the number of successful candidates in matriculation examinations rose to 12,392 in Calcutta, 5,502 in Madras and 2,703 in Bombay. The annual output of the recipients of the bachelor's degree also

81. University of Calcutta, *Hundred Years*, p. 127.
82. Appendix M, Statement 3, in *Report of the Public Service Commission, 1886–87*, Calcutta, 1888, p. 81.
83. Ibid.

increased after 1857. There were 175 graduates by 1870, 404 by 1880, and 470 by 1884.[84] The number of failures in the 'first arts' examination were 570 in 1870, 1,110 in 1880, and 1,289 in 1884.[85] Sir Henry Maine estimated the number of successful candidates for the 'first arts' examinations and the holders of BA and MA degrees from 1853 to 1883 to be 25,000 out of an estimated population of 250,000,000.[86]

Having received a good secondary school education up to the level of matriculation, and having attended university, these men were certainly highly educated, compared to the illiterate town-dwellers and villagers. They themselves were very much aware of this difference. What was the prospect open to the large number of students who had received such higher education? A career in the ICS was virtually never open to them, though the principle had been asserted time and again in the Charter Act of 1833 and the Queen's Proclamation of 1858 after the mutiny. Some avenues like the army and the legislatures were closed altogether. Agriculture offered no temptation to an educated person, and neither did manufacturing and commerce, since the latter was almost impossible without skill, capital and equality, in terms of competition with European businessmen.

The very nature of the courses of study with their 'unique and disproportionate attention' to literature and philosophy,[87] compared with technological and cognate branches of practical instruction, tended to limit the choice of a career to government service or similar employment.[88] 'What also can he do but qualify himself', lamented a Calcutta newspaper, 'or, if he is [a] father, train his son for the public service or one of the learned professions?'[89] In theory, the covenanted

84. Ibid.
85. Ibid., Appendix M, Statement 4, p. 82.
86. Lytton Strachey, *India*, London, 1903, p. 187.
87. For detail of the courses, see Richey, *Selections from Educational Records*, pp. 371 ff.
88. Richard Temple, *Men and Events of my Time in India*, London: Murray, 1882, pp. 432–33.
89. *Indian Mirror*, Calcutta, 13 February 1878.

civil service[90] had been open to Indians since 1853; but in practice, difficulties stood in their way. These included the low upper age-limit for the examination, the content of the syllabus, the expense of going to London where the examination was conducted, the Hindu prejudice against crossing the 'black water', and the official reluctance of the British to admit Indians into this vital service. Educated Indians could only avail themselves of posts at the lower level of the uncovenanted service which continued to remain open of them. The salaries in these posts were very low, prospects for promotions negligible, and conditions of service poor.[91]

Since men were not often employed outside their own provinces, less than 2,000 posts were available in the uncovenanted executive and judicial branches in Bengal, Bombay and Madras for the graduates of each of the universities in these areas. Not all of these were given to the educated. In Bombay and Madras, less than half of the uncovenanted civil servants had the qualifications offered by the new education, while in the North-Western Provinces and in Punjab most of these posts went to those without any educational qualifications.[92]

The creation of nine departments of education by 1879 in accordance with the provision of the Education Despatch of 1854, and the gradual development of a graded Indian educational system to serve these departments and the colleges under them, opened new vistas for employment in British India. Still, the posts in the uncovenanted service were not normally open to the educated Indians, but to the Europeans with qualifications from British universities, particularly from Oxford and Cambridge. In the whole of British India by 1879, only 5 per cent of the employees in the

90. For the origin of the elite service, see S. C. Ghosh, *The Social Condition of British Community in Bengal, 1757–1800*, Leiden: E. J. Brill, 1971, p. 11.
91. B. B. Misra, *The Central Administration of East Indian Company*, London: Manchester University Press, 1959, pp. 404 ff.
92. See Appendix 1 of the *Report of the Public Service Commission 1886–87*, pp. 51–55.

uncovenanted service were educated Indians, while the British made up 95 per cent.[93]

The paucity of suitable openings in the public service naturally compelled many to turn to independent professions such as teaching, law, journalism and medicine. Unlike the government servants who were inhibited by their dependence on the goodwill of the government which employed them, in these professions there was some opportunity to participate in public life. By the end of the 1870s, there was hardly any important town in India which did not possess a sprinkling of teachers, lawyers, journalists and physicians who took a very lively interest in the social, political, economic and religious problems of the day.[94] This group of persons later formed the backbone of the early Congress. Because of their complaints against the government, they were often distrusted and ridiculed by the European officials and the English press.[95]

What had been moderate difficulties of educated Indians in finding suitable employment in the 1850s had become an acute problem by the 1870s. A year before the establishment of the universities in India, the *Friend of India* had warned of the problem: 'Native education had gone so far that it has become one of the most serious problems of the day. What to do with our educated men.'[96] After 1857, higher education in India began to expand and the problems of finding employment also became aggravated. By 1877, it had reached such dimensions that Sir Richard Temple, the lieutenant-governor of Bengal, recorded the following minute:

> It is melancholy to see young men, who once appeared to receive their honours in the university convocation now applying for some

93. J. P. Naik and S. C. Ghosh (eds.), *Development of Educational Service 1854–74*, Delhi: Zakir Husain Centre for Educational Studies, Jawaharlal Nehru University, pp. 361–70.
94. Anil Seal, *The Emergence of Indian Nationalism*, Cambridge: Cambridge University Press, 1968, pp. 114–30.
95. 'Wretched pettifogger'—this is how Bengali lawyers were described by the *Pioneer* in July 1888, see Prem Narian, *Press and Politics in India*, Delhi: Munshiram Manoharlal, 1976, p. 196.
96. *Friend of India*, Calcutta, 11December 1856.

> lowly-paid appointment, almost begging from office to office, from department to department, or struggling for the practice of petty practitioner, and after all this returning baffled and disheartened to a poverty-stricken home, and then to reflect how far happier their lot might have been had they, while at school or college, been able to move in a healthier atmosphere of thought and freer walks of life. Nevertheless, with these examples before their eyes, hundreds, perhaps thousands of young men persist in embarking on the same course, which can lead only to the same sad ending.[97]

Unemployment among educated Indians made them discontented with the British Raj, which not only gave them no relief or sympathy, but excluded them from higher posts in the army, education and the civil service. They saw thousands of foreigners being given precedence in all the best appointments under the administration. In the press and on the platform, the professionals joined the educated unemployed in waging an acrimonious war of criticism against the Government of India whom they held responsible for the prevailing unemployment. The object of the attack against the government was twofold: it was directed against the kind of education provided by the government, and against the failure to employ those who had been trained by it. In 1882, the year which saw the appointment of an education commission, Dadabhai Naoroji wrote to the secretary of state for India on the subject of unemployment among the educated Indians:

> The thousands that are being sent out by the universities every year find themselves in a most anomalous position. There is no place for them in their motherland. They may beg in the streets, or break stones in roads for aught the rulers seem to care for their natural rights, position and duties in their own country. They may perish or do what they like or can, but scores of Europeans must go from this country to take up what belongs to them, and that in spite of every profession for years and years past and up to the present day,

97. Extract from the minute by the lieutenant-governor of Bengal on 5 January, 1877, in *Report on the Administration of Bengal, 1875–77*, Calcutta, 1877, p. 59.

> of English statesman, that they must govern India for India's good by the words of the august Sovereign herself.[98]

The following year, a contributor to the *Indian Spectator* brought out more clearly the difference between the prospect of an educated Indian and that of an educated Englishman:

> How many university graduates go without work? The luckiest of them is often too glad to begin life as a Mamlatdar's[99] clerk. Now look at his English contemporary. The very first appointment he holds is that of Assistant Judge or Collector. What a difference when both had worked equally hard! The native graduate knows his importance, he feels his neglect all the more bitterly. He has the power to do harm, and may exercise that power. The uneducated does not feel neglect, he can get some work or other [of] which he is not too proud. Not so that educated youth. He knows his marketable value and when neglected, he frets and fumes.[100]

Such criticisms were likely to arouse the suspicions of the Government of India, the provincial authorities and the British press. As *The Englishman* wrote in 1870:

> The number of thinly veneered, but highly polished, students who are every year turned adrift into the world from our Anglo-Indian schools and colleges is perfectly appalling. Puffed up with a notion of superiority to the rest of their countrymen, they are no longer content to apply themselves to the industrial pursuits of their forefathers but demand employments more suited to the educational aroma with which they are imbued. Failing this, they spread abroad over the land, diffusing a feeling of discontent wherever they settle down, and stirring up disaffection to the very Government whose fond weakness has given them whatever strength they possess.[101]

In the year *The Englishman* made these comments, official circles began to be sceptical about the value of higher education. This scepticism was presumably provoked by the fact that three Indians

98. *Journal of the East India Association*, XIV, 1882, pp. 171–72.
99. A subordinate collectorship, normally held by an Indian.
100. *Indian Spectator*, Bombay, 27 May 1883.
101. *Englishman*, Calcutta, 28 February, 1870.

had qualified for the ICS in 1869.[102] It was argued that had more money been spent on higher education, many more Indians could have entered the ICS which had hitherto been a British preserve. In May 1870, the supplement to the *Gazetteer of India* carried a resolution by the Government of India (finance department) dated 31 March 1870. After referring to the resolution of 8 September 1869, which mentioned the withdrawal of governmental financial assistance for the instruction of the people of Bengal in the English language, the resolution went further: it declared that the motives which induced the people to seek instruction in the English language were prima facie sufficient to contribute to its rapid development without any contribution by the imperial government—in contrast with this, the desire for vernacular education required much artificial stimulus and encouragement. Therefore, 'it should be, in accordance with the view expressed by successive Secretaries of State, the constant aim of the Supreme and the Local Governments ... to reduce to the utmost the charge upon the state of English education in the view of rendering it as self-supporting as possible'.[103]

The publication of this resolution was the signal for an agitation in Bengal which was unprecedented in its intensity and magnitude. Without governmental assistance, most of the Indian secondary schools and colleges which drew the majority of their students from the middle and lower income groups, and which depended for their existence on the grants-in-aid system, would have had to close. The Bengali press raised the cry of 'higher education in danger', and in view of the agitation carried out by the British Indian Association in Calcutta and in the *mofussil*, the government withdrew the resolution and attempted to reassure the public by denying that it had any intention of discontinuing its assistance to higher education. All the while, the English-language press, owned and managed by Europeans, severely criticised the government's policy of supporting higher education. It pointed to the existence of a reaction against

102. All three—Romesh Chunder Dutt, Bihari Lal Gupta and Surendranath Banerjee—were Bengalis. See L. S. S. O'Malley, *The Indian Civil Service*, London: John Murray, 1931, pp. 204–10.
103. Supplement to the Government of India, 7 May 1870, pp. 715–17.

it among the Englishman in India and in Great Britain, including those who had earlier supported the spread of English education in India. The press openly said that the time would soon come when the Government of India would have to revise its policy regarding the education of Indians in English.

However, the revision of its policy towards English education did not occur until the end of the 1870s, when the movement in many parts of India against the reduction from twenty-one to nineteen of the maximum age at which the ICS examination could be taken grew in vigour. This lowering of the age-limit by Lord Salisbury in 1876 had been aimed primarily at making it more difficult for Indians to come to London to compete in the examination. As early as 1866, educated Indians had opposed the reduction of the maximum age-limit from twenty-two to twenty-one because they thought it prejudicial to Indian aspirants; they found the further reduction from twenty-one to nineteen even more unacceptable. They looked upon it as a manoeuvre on the part of the Government of India to thwart the ambition of Indians to enter the ICS. A national protest was organised under the leadership of Surendranath Banerjee to invoke the Charter Act of 1833 and the Queen's Proclamation of 1858, in which the rights of the Indians to serve in the administration, irrespective of class, creed, caste and colour, had been proclaimed.

On 24 March 1877, a public meeting was held in the Albert Hall, Calcutta, and a committee consisting of the representatives of educated sections of the Indian community in Calcutta was appointed to draw up a memorial attracting attention to the principles and pledges contained in the Charter Act of 1833 and the Queen's Proclamation of 1858, and to forward it to Parliament. Surendranath Banerjee was assigned the task of travelling across the country to gain support for the memorial. In April 1879, Lal Mohan Ghose was asked by the Indian Association to go to Great Britain as its representative to lay before the British public the grievances of the Indian people regarding access to appointments in the civil service.[104] This agitation, which was supported by educated Indians throughout the country, was organised and conducted with such care

104. Banerjee, *A Nation in the Making*, pp. 40 ff.

and in such a constitutional manner that it drew admiration from the Englishmen. 'The really remarkable feature of the whole movement is the moderation, the good sense, and political tact which have distinguished it from first to last.... A race that can conduct a political campaign with such ability has already won half the battle.'[105] The gradual extension of the use of Western methods of agitation and organisation acquired through universities by the educated Indians posed a 'real danger to our rule in India', as Hamilton pointed out several decades later to Curzon.[106]

The Encouragement of Private Enterprise in Higher Education

The commotion in Indian public opinion gave pause to the Government of India and induced it to consider the revision of its policy towards the education of Indians. 'The present system', wrote the Rev. James Johnston in 1880, 'is raising a number of discontented and disloyal subjects.'[107] Against this background, a liberal viceroy, Lord Ripon, took the bold step of appointing the first education commission in 1882—called the Hunter Commission—to review the whole field of primary and secondary education in India. Its president, Sir William Hunter, thought that governmentally supported education was producing, among educated Indians, a revolt against three principles which represented 'the deepest wants of human nature—the principle of discipline, the principle of religion, the principle of contentment'.[108] On the recommendations of the commission, and nominally as a measure of economy, it encouraged

105. *The Times of India*, Bombay, 24 December 1877.
106. Hamilton to Curzon, 20 September 1899, Hamilton Papers, Reel 1. (Hamilton Papers on microfilm in the National Archives of India, New Delhi.)
107. James Johnston, *Our Education Policy in India*, Edinburgh, 1880, 'Introduction' quoted in *University of Calcutta*, p. 150.
108. *Report of the Indian Education Commission, 1881–82* quoted in Haridas and Uma Mukherjee, *The Growth of Nationalism in India*, Calcutta: Presidency Library, 1957, p. 25.

private enterprise in the field. It directed the provincial governments to close down or hand over to 'a suitable agency, public or private', control over some of the government colleges in the mofussil, while deciding to continue the financial support of the Presidency—i.e., governmental—colleges, 'on which the higher education of the country mainly depends'.[109] A stronger reason for the withdrawal was more political than economic. Lord Ripon, in his convocation address at the University of Bombay in 1884 intimated, rather sympathetically to the Indian cause:

> That...it is little short of folly that we should throw open to increasing numbers the rich stores of Western learning; that we should inspire them with European ideas, and bring them into the closest contact with English thought, and that then we should as it were, pay no heed to the growth of those aspirations which we have ourselves created, and the pride of those ambitions we have ourselves called forth.[110]

However, as the Government of India diminished its role in higher education, Indians became more active. Higher education, instead of declining continued to expand. In 1881, for example, the number of colleges was seventy-five; in 1886, the number increased to 110; and in 1893, it was 156. Similarly, the number of students in these colleges rose from 7,582 in 1881 to 10,538 in 1886 and 18,571 in 1893.[111] Thus, within the decade following the withdrawal of governmental support for higher education other than the Presidency colleges, the number of colleges almost doubled and the number college students nearly trebled. The number of secondary schools in Bengal also rose, but not to the same extent: from 4,122 in 1881 to 5,097 in 1893—i.e., nearly 25 per cent in twelve years—while

109. For details, see *Report of the Indian Commission, 1881–82.*
110. Quoted in University of Calcutta, *Hundred Years*, p. 152.
111. In Bengal alone between 1882 and 1893, seven new colleges emerged including those set up by Anand Mohan Bose (City College), Surendranath Banerjee (Ripon College) and Girishchandra Bose (Bangabasi College). See J. Ghosh, *Higher Education in Bengal under British Rule*, Calcutta: The Book Co., 1926, p. 165.

the number of secondary school students increased from 222,000 to 511,000 during the same period.[112]

Within these same twelve years, despite the desire of the Government of India to reduce its role in higher education, the University of Punjab was established at Lahore in 1882 and the University of Allahabad in 1887; though obviously to reduce the burden on University of Calcutta, the main reason for their establishment was because of the increasing demand in these places for higher education, including 'Oriental' as well as modern European education.

The expansion of higher education in India in the decades following the report of the Hunter Commission was accompanied by an aggravation of the problem of unemployment among Indians educated in English. A district officer in Bihar suggested in 1882 that the establishment of technical schools could alleviate the problem of unemployment and consequent discontent: 'Unless technical schools are provided as outlets, the mere scholastic element will breed political discontent.'[113] In any case, the senior staff in jute mills, coal mines and iron foundries was recruited from Great Britain; the government therefore did not anticipate any improvement in the near future. There would have to be a long period of industrial development before there would be any large number of opportunities for the employment of Indians with technical training. In a resolution of 18 June 1888, the Government of India declared:

> In India at the present time application of capital to industry has not been developed to the extent which in European countries has rendered the establishment of technical schools on a large scale an essential requisite of success. But the extension of railways, the introduction of mills and factories, the expansion of external trade

112. The data are from (a) *Report of the Hunter Commission*, pp. 256–312, (b) *Quinquennial Review of the Progress of Education* by A. Croft, pp. 136–60, 161–94 (1886); A. M. Nash, pp. 51–83 and 85–132 (1887–88 to 1891–92) and J. S. Cotton , pp. 70–115 and 121–70 (1892–93 to 1896–97); (c) *Statistical Abstract Relating to British India*, 1881–82, 1886–87 and 1893–94.
113. *Statement Exhibiting the Moral and Material Progress and Condition of India*, 1882–83, p. 148.

> and the enlarged intercourse with foreign markets, ought in time to lead to the same results in India as in other countries, and create a demand for skilled labour and for educated foremen, supervisors and managers. It may be conceded that the effect of these various influences on an Asiatic people is very gradual, and that it would be premature to establish technical schools on such a scale as in European countries and thereby aggravate the present difficulties by adding to the educated unemployed a new class of professional men for whom here is no commercial demand.[114]

In January 1889, Lansdowne drew attention to the problem of unemployment when he addressed the University of Calcutta as its chancellor:

> I am afraid we must not disguise from ourselves that if our schools and colleges continue to educate the youth of India at the present rate, we are likely to hear even more than we do at present of the complaint that we are turning out every year an increasing number of young men whom we have provided with an intellectual equipment admirable in itself but practically useless to them on account of the small number of openings which the professions afford for gentlemen who have received this kind of education.[115]

The Intensification of Nationalist Sentiment

The growing unemployment among young English-educated Indians and their disaffection with the Government of India which they

114. See *Papers Relating to Technical Education in India, 1880–94*, Calcutta, 1904 quoted in Robert I. Crane, 'Technical Education and Economic Development in India before World War I', in *Education and Economic Development*, ed. C. Arnold Anderson and Mary Jean Bowman, Chicago: Aldine Publishing Co.: 1966, pp. 167–68, 180–81. See also *Papers Relating to Technical Education in India, 1880–94*; K. D. Bhargava, (ed.), *Selections from the Educational Records from the Government of India* Delhi: Manager of Publication, Government of India, 1968, vol. IV, p. 86.
115. Marquis of Lansdowne's convocation address at Calcutta on 19 January 1889, in *University of Calcutta Convocation Address*, vol. II, p. 579.

held responsible for their plight, intensified nationalist sentiments. Thus was forged a collective consciousness and solidarity through common plight and the common objects of grievance. They began to write letters to English newspapers and form associations to demand rights for educated Indians, especially the rights of representation and employment.[116] In 1885, the Indian National Congress, which Hume considered a 'safety-valve' for the growing discontent with British rule, was formed.[117] It adopted 'wider employment of our people in the public service', as one of 'the three important questions' constituting 'the chief planks in the Congress platform'.[118]

Hardly any annual session of the Indian National Congress took place without discussion on the subject of employment of English-educated Indians and the passage of resolutions on it.[119] In December 1885, at the first session of the Indian National Congress in Bombay, Dadabhai Naoroji, speaking in support of the fourth resolution which demanded that simultaneous examinations for the ICS be held in England and India in accordance with the views of the India Office Committee of 1860, observed: 'It is the most important key to our material and moral advancement. All our political reforms will benefit us but very little indeed if this reform of all reforms is not made. It is the question of poverty or prosperity. It is the question of life and death to India. It is the question of questions.'[120]

The Aitchison Commission which met the next year to report on the state of the public services in India, rejected the demand for simultaneous examinations in England and India for the ICS; but it

116. Martin Briton, Jr., 'Lord Duffer in and the Indian National Congress, 1885–88', *Journal of British Studies* VII, November, 1967, pp. 68–96.

117. See Martin Briton, Jr., *New India, 1885*, Bombay: Oxford University Press, 1970 on the birth of the Indian National Congress.

118. Report of the Proceedings of the Sixteenth Session of the Indian National Congress, 1900. See p. 59.

119. See reports of the proceedings of the sessions of the Indian National Congress between 1885 and 1899.

120. See Proceedings of the First session of the Indian National Congress, 1885, p. 81.

proposed a scheme for doing 'full justice to the claims of natives of India to higher employment in the public service'. It recommended that the ICS should be a *corps d'elite* with its numbers limited to what was necessary to fill the chief administrative appointments of the Government of India, and by transferring a corresponding number of appointments to provincial governments which were to be separately recruited in each province. The latter service, known as the Provincial Civil Service, should include 108 posts hitherto reserved for the ICS, and also the higher posts held by the uncovenanted service (which the commission now abolished). The lower posts of the former uncovenanted service were, however, to be relegated to a subordinate civil service.[121]

In 1889, 56 per cent of the total appointments, which numbered 25,370 and which were paid salaries of at least Rs. 75 a month, were held by the Indians; only 14 per cent of the appointments carrying salaries of Rs. 1,000 and over 'fall to our lot', said Surendranath Banerjee, commenting on these statistics, 'although the country is ours, the money is ours and the bulk of the population is ours.'[122]

> If you look at the statistics connected with these Departments you will find that the higher offices, the bulk of the higher offices—I should not be guilty of the smallest exaggeration if I say that at least 90 per cent of the higher offices—are filled by Europeans and Anglo-Indians... Imperialists, somebody says. They may be imperialists or not but at any rate, these Departments constitute the close preserve, the absolute monopoly of these gentlemen. We are excluded. And why? Because of our race. Our colour is our disqualification.[123]

121. See *Report of the Public Service Commission, 1886–87*, Calcutta, 1888 for details. See also S. C. Ghosh, 'Indian Nationalism and the Emergence of the Public Service Commission', in the *Union Public Service Commission Souvenir Volume*, Delhi, November, 1976, p. 6.
122. In 1903, Curzon had ordered a survey of appointments for the thirty-six years from 1867 to 1903; Surendranath Banerjee made this comment at the twentieth session of the Indian National Congress, 1904. See pp. 63–64.
123. Report of the Proceedings of the Sixteenth Session of the Indian National Congress, 1900. See pp. 61–62.

While the 'discontented BAs and MAs' must have shared Banerjee's views of the policy of the Government of India with regard to the appointment of Indians to the ICS and the lesser services, some of them were becoming advocates of a more militant nationalism. The latter became adherents of the new generation of leaders like Bal Gangadhar Tilak, Lala Lajpat Rai and Bepin Chandra Pal, who were more 'extremist' that the previous leadership. In Bengal, the extremist challenge began with Aurobindo's fierce attack on the Congress in 1893.[124] Next year, Alfred Croft reported in his convocation address at Calcutta in 1894 that lack of any suitable openings for those who had just been able to take their degrees as well as those who had failed was posing a grave problem. Quoting from Bacon's *Of Seditions and Troubles,* he underlined the danger by warning that one of the chief causes of discontent was 'when more are bred scholars than preferment can take off'.[125] In 1897, the last year of Elgin's viceroyalty when Bombay was threatened with an outbreak of plague, two educated young men, Damodar and Balkrishna Chapekar, murdered Rand, the collector and plague officer of Poona and his associate, Lieutenant Ayerst. As a reaction to the murders in Poona, in 1898, the Government of India enacted the 'Sedition Law'.[126] After going through the papers documenting the events leading to the murders, Hamilton found it impossible to dissociate these young men's ideas and hatred of Great Britain from the course of education and training through which they had passed.[127] He and his advisers regarded Fergusson College at Poona, where Damodar and Balkrishna had been students, as the source of a small but deep-rooted political conspiracy in the Deccan.[128]

124. For details, see A. Tripathi, *The Extremist Challenge*, Calcutta: Orient Longman, 1967.
125. *University of Calcutta Convocation Address*, vol. II, pp. 735–36.
126. R. C. Dutt, in his presidential address at the Lucknow Congress session on 27 December 1899, commented that by passing this law, the Raj made 'the blunder of committing sedition with the spread of education'. See Report of the Proceedings of the Fifteenth Session of the Indian National Congress 1899, p. 10.
127. Hamilton to Curzon, 11 October 1899, Hamilton Papers, Reel 1.
128. Hamilton to Curzon, 10 August 1899, Hamilton Papers, Reel 1.

Hamilton's views on the murders in Poona thus brought to a head the sentiments of those British officials who had since the early 1870s been pondering over the utility of spreading English education in India. Gustave Le Bon, the French publicist and social scientist who visited India in the early 1880s, commented that English education was not at all suitable for Indians who were steeped in the traditional culture. The latter could not satisfy the wants created by English education. The 'English-educated' also wrote to the Indian press in the same vein, bitterly attacking the Raj. The 'Babus', as LeBon called the English-educated Indians in Bengal, were the enemies of British rule, and it was silly to rule the country through them: 'Le pireennemi de I' Angleterre, place sur le trone des Indes, n'aurait pas porte a la metropole un plus grave prejudice.'[129]

In the decades following the birth of the Congress, it began to be thought that the decision to promote education in English, ever since the days of Macaulay, was a 'story of grave political miscalculation' containing a lesson 'that has its significance for other nations which have undertaken a similar enterprise'.[130] English education, which was identified with higher education in India, had given birth to a state of mind and a type of character that was 'ill-regulated, averse from discipline, discontented, and in some case actually disloyal'. In short, it had raised 'a fighting cock' when it was expected to raise 'an innocuous hen'. As Curzon later declared in connection with his scheme for educational reform at a conference in Simlain September 1901:

> When Erasmus was reproached with having laid the egg from which came forth the Reformation, 'Yes', he replied, 'but I laid a hen's egg, and Luther had hatched a fighting cock'. This, I believe, is pretty much the view of a good many critics of English education in India.'[131]

Curzon himself fully subscribed to this view. Five weeks after landing in Calcutta, while delivering his first convocation address at the

129. Gustave Le Bon, *Les Civilizations de I'Inde*, Paris: Firmin Didot, 1887, pp. 707–12.
130. See Sir Alfred C. Lyall's 'Introduction' to Valentine Chirol's *Indian Unrest*, London: Macmillan, 1910, pp. xii–xvi.
131. Home Education, October 1901, no. 19, Appendix A, p. 12.

university as its chancellor on 11 February 1899, he observed that he knew:

> That our system of higher education in India is a failure; that it has sacrificed the formation of character upon the altar of cram; and that the Indian University turn out only a discontented horde of office seekers, whom we have educated for places which are not in existence for them to fill.[132]

Since it was now too late to undo Macaulay's or Bentinck's decisions to offer English education in India, the best that could then be done was to devise means to restrict its disadvantages. One of the means could have been to divert the attention of the young Indians from Western education to Oriental education, which Annie Besant's Hindu College in Banaras proposed to impart 'by undertaking the task of giving religious and moral education on Hindu lines to its Youths'.[133] Hamilton was willing to 'encourage' Annie Besant's scheme of education.[134] As he wrote to Curzon in connection with Mrs Besant's Hindu College:

> I think the real danger to our rule in India, not now but say 50 years hence, is the gradual adoption and extension of Western agitation and organization; and if we could break the Hindu party into two sections holding widely different views, we should, by such a division, strengthen our position against the subtle and continuous attack which the spread of education makes upon out present system of Government.[135]

Another means would be to give more attention to education at the lower levels and less to higher education, as had been unsuccessfully done by the government before in the 1870s and in 1882. Anything, Hamilton remarked rather gloomily, would be

132. C. S. Raghunatha, Rao (ed.), *Notable Speeches of Lord Curzon*, pp. 98–99, *University of Calcutta Convocation Address*, vol. III, pp. 841–47.
133. Besant to Curzon, 17 January 1899, Letter 18, Curzon Papers, Reel 7.
134. Hamilton to Curzon, 20 September 1899, Hamilton Papers, Reel 1.
135. Hamilton to Curzon, 20 September 1899, Letter 47, Curzon Papers, Reel 1.

better than the expansion of purely literary education, 'joy of the Babu and anglicized Brahmin', which 'produces a wholesale mass of discontented individuals who, if they cannot find government employment spend their time in abusing the government which has educated them'.[136]

Curzon was uneasy about Mrs Besant's scheme because it was associated with 'not merely active, but disloyal politicians', though she 'herself had no political motives'.[137] He thought, however, that the best way to slow down what Hamilton later described in his reminiscences as the 'educational juggernaut'[138] was to bring higher education under effective governmental control.[139] This was exactly what was done by Curzon in carrying through the Indian Universities Act in March 1904; and his plan to effect this reform through 'legislation' after appointing 'a small preliminary commission' had been disclosed to Hamilton in August 1901, after he had allowed himself sufficient time to study the problems of university education in India.

Conclusions

Curzon's university reform has never been studied in the context of the developments affecting the interests of the British Raj in the decades immediately preceding it. The universities in India were not free from defects and they did need reform, though one may be inclined to agree with the observation made by the Indian Universities Commission of 1902 that 'we are not disposed to confirm the sweeping condemnation which has sometimes been passed upon our University system'.[140]

136. Hamilton to Curzon, 13 August, 1899, Hamilton Papers, Reel 1, quoted in David Dilks, *Curzon in India*, London: Rupert Hart-Davis, 1969–70, vol. 1, p. 244.
137. Curzon to Hamilton, 30 August 1899, Letter 38, Reel 1.
138. G. Hamilton, *Parliamentary Reminiscences and Reflections*, London: 1916–24, vol. 1, p. 278.
139. Hamilton to Curzon, 18 May 1899, *Hamilton Papers*, Reel 1.
140. *Report of the Indian Universities Commission 1902*, p. 15.

The universities suffered from the same limitations as the University of London which had acted as a model in 1857. In the conditions peculiar to India, these limitations assumed such gigantic dimensions as to invite the attention of all those authorities directly concerned with the state of higher education in the country. So, when in 1898, a royal commission was appointed under Lord Davey, and the University of London became a teaching university after the recommendations of the Davey Commission had been approved by Parliament,[141] it was only a matter of time before the issue of modifying the character of the universities in India came up.[142]

It is indeed an interesting coincidence that the person appointed to head the Government of India immediately after the appointment of a royal commission to report on the University of London was someone very much concerned with university education. 'I will not conceal from you', Curzon told the graduates of the University of Calcutta in his first convocation address, 'that I am a University man to the core of my being... I have been an undergraduate of a university, a Bachelor of Arts, a Master of Arts, a Fellow of a College and a Member of Convocation. But a Chancellor I have never been until today.'[143]

Indian intellectuals could easily see his attempt to control higher education in the country as an attempt to stop the spread of the Western education which had contributed to their progress. As Surendranath Banerjee observed in his presidential address at the Ahmedabad session of the Indian National Congress on 23 December 1902:

> [Higher education] lies at the root of all our progress. It is the mainspring, the motive power, the germinal source of all those forces which make for progress....It is English education which has overcome the barriers of race, religion, and language, has dissipated the prejudices and misunderstandings of ages and has created those

141. *University of Calcutta Convocation Address*, vol. III, p. 938.
142. *Report of the Calcutta University Commission, 1917–19*, vol. 1, p. 65
143. *University of Calcutta Convocation Address*, vol. III, p. 841–47. See also C. S. Raghunatha Rao (ed.), *Notable Speeches of Lord Curzon*, pp. 98–99.

> unifying influences which find a living expression in this vast, this stupendous, this majestic organization of the National Congress. Could this educated community submit to the curtailment of this boon—to the restriction of its beneficent area?[144]

If the British administration thought that the universities in India were breeding 'fighting cocks' which threatened British interests in India, why did it not abolish the universities altogether instead of attempting to bring them under governmental control? The abolition of the universities would have been contrary to their interests. The British in India always needed men like Syed Ahmad Khan, Bepin Behari Bose and R. G. Bhandarkar,[145] and a host of officials trained through these universities, to help them conduct their administration in the country.

Indeed, one of the specific objects of the 'encouragement' of higher education in India as mentioned in the Education Despatch of 1854 addressed to the governor-general of India was 'to supply you with servants to whose probity you may with increased confidence commit offices of trust'.[146] However, the demand for such servants in India was obviously limited. When supply steadily exceeded demand, discontent became common among educated Indians, especially among those who had adopted independent professions like law, teaching and journalism, often reluctantly and under difficult circumstances. It was natural for the educated unemployed as well as for those professionals who were not patronised by the British establishments to become increasingly alienated from the British Raj.[147]

144. See Report of the Proceedings of the Eighteenth Session of the Indian National Congress, 1902, pp. 18–20.
145. Syed Ahmad Khan, as founder of the Anglo Mohammadan Oriental College at Aligarh, out of which grew the Aligarh Muslim University had provided an antidote to Congress Movement since 1885. Syed A. Bilgrami, Bepin Behari Bose and R. G. Bhandarkar supported Curzon's university reforms.
146. Richey, *Selections from Educational Records*, p. 365.
147. Curzon himself admitted in his inaugural address at a conference in Simla on 2 September 1901 that the students went to universities

Such alienation, however, was not a phenomenon peculiar to India alone, despite her colonial character in the late nineteenth century. In Russia, for example, the spread of higher education, accompanied by a lack of suitable opportunities for employment, increasingly alienated young educated Russians from the Tsarist regime. The case of Russia was repeatedly cited by the members of Curzon's council while debating on the draft Universities Bill in 1903. In a minute on 23 July 1903, Edward Law observed that: 'In India the University system must lead to the same class of results as in Russia though it will take some time before it shows any acute and violent forms.'[148] He suggested that the situation could be remedied 'by raising fees so that only richer class could afford to send their sons to the university'.[149] E. R. Ellis, another member of the council, who also saw a parallel between Russia and Bengal as far as higher education was concerned, fully agreed with Law that high fees could probably get rid of 'riff-raff'.[150]

In a letter to Dalhousie on 6 June 1854, Wood pointed out that he was unwilling to provide higher education for all, since this would create a 'discontented class unless they are employed' and would ultimately ruin British prospects in India.[151] In a letter to Halliday, the lieutenant-governor of Bengal, in July 1854, he further clarified his views about the spread of higher education in India:

> I do not see the advantage of rearing up a number of highly educated gentlemen at the expense of the state whom you cannot employ, and who will naturally become depositories of discontent. If they choose

(colleges), 'not to learn but to earn'. The full text of Curzon's speech is in Home Education, October 1901, no. 19, Appendix A, pp. 11–23.

148. See Home Education, December 1903, nos. 67–86.

149. Ibid.

150. See minute of E. R. Ellis on 25 July 1903, in ibid.

151. Wood to Dalhousie, 8 June 1854, Dalhousie Papers 57, p. 2, (Dalhousie Papers at the Scottish Record Office, Edinburgh.)

> to educate themselves, well and good but I am against providing our own future detractors and opponents and grumblers.[152]

By his attempt to bring higher education under effective governmental control through the Indian Universities Act of 1904, Curzon tried to tackle the realities of the problem visualised by Wood nearly half a century earlier.

152. Wood to Halliday, 24 July 1854, Wood Papers, *India Board Letter Book*, vol. IV, (Wood Papers at the India Office Library, London). Also see Ghosh, 'Dalhousie, Charles Wood and the Education Despatch of 1854', p. 42.

9

The Transformation of Schooling in Colonial Punjab, 1854–1900

Preeti

The education system of any society is shaped not only by its needs at a particular point in time, but also by larger historical events and processes. The system is often made subservient to the needs and demands of the ruling classes in any historical period. The education system in colonial India was aimed at reducing the economic costs of empire by placing Indians in subordinate posts; training revenue officers who would ensure efficient and timely revenue collection;[1] creating a taste for British goods among Indians, and producing a loyal class of Indians,[2] in the name of the moral and intellectual progress of the Indian people at large. However, this attempt was not confined just to English-language education, but also encompassed the transformation of the entire system of education, resulting in

1. In 1833, the East India Company was in the midst of a grave financial crisis. One of Governor-General Bentinck's principal problems was the high pay of English officers. He, therefore, considered employing Indian subordinates in the judicial and revenue offices. Revenue extraction was the main source of income for the company; so, he wanted to train native revenue officers in a more efficient way. This objective guided the design of school curricula, which included subjects such as geography, arithmetic and geometry. See Aparna Basu, *Essays in the History of Indian Education*, New Delhi: Concept Publishing Company, 1982, pp. 7–9.
2. Colonial officers in favour of English education argued that it would provide legitimacy to colonial rule and that Indians would not feel the alienness of the masters. See Thomas R. Metcalf, *Ideologies of the Raj*, Cambridge: Cambridge University Press, 1996.

a new system—one that had not been prevalent in pre-colonial India. Although there were some overlaps between the indigenous education system and the colonial education system, the colonial state transformed the indigenous system and modified it according to its needs.

As mass schooling gradually became the norm in the nineteenth century, enormous institutional changes were effected in the physical and material sense (for example, the introduction of buildings only meant to serve as schools, the use of classroom furniture, and the division of schools into age-specific classes); in the fee structure; in the homogenised curricula (for example, the introduction of new subjects, timetables, new pedagogies, new teacher-pupil relationships, physical training, and sanitation), and in the introduction of textbooks, examination systems, inspections and scholarships. Through these extremely partial and limited changes, the colonial state asserted its power over the Indian subcontinent and its inhabitants. The changes that were introduced by the colonial state were intended to fulfil the needs of colonial control and rule, rather than the needs of industrial capital, although the effects on the indigenous education system were irreversible, shifting the burden of education to the state and to its agencies.

Indigenous Schools in Punjab

Prior to the advent of colonialism in India, robust and flourishing systems of education existed in Punjab, although they were not necessarily inclusive of all sections of society and only rarely stretched beyond the goal of serving local needs.[3] Colonialism irrevocably altered

3. Indigenous schools were defined by the 1882 Indian Education Commission as educational institutions that were established or conducted by the natives of India using indigenous methods. Such institutions were either of an advanced character or were purely elementary. (*Report of the Indian Education Commission, appointed by the resolution of the Government of India, dated 3rd February, 1882*, Calcutta: Superintendent of Government Printing, 1883, hereafter Hunter Commission Report), p. 53. Hunter was the president of the Indian Education Commission of 1882.

these systems. Following the annexation of Punjab by the British in 1849, the indigenous education system underwent various changes. Although colonial rule did not result in the complete dismantling of the indigenous education system, it resulted in its partial decline. Some indigenous schools continued to function until the end of the nineteenth century, although their number fell dramatically as a result of the adoption of certain colonial policies. Those schools that were able to survive, lost their 'own real character'.[4]

There were several types of schools in pre-colonial Punjab: Gurmukhi, Persian, Arabic and *lande* schools Koran schools that were primary schools for Muslim children, and schools that imparted education in Sanskrit and Hindi (*pathsalas*). All these schools catered to the needs of specific communities, and some were closely linked to certain religions. The religious content and orientation of the educational system was evident not only in the content of the curriculum, but also in various other aspects of schooling, such as the salaries of teachers, and the organisation and plan of learning spaces.[5] Indigenous schools imparted knowledge that was value-oriented, and their curricula included instruction in reading, writing, and arithmetic (the three 'R's), alongside religious instruction and professional training for account keeping, record maintenance, etc. It was a completely decentralised system. There was neither any direct

4. This term is used by Kazi Shahidullah. He argues that schools that accepted grants-in-aid policies lost their own character as 'indigenous' schools and came under government rules and regulations. See Kazi Shahidullah, *Patshalas into Schools: The Development of Indigenous Elementary Education in Bengal, 1854–1905*, Calcutta: Firma KLM Private Limited, 1987.
5. Learning spaces in religious schools were mostly attached to religious buildings such as temples, mosques and gurdwaras. Teachers were selected from within religious communities. They were largely religious men and imparted education alongside performing their priestly functions. Most teachers taught gratuitously and in the service of god, although, as we shall see, informal modes of payment were also known. G. W. Leitner, *History of Indigenous Education in the Panjab since Annexation and in 1882*. Patiala: Languages Department, Punjab, 1883, reprinted 1971.

state control nor any centralised administrative structure to monitor the system. The state's role was limited to giving endowments to some indigenous schools, and it did not otherwise interfere in matters of education. These institutions were established mainly through private initiative with social and community support. Indigenous schools employed one or two teachers. The number of pupils varied according to the type of instruction, its utility, and its specific location.[6]

Colonial officials who were familiar with Western notions of schooling, systems of pedagogy, curricula, subjects, classrooms, and language-use, only saw weaknesses in the indigenous education system and wanted to introduce colonial education, which they considered superior. The colonial education policy in the initial phase (after 1854) tried to absorb indigenous schools into the new system through a grants-in-aid policy and thereby changed their character completely. The colonial state resumed the lands of indigenous educational authorities and institutions after the annexation to increase revenue assessments and inflows. This threw the indigenous schools—which had been maintained on the revenue from rent-free lands endowed by either the state or by private individuals—into a state of dependence on the colonial government. The resumption after the annexation of all lands granted to indigenous schools led to the decline of such schools and increased their dependence on the colonial state.[7] Any school that continued to exist had to face competition from the colonial schools.

Colonialism and Schooling in Punjab

As the colonial government engaged itself in building the infrastructure of its rule after the annexation of Punjab only gradually, there was not much emphasis on education until 1854, when

6. For instance, the number of pupils in lande schools used to be larger as these schools imparted practical instruction. The number of pupils was usually smaller when teachers instructed at home. See Leitner, *History of Indigenous Education*.
7. Ibid.

the Department of Public Instruction was created.[8] Before the intervention of the government in the arena of education, it was largely the concern of missionaries and indigenous authorities. Although the government had established some government schools to educate the people of Punjab before 1854, it was in that year that there was a formal declaration of a policy for educating the masses. Prior to the organisation of the Education Department in Punjab, only thirty-four schools were directly and indirectly maintained by the government.[9] At the close of 1855, W. D. Arnold was appointed Director of Public Instruction for Punjab, and he declared a policy suitable to the requirements of the province. He copied the scheme of the *halkabandi* system, which had already been introduced in the North-West Provinces (later United Provinces). The scheme was based on the principle of making existing indigenous village schools 'the nucleus of a new, improved and organized system'.[10] It was proposed to search out and foster existing indigenous schools, and to support them by imposing a 1 per cent cess on land revenue.[11] So the schools were partly supported by the government, and were open to government supervision.[12] The aim of the government was to make

8. Harbans Rai Mehta, *A History of the Growth and Development of Western Education in the Punjab, 1846–1884*, Patiala: Languages Department, Punjab, 1971.
9. J. A. Richey, *Selections from Educational Records, Part-ii*, Calcutta: Superintendent of Government Printing, 1922, p. 289.
10. *Report by the Punjab Provincial Committee with Evidences taken Before the Committee and Memorials Addressed to the Education Commission*, Calcutta: Superintendent of Government Printing, 1883, pp. 1–8. Hereafter *Report by the Punjab Provincial Committee to the Education Commission*.
11. Ibid.
12. According to grants-in aid rules, institutions had to adhere to government rules and regulations regarding curricula and other infrastructure of schools. Schools came under the supervision of the colonial state. See *The Despatch of* 1854 on *"General Education* in *India"*. reprinted by the *General Council of Education in India from a return to an order of the honourable the House of Commons*, London: John Maclaren & Sons, 1880, pp. 23–25.

changes in the indigenous schools and substitute their curricula with a more useful and practical education.[13] Through a system of grants-in-aid, the colonial government grafted its own rules and regulations onto indigenous schools. In accepting financial help from the government, such schools also had to follow a common methodology of teaching, curricula and subjects, fee structure, textbooks, written examination system, and other rules and regulations. Indigenous educational institutions lost their freedom as they came under the colonial educational system.[14]

By and large, this system proved unsuccessful. In many localities, it was found that the people tried to rid themselves of the responsibility of maintaining their own schools and sought to shift the entire burden of their support on the state. In other localities, it was found that the additional funds supplied led to no improvement in the schools; and that the teachers readily accepted the increase in pay, but did not adhere to the rules prescribed by the Education Department. Efforts were then made to introduce the new system in the new village schools that were supported entirely on the 1 per cent cess. The most respectable and well-known teachers of the indigenous system were selected by the subordinate officers. However, this did not change the character of the indigenous schools because religious education remained an important part of their curriculum. Finally, an entirely new British-based education system, parallel to the indigenous system, was introduced after February 1859.[15] All schools were physically removed from the premises of mosques and other buildings of a religious character. Old and inefficient teachers, and those who had been selected largely for their priestly merit, were removed. The state created its own infrastructure of education encompassing textbooks, examinations, physical spaces of schools and classrooms, sanitation, technology of education, and inspection

13. *Report by the Punjab Provincial Committee to the Education Commission*, pp. 1–8.
14. As per the grants-in-aid rules of Charles Wood's Despatch of 1854. In J. A. Richey, *Selections from Educational Records, Part-ii*, pp. 378–81.
15. 'Memorandum No. 155 dated 9th August 1859', in *Report by the Punjab Provincial Committee to the Education Commission*, pp. 7–8.

system. This new system was substantially different from the system of indigenous education. Through its policies, the colonial state, on the one hand, introduced standardisation and uniformity into the system, and on the other hand, produced new kinds of hierarchies.

Homogenisation through the Textbook

The introduction of textbooks was an important means by which uniformity and systematisation were achieved in the educational system in colonial Punjab. The systematisation of textbooks can be traced to the establishment of the Punjab Textbook Committee in 1877.[16] The committee was responsible for recommending suitable textbooks in all subjects for use in government schools and colleges. It had the power to take steps for the preparation, translation and publication of textbooks in all subjects for school and college education where suitable books were not available. [17]

There were also eight subcommittees, each of which dealt with a particular branch of the work of the general committee, that is, the Punjab Textbook Committee. The branches were English language, literature and grammar; mathematics, natural science and technical education; history and geography; Urdu language and literature; Hindi and Sanskrit; Arabic and Persian; Gurmukhi, and libraries of school and reference libraries. An author approved by the subcommittee was encouraged either to publish the book or to contribute towards the cost of publication, while the committee charged a percentage on the sale of the work. These publication rules were designed to

16. Before the establishment of the Punjab Textbook Committee, a committee was appointed in 1875 to suggest books that should be adopted as textbooks. Its progress was slow and the need to establish a permanent committee of gentlemen was felt. This resulted in the setting up of the Punjab Textbook Committee in 1877, which finalised the textbooks to be used in schools in the province.
17. 'Memorandum of Association or textbook committee', cited in *Punjab Education Code*, fifth edition, and *Proceedings of the Government of Punjab in the Home Department (Education) for the Year 1899*, Lahore: Punjab Government Press, 1899, pp. 58–59. Hereafter *Proceedings of Education of the Punjab*.

ensure that 'the committee is giving [a] guarantee of excellence of the book' while assuring the author of a profit on all copies sold.[18] The subcommittee also took care to ensure that the book was printed in a 'creditable manner' with regard to the quality of paper, printing and content. Through these rules, the state scrutinised textbook publishing and ensured that no book could spread ill-feeling against colonial rule. On the other hand, the managers of aided schools were free to choose their own books, subject to the proviso that they would not prescribe any books that offended pupils or that promoted lax moral standards.[19] Aid was given to schools on the condition that they would not prescribe any books that were not included in the list of textbooks authorised by the local government. Through its textbook scheme, therefore, the government controlled every school, whether aided or not.

The colonial regime did not conceive of India as a nation, seeing it instead as a congeries of various religious communities, essentially exclusive of each other. It did not see these communities as rational agents but only as subjects of feeling.[20] The textbook policy exemplified this viewpoint. In the aftermath of the uprising of 1857, the colonial state became particularly sensitive to the consequences of disturbing 'native' sensibilities, and was against prescribing books that could offend the religious feelings of any community and lead to unrest. In 1882, the first Indian Education Commission, also called the Hunter Commission, stated that

> [C]omplaints have also reached us that sufficient care is not always taken in the selection of text-books to see that they contain no matter which is likely to give offence to any class of pupils, and we accordingly recommend that care be taken to avoid as far as possible the introduction of text-books which are of an aggressive

18. 'Proceedings of a meeting of the Punjab Textbook Committee held on Friday, the 20th April 1888', in *Proceedings of Education in the Punjab for the Year 1888*, pp. 167–73.
19. 'Resolution of the Government of India in 1881', cited in *Proceedings of Education in the Punjab for the Year 1890*, pp. 101–07.
20. Vikas Gupta, 'The World of Education and the Processes of Identity Formation', unpublished M. Phil. dissertation, Department of History, University of Delhi, 2007, pp. 33–34.

character, or are likely to give unnecessary offence to any section of the community.[21]

Alfred Croft,[22] a senior official connected with the drafting of the colonial educational policy, referring to the Education Commission of 1882, however, clarified that while books that were against the religious feelings of other creeds should not be prescribed, books that simply explained the religion of the author, compiler or publisher should not be excluded from the list of textbooks authorised by the government.[23] Hence, at specific political junctures, religion and morality shaped decisions about the prescription of textbooks by the colonial state.

By preparing and prescribing textbooks, the state decided what should be taught and how it should be taught, namely what was worthy of being designated as knowledge. Although the Punjab Textbook Committee set up various subcommittees for vernacular literature, the production of vernacular literature did not improve, since the headmasters of schools had no right to prescribe books or to set aside those prepared by the Department of Public Instruction. In addition, books written by private individuals very rarely found a place alongside the prescribed textbooks. Individuals were unable to offer cheap prices in comparison with the books issued by the Director of Public Instruction of Punjab, who ordered several thousands of copies at once, which reduced their price. Hence, the state policy promoted textbooks in English rather than those in the vernaculars.[24]

21. 'Memorandum by Alfred Croft on June 25th 1890', cited in *Proceedings of Education in the Punjab for the Year 1890*, pp. 101–07.
22. Alfred Croft was Director of Public Instruction in Bengal in the late nineteenth century. The Governor-General in Council gave him a special duty to review the Indian Education Commission for the future guidance of local government in regard to education. He submitted an extensive report titled *Review of Education in India in 1886 with Special Reference to Report of the Indian Education Commission.*
23. *Proceedings of Education in the Punjab for the Year 1890*, pp. 101–07.
24. 'Answer of Lahore Arya Samaj', in *Report by the Punjab Provincial Committee to the Education Commission*, pp. 476–77.

Textbooks were central to the new education system as opposed to the indigenous system of education. If the teacher's role was authoritative in the indigenous system, textbooks now became pre-eminent and led to the teacher's subservient status in the new educational culture.[25]

Syllabi

Another means of standardisation was through the syllabi prescribed for schools. Schools were divided primarily into vernacular and Anglo-vernacular schools, reflecting the languages taught in these institutions. In the Anglo-vernacular schools, English was part of the syllabus, to which more time was given than other subjects. In the vernacular schools, Urdu was taught in the place of English. New subjects like geography, science, physical education, sanitation, history and mathematics were also introduced. Mathematics was also a subject that increased the gap between the vernacular and Anglo-vernacular schools, since students who chose mathematics in the middle-school classes of Anglo-vernacular schools were introduced to new professional subjects such as letter and précis (comprehensive) writing, calligraphy, bookkeeping and accounts. Students of vernacular schools could take mathematics only at a higher level because they did not usually have mathematics at the middle-school level. Students of vernacular schools were taught classical languages like Arabic and Sanskrit. Moreover, vernacular schools had no higher sections, as it was assumed that education at the high-school level could only be imparted through the English language,[26] as had been stated in Wood's Despatch of 1854.[27]

Unlike the policies followed in Britain, the colonial state in India adopted a filtration policy that was opposed to mass education. Only

25. Krishna Kumar, 'Textbooks and Educational Culture', *Economic and Political Weekly*, vol. 21, no. 30, 26 July 1986, pp. 1309–11.
26. 'Resolution on the Proceedings of the General Education Conference', cited in the *Proceedings of Education in the Punjab for the Year 1887*, pp. 197–204.
27. J. A. Richey, *Selection from Educational Records, Part-ii*, pp. 365–69.

those children whose parents could afford to arrange private tutors for them were able to continue on to the higher classes.[28] In addition, the colonial regime discouraged the study of classical languages like Arabic and Sanskrit not only in Anglo-vernacular schools, but also in vernacular schools. While Arabic and Sanskrit were optional subjects, Persian and Urdu were taught in both kinds of schools.

Language became a major determining factor in attaining employment. It was necessary to master English for government employment and higher education. In the indigenous system, education was skill-oriented; but colonial education was not based on vocational skill-building among particular classes, and hence it proved less useful to some classes and castes.[29] As Manu Goswami has shown, geography, surveying, mensuration and arithmetic were important subjects in the reconstitution of local knowledge. The introduction of these new subjects was linked to the need to further the colonial interest in the area of revenue collection, since a sound knowledge of Indian land settlement was imperative for increasing revenues. For the investigation of land and for the collection of land revenue, modern and scientific techniques of mapping, surveying and calculation, and spatial knowledge of India were taught to the natives as parts of new subjects such as mensuration, arithmetic, mathematics, geography and surveying. Subjects like science were introduced to encourage pupils to ask questions and develop their observational skills. History was introduced to contrast the history of the colony with the history of Europe, or to differentiate between Indian and European knowledge. The introduction of geography and mapping created a new colonial spatial knowledge, which was also a systematic critique of Puranic

28. See *Report by Provincial Committee to the Education Commission.* Questions relating to home instruction were asked, and it became clear that many Indians preferred home instruction.
29. Unlike lande schools and schools for language learning, which were not only connected to the professions of people but also to their day-to-day lives, these schools taught religion, an important part of people's lives. In contrast, colonial education was useful to those who were engaged in the activities of revenue assessment, such as *patwaris*, *lambardars* and other members of the subordinate revenue classes.

understanding of space and time.[30] Subjects like physical education were introduced in the 1880s. In England, these were emphasised to improve the sanitary habits of industrial workers and to safeguard general public health and well-being. But in India, these measures were driven by a fear of epidemics. Physical education included the moral, physical and intellectual development of children, as well as the knowledge and practice of basic hygiene.

This syllabus was not found appropriate by all communities and classes in Punjab. The priestly classes, village elites, moneylenders, shopkeepers, agriculturists, and religious groups like the Muslims stayed away from the government schools. Baden-Powell[31] stated that education was neglected among agriculturists, village moneylenders and shopkeepers. All those who went to school were either the sons of *lambardars* and *patwaris* (who sought employment as village revenue officials), or else the sons of others who desired to leave the village for 'service' of some kind for which a little knowledge of English or Persian was useful. He further stated that only those boys went to school who desired to leave the village; since the majority were agriculturists, the nature of colonial education forced them to leave the plough. Baden-Powell criticised the nature of education, which was not meant for all. The value of subjects like geography and history was not understood by most, who largely did not get beyond the primary education level.[32] Similarly, Lala Mulraj of the Arya Samaj stated that the primary instruction of colonial schools

30. Manu Goswami, *Producing India: From Colonial Economy to National Space*, New Delhi: Permanent Black, 2004, pp. 132–53.
31. S. C. Baden-Powell was commissioner of Lahore division. He established Punjab University College and its committees, and generally participated in government educational and textbook committees. Evidence of Baden-Powell to the Education Commission, *Report by the Punjab Provincial Committee to the Education Commission*, pp. 150–51.
32. Most people in Punjab did not receive education beyond the primary level. The new subjects introduced failed to arouse interest among Indians, and many regarded the pursuit of education as a useless investment of time and money.

was very difficult to acquire and took up many years and made the students unfit for pursuing their own hereditary callings. They, therefore, became post-hunters; and even if the boys returned to their occupations after school, their education was of little use. So the impracticality of the system led to the neglect of education.[33]

Hence, Baden-Powell suggested that useful learning should be conveyed on morals, health, natural phenomena and the properties of things through the teaching of reading. He proposed the use of object lessons, during which pupils were shown pictures and objects to create interest among them and to develop their intellectual and reasoning faculties.[34] Children were encouraged to observe the objects presented to them and to carefully describe their observations, as a way of teaching them to classify and arrange things. In nineteenth-century Britain and India, government officials, missionary educators and radical pedagogues regularly evoked the object lesson as a means of modernising and elevating both primary schooling and teacher training.[35]

Unlike the influential classes of England which did a lot for the expansion of education in England, the influential classes in Punjab, said the Anjuman-i-Rifa'i-am, were not well-educated themselves and were indifferent to education and its benefits and advantages.[36] The Anjuman-i-Rifa'i-am told the Hunter Commission that education was meant for those who wanted to get government employment. The upper classes like *nawabs*, *shahzadas* and *jagirdars* did not send their children to school because they considered education an unnecessary burden. The lower classes were not able to afford

33. Evidence of Lala Mulraj to the Hunter Commission, *Report by the Punjab Provincial Committee to the Education Commission*, pp. 314–15.
34. Ibid.
35. Parna Sengupta, 'An Object Lesson in Colonial Pedagogy', *Comparative Studies in Society and History*, vol. 45, no. 1, 2003, pp. 96–102.
36. Evidence of Pandit Ishwar Prasad to the Hunter Commission. Pandit Ishwar Prasad had been a teacher for twenty years, before running a school up to the high-school level at his own cost. *Report by the Punjab Provincial Committee to the Education Commission*, pp. 329–37.

education for their children, and wanted to employ their sons in their respective family professions. Traders, shopkeepers and artisans found modern or colonial education useless and were content with their own professions.[37]

Similarly, the priestly classes of various religious communities excluded themselves voluntarily from the colonial education system because they did not receive religious and moral instruction, which they considered most important.[38] The Muslims generally believed that the absence of religious instruction in government schools and colleges was the cause of their low enrolment.[39] Brahmans were neither imparted religious education nor instructed in Sanskrit or the Devanagari script, which they studied in their homes or in private schools. Among the Sikhs, *bhais*, *granthis*, Akalis and other Sikh artisans and cultivators also remained aloof from the educational system because their sacred books were not taught, and also because Persian and Urdu were quite useless to them.[40]

The Grid of Examinations

The examination system introduced by the colonial government determined the student's academic progress, assessed the pupil's

37. Evidence of Anjuman-i-Rifa'i-am to the Hunter Commission, *Report by the Punjab Provincial Committee to the Education Commission*, p. 458.
38. Evidence of Lala Mulraj to the Hunter Commission, *Report by the Punjab Provincial Committee to the Education Commission*, pp. 314–15.
39. Sir Syed Ahmad Khan, *Report of the Members of the Select Committee for the Better Diffusion and Advancement of Learning among Muhammadans of India*, Banares: Medical Hall Press, 1872, pp. 5–8.
40. Evidence of Anjuman-i-Punjab to the Hunter Commission, *Report by the Punjab Provincial Committee to the Education Commission*, pp. 500–01. It included the opinions of members who were connected with Government College, Oriental College, and the Department of Public Instruction. Some of them were parents of pupils of these colleges and of public and private schools.

attainment of knowledge, and further systematised the educational system. The written examination was introduced at the middle-school level, although there were signs of the written examination being introduced at the primary-school level during inspections. At the primary-school level, examinations were held during the visits of the school inspector. As Krishna Kumar notes:

> The policy of centralised examinations made a major contribution to the culture of reutilised textbook-centred teaching. Examination was impersonal in the sense that students were examined by someone other than their own teacher. Secrecy was maintained over question papers and the identity of the examiner. With its aura of strictness and impartial treatment of all examinees, the examination system played an important role in the development of a bureaucratic system of education.[41]

The written examination not only tested the acquisition of knowledge by the student, but was also the basis for the awarding of scholarships. Examinations were conducted through written questions and answers, and secrecy was maintained in the arrangement and distribution of question papers, with punishment being meted out to those who cheated. The procedures introduced included specifications about the timings, answer sheets, processes for writing the answers, medium of examination, passing marks for pupils of vernacular and Anglo-vernacular schools, and subjects.[42] The new

41. Krishna Kumar, 'Textbooks and Educational Culture', *Economic and Political Weekly*, vol. 21, no. 30, 26 July 1986, pp. 1309–11; see also S. Shukla, 'Economy and Society in British India', *Varanasi National Journal Education*, vol. 1, nos. 1 and 2, 1978, pp. 7–80, 112–25.
42. Students were allowed to write the examination in any one of four languages—English, Urdu, Hindi and Punjabi—according to their preference. Anglo-vernacular candidates were required to obtain 33 per cent marks in English, 25 per cent in all other subjects, and 33 per cent in aggregate of the compulsory subjects to pass the examination. Candidates of vernacular schools were required to obtain 33 per cent in Euclid and Algebra, 25 per cent in all other subjects, and 33 per cent in aggregate of the compulsory subjects to pass. This distinction was maintained since English was compulsory in Anglo-vernacular schools

system of written examinations marked a sharp shift away from the indigenous examination system, which emphasised oral testing.

Rule by Inspection

The monitoring and regulation of schools through inspection was introduced. Inspectors, who were usually Europeans, evaluated the sanitary conditions of the classroom and the school; assessed the behaviour and discipline of pupils; tested the knowledge of pupils, and checked the attendance registers of pupils and teachers. Reports sent by the inspectors to the Director of Public Instruction became the basis for deciding which schools were working under the government rules and regulations, and decisions to provide grants-in-aid were made on the basis of this.

Despite the fact that inspection tours continued from October to March, Leitner argued that the inspection system was inadequate and inefficient. Vernacular primary and middle schools were meant to be inspected once every quarter by the district inspector or the chief *muharrir*, and once every year by the assistant inspector or the inspector of a circle of schools. English schools, both high and middle, were meant to be inspected twice a year. However, some schools were not visited by the inspector even once in three years, while the bulk of village schools were never visited by him. The inspector of schools often summoned pupils from different schools to his camp instead of going from village to village. The inspector's *munshi* or the chief muharrir was ordered to examine the children in a very cursory way. The inspectors judged teachers' and pupils' ways of dressing, their speech, etc., which only showed the moral side of the students and not their intellect. This time- and money-saving way of inspection undermined the very purpose of the exercise.[43] Hence, the Anjuman-

---

while Euclid and Algebra was compulsory in vernacular schools. *Proceedings of Education in the Punjab for the Year 1890*, pp. 73–77.

43. Memorial of G. W. Leitner to the Hunter Commission, *Report by the Punjab Provincial Committee to the Education Commission*, pp. 371–72.

i-Rifa'i-am suggested that the commission appoint Indian inspectors on grades different from those of Europeans for purely vernacular schools while Europeans be left to inspect English middle and high schools.[44] Likewise, there were many memorials from various social and political associations demanding that the work of inspection be given to Indians on the grounds that this would be both economical and efficient.[45]

The inspection format included detailed comments on seating arrangements, the display of teaching apparatuses and furniture (like maps, floor cloths, mats, blackboards, chairs and tables), the neatness, order and cleanliness of pupils, and the maintenance of the school building and other government property. The deputy commissioner also suggested to the inspectors that boys should be taught to be quiet and respectful in their demeanour and implicitly obedient to teachers. Teachers were thus meant not merely to impart instruction but also to maintain order, regularity and cleanliness in the classroom. Inspectors used to observe these kinds of things too. If the inspector found conditions unfavourable, his report could lead the Director of Public Instruction to withdraw the grants-in-aid.[46]

44. Answers of the Anjuman-i-Rifa'i-am of Jhang to the Education Commission, *Report by the Punjab Provincial Committee to the Education Commission*, p. 463.
45. See *Report by the Punjab Provincial Committee to the Education Commission*, on the question of inspection. Most of these associations demanded that the responsibility of the inspection of vernacular schools should be in the hands of the natives, because they knew the language of the people and could inspect properly. On the other hand, European officers did not know the language of the people; their assessment of the students was usually based on their expression, clean habits, sitting arrangement, and performance in the written examination: and all this was done with the help of *muharrirs*.
46. *The Despatch of 1854* on the *"General Education* of *India"*, p. 24.

Physical and Sanitary Education and the Technologies of Education[47]

From the 1880s onwards, the question of physical education engaged the attention of colonial educational authorities, who foregrounded the complete development of the child and her/his mental, moral and physical faculties. Wrestling and other indigenous games had always been popular in Punjab, and had naturally found their way into the schools; but now, sports officially became part of the curriculum.

The sports culture in English public schools in the nineteenth century included cricket, football, swimming and athletics.[48] The influential educational ideology of athleticism in Britain in the latter half of the nineteenth century was an attempt to curb the undisciplined behaviour of British public schoolboys and channelise their energies into more fruitful pursuits. Public schools as sites of training the next generation of leaders and of character-building played a crucial role in the construction and maintenance of empire. Games and sports—as parts of curricular reforms aimed at fostering organisation and discipline—were used as a means of social control, character-building and leadership-training.

Likewise, the colonial state recognised the importance of sports for schools in the colonies and tried to incorporate physical education in the school curricula. English games such as cricket and activities such as gymnastics were introduced in some schools in Punjab. Lala Mulraj, the officiating extra commissioner of Gujarat district, stated

47. The phrase 'technology of education' refers to the rituals like timetables, discipline, infrastructure, classroom furniture, and teaching aids that were introduced under the colonial educational system. Nita Kumar, *Lessons from Schools: The History of Education in Banaras*, New Delhi: Sage Publications, 2000.
48. See Colm Kerrigan, *Teachers and Football: Schoolboy Association Football in England, 1885–1915*, London: Routledge Falmer, 2005. Although the book is about the history of football, it also describes the changes in the attitude of the British Education Department towards physical education and the sports culture in England in the nineteenth century.

to the Education Commission that the existing conditions in schools affected the health of students adversely. He said:

> In the government district schools, there are parallel bars, swinging poles, cricket provided for physical exercise and some district officers such as Mr. Wakefield, Deputy Commissioner of Ludhiana take special interest in the physical exercises of the students; but, as a general rule, teachers and the district officers are indifferent to the physical development and wellbeing of the students. The physical condition of the students generally is found to suffer on account of the education they receive in the colleges and schools. The reasons appear to be that boys are not yet alive to this; that sedentary habits tell upon the health, and that examiners in almost all examinations put such questions which require great cramming and that in some examinations a very high percentage is required for passing. *The teaching of Persian as a compulsory subject in the schools adds to the work of the boys and thus injures their health*. The attendance at schools for so many hours is also not consistent with the physical development of the boys. Special certificates, marks, and prizes should be given in all schools and colleges to those students who distinguish themselves in physical exercise, and some few marks might be deducted in the school examination in case of candidates who do not look to their health.[49] [emphasis added]

It is clear that while provisions were made for encouraging physical education, the burdens of learning were used to explain or rationalise the poor use of the facilities provided; ill health was even blamed on the taxing nature of the study of Persian. The deputy commissioner of Hoshiarpur, W. Coldstream, ordered that every school should have one 'decent' chair, and that schools in towns or middle schools should have more than one chair, and should also be provided with a small table. Blackboards were supplied wherever they seemed useful. Maps were mounted neatly on cloth and rollers

49. Evidence of Lala Mulraj to the Hunter Commission, *Report by the Punjab Provincial Committee to the Education Commission*, p. 324. In addition to being the officiating extra assistant commissioner in Gujarat District in Punjab, he was an assistant professor in the Oriental College, Lahore, on the Hindi side. He also started some small schools in Punjab.

with rings by which they could be hung. The cleanliness of the walls, door frames, maps, floor cloths, and mats of the school were also considered important issues worthy of scrutiny by the inspector. Masters were therefore punished if they were found responsible for lax discipline and improper maintenance of school property and equipment.[50]

The new education system also produced novel ailments and problems among students. In Punjab, school inspectors were given the authority to note sanitary defects and request the district medical and sanitary officers as to situations where the opinion of a specialist was required. According to the sanitary commissioner of Madras, the chief requirements of an educational institution were clean surroundings, effective drainage and free circulation of air. (The Government of Madras was the first to take measures for ensuring better sanitary conditions in schools; these measures were later adopted by other provincial governments, including that of Punjab.) Existing schoolrooms had two types of problems. Most were overcrowded, hot and badly ventilated. The second problem was the lack of proper lighting. These conditions increased the risk of infection on the one hand, and resulted in anaemia because of hard work on the other.[51]

Yet, the increased demand for education led to the appropriation of old buildings for classrooms, even though these were considered ill-suited and insufficient for the purpose of education. Inappropriate buildings, along with long hours of study, sometimes insufficient food, and emotional and mental strain affected both the minds and the bodies of the young. Dyspepsia and headache were common ailments among the young, even though they were rare among the

50. 'Extracts from Deputy Commissioner's Educational Order Book, Hoshiarpur District, No. II and III', cited in the Evidence of W. Coldstream to the Hunter Commission, *Report by the Punjab Provincial Committee to the Education Commission*, pp. 176–83.
51. According to the Madras sanitary commission of 1886, overcrowding and exposure to foul air created risk of infection from itching and other diseases. In its opinion, 'chaotic poisoning' as much as overwork were the causes of anaemic conditions.

older generation. In addition, many students had defective eyesight as a result of straining their eyes by bending over unsuitable desks, or deciphering small or poor print in a badly-lit room. The size and height of the classroom, the shape and size of the furniture, and the location of latrines and urinals were all scrutinised as part of the effort to keep schoolrooms and the surroundings clean and sanitary, and to ensure that they were conducive to learning. Yet, the effort to tutor students in the new habits and values deemed appropriate by the colonial state was equally important, and the school became a site for instruction on new norms of cleanliness. The amount of time spent on study, leisure, sleep and exercise was staggered according to the age of students as well as their individual differences.[52] To encourage the all-round development of the child, the school was supposed to be equipped with a playground, although most schools did not provide any such space.

Local bodies were given the duty of supplying important equipments to schools. There were important differences, not only between Anglo-vernacular and other schools, but also between boys' and girls' schools. For the boys' schools, *tats* for scholars (one square yard per scholar), small diaries for teachers, one chair, one table, maps (of the district, Punjab, India, Europe, Asia, Africa, America and the world), alphabetical sheets, blackboards (at least two), a box or rack for maps, and simple gymnastic apparatus, where possible, were the chief articles required. At the vernacular middle-school level, certain things, such as two extra blackboards, two extra chairs, and a clock were needed along with everything that was used at the primary-school level.[53] The girls' schools were provided with furnishings and equipment just like the boys' schools, except for gymnastic equipment. On the other hand, their schools were provided *takhtis* and slates (one takhti and one slate for each student), and materials to teach the girls needlework. They were also given textbooks when they were unable to supply their own. The strength of the class could

52. 'Extracts of Madras Sanitary Commission', cited in *Proceedings of Education in the Punjab for the Year 1888*, p. 145.
53. 'Proceedings of General Education Conference of 1887, July', cited in *Proceedings of Education in the Punjab for the Year 1887*, p. 164.

not exceed forty, since it was believed that efficient teaching could take place only when the strength of the class was not large.

Thus, infrastructure itself became a site for the creation of new hierarchies, between Anglo-vernacular and vernacular schools, and between boys' and girls' schools. Yet, no homogeneity was imposed on all schools, since the type of instruction imparted in each school called for different things. The introduction of desks increased this hierarchy because only Anglo-vernacular students were provided desks. Since Anglo-vernacular schools used desks and benches, the classrooms had to be designed to allow superficial space of 10 square feet for each student learning English as opposed to vernacular schools which did not have desks and benches for their pupils. Indigenous schooling took place largely in the open air, involved the use of natural light and natural surroundings, and was based on flexible learning and teaching hours. In the new systems, even the chair was considered a way of raising the status of the teacher; the Anjuman-i-Rifa'i-am and the Arya Samaj petitioned that chairs should be allowed for the teachers to raise their status in front of villagers and before officials.[54]

The Transformation of Time

Notions of time are determined by patterns of employment and by general social and cultural norms. Notions of time differ greatly in agrarian and non-agrarian societies. As E. P. Thompson points out, agrarian time is measured by the seasons, by the planting of crops and by the position of the sun, while non-agrarian time in an industrial society is a way of controlling labourers and making

54. The Anjuman-i-Rifa'i-am and the Arya Samaj considered that the status of teachers was very low. The two organisations believed that the status of teachers could be raised if they were officially recognised in the presence of lambardars and patwaris during the visits of the commissioner to schools. Chairs were given only to some successful teachers, and not to all. Evidences of Arya Samaj and Anjuman-i-Rifa'i-am to the Hunter Commission, *Report by the Punjab Provincial Committee to the Education Commission*, pp. 459, 470.

them perform more work in a shorter duration. Time was measured by the minute, disciplining workers and monitoring their activities, since it was necessary to convert time into money.[55] Foucault points out that in the elementary schools of modern societies, the division of time became increasingly smaller and activities were governed by detailed rules that had to be obeyed. Control of time was maintained by preparing and following timetables. The bell signalled the division and passage of time. Through constant supervision and monitoring, supervisors ensured that the time was used properly and efficiently, thereby ensuring the quality of this time.[56]

The colonial state introduced similar notions of time by dividing the scheme of studies into short time frames and deciding what should be taught and when. Unlike the indigenous schools, which were task-oriented, the colonial school adopted the new timetable which was oriented to the use of capsules of time, which allowed for the completion of the syllabus in the prescribed time frames. The school timetable was maintained to ensure the optimum use of the scheme of studies. In the General Education Conference of July 1887, headmasters and district inspectors were given the right to fix the hour at which school would begin in the summer and winter sessions in the case of Anglo-vernacular and vernacular schools. The time for instruction was fixed at not less than five hours in the primary school and at not less than six hours in the high and middle schools, with a concession of half an hour in case of excessive heat. The time for games and gymnastics were also fixed. A roll call was recommended both when the school opened and at final dismissal.[57] However, extension of education was not possible, since teaching hours were not flexible enough to accommodate the different schedules of agricultural and industrial labourers. Even when the colonial authorities tried to make timetables flexible, it did not result in greater attendance or in increased adherence to the schedule. In

55. E. P. Thompson, 'Time, Work-Discipline, and Industrial Capitalism', *Past and Present*, No. 38, December 1967, pp. 56–97.
56. See Michel Foucault, *Discipline and Punish: The Birth of the Prison*, New York: Vintage Books, 1995.
57. *Proceedings of Education in the Punjab for the Year 1887*, pp. 156–73.

some other provinces, like Bombay and Bengal, the government established night schools for industrial labourers; but since Punjab was largely agricultural, these measures were not introduced in the province.

Holidays and vacations were also fixed at the beginning of the school year. There were as many as thirty-seven holidays during the year exclusive of Sundays, since provision had to be made for a variety of religious holidays. The gazette holidays for the English were New Year's Day, Ash Wednesday, Good Friday, the Queen-Empress's Birthday, and Christmas Vacation (25 to 31 December, or seven days). Holidays on Nauroz, Id-ul-Fitr, Id-uz-Zuha, Muharrum (three days), and Bara Wafat were called Muhammadan holidays. Hindu holidays included Basant Panchami, Sheoratri, Holi, Baisakhi, Salono, Janam Ashtmi, Dushara (four days), and Diwali. Seven local and special holidays were also given.[58]

Reduction of Disparity and Production of New Hierarchies

In the indigenous education system, the differences between schools arose as the result of differences in community needs and the various subjects taught. For instance, Sanskrit schools were different from Arabic schools because as schools of language-learning, they taught different languages. Lande schools were meant for training the children of a specific class of merchants and traders to develop the skills required for pursuing their work. In the colonial education system, these types of disparities were reduced and new types of hierarchies were produced in terms of the levels of schools, the facilities available, and the re-inscribed hierarchies of gender.

Schools were divided into various categories based on the geographical region they served, with village schools at the base, followed by *tehsil* schools (tehsil was a sub-district, or a collection of villages), and then *zillah* schools (located at the headquarters of each district). At the top of the scheme or pyramid, was a college

58. Ibid.

in Lahore—Government College, established in 1864.[59] The classification of schools into high, middle and primary schools was adopted in 1868–69. A new system of classification for India was introduced in 1879–80, in which English schools were classed separately from vernacular ones. The classification of schools after 1879–80 was as follows: secondary and primary schools, which were further divided into two groups, English and vernacular, which were further classified into government institutions and aided institutions.

Institutions imparting education up to the primary level were indigenous schools, village schools and tehsil schools. Some indigenous schools accepted aid from the government, thereby coming under its control. Vernacular schools were then classified as town schools and village schools, corresponding to the middle and the primary levels. At the secondary school level, that hierarchy was also maintained. The government established zillah or Anglo-vernacular schools of two classes, namely superior schools in which the medium of instruction was chiefly English, and inferior schools in which the medium of instruction was the vernacular. According to Mr Arnold, the first Director of Public Instruction of Punjab:

> The establishment of Zillah School was larger than Tehsil School: that the course of instruction was to be higher, and that [the] main business of the school was always to be conducted in and through the medium of Urdu[,] yet in a Zillah School[,] English was always to be taught as an accomplishment to those who were willing to pay for learning it.[60]

So, new divisions were created through the introduction of English and the adoption of fees. According to the Rules for the Classification of Educational Institutions issued in 1879, all educational

59. Farina Mir, *The Social Space of Language: Vernacular Culture in British Colonial Punjab*, Berkeley: University of California Press, 2010, pp. 53–56.
60. 'Extracts from Mr. Arnold's Second Report dated 25th June 1858', cited in J. A. Richey, *Selections from Educational Records, Part-ii*, p. 300.

institutions were classified into government, aided and unaided colleges or schools.[61]

As I have already shown, the principal difference between the vernacular and Anglo-vernacular schools was the teaching of English. But the government maintained the difference between English and vernacular knowledge in its policies. While Macaulay had emphasised English as a medium of instruction, Wood's Despatch gave equal weight to the vernaculars until middle school. It was generally believed that knowledge could not be imparted to the masses in English, while higher education was to be imparted in English only. So both languages were emphasised at different levels. To prevent the feeling of alienation or disorientation caused by a complete change, the Punjab government introduced Urdu as the medium of instruction in Punjab in the place of Persian.

In the 1880s, language became a site of resistance connected with identity issues. As Kenneth Jones has shown, various associations and *samaj*s were established in the latter half of the nineteenth century among Hindus and Muslims.[62] The most contentious issue was language: Hindus wanted Hindi (in the Devanagari script) to be taught in schools, while Muslims wanted Urdu, and Sikhs wanted Punjabi as the medium of instruction. All communities linked religion with language. In other words, through the official promotion of their chosen language, these groups wanted to spread their respective religions. The debate on the medium of instruction was connected with the debate on the 'real dialect of the province'. Punjabi, Urdu, Hindi, Pahari, and other languages were spoken in Punjab. Every community wanted to make its language the medium of instruction. But the fact is that the people of Punjab also wanted to gain knowledge of English since it was the language of the rulers, opening doors to prosperity and employment. As Tariq Rahman has argued, control over or possession of language is a source of power

61. 'Rules for the Classification of Educational Institutions and the Preparation of Statistics Returns', File no. 11, 1879, H. R., Delhi, General Department, Haryana State Archive, Punchkula, Haryana.
62. Kenneth W. Jones, *Arya Dharm: Hindu Consciousness in Nineteenth-century Punjab*, New Delhi: Manohar, 1976.

by which one retains social position and creates hierarchies, even up to the present day, and governments in multilingual societies always ration language-teaching to keep up with the demand in the 'market of language'.[63]

The colonial state intervened in the gender issue and created new kinds of hierarchies and reduced the earlier disparities. Before the onset of colonial rule in Punjab, girls' education had been primarily in the hands of missionaries and indigenous authorities. At the beginning of the nineteenth century, some women belonging to aristocratic families received elementary education to help them in the management of their estate. Their number, of course, was not large; but the situation was encouraging compared to other parts of India. G. W. Leitner wrote that female education in colonial Punjab needed to be revived.[64] According to him, the number of literate females in Punjab had been higher before the annexation. But he could not provide statistics because many females received instruction at home.[65] The girls and the teachers (also females) belonged to the three religions of Punjab, namely Hinduism, Islam, and Sikhism.[66] They were educated at home by their relatives, *maulvi*s and *pundit*s. In some cases, some females received co-education, especially in the case of Koran schools and Gurmukhi schools. The reason for allowing co-education in these schools was that it enabled girls to read religious books and inculcated morals among them. There were a few indigenous girls' schools in Punjab, chiefly for teaching the Koran and the Guru Granth Sahib. Parents paid teachers to impart

63. Tariq Rahman, *Language, Ideology, and Power: Language Learning among the Muslims of Pakistan and North India*, Oxford: Oxford University Press, 2002, pp. 34–64.
64. Cited in Nirmala Devi, 'Development of Education of Punjab in the Latter Half of the Nineteenth Century', unpublished Ph.D. thesis, Indian Institute of Advanced Study, Shimla, 1985, p. 24.
65. G. W. Leitner, *History of Indigenous Education*, pp. 96–112.
66. Cited in G. S. Chhabra, *Social and Economic History of the Panjab (1849–1901)*, Jullundur City: S. Nagin & Co., 1965, p. 136.

religious instruction to their daughters.[67] Hardly any girls were educated beyond the bounds of religion, morality, and the two 'R's (reading and writing) in the indigenous schools.[68]

But extensive progress could not be made in this field due to social prejudices of the pre-colonial and colonial periods.[69] In the late nineteenth century, girls' schools in Punjab were only vernacular primary schools, whether they were maintained by local people or whether they were aided or government schools. Girls were taught the three 'R's—reading, writing and arithmetic. The people of Punjab regarded missionary schools with some suspicion, believing that they were teaching their children Christian songs. This was seen as an attempt to shake the faith of the girls in their religion, and religion was intimately connected with morality. However, at least some elites admitted that the primary girls' schools maintained by the government and by the missionaries resulted in great savings and did no harm to society.[70] But Hindus generally dreaded the prospect of not finding a good match for daughters after a certain age, and also feared the incompatibility of ignorant husbands and educated wives. Muslims restricted female education through the *purdah* system. Generally, it was believed that the age of puberty was lower

67. Evidence of Miss Wauton to the Hunter Commission. She was engaged in the superintendence of female primary and Normal schools for eight years. She was connected with the Zanana Mission. *Report by the Punjab Provincial Committee to the Education Commission*, p. 450.
68. Evidence of Arya Samaj to the Education Commission. *Report by the Punjab Provincial Committee to the Education Commission*, pp. 479–80.
69. Evidence of Pandit Ishwar Prasad to the Education Commission. He explained that social problems like early marriage, superiority of males over females and notions of men towards female education, dependence on parents, early age of puberty, and the *purdah* system, especially among Muslim ladies, were the main causes for the backwardness of female education, along with lack of female teachers, bad mistresses, and the occasionally shameful behaviour of male staff members. *Report by the Punjab Provincial Committee to the Education Commission*, p. 343.
70. Ibid.

in India than in other colder countries.[71] It was also believed that 'female education among the masses will [be] spread by sisters and daughters picking up knowledge from their brothers at home and not much by means of school'.[72] Finally, even many large towns had no girls' schools, while villages were entirely neglected. Quoting the report of a schoolmaster, G. W. Leitner said:

> The progress made by the Educational Department in the matter of female education is very meagre. The character of instruction is in some schools Deva Nagari, in others Gurumukhi, and in others Persian. Practical teaching in needle-work, lace making, &c., &c., if introduced into our schools, is likely to make them more attractive and useful. Besides, a better class of teachers should be provided.[73]

Another schoolmaster wrote to Leitner:

> Some progress has, of course, been made by the department in instituting female schools, and the instruction given in them is the same as in the schools for boys. This kind of instruction, however, is not suited to female schools; there should not be any Persian in them, and not so much of arithmetic. Female education in this country is purely and simply a forced thing, and almost a farce, because girls cannot stay long on account of early marriage because some instruction in their own religion is of necessity to be given them in the school-hours, otherwise they would not attend, and because efficient teachers (females) cannot be readily had for them.[74]

However, he added:

> The schools in the city of Jalandhar itself and in [the] *suburbs* (called *bustees*) have, under the untiring zeal, efficiency, diligence, and

71. Ibid.
72. This was stated in the memorial of the residents of Rupar district along with members of the Gujarat Bhasha Pracharini Sabha, 16,609 residents of Jagadhari of Ambala district, and 1,139 residents of Ferozpur district. *Report by the Punjab Provincial Committee to the Education Commission*, p. 542.
73. Evidence of G. W. Leitner to the Hunter Commission, *Report by Punjab Provincial Committee to the Education Commission*, p. 380.
74. Ibid.

> supervision of the Inspectress, Mrs. Mitter, made the most marked improvements and are *the most promising in the Province* (Director's Report 1880–81). These last are not only the *best schools in the province*, but are *representative* schools, and will no doubt, in time, create a desire among the neighbouring people all round to have similar institutions among them also.[75] [emphasis added]

A missionary lady named Miss Mary R. Boyd told the commission that the attendance of pupils in the female primary schools depended entirely on the payment of scholarships, which were given as incentives to attend school. The scholarships made up what the child would have earned by working at home, so the discontinuance of scholarships often resulted in the closure of schools. In some exceptional cases, as in Amritsar, it was found that some high-caste girls were studying without scholarships.[76]

The policies themselves embodied specific gendered notions about education. The curricula of boys' schools and girls' schools were separate, and girls largely received only primary education. In the education of females, circumstances, needs and environment were kept in mind by the educational authorities, with an emphasis on moral education, which would be useful in their married life because it would make them better wives and mothers. In the Gurmukhi and Koran schools, boys and girls studied together. Generally, the people of Punjab, including the missionaries, believed that women's education should be differentiated from that of men's education. Usually, they had less time for studying due to the practice of early marriage, so their curriculum was quite different from that of men. All were against the learning of foreign languages, especially for girls, when their time could be utilised in activities such as cooking, needlework, and knitting. However, government vernacular primary schools included subjects such as arithmetic, history, geography,

75. Ibid.
76. Evidence of Miss Mary R. Boyd, who was connected with the Zanana S. P. G. Mission of Delhi. She was then working as a superintendent of the Muslim female schools, which had been opened by the late Mrs. Winter. *Report by the Punjab Provincial Committee to the Education Commission*, pp. 183–84.

and literature taught in the four languages (that is, Hindu and Sikh girls were taught in Hindi and Gurmukhi, and Muslim girls were taught in Urdu and Persian). Even the examinations for girls were less rigorous than those for boys. It should be kept in mind that girls did not pay fees; on the other hand, schools in most cases gave monetary incentives to girls to study, or at least to enrol in schools. Despite this differentiation, the inspection of girls' schools presented specific problems. Muslim girl pupils were *purdahnashin*. Moreover, as was pointed out by Miss Wauton, who was attached to the Zanana Mission, inspection was fair only when the inspector knew the languages and dialects spoken by the girls. Males could not be inspectors, and hence emerged the demand for indigenous lady inspectors.[77]

Conclusion

The education system in Punjab in the latter half of the nineteenth century was transformed by political changes after the province was annexed by the British. New innovations and measures were adopted that were not part of the indigenous education system. An important goal of colonial rule was disciplining the subjects, and this was achieved through the new system of colonial education. The colonial state sought to impose standardisation and uniformity on the education system in the areas of textbook preparation and adoption, examination, inspection, and the space and physical structure of classroom and school to fulfil their aims. The imposition of this uniformity reduced some disparities of the indigenous education system, but created new kinds of divisions: the vernacular–Anglo-vernacular division; standards and divisions (primary, middle and high schools); classes (first, second, third, etc., classes); academic success or progress based on an examination system, and schools based on gender (separate schools for boys and girls).

77. Evidence of Miss Wauton to the Hunter Commission, *Report by the Punjab Provincial Committee to the Education Commission*, pp. 449–51.

Consolidated Bibliography

Acharya, Poromesh. 'Bengali Bhadralok and Educational Development in Nineteenth-Century Bengal', in *Education, Development and Underdevelopment*, edited by S. C. Shukla and Rekha Kaul. New Delhi: Sage, 1998, pp. 28–35.

Adam, William. *Reports on the State of Education in Bengal 1835 and 1838*, Reprint edition. Calcutta: University of Calcutta, 1941.

Adamoski, Robert, Dorothy E. Chunn and Robert Menzies (eds.). *Contesting Canadian Citizenship: Historical Readings.* Peterborough, Ontario: Broadview Press, 2002.

Aldrich, Richard. *Lessons from the History of Education: The Selected Works of Richard Aldrich.* Oxford: Routledge, 2006.

Alexander, E. S. *The Attitudes of British Protestant Missionaries Towards Nationalism in India.* New Delhi: Konark Publishers, 1994.

Allen, Theodore W. *The Invention of the White Race.* London: Verso, 1994.

Aloysius, G. *Religion as Emancipatory Identity: A Buddhist Movement among the Tamils under Colonialism.* New Delhi: New Age International, 1998.

Ambedkar, B. R. *Dr. Babasaheb Ambedkar, Writings and Speeches: Unpublished Writings* (vol. 5). Government of Maharashtra: Education Department, 1989.

———. *Dr. Babasaheb Ambedkar, Writings and Speeches: Correspondence* (vol. 21). Government of Maharashtra: Dr. Babasaheb Ambedkar, Mahatma Phule and Rajarshi Shahu Source Material Publication Committee, 2006.

Anderson, C., and Mary Jean Bowman (eds.). *Education and Economic Development.* Chicago: Aldine Publishing Co., 1966.

Anderson, Kay J. *Vancouver's Chinatown: Racial Discourse in Canada, 1875–1980.* Montreal and Kingston: McGill Queen's University Press, 1991.

Andrews, C. F. 'The Effect of the Japanese Victories upon India'. *The East and the West*, 1905.

Anthony, Arblaster. *The Rise and Decline of Western Liberalism*. Oxford: Basil Blackwell, 2001.

Armstrong, Karen. *Buddha*. New York: Penguin, 1987.

Arnold, Edward. *Education in India: A Letter from the Ex-principal of an Indian Government College to His Appointed Successor*. London: Bell & Daldy, 1860.

Aryanayakam, E. W. *The Story of Twelve Years*. Sevagram (Wardha): Hindustani Talimi Sangh, 1950.

Baber, Zaheer. *The Science of Empire: Scientific Knowledge, Colonization and Colonial Rule in India*. Albany: State University of New York Press, 1995.

Bagchi, A. K. *Private Investment in India, 1900–1939*. Cambridge: Cambridge University Press, 1972.

Ballhatchet, Kenneth. *Social Policy and Social Change in Western India, 1817–1830*. London: Oxford University Press, 1961.

———. *Race, Sex and Class under the Raj: Imperial Attitudes and Policies and their Critics*. London: Weidenfeld and Nicolson, 1980.

Banerjee, Surendranath. *A Nation in the Making*. New York: Oxford University Press, 1925.

———. *Speeches and Writings of Babu Surendranath Banerjea*, Madras: G. A. Natesan and Co., 1940.

Banks, Margaret A. *Sir John George Bourinot, Victorian Canadian: His Life, Times and Legacy*. Montreal and Kingston: McGill-Queen's University Press, 2001.

Bannerjee, Sukanya. *Becoming Imperial Citizen: Indians in the Late Victorian Empire*, Durham and London: Duke University Press, 2010.

Barman, Jean. *The West Beyond the West: A History of British Columbia*. Toronto: University of Toronto Press, 1991.

Barman, Jean, Jill Wade and Robert A. J. McDonald (eds.). *Readings in the History of British Columbia*. Burnaby, British Columbia: Open Learning Agency, 1997.

Barman, Jean, and Mona Gleason (eds.). *Children, Teachers and Schools in the History of British Columbia*, Calgary, Alberta: Detselig, 2003.

Basu, Aparna. *The Growth of Education and Political Development in India, 1898–1920*. New Delhi: Oxford University Press, 1974.

———. *Essays in the History of Indian Education*. New Delhi: Concept, 1982.

Basu, Subho. 'The Dialectics of Resistance: Colonial Geography, Bengali Literati and the Racial Mapping of Indian Identity'. *Modern Asian Studies* 44, no. 1, 2010, pp. 53–79.

Bates, Crispin. *Race, Caste and Tribe in Central India: The Early Origins of Anthropometry*. Edinburgh: Centre for South Asian Studies, 1995.

Bayly, C. A. *Empire and Information: Intelligence Gathering and Social Communication in India, 1780–1870*. Cambridge: Cambridge University Press, 1996.

Becker, Gary S. *Human Capital: A Theoretical and Empirical Analysis, with Special Reference to Education*. New York: Columbia University Press, 1964.

Bellenoit, Hayden. *Missionary Education and Empire in Late Colonial India, 1860–1920*. London: Pickering & Chatto, 2007.

Benoit, Paul. 'The Politics and Ethics of John George Bourinot'. *Canadian Parliamentary Review* 7, no. 3, 1984, pp. 6–10.

Bertrand, Marianne, and Sendhil Mullainathan. 'Are Emily and Greg More Employable than Lakisha and Jamal? A Field Experiment on Labor Market Discrimination'. *Working Paper Series WP 03–22*. Department of Economics, Massachusetts Institute of Technology, 2003.

Bhagavan, Manu. *Sovereign Spheres: Princes, Education and Empire in Colonial India*. New York: Oxford University Press, 2003.

Bhagavan, Manu, and Anne Feldhaus (eds.). *'Speaking Truth to Power': Religion, Caste and the Subaltern Question in India*. New Delhi: Oxford University Press, 2008.

Bhargava, K. D. (ed.), *Selections from Educational Records of the Government of India: Technical Education in India, 1886–1907* (vol. 4). New Delhi: Manager of Publication, Government of India, 1968.

Bhaskar, Pabitra. 'Dr. Sachchidanand Sinha's Role in the Creation of the Province of Bihar', in *Souvenir*, edited by K. K. Datta. Patna: Dr. Sachchidanand Sinha Library, 1972.

Bhattacharya, Mita, Russel Mythe and Marika Vicziany (eds.). *South Asia in the Era of Globalization: Trade, Industrialization Welfare*. New York: Nova Science, 2004.

Bhattacharya, Sabyasachi. (ed.). *Education and the Disprivileged: Nineteenth and Twentieth Centuries*. New Delhi: Orient Longman, 2001.

———. *Development of Modern Indian Thought and the Social Science*. New Delhi: Oxford University Press, 2007.

Bhattacharya, Sabyasachi, Joseph Bara and Chinna Rao Yagati (eds.). *Educating the Nation: Documents on the Discourse of National Education in India, 1880–1920*. New Delhi: Kanishka, 2003.

Blue, Gregory, Bunton Martin and R. Croizier (eds.). *Colonialism and the Modern World.* New York: Armonk, 2002.

Bob, Clifford (ed.). *The International Struggle for New Human Rights.* Philadelphia: University of Pennsylvania Press, 2009.

Bolt, Christine. *Victorian Attitudes to Race*. London: Routledge and Kegan Paul, 1971.

Boman-Behram, B. K. *Educational Controversies of India: The Cultural Conquest of India under British Imperialism.* Bombay: D. B. Taraporevala, 1943.

Borthwick, Meredith. *The Changing Role of Women in Bengal, 1849–1905.* Princeton: Princeton University Press, 1984.

Bose, Joges. *Surendranath Banerjee*. Dacca: Baroda Ganguli, 1939.

Bourinot, John George. *Canadian Studies in Comparative Politics*. Montreal: Dawson Brothers, 1890.

______. *How Canada is Governed: A Short Account of its Executive, Judicial and Municipal Institutions with a Historical Outline of Their Origins and Development.* Toronto: Copp, Clark and Co., 1895.

Brehony, Kevin. 'A New Education for a New Era: The Contribution of the Conferences of the New Education Fellowship to the Disciplinary Field of Education (1921–1938)'. *Paedagogica Historica* 40, no. 5, 2004, pp. 191–205.

Briton, Martin. 'Lord Dufferin and the Indian National Congress, 1885–88'. *Journal of British Studies* 7, no. 1, November 1967, pp. 68–96.

Brock-Utne, B. *Whose Education for All? The Recolonization of the African Mind.* New York: Falmer Press, 2000.

Brown, C. (ed.). *Central Provinces and Berar District Gazetteers, Akola District, vol. A–Descriptive.* Calcutta: Baptist Mission Press, 1910.

Burton, Antoinette. *Burdens of History: British Feminists, Indian Women and Imperial Culture, 1865–1915.* Chapel Hill: University of North Carolina Press, 1994.

Carnoy, Martin. *Education as Cultural Imperialism.* New York: Longman, 1974.

Carty, R. K. (ed.). *Politics, Policy and Government in British Columbia.* Vancouver: University of British Columbia Press, 1996.

Caruso, Marcelo. 'Latin American Independence, Education, and the Invention of New Polities'. *Paedagogica Historica* 46, no. 4, 2010, pp. 409–17.

Casolari, Marzia. 'Hindutva's Foreign Tie-up in the 1930s Archival Evidence.' *Economic and Political Weekly* 35, no. 4, 22 January 2000.

Census of India 1931: Central Provinces and Berar (vol. 12, part 1). Nagpur: W. H. Shoobert, 1933.

Chaiton, Alf, and Neil McDonald (eds.). *Canadian Schools and Canadian Identity*. Toronto: Gage, 1977.

Chakrabarty, Dipesh. 'Limits of the Bourgeois Model', in *The Middle Class in Colonial India*, edited by Sanjay Joshi. New Delhi: Oxford University Press, 2010.

Chakravarti, Uma. *Rewriting History: The Life and Times of Pandita Ramabai.* New Delhi: Kali for Women, 1998.

Chakravarti, Uma, and Preeti Gill (eds.). *Shadow Lives: Writings on Widowhood.* New Delhi: Kali for Women, 2001.

Chanana, Karuna. *Socialization, Education and Women: Explorations in Gender Identity*. New Delhi: Orient Longman, 1988.

———. *Interrogating Women's Education: Bounded Visions, Expanding Horizons.* Delhi: Rawat Publications, 2001.

Chandra, Satish. (ed.). *Religion, State and Society in Medieval India.* New Delhi: Oxford University Press, 2008.

———. *History of Medieval India.* Hyderabad: Orient BlackSwan, 2009.

Chandra, Sudhir. 'Rukhmabai: Debate over Woman's Right to Her Person'. *Economic and Political Weekly* 31, no. 44, November 1996, pp. 2937–47.

———. *Enslaved Daughters: Colonialism, Law and Women's Rights*. Delhi: Oxford University Press, 1998.

Chatterjee, Nandini. *The Making of Indian Secularism: Empire, Law and Christianity, 1830–1960*. Basingstoke: Palgrave Macmillan, 2011.

Chatterji, H. L. *Pt. Bishan Narain Dhar: Speeches and Writings.* Lucknow: Anglo-Oriental Press, 1921.

Chattopadhyaya, Kamaladevi. *Indian Women's Battle for Freedom*. Delhi: Abhinav, 1983.

Chaudhuri, Maitrayee (ed.). *Feminism in India.* New Delhi: Kali for Women and Women Unlimited, 2004.

Chhabra, G. S. *Social and Economic History of Punjab (1849–1901).* Jullundhur: S. Nagin & Co., 1965.

Chirol, Valentine. *Indian Unrest.* London: Macmillan, 1910.

Clarke, J. J. *Oriental Enlightenment: The Encounters Between Asian and Western Thought*. London: Routledge, 1997.

Clarke, Linda, and Christopher Winch. *Vocational Education, International Approaches, Developments and Systems.* London and New York: Routledge, 2007.

Cohn, B. S. *Colonialism and its Forms of Knowledge*. Princeton: Princeton University Press, 1996.

Constable, Philip. 'Sitting on the School Verandah: The Ideology and Practice of "Untouchable" Educational Protest in Late Nineteenth-century Western India'. *Indian Economic and Social History Review* 37, no. 4, 2000, pp. 383–422.

Copley, A. *Religions in Conflict: Ideology, Cultural Contact and Conversion in Late Colonial India*. New Delhi: Oxford University Press, 1997.

Cotton, J. S. *Progress of Education in India 1892–97, Third Quinquinnneal Review*. London: Her Majesty's Stationery Office, 1898.

Cox, J. *Imperial Fault Lines: Christianity and Colonial Power in India, 1818–1940*. Princeton: Princeton University Press, 2002.

Crane, Robert I. *Technical Education and Economic Development in India before World War I*. Durham, North Carolina: Commonwealth Study Center, Duke University, 1965.

Crease, Gillian, and Veronica Strong-Boag (eds.). *British Columbia Reconsidered: Essays on Women*. Vancouver: Press Gang Publishers, 1992.

Crook, N. *The Transmission of Knowledge in South Asia: Essays on Education, History, Religion and Politics*. New Delhi: Oxford University Press, 1996.

Cust, R. N. *Linguistic and Oriental Essays: Written from the Year 1847 to 1887*. London: Trubner & Co., 1887.

Cutts, Elmer H. The Background of Macaulay's Minute. *The American Historical Review* 58, no. 4, 1953.

Dangle, Arjun (ed.). *Poisoned Bread: Translations from Modern Marathi Dalit Literature*. Bombay: Orient Longman, 1994.

Datla, Kavita. 'A Worldly Vernacular: Urdu at Osmania University', *Modern Asian Studies* 43, no. 5, 2009, pp. 1117–48.

Dent, V. F., and L. Yannotta. 'A Rural Community Library in Uganda: A Study of its Use and Users'. *Libri* 55, no. 1, 2005, pp. 39–55.

Desai, A. R. (ed.). *Peasant Struggles in India*. Bombay: Oxford University Press, 1979.

Deshpande, G. P. (ed.). *Selected Works of Jotirao Phule*. New Delhi: LeftWorld, 2002.

Despatch of 1854 on General Education of India (Reprint edition), London: John Maclaren & Sons, 1880.

Dey, Lal Bihari. *Recollections of Alexander Duff*. London: T Nelson and Sons, 1879.

Dirks, Nicholas. *Castes of Mind: Colonialism and the Making of Modern India*. Princeton: Princeton University Press, 2001.

Edwards, Elizabeth (ed.). *Anthropology and Photography*. London: Yale University Press in Association with the Royal Anthropological Institute, 1992.

Edwards, Michael. *Warren Hastings: King of Nabobs.* London: Hart – Davis, MacGibben, 1976.

Engels, Dagmar. *Beyond Purdah? Women in Bengal, 1890–1939.* New Delhi: Oxford University Press, 1996.

Engels, Dagmar, and Shula Marks (eds.). *Contesting Colonial Hegemony: State and Society in Africa and India.* London: British Academic Press, 1994.

Faruqui, Ziaul Hasan. *Dr. Zakir Hussain. Quest for Truth*. New Delhi: APH Publishing Corporation, 1999.

First Annual Report of the Bombay Education Society. Bombay: Samuel Rans, 1816.

Fiske, Adele. 'Scheduled Caste Buddhist Organizations', in *The Untouchables in Contemporary India*, edited by J. Michael Mahar, Tucson: University of Arizona Press, 1972.

Forbes, Geraldine. *Women in Colonial India: Essays on Politics, Medicine and Historiography*. New Delhi: Chronicle Books, 2005.

Forbes, Geraldine, and Tapan Raychaudhuri (eds.). *The Memoirs of Dr. Haimabati Sen: From Child Widow to Lady Doctor*. New Delhi: Roli Books, 2000.

Forster, E. M. *A Passage to India.* New York: Harcourt, Brace and Co., 1924.

Forrester, D. B. *Caste and Christianity: Attitudes and Policies on Caste of Anglo-Saxon Protestant Missions in India*. London: Curzon Press, 1980.

Foucault, Michel. *Discipline and Punishment: The Birth of the Prison*. New York: Vintage Books, 1996.

Francis, Daniel. *The Imaginary Indian: The Image of the Indian in Canadian Culture*. Vancouver: Arsenal Pulp Press, 1992.

_______. *National Dreams: Myth, Memory and Canadian History*. Vancouver: Arsenal Pulp Press, 1997.

Frankenberg, Ruth. *White Women, Race Matters: The Social Constitution of Whiteness*. London: Routledge, 1993.

Frykenberg, R. *Christians and Missionaries in India: Cross-Cultural Communication and Consequences since 1500*. Cambridge: W. B. Eerdmans Publishing, 2003.

Frykenberg, R. (ed.). *Delhi Through the Ages: Essays in Urban History, Culture and Politics.* New Delhi: Oxford University Press, 1986.

Gandhi, M. K. *Hind Swaraj.* Ahmedabad: Navajivan Publishing House, 1946.

———. *The Problem of Education.* Ahmedabad: Navajivan Publishing House, 1962.

———. *Varnashramadharma.* Ahmedabad: Navajivan Publishing House, 1962.

———. *The Collected Works of Mahatma Gandhi* (98 vols.), (vol. 91). New Delhi: Publications Division, Ministry of Information and Broadcasting, Government of India, 1999.

Gazetteer for Chanda District. Allahabad: The Pioneer Press, 1909.

Gellner, Ernest. *Conditions of Liberty: Civil Society and its Rivals.* London: Hamish Hamilton, 1994.

General Report on Public Instruction in the United Provinces of Agra and Oudh. Allahabad: Government Press, 1912.

Ghosh, Durba, and Dane Kennedy (eds.). *Decentering Empire: Britain, India and the Transcolonial World.* Hyderabad: Orient Longman, 2006.

Ghosh, J. *Higher Education in Bengal under British Rule.* Calcutta: The Book Co., 1926.

Ghosh, S. C. *The Social Condition of British Community in Bengal, 1757–1800.* Leiden: E. J Brill, 1971

———. *Dalhousie in India, 1848–56.* New Delhi: Munshiram Manoharlal, 1975.

———. 'Dalhousie, Charles Wood and the Education Despatch of 1854'. *History of Education* 4, no. 2, 1975, pp. 37–47.

———. *History of Education in Modern India, 1757–1986.* New Delhi: Orient Longman, 1975.

———. 'Formation of an Education Policy of the British Raj between 1757 and 1857', in *The Supply of Schooling,* edited by W. Frijhoff. Paris: Pulications de la Sorbonne, 1983.

Ghosh, S. C., and J. P. Naik (eds.). *Development of Educational Service 1854–74.* New Delhi: Sterling Publishers, 1976.

Gokhale, Jayashree. *From Concessions to Confrontation: The Politics of an Indian Untouchable Community.* Bombay: Popular Prakashan, 1993.

Goodson, I. (ed.). *Social Histories of Secondary Curriculum: Subjects for Study.* London: The Falmer Press, 1985.

Gore, M. S. *Vitthal Ramji Shinde: An Assessment of His Contribution.* Bombay: Tata Institute of Social Sciences, 1990.

Goswami, Manu. *Producing India: From Colonial Economy to National Spaces*. New Delhi: Permanent Black, 2004.

Gregory, R. *India and East Africa: A History of Race Relations within the British Empire*. Oxford: Clarendon Press, 1971.

Gupta, N. *Delhi Between Two Empires, 1803–1931: Society, Government and Urban Growth*. New Delhi: Oxford University Press, 1981.

Gupta, S. H. *The Arya Samaj and the Raj, 1875–1920*. New Delhi: Gitanjali Publishing House, 1991.

Gutek, Gerald Lee (ed.). *The Montessori Method: The Origins of an Educational Innovation: Including an Abridged and Annotated Version of Maria Montessori's 'The Montessori Method'*. Oxford: Rowman & Littlefield. 2004.

Habib, Irfan, and Dhruv Raina. *Domesticating Modern Science: A Social History of Science and Culture in Colonial India*. New Delhi: Tulika Books, 2004.

Hall, Catherine. 'Gender and Ethnicity in the 1830s and 1840s', in *White, Male and Middle-Class: Explorations in Feminism and History*, edited by Catherine Hall. London: Polity Press, 1992.

Hasan, Mushirul (ed.). *Knowledge, Power and Politics: Educational Institutions in India*. New Delhi: Lotus Collection, 1998.

Hardtmann, Eva-Maria. *The Dalit Movement in India: Local Practices, Global Connections*. New Delhi: Oxford University Press, 2009.

Harrington, Jack. *Sir John Malcolm and the Creation of British India*. New York: Palgrave Macmillan, 2010.

Headrick, Daniel R. *The Tentacles of Progress Technology Transfer in the Age of Imperialism, 1850–1940*. New York: Oxford University Press, 1988.

Heater, Derek. *Citizenship in Britain: A History*, Edinburgh: Edinburgh University Press, 2006.

Heimsath, C. H. *Indian Nationalism and Hindu Social Reform*, Princeton: Princeton University Press, 1964.

'The Hindu Character'. *Asiatic Journal*, 1828.

Hobsbawm, Eric. *On History*. London: Weidenfeld and Nicolson, 1997.

Holland, W. *The Goal of India*. London: United Council for Missionary Education, 1917.

———. *The Indian Outlook*. London: Edinburgh House Press, 1926

Huttenback, R. A. *Racism and Empire: White Settlers and Colored Immigrants in the British Self-Governing Colonies, 1830–1910*. Ithaca: Cornell University Press, 1976.

Ibbetson, D. *Outlines of Panjab Ethnography: Being Extracts from the Panjab Census Report of 1881, Treating Religion, Language and Caste*. Calcutta: Superintendent of Government Printing, 1883.

Ignatieff, Noel. *How the Irish Became White: Race and the Intimate in Colonial Rule*. New York and London: Routledge, 1995.

Ikoja-Odongo, J. R. 'Public Library Politics: The Ugandan Perspective', *Information Development* 20, no. 3, 2004, pp. 169–81.

Inden, R. *Imagining India*. Oxford: Basil Blackwell, 1990.

Ingleby, J. *Missionaries, Education and India: Issues in Protestant Missionary Education in the Long Nineteenth Century*. Delhi: International Society for the Propagation of Christian Knowledge, 2000.

Jadhav, Narendra. *Untouchables: My Family's Triumphant Escape from India's Caste System*. Berkeley: University of California Press, 2005.

Jakobsh, Doris R. *Relocating Gender in Sikh History: Transformation, Meaning and Identity*. New Delhi: Oxford University Press, 2003.

Jayawardena, Kumari. *The White Woman's Other Burden: Western Women and South Asia during British Colonial Rule*. New York: Routledge, 1995.

Jenkins, Laura Dudley. 'Race, Caste and Justice: Social Science Categories and Antidiscrimination Politics in India and the United States', *Connecticut Law Review* 36, no. 3, 2004, pp. 747–84.

———. *Identity and Identification in India: Defining the Disadvantaged*. London and New York: Routledge, 2009.

Jenkins, R. S. *Canadian Civics*. Toronto: Clark & Co., 1910.

Jodhka, Surinder S. 'Nation and Village: Images of Rural India in Gandhi, Nehru and Ambedkar'. *Economic and Political Weekly* 37, no. 32, 2002 , pp. 3343–54.

Johnson, Gordon. 'Partition, Agitation and Congress, Bengal 1904–1908'. *Modern Asian Studies* 7, no. 2, 1973, pp. 533–88.

Johnson, Henry. *John Jessop, Gold Seeker and Educator: Founder of the British Columbia Educational System*. Vancouver: Mitchell Press, 1971.

Jones, Kenneth W. *Arya Dharm: Hindu Consciousness in the Nineteenth Century*. New Delhi: Manohar, 1976.

———. (ed.). *Religious Controversy in British India: Dialogues in South Asian Languages*. New York: State University of New York Press, 1992.

Kadam, K. N. *Dr. Babasaheb Ambedkar and the Significance of His Movement: A Chronology*. Bombay: Popular Prakashan, 1991.

Kaikini, L. V. *The Speeches and Writings of Sir Narayan G. Chandavarkar*. Bombay: MGPM, 1911.

Kakarambe, S. A. *Karmaveer Bhaurao Patil*. Bombay: Somaiya Publications, 1983.

Kane, Pandurang Vaman. *History of Dharmasatras* (vol. 1). Poona: Bhandarkar Research Institute, 1968.

Keer, Dhananjay. *Dr. Ambedkar: Life and Mission.* Revised edition, Bombay: Popular Prakashan, 1962.

______. *Mahatma Jotirao Phooley: Father of our Social Revolution.* Bombay: Popular Prakashan, 1964.

______. *Shahu Chatrapati, A Royal Revolutionary.* Bombay: Popular Prakashan, 1976.

Kendrick, M. and S. Jones. 'Girls' Visual Representations of Literacy in A Rural Ugandan Community'. *Canadian Journal of Education* 31, no. 2, 2008, pp. 371–404.

Kerrigan, Colm. *Teachers and Football: Schoolboy Association Football in England, 1885–1915.* London: Routledge Falmer, 2005.

Khan, Syed Ahmad. *Report of the Member of Select Committee for the Better Diffusion and Advancement of Learning among Muhammadans of India.* Benares: Medical Hall Press, 1872.

Khanolkar, Vaman Pandurang. *Indigenous Elementary Education in the Bombay Presidency in 1855 and Thereabouts.* Bombay: Indian Institute of Education, 1965.

Kishwar, Madhu. 'Arya Samaj and Women's Education Kanya Mahavidyalaya, Jalandhar', *Economic and Political Weekly*, vol. 21, no. 17, April 1986, pp. 9–24.

Knowles, Valerie. *Strangers at Our Gates: Canadian Immigration and Immigration Policy, 1540–2006.* Toronto: Dundurn Press, 2007.

Kopf, David. *British Orientalism and Bengal Renaissance: The Dynamics of Indian Modernisation, 1773–1835*, Berkeley: University of California Press, 1960.

Kosambi. Meera (ed.). *Pandita Ramabai Through Her Own Words: Selected Works.* New Delhi: Oxford University Press, 2000.

Kozol, Jonathan. *Savage Inequalities: Children in America's Schools.* New York: Harper Perennial, 1992.

Kshirsagar, R. K. *Dalit Movement in India and Its Leaders, 1857–1956.* New Delhi: M D Publications, 1992.

Kumar, Deepak (ed.). *Science and Empire: Essays in Indian Context, 1700–1947.* New Delhi: Anamika Prakashan, 1991.

Kumar, Krishna. 'Textbooks and Educational Culture'. *Economic and Political Weekly* 21, no. 30, 1986, pp. 1309–11.

______. *Political Agenda of Education: A Study of Colonialist and Nationalist Ideas.* New Delhi: Sage Publications, 1991.

Kumar, Neelam (ed.). *Women and Science in India: A Reader*. New Delhi: Oxford University Press, 2009.

Kumar, Nita (ed.). *Women as Subjects: South Asian Histories*. New Delhi: Stree, 1994.

———. *Lessons from Schools: The History of Education in Banaras*. New Delhi: Sage Publications, 2000.

Kumarappa, Bharatan (ed.). *Towards New Education*. Ahmedabad: Navajivan Publishing House, 1963.

Laird, M. A. *Missionaries and Education in Bengal*. Oxford: Oxford University Press, 1972.

Laut, Agnes C. *Am I My Brother's Keeper? A Study of British Columbia's Labor & Oriental Problems*. Vancouver: Subway, 2003.

Leitner, G. W. *History of Indigenous Education in Punjab since Annexation in 1882*. Lahore: Language Department, 1883.

Lelyveld, D. *Aligarh's First Generation: Muslim Solidarity in British India*. Princeton: Princeton University Press, 1978.

Leonard, Victoria. *Politicians, Pupils, and Priests: Argentine Education since 1943*. New York: Peter Lang, 1989.

Lewis, Maureen A., and Marlaine E. Lockheed (eds.). *Exclusion, Gender and Education: Case Studies from the Developing World*. Washington, D.C.: Center for Global Development, 2006.

Macpherson, C. B. *Political Theory of Possessive Individualism*. London: Oxford University Press, 1977.

Madhukar, K. H. *Dr Sachidanand Sinha: A Maker of Bihar and Modern India*. New Delhi: Northern Book Centre, 1996.

Magara, E., and C. Batambuze. 'Towards a Reading Culture for Uganda'. *African Journal of Library, Archive and Information Science* 15, no. 1, 2005, pp. 35–42.

Magara E., and J. B. Nyumba. 'Towards a School Library Development Policy for Uganda'. *Library Review* 53, no. 6, 2004, pp. 313–22.

Majumdar, Bhagaban Prasad. *First Fruits of English Education*. Calcutta: Bookland, 1973.

Malhotra, Anshu. *Gender, Caste and Religious Identity: Restructuring Class in Colonial Punjab*. New Delhi: Oxford University Press, 2002.

Mangan, J. A. *The Imperial Curriculum: Racial Images and Education in the British Colonial Experience*. Manchester: Manchester University Press, 1990.

———. (ed.). *Making Imperial Mentalities: Socialisation and British Imperialism*. Manchester: Manchester University Press, 1990.

Mani, Lata. *Contentious Traditions: The Debate on Sati in Colonial India.* Berkeley: University of California Press, 1988.

Matthew, Anjilvel V. *Karmaveer Bhaurao Patil.* Satara: Rayat Shikshan Sanstha, 1957.

Mayhew, A. *The Education of India: A Study of British Educational Policy in India 1835–1920.* London: Faber & Gwyer, 1928.

McClintock, Anne. *Imperial Leather: Race, Gender and Sexuality in the Colonial Context.* New York: Routledge, 1995.

McCully, Bruce T. *English Education and the Origins of Indian Nationalism.* Glouchester, Mass, Peter Smith, 1966.

McDonald, Neil, and Alif Chaiton (eds.). *Egerton Ryerson and His Times.* Toronto: Macmillan of Canada, 1978.

McKaque, Ormond (ed.). *Racism in Canada.* Saskatoon, Saskatchewan: Fifth House Publications, 1991.

McLeod, W. H. *Who is a Sikh? The Problem of Sikh Identity.* New Delhi: Oxford University Press, 1989.

Mehta, H. R. *A History of the Growth and Development of Western Education in Punjab 1846–1884.* Punjab: Language Department, 1971.

Menon, Visalakshi. *Indian Women and Nationalism: The UP Story.* New Delhi: Shakti Books, 2003.

Meston, W. *Indian Educational Policy.* Madras: Christian Literature Society for India, 1936.

Metcalf, Thomas R. *Ideologies of the Raj*, New Delhi: Cambridge University Press, 1996.

Midgely, Clare (ed.). *Gender and Imperialism.* Manchester: Manchester University Press, 1998.

Miller, Barbara. D. *The Endangered Sex.* London: Cornell University Press, 1981.

Miller, William. *Unrest and Education in India.* Edinburgh: Edinburgh & Co., 1911

Millington, C. M. *'Whether we be Many or Few': A History of the Cambridge/Delhi Brotherhood.* Bangalore: Asian Trading Corporation, 1999.

Minault, Gail. 'Sayyid Mumtaz Ali and Tahzib un-Niswan: Women's Rights in Islam and Women's Journalism in Urdu'. In *Religious Controversy in British India: Dialogues in South Asian Languages*, edited by Kenneth W. Jones. New York: State University of New York Press, 1992.

———. *Secluded Scholars: Women's Education and Muslim Social Reform in Colonial India.* New Delhi: Oxford University Press, 1998.

———. 'Sayyid Ahmad Dehlavi and the Delhi Renaissance', in *The Delhi Omnibus.* New Delhi: Oxford University Press, 2007.

Mir, Farina. *The Social Space of Language: Vernacular Culture in British Colonial Punjab*. Los Angeles and London: University of California Press, 2010.

Misra, B. B. *The Central Administration of East Indian Company*. London: Manchester University Press, 1959.

Mital, K. V. *History of the Thomson College of Engineering, 1847–1949*. Roorkee: University of Roorkee, 1986.

Mohamad, Shan. *Writings and Speeches of Sir Syed Ahmad Khan*. Bombay: Nachiketa, 1972.

Mohanty, Chandra Talpade. '"Under Western Eyes": Feminist Scholarship and Colonial Discourses'. *Boundary* 12/13, nos. 3/1, Spring/Fall 1984, pp. 352–57.

Monk, F. F. *A History of St. Stephen's College, Delhi*. Calcutta: Mission Press, 1935.

Mostert, B. J. 'Community Libraries: The Concept and its Application; with Particular Reference to a South African Community Library System'. *International Information & Library Review* 30, no. 1, 1998, pp. 71–85.

Mukherjee, Bhudev. *Report on the Village Schools in North-Western Province and Punjab*. Calcutta: Calcutta Central Press, 1868.

Mukherjee, Haridas and Uma Mukherjee. *The Growth of Nationalism in India*. Calcutta: Presidency Library, 1957.

______. *The Origins of the National Education Movement, 1905–1910*. Calcutta: Jadavpur University, 1957.

Mukherjee, S. N. *History of Education in India*. Baroda: Acharya Book Depot, 1951.

Mukherjee, T. N. *Selections from the Writings and Speeches of the Late Raja Peary Mohan Mukerjee*. Calcutta: Tarak Nath Mukherjee, 1914.

Murthy, B. Srinivasa. *Mahatma Gandhi and Leo Tolstoy Letters*. Long Beach: Long Beach Publications, 1987.

Muwanga, N. K., J. N. Aguti, J. F. Mugisha, A. N. Ndidde, and S. N. Siminyu. *Literacy Practices in Primary Schools: Lessons for Future Interventions*. Kampala: Fountain Publishers, 2007.

Naik, J. P. (ed.). *Selections from Educational Records*, (vol. 2). Delhi: Manager of Publication, 1963.

Nair, Janaki. *Women and Law in Colonial India: A Social History*. New Delhi: Kali for Women, 1996.

Nanda, B. R. (ed.). *The Collected Works of Lala Lajpat Rai*, (2 vols.). New Delhi: Manohar, 2003.

Nevison, H. *The New Spirit in India*. London: Harper & Brothers, 1908.

Newman, Peter C. and Peter Christopher. *Canada 1892: Portrait of a Promised Land.* Toronto: McClelland & Stewart, 1992.

Nicholas, Andrea Bear. 'Citizenship Education and Aboriginal People: The Humanitarian Art of Cultural Genocide'. *Canadian and International Education* 25, no. 2, December 1996, pp. 59–107.

Oberoi, Harjot. *The Construction of Religious Boundaries: Culture, Identity and Diversity in the Sikh Tradition.* New Delhi: Oxford University Press, 1994.

O' Connell, Joseph (ed.). *Sikh History and Religion in the Twentieth Century.* New Delhi: Manohar Publications, 1990.

O'Conner, D. and others. *Three Centuries of Mission: The United Society for the Propagation of the Gospel, 1701–2000.* London: Continuum, 2000.

Oddie, G. A. *Social Protest in India: British Protestant Missionaries and Social Reform.* New Delhi: Manohar, 1979.

———. *Missionaries, Rebellion and Proto-Nationalism: James Long of Bengal, 1814–1870.* Richmond: Curzon Press, 1999.

O'Hanlon, Rosalind. *Caste, Conflict and Ideology: Mahatma Jotirao Phule and Low Caste Protest in Nineteenth-century Western India.* Cambridge: Cambridge University Press, 1985.

———. *A Comparison between Women and Men: Tarabai Shinde and the Critique of Gender Relations in Colonial India.* New Delhi: Oxford University Press, 1994.

Olden, A., and M. Wise (ed.). *Information and Libraries in Developing World, vol. 1: Sub-Saharan Africa.* London: Library Association, 1990.

O'Malley, L. S. S. *The Indian Civil Service.* London: John Murray, 1931.

Omvedt, Gail. *Cultural Revolt in a Colonial Society: The Non-Brahman Movement in Western India, 1873 to 1930.* Bombay: Scientific Socialist Education Trust, 1976.

Otiso, K. M. *Culture and Customs of Uganda.* Westport, Connecticut: Greenwood Press, 2006.

Page, D. *Prelude to Partition: The Indian Muslims and the Imperial System of Control, 1920–1932.* New Delhi: Oxford University Press, 1982.

Panigrahi, Lalitha. *British Social Policy and Female Infanticide in India.* New Delhi: Munshiram Manoharlal, 1972.

Paranjape, M. R. *A Source Book of Modern Indian Education, 1797–1902.* London: MacMillan, 1938.

Parry, K. (ed.). *Language and Literacy in Uganda.* Kampala: Fountain Publishers, 2000.

Parulekar, R. V. (ed.). *Survey of Indigenous Education in the Province of Bombay, 1820–1830*, Bombay: Asia Publishing House, 1951.

Parulekar, R. V. (ed.). *Selections from Educational Records (Bombay), 1826–1840* (part III). Bombay: Asia Publishing House, 1957.

Parulekar, R. V. and C. L. Bakshi (eds.). *Selections from Educational Records: Bombay, 1815–1840* (part II). Bombay: Asia Publishing House, 1955.

Pawar, Kiran (ed.). *Women in Indian History*. New Delhi: Vision and Venture, 1996.

Pawde, Kumud. 'The Story of My Sanskrit', in *Poisoned Bread: Translations from Modern Marathi Dalit Literature*, edited by Arjun Dangle. Bombay: Orient Longman, 1994.

Philips, C. H. *The East India Company, 1784–1834*. Manchester: Manchester University Press, 1961.

Pickles, Katie. *Female Imperialism and National Identity: Imperial Order Daughters of the Empire*. Manchester: Manchester University Press, 2002.

Pillai, K. P. K. *History of Higher Education in South India*. Madras: University of Madras, 1957.

Pineau, Pablo. 'Peronism, Secondary Schooling and Work in Argentina, 1944–1955: An Approach through Cultural Hierarchies'. *Paedagogica Historica* 40, nos. 1–2, 2004, pp. 183–91.

Popkewitz, S. (ed.). *The Formation of School Subjects: The Struggle for Creating an American Institution*. London: The Falmer Press, 1987.

Popplewell, R. J. *Intelligence and Imperial Defence: British Intelligence and the Defence of the Indian Empire, 1904–1924*. London: Frank Cass, 1995.

Porter, A. *Religion Versus Empire? British Protestant Missions and Overseas Expansion, 1700–1914*. Manchester: Manchester University Press, 2004.

Powell, A. *Muslims and Missionaries in Pre-Mutiny India*. Richmond: Curzon Press, 1993.

Prasad, Rajendar (ed.). *Speeches and Writings of Dr. Sinha*, Allahabad: Ram Narain Lal, 1965.

Prior, Katherine, Lance Brennan and Robin Haines. 'Bad Language: The Role of English, Persian and Other Esoteric Tongues in the Dismissal of Sir Edward Colebrooke as Resident of Delhi in 1829.' *Modern Asian Studies* 35, no. 1, 2001, pp. 75–112.

Rahman, Tariq. *Language, Ideology and Power: Language-learning among the Muslims of Pakistan and North India*. Oxford: Oxford University Press, 2002.

Rao, Parimala V. 'Women in the Nationalist Discourse: A Case Study of Tilak's Approach to Women's Education and Emancipation', in *Development of Modern Indian Thought and the Social Sciences,* edited by Sabyasachi Bhattacharya. New Delhi: Oxford University Press, 2007.

———. 'New Insights into the Debates on Rural Indebtedness in the Nineteenth Century Deccan'. *Economic and Political Weekly* 44, no. 4, January 2009, pp. 24–30.

———. *Foundations of Tilak's Nationalism: Discrimination, Education, and Hindutva.* New Delhi: Orient BlackSwan, 2010.

———. 'Promiscuous Crowd of English Smatterers': The "Poor" in the Colonial and Nationalist Discourse on Education in India, 1835–1912.' *Contemporary Education Dialogue* 10, no. 2, 2013.

Rao, Raghunatha (ed.). *Notable Speeches of Lord Curzon.* Madras: Arya Press, 1905.

Rattu, Nanak Chand. *Dr. Ambedkar Important Messages, Sayings, Wit and Wisdom.* New Delhi: Rajgriha, 2001.

Ray, Bharati (ed.). *From the Seams of History: Essays on Indian Women.* New Delhi: Oxford University Press, 1995.

———. *Early Feminists of Colonial India: Sarala Devi Chaudhurani and Rokeya Sakhawat Hossain.* New Delhi: Oxford University Press, 2002.

Raya, B. B. *Zenana Mission: The Role of Christian Missionaries for the Education of Women in Nineteenth Century Bengal.* Delhi: Indian Society for Promoting Christian Knowledge, 1998.

Razack, Sherene (ed.). *Race, Space, and the Law: Unmapping a White Settler Society.* Toronto: Between the Lines, 2002.

Rein, Monica Esti. *Politics and Education in Argentina, 1946–1962.* New York: M. E. Sharp, 1998.

Report of the General Committee of Public Instruction of the Presidency of Fort William in Bengal, 1841

Report of the Indian Education Commission. Calcutta: Superintendent of Government Printing, 1882.

Rich, R. *Race and Empire in British Politics.* Cambridge: Cambridge University Press, 1986.

Richey, J. A. *Selections from the Educational Records,1840–1859,* (part 2). Calcutta: Superintendent Government Press, 1922.

Riendeau, Roger. *A Brief History of Canada.* New York: Facts on File, 2007.

Robb, P. (ed.). *The Concept of Race in South Asia*, New Delhi: Oxford University Press, 1995.

Rodríguez, Miguel Somoza. 'Poverty, Exclusion and Social Conflict in the Schoolbooks of Argentina during the First Peronist Period'. *Paedagogica Historica* 43, no. 5, 2007, pp. 633–52.

Roediger, David R. *The Wages of Whiteness: Race and the Making of the American Working Class*. London: Verso, 1991.

Röhrs, Hermann. 'The New Education Fellowship: An International Forum for Progressive Education' in *Progressive Education Across the Continents: A Handbook*, edited by Hérmann Röhrs and Volker Lenhart. Frankfurt: Peter Lang. 1995.

Roy, Anupama. *Gendered Citizenship: Historical and Conceptual Explorations*. New Delhi: Orient Longman, 2005.

Roy, Macleod, and Deepak Kumar (eds.). *Technology and the Raj: Western Technology and Technical Transfer in India*. New Delhi: Sage Publication, 1995.

Roy, Patricia E. *A White Man's Province: British Columbia Politicians and Chinese and Japanese Immigrants, 1858–1914*. Vancouver: University of British Columbia Press, 1989.

Ruskin, John. *Unto This Last*. Lincoln: University of Nebraska Press, 1967.

Russell, R. V., and Hira Lal. *The Tribes and Castes of the Central Provinces of India* (Reprint edition, 1916). Delhi: Cosmo Publications, 1975.

Sandor, David. '"Black is as Good a Color as White": The Harriet Beecher Stowe School and the Debate Over Separate Schools in Cincinnati'. *Ohio Valley History* 9, no. 2, Summer 2009, pp. 27–53.

Sangari, Kumkum, and Sudesh Vaid (eds.). *Recasting Women: Essays in Indian Colonial History*. New Delhi: Kali for Women, 1985.

Sarkar, Sumit. *Swadeshi Movement in Bengal, 1903–1908*. New Delhi: People's Publishing House, 1973

Sarkar, Sumit and Tanika Sarkar (eds.). *Women and Social Reform in Modern India: A Reader* (vol. 1). New Delhi: Permanent Black, 2007.

Schwarz, Henry, and Samgeeta Ray (eds.). *A Companion to Postcolonial Studies*. Oxford: Blackwell Publishers, 2000.

Sharpe, E. J. *Faith Meets Faith: Some Christian Attitudes to Hinduism in the Nineteenth and Twentieth Centuries*. London: SCM Press, 1977.

______. *Not to Destroy But to Fulfil: The Contribution of J. N. Farquhar to Protestant Missionary Thought in India*. Lund: Gleerup, 1965.

Scott, W. *The History of Canada*. New York: Grey House Publishing, 2010.

Sen, S. N. *Scientific and Technical Education in India, 1781–1900*. New Delhi: Indian National Science Academy, 1991.

Sengupta, Parna. 'The Object Lessons in Colonial Pedagogy'. *Comparative Studies in Society and History* 45, no. 1, 2003, pp. 96–121.

Seth, Sanjay. *Subject Lessons: The Western Education of Colonial India*. New Delhi: Oxford University Press, 2007.

Shah, A. B. 'Dalit Movement and Its Historical Background'. *Bulletin of the Indian Educational Institute* 11, 1981, pp. 22–35.

Shahidulla, Kazi. *Pathsalas into School: The Development of Indigenous Elementary Education in Bengal (1854–1905)*. Calcutta: Firma KLM Private Limited, 1987.

Shamasastri, R. *Kautilya's Arthasastra*. Mysore: Mysore Publishing and Printing House, 1967.

Sharma, Sonali. 'Reformist Ideas and Emergence of Feminism in Marathi Fiction, 1850s–1920s.' M.Phil. dissertation, Centre for Historical Studies, Jawaharlal Nehru University, 2008.

Sheehan, Nancy. 'Philosophy, Pedagogy and Practice: the IODE and the Schools in Canada 1900–1945'. *History of Education Review* 2, no. 2, pp. 307–21.

Shende, N. R. *A Collection of Bansode's Poetry*. Nagpur: Shamrao Bansode, 1958.

Sherring, M. *Hindu Tribes and Castes as Represented in Benares* (3 vols.), Calcutta: Thacker, Spink & Co., 1872.

Shinde, J. R. *Dynamics of Cultural Revolution: 19th Century Maharashtra*. Delhi: Ajanta Publications, 1985.

Shukla, S. 'Economy and Social in British India'. *Varanasi National Journal Education* 1, nos. 1 and 2, 1978, pp. 70–80.

Singh. Ganda (ed.). *The Singh Sabha and Other Socio-Religious Movements in the Punjab (1850–1925)*. Patiala: Punjab University, 1997.

Singh, Madhu. 'How Equal are the Scheduled Castes? Some Aspects of Their Educational Development'. *Bulletin of the Indian Institute of Education* 2, 1981, pp. 85–97.

Sinha, Bageswar. *Builders of Modern India: Sachchidanand Sinha*, Faridabad: Publications Division, Ministry of Information and Broadcasting, Government of India, 1969.

Sinha, Jagdish N. *Science, War and Imperialism: India in the Second World War*. London: Brill, 2008.

Sinha, Sachchidanand. *Speeches and Writings: Hindustani as a Medium of Primary Education*. Calcutta: Thacker, Spink & Co., 1933.

———. *Some Eminent Behar Contemporaries*. Patna: Himalaya Press, 1944.

Smedley, Audrey. *Race in North America: Origin and Evolution of a World View*. Boulder, Colorado: Westview Press, 1999.

Solanki, A. B. *The Technique of Correlation in Basic Education*. Ahmedabad: Navajivan Publishing House, 1958.

Srivastava, Sanjay. *Constructing Post-Colonial India: National Character and the Doon School*. London: Routledge, 1998.

Stasiulis, Daiva, and Nira Yuval-Davis (eds.). *Unsettling Settler Colonies: Articulations of Gender, Race, Ethnicity and Class*. London: Sage, 1995.

Stilwell, C. 'Community Libraries: A Brief Review of their Origins and Nature with Particular Reference to South Africa'. *Journal of Librarianship* 21, no. 4, 1989, pp. 260–69.

Stoler, Ann Laura. *Carnal Knowledge and Imperial Power*. Berkeley: University of California Press, 2002.

Studdert-Kennedy, G. *British Christians, Indian Nationalists and the Raj*. New Delhi: Oxford University Press, 1991.

———. *Providence and the Raj: Imperial Mission and Missionary Imperialism*. New Delhi: Sage Publications, 1998.

Sutherland, Neil. *Children in English-Canadian Society: Framing the Twentieth Century Consensus*. Waterloo, Ontario: Wilfred Laurier University Press, 2000.

Szreter, R. 'The Origins of Full-Time Compulsory Education at Five'. *British Journal of Educational Studies* 13, no. 1, November 1964, pp. 16–28.

Szuchman, Mark D. 'Childhood Education and Politics in Nineteenth-Century Argentina: The Case of Buenos Aires'. *Hispanic American Historical Review* 70, no. 1, 1990, pp. 109–38.

Tagore, Rabindranath. *The English Writings of Rabindranath Tagore*. New Delhi: Sahitya Akademi, 1996.

Thapar, Romila. *From Lineage to State: Social Formations of the Mid-First Millennium B.C. in the Ganges Valley*. New Delhi: Oxford University Press, 1985.

Tharu, Susie, and K. Lalitha (eds.). *Women Writing in India: 600 B.C. to the Present* (vol. 1). New York: Feminist Press at the City University of New York, 1991.

Thavaraj, M. J. K. 'Framework of Economic Policies under British Rule'. *Social Scientist* 7, no. 5, 1978, pp. 13–44.

Thobani, Sunera. *Exalted Subjects: Studies in the Making of Race and Nation in Canada*. Toronto: University of Toronto Press, 2007.

Thompson, E. P. 'Time, Work-Discipline and Industrial Capitalism'. *Past and Present* 38, no. 1, December 1967, pp. 56–97.

Thorat, S. K., and Paul Attewell. 'The Legacy of Social Exclusion: A Correspondence Study of Job Discrimination in India'. *Economic and Political Weekly*, vol. 27, bo. 14, 13 October 2007, pp. 4141–45.

Tilak, Jandhyala B. G. *Women's Education and Development*. New Delhi: Gyan Publishing House, 2007.

Tomkins, G. S. 'The Curriculum in Canada in Historical Perspective'. *Canadian Society for the Study of Education*, Sixth Yearbook (vol. 7), 1979.

———. *A Common Countenance: Stability and Change in the Canadian Curriculum*, Scarborough: Prentice-Hall, 1986.

Trevelyan, Charles E. *On the Education of the People of India*. London: Longman, Orme, Brown, Green and Longman, 1838.

Trivedi, Lisa. *Clothing Gandhi's Nation: Homespun and Modern India*. Bloomington: Indiana University Press, 2007.

Valverde, Mariana. *The Age of Light, Soap and Water: Moral Reform in English Canada 1885-1929*. Toronto: McClelland & Stewart Inc., 1991.

Varma, Mahadevi. *Sketches from My Past*, translated by Neera Kuckreja Sohoni. New Delhi: Kali for Women, 1994.

———. *Links in The Chain*, translated by Neera Kuckreja Sohoni, New Delhi: Katha, 2005.

Velaskar, Padma. 'Ideology, Education and the Political Struggle for Liberation: Change and Challenge among the Dalits of Maharashtra' in *Education, Development and Underdevelopment*, edited by S. C. Shukla and Rekha Kaul. New Delhi: Sage Publications. 1998.

Verkey, C. J. *The Wardha Scheme of Education: An Exposition and Examination*. London: Oxford University Press, 1940.

Viswanathan, Gauri. *Masks of Conquest: Literary Study and British Rule in India*. New York: Columbia University Press, 1989.

Walsh, Judith. *What Women Learned When Men Gave Them Advice*. New Delhi: Oxford University Press, 2004.

Ward, M., A., Penny and T. Read. *Education Reform in Uganda, 1997–2004: Reflections on Policy, Partnership, Strategy and Implementation*. London: Department for International Development, 2006.

White, Randall. *Ontario 1610–1985: A Political and Economic History*. Toronto: Dundurn Press, 1985.

Wilson, J., and David Jones (eds.), *Schooling and Society in Twentieth Century British Columbia*, Calgary, Alberta: Destelig Enterprises Ltd., 1980.

Woolf, Virginia. *A Room of One's Own*. New York: Harcourt, 1989.

Wright, Ronald. *Stolen Continents: The 'New World' Through Indian Eyes*. Toronto: Penguin, 1993.

Young, Robert. *Colonial Desire: Hybridity in Theory, Culture and Race*. London: Routledge, 1995.

Zastoupil, L., and M. Moir, *The Great Indian Educational Debate: Documents Related to the Orientalist-Anglicist Controversy, 1781–1843*. Richmond: Curzon Press, 1999.

Zelliot, Eleanor. 'Dr. Ambedkar and the Mahar Movement'. Unpublished Ph.D. dissertation, University of Pennsylvania, 1969.

Zelliot, Eleanor, and Maxine Berntsen (eds.). *The Experience of Hinduism*. Albany: State University of New York Press, 1988.

Notes on the Contributors

HAYDEN BELLENOIT teaches history at the United States Naval Academy, Maryland, USA.

RADHA GAYATHRI works at the Educational Records Research Unit, Jawaharlal Nehru University, New Delhi.

SURESH CHANDRA GHOSH is a former member of the editorial advisory board of *Paedagogica Historica* (Belgium). He held the chair of History of Education at Jawaharlal Nehru University, New Delhi till 2002.

SIMONE HOLZWARTH is a research scholar at the Centre for Collaborative Research, Humboldt University of Berlin.

LAURA DUDLEY JENKINS teaches political science at the University of Cincinnati, USA.

MAHIMA MANCHANDA is a research scholar of modern Indian history at the University of Mississippi, USA.

VERÓNICA OELSNER is currently at the University of Applied Sciences Neubrandenburg, Germany.

PREETI is a research scholar of modern Indian history at the Centre for Historical Studies, Jawaharlal Nehru University, New Delhi.

PARIMALA V. RAO teaches history of education at the Zakir Husain Centre for Educational Studies, Jawaharlal Nehru University, and currently holds a fellowship at the Nehru Memorial Museum and Library, both in New Delhi.

ELEANOR ZELLIOT is professor emerita, Carleton College, Minnesota, USA.

Index

Abbas, Abdul Haq, 131
Acts of Incorporation, 227–32, 24
  and appointment to the Senate, 239–40
Adam, William, 16, 151, 152
Adi Dharm, 61
Adi Dravida Education Society, 60
Adi Granth, 139–40
adult education programmes, 223
African American students, 31, 32, 69, 71
  discrimination of, 83
Agarkar, Gopal Ganesh, 34, 51
Age of Consent Act, 1891, 93n
  debate surrounding, 116
  opposition to, 166
Aher, Shuddhodhan, 85
Ahmad, Moulvi Nazir, 132
AIIMS, ragging incident at, 73, 74
Aitchison Commission, 259
Akbar, education during rule of, 225
Aldrich, Richard, 42
Ali, Sayyid Mumtaz, 24, 167
Ali, Syed Ameer, 154, 158, 161
  opposition to Bengal Rent Bill Act, 166
Aligarh Muslim University, 266n
All India Education Board, 211
All India Matang Seva Sangh, 57
All India Scheduled Castes Students Federation Conference, 1946, 89
Allnutt, Rev. Samuel Scott, 185
Ambadevi Temple Entry Satyagraha, 56
Ambedkar, B. R., 32, 45, 50, 63, 71, 75, 89
  Chairman of Drafting Committee of Constituent Assembly, 46
  conversion to Buddhism, 46
  on Gandhian education, 29
  People's Education Society of, 55, 63–67, 72, 77
  quitting Hinduism, 56
  support to modern education, 31
Ambedkar Open University, Gujarat, 59
Ambedkar Physical Education College, Aurangabad, 67
American Presbyterian Mission, establishment of schools for girls in Punjab, 124
Amir Chand, 185
Anand Karaj Act, 1909, 139

anandkaraj ceremony, 140
Anderson, Mrs, 124
Andrew, C. F., 37, 181, 184, 191, 192
Anglo-Mohammadan Oriental College, Aligarh, 266n
Anglo-Indian Vidyalaya College, 10–11
    see also Presidency College
Anglo-vernacular schools
    English as compulsory subject in, 42, 283n
    and other schools, 289
    syllabus of, 278
Anjuman-i-Punjab, 123
    evidence before Hunter Commission, 282n
Anjuman-i-Raifa'i-am, 281, 284, 290
Anjumans, schools established by, 32
Anson, William, 237
Apartheid, 70
Arabic schools, 174, 292
Argentina, coup of 1943 in, 37
    manual work in, 212–14
    political upheaval in 1920s to 1940s in, 201–05
    structural changes in education in, 37
    vocational education in, 201, 206–07
Arnold, Thomas, 31
    reform of, 15, 16
Arnold, W. D., Director of Public Instruction, Punjab, 24–25, 31, 273, 293
    halkabandi system of education of, 273
'Arya', notion of, 35
Arya Samaj, 121, 125, 131, 134, 141, 146–47, 164–65, 194, 281, 290
    on caste, 127
    ideology, 142
    schools set up by, 32, 122ff.
    role of women in, 135, 140–41
Aryanayakam, E. W., 220n
Asiatic Society of Bengal, 225
Attewell, Paul, 82
Auckland, Governor-General, 31, 152, 153
Audiah, M. L., 59
Avellaneda, Nicolás, 37
Ayerst, Lieutenant, 261

Babasaheb Ambedkar Marathawada University, Aurangabad, 66
bachelor's degree, increase in recipients of, 247–48
Baden-Powell, S. C., on education in Punjab, 280–81
Dr. Babasaheb Ambedkar Memorial Law College, Dhule, 56
'*bande mataram*' slogan, 183–184
Banerjee, Gooroodas, 242–43
Banerjee, Surendranath, 159, 241, 254, 260, 265
Bansode, Kisan Phagoji, 31
Barve, Vishnu Hari, 142
Basavalingappa, B., 67
'basic' schools, in India, 222–23
Battle of Plassey, 135
Bell, Commissionner for Punjab, 242
Bengal (Presidency), agitation in, 253
    compulsory and free education in, 154
    partition of, 224

protest against partition of, 192, 219
Bengal Rent Bill, 1884, opposition to, 166
Bengal Sati Regulation Act, 1829, 93n
Bentham, Jeremy, 11
Bentinck, Governor-General, 152, 263, 269n
see also Government of India Resolution
Berar Provincial Association, 171
Besant, Annie, scheme of education, 263–64
Bhandarkar, Ramakrishna Gopal, 97, 154, 155, 276
Bhansode, Kisan Phagoji, 50, 51–53, 55
Bhatia, Pritam Kaur, 147
Bhatkar, L. S., 55
Bhatkar, P. N., 56
Bheem Patrika (journal), 59
Bhikaji, Dadaji, 98
Bhole, Justice, 55, 66
Bible, study of, 17
Bilgrami, Syed H., 241, 266n
on education, 163
Black Panthers, 45n
Bombay (Presidency), schools in, 15
Bonaparte, Napoleon, 23
Bose, Bepin Behari, 266
Boyd, Mary R., 298
'Brahmanical-cum-Colonial Paradigm', 208
Brahmo Samaj, 188
bride price, 93
British colonial government, control over schools in Punjab, 276
education policy in Punjab, 272
English-educated Indians on, 262
expenditure on education, 159
on missionaries, 9
on reforming women's education, 115–19
and schooling in Punjab, 272–75
British colonialism/imperialism, 92
in Central Asia, 224
interest in India, 266
British rule, movement against, 176
Buddhism, 3, 64, 66, 75–76
conversion to, 57

Calcutta, college students in, 29
Calcutta Madrassa, 17, 18
Calcutta Missionary Conference, 1903, 189
Campbell, George, lieutenant-governor of Bengal, 154
Cambridge Mission to Delhi, 177, 179
Canning, Viceroy, 227, 247
Carpenter, B. E., 99
Carnoy, Martin, 3, 6–7, 19, 21
caste-based society, in India, 17
distinction, 73
see also 'Untouchables'
Caveeshar, Sardul Singh, 127
Chambhar community, 53
Chandavarkar, N. G., 11
Charter Act of 1813, 1, 2, 4
Charter Act of 1833, 225, 254
Chandavarkar, N. G., 11, 242
Chatterjee, A. K., 185
Chaudhary, Jaibai, 52, 55
Chaudhry, Prem, 135

Chikkalingaiah, M., 60
child labour, 36
child marriages, 92–93, 108
 defenders of, 166
Child Marriage Restraint Act, 1929, 93n
Chitnis, M. B., 64
Chitnavis, Gangadhar, 171
Church Missionary Society, 177, 179
 on education, 220
civil services, appointments to, 249, 254
Cokhamela Boarding, Nagpur, 56
Cokhamela Girls' School, Mopla, 52
Cokhamela Vidyavardak Mandal, 51
Coldstream, W., 287
colonialism, *see* British colonial government
communal riots, in India, 43
compulsory and free education, 154
 criticism of, 160–63, 165–68
 and political leadership in Colonial India, 151ff.
 supporters of, 167–68
Congress, *see* Indian National Congress
Cornwallis, Governor-General, 23
Cotton, Henry, 243
Critical Study Team for Secondary Education, Karnataka, 22
Crosthwaite, Rev. Charles, 191
Croft, Alfred, 261, 277
'cultural imperialism', 3, 8
curriculum, in colonial India, 161–62
 in Punjab schools, 145, 298
Curzon, Viceroy, 40
 on appointments to public service, 260n
 confrontation with University of Bengal, 234–37
 Council of, 267
 educational reforms of, 188, 262–64
 and Hamilton, 240, 242
 University Reforms of 1899–1905, 39, 224ff., 245
Cust, Robert Needham, 178

Dadabhai, M. B., 171
Dalhousie, Governor-General, 224, 228, 246, 267
Dalits
 colleges for, 32, 68ff., 87, 89
 conversion to Buddhism, 72
 early educators, 47–50, 55–58
 education of, 30–32, 55–58
 empowerment, 84
 Gujarati literary movement, 49
 initiatives in education, 45, 50, 61–63
 Maharashtra, Dalits initiatives in education in, 55–58
 Nagpur, Dalit activists in, 50, 54
 resources and opportunity, 78–83
 study centres for, 83–87
 Students' Movement, 1989, 59
 in Uttar Pradesh, 59
 Uttar Pradesh, Dalit student groups in, 59
Dalit Open University, Andhra Pradesh, 58
Dani, Shantabai, 56
Darwin, Solomon, 61, 62

Davey Commission, 265
Davis, Patrick, 185
Dawkins, C. E., 238
Dayanand, Swami, rejection of caste by, 127
  Satyarth Prakash by, 126, 127
Deb, Radha Kanta, 10, 153
Deccan Agriculturalists Relief Act, 1879, 166
Deepankar, Rahul, 61
Deepankar Kanya Inter College, US, 61
Departments of Education, creation of (1879), 249
Department of Instruction, Punjab, creation of, 273, 277
Deshpande, J. V., 65
Deshpande, Satish, 85
'Depressed Classes', 45n, 46
Depressed Class Mission, 31, 49, 50, 57
Depressed Classes Hostel, Sangamner, 57
devadasi system, 51
Devraj, Lala, 121, 138–39, 141, 143, 145
  founding of Kanya Mahavidyalaya, 131
Dey, Lal Behari, 16–17, 19
Dhar, Bishan Narain, on education, 163
Dharma Sabha, 153
Director of Public Instruction, 284, 285
Dongre, Anant Shastri, 97
dowry, 93
Dr Ambedkar College, Nagpur, 56
Dr Ambedkar's College of Arts and Commerce, Pune, 66, 67
Dr. Ambedkar National Institution, Madhya Pradesh, 59
Dravidian School, Madras, 61
Duff, Alexander, 16–17
Dufferin Scheme, 98
Durrant, Rev. Henry, 188–89
Dutta, Nonica, 147

East India Company, 7, 13, 14, 41, 176–77, 245, 269n
  Court of Directors, 18
  on English education, 246
education, in colonial India, 177–78
  female, 90, 93, 111
  'holistic', 220
  human interaction and 'colonial knowledge', 177–80
  Indian English concept of, 24
  legislation, controversy over, 188
  missionaries and Indian nation, 176ff.
  and nationalism, 185
  politicisation of, 39
  pre-colonial and colonial, 20
  reforms, as a law, 244–45
  reforms in universities, 237–41
  and religious identity, 122
  system, standardisation and uniformity under colonial rule, 269, 299
  value of, 45
  two-tier system of, 160–63
Education Commission, 188, 277, 287
  Appointment of First, 155, 255
Educational Conference, First, 1901, 238, 240–41

Educational Despatch (1854), 43, 227–29, 233, 249, 266, 278
see also Wood's Despatch
Ekalavya and Upamanyu, stories of, 27–28
Elementary Education Act (England), 36, 154
Elementary Education Bill, 1910, 168–71
opposition to, 170
Ellenborough, Viceroy, 153
Elgin, Viceroy, 261
Ellwood, John, 184
Ellis, E. R., 267
Elmhirst, Leonard, 220
Elphinstone College, Mumbai, 11, 25
Elphinstone, John, 14
Elphinstone, Mountstuart, 20
'English educated Indians', 19, 25, 262
English education, 25, 134, 156, 160, 265
benefits of, 246
in schools in Punjab, 134
English language, financial assistance to learn, in Bengal, 253
as official language of British India, 246
English schools, established by Indians, 20
Enlightenment, 3–4
European fascism, 217
European nationalism, 5, 6
examinations, colonial government's introduction of, 282
for girls in Punjab, 299
grid of, 282–83
and passing marks, 283n
written, 42, 283
Extremists, 160

Factory Act, 1881, 165
Factory (Amendment) Act 1891, 165
factory system, children working in, 151
fellowship, to universities, 229–30
female infanticide, 33, 92, 93, 104–07, 118, 245
female literacy rate, 90
female teachers, lack of, 128
Fergusson College, Pune, 261
Figuerola, Jose, 217
financial assistance, to Indian universities, 244
'fine arts' exams, successful candidates of, 248
Forster, E. M., 180
Fosse, Charles de la, 185
Foucault, Michel, 292
Francis, Mrs, 137
Fraser, Andrew, 182, 184
Fraser, William, 152
French Revolution (1789), 23

Gaikwad, D. K. 'Dadasaheb', 56
Gajendragadkar, A. B., 65
Gandhi, M. K., 45n, 54, 194, 195, 202
arrival on national scene, 181
'Basic Education' of, 28–29, 171–75, 210–11, 222
on caste system, 205n
on colonial legacy in education, 208
concept of new social order, 204–05, 218

on education, 38, 48, 196, 219
on education and manual work, 207, 215
Hind Swaraj by, 172
on modern education, 36
Nai Talim of, 174, 207, 209–10, 216, 219, 221–23
opposition to compulsory education, 171
Peronist ideas and Gandhi's ideas compared, 38–39, 196
'rural reconstruction' of, 219
schools of, 38
on spinning yarn, 209
and Tagore, 250
Gandhian educational reform, 210
Gandhian Hostel, Ahmedabad, 61
Gautam Centre for Buddhism, Nashik, 46
Gautam Vidyalaya, Pandharpur, 66
Gawai, G. A., 48
Gellner, Ernest, 181
General Education Conference, 1887, 291
Germany, traditional apprenticeship in workplace and vocational schools, 200
Ghioldi, Américo, 218
Ghose, Lalmohan, 254
Ghosh, Aurobindo, 161, 164
Ghosh, Motilal, 159, 166
on women's education, 167
girls' high schools
establishment of, 166
opening of, in Punjab, 125, 297, 298
Gokhale, Gopal Krishna, 6, 34, 36, 64, 159, 168, 245
on education of girls, 169
Gandhi and, 172
introduction of Elementary Educational Bill by, 168–71
Godley, Arthur, 235
Goswami, Manu, 279
Gotama, 19
Government College, Lahore, 293
Government of India Resolution, 1835, 14, 15
government schools
for Mahars, 18
in Punjab, 125, 128
low quality of vernacular, 42
unpopularity of, 126
graduates, increase in number of, 248
grants-in-aid rules, 273n, 274
Gurdwara Committee of Shri Nanak Sahib, 63
Gurmukhi, teaching of, in Punjab, 126
Gurmukhi schools, in Punjab, 298
girls' education in, 295
Guru Granth Sahib, 138, 147
teaching in Punjab, 295
Guruji, Mohiti, 64
Guruji, Parmar, 64
gurukul tradition, of education, 174
Guruswami, L. K., 60

halkabandi schools, in North-West Provinces and Oudh, 41
in Punjab, 273
Halliday, F. J., 267
Hamilton, George, 255, 261–64
Curzon and, 240, 242–43, 249
as Secretary of State for India, 235
Hardas, L. N., 53

Hardinge, Governor-General, 17, 21, 153
  on English education, 18
Hardinge Resolution, 1844, 18
'Hardinge schools', Bengal, 41
Haridas, 55
'Harijan', 45n
Harijan Sevak Sangh, 32, 79
Harris, Jane, 124
Hastings, Warren, Governor-General, 7, 23
  encouraging Brahmanism, 7
  establishment of Calcutta Madrassa, 7–8
Haythornwaite, John, 186–88
Hewett, J. P., 241
Hewlett, John, 188
Hibbert-Ware, George, 192
higher education, effects of the spread of, 245–55
  private enterprise in, 255–58
  of women, 114
Hindi, teaching of, in Punjab, 133
Hindu Code Bill, 46
Hindu College, Benaras, 10, 246, 263
Hindu educational tradition, 28
Hindu laws, 115–16
Hindu Mahasabha, 52
Hindu matrimonial laws, 116
Hindu patriarchal system, 96
Hindu society, reform of, 93
Hindu Union Club, 162
Hindu Widow's Remarriage Act, 1856, 47n
Hinduism, 53, 146, 147
Hindustani Talimi Sangh, 211
Hobart, William W., 105–06
Hobsbawm, Eric, 8, 9, 30, 42
holidays and vacation, for schools in Punjab, 292
Holland, Rev. William, 182, 192–93
Hooper, Rev. William 'Pundit', 190
Hossein, Rokeya Sakhawat, 32, 91, 101–02
  Aborodhbashini by, 101
  Ardhangi by, 101
  Griha by, 101
  Narir Adhikar by, 101
  Stree Jatir Abanati by, 101
  Sultana's Dream by, 101
Hostel for Depressed Classes Students, Kolhapur, 55
Hume, Allen Octavian, 6
Hume, David, 11, 24, 259
Hunter, W. W., 14, 155, 255
Hunter Commission, on Education, 112, 156, 158, 167, 255, 257, 276, 281
  on affiliated colleges, 233
  see also Education Commission
Husain, Zakir, 210, 221
  report by, 216

Ibbetson, Denzil, 178, 244
Ibn Khaldun, 4
Imperial Library, 225
Independent Labour Party, of Ambedkar, 53
Indian Civil Service, age for joining, 254
  demands for exams in England and India, 259–60
  Indians qualifying for, 252–53
Indian Councils Act, 1909, 185
Indian Education Commission, 1882, 14, 276

Indian Institute of Dalit Studies, 74
Indian languages, scripts of, 24
Indian National Congress, 5, 6, 29–30, 50, 54, 159, 160, 195, 262, 266
  Ahmedabad session of, 265
  educated Indians in, 250
  establishment of, 158–59
  National Planning Committee of, 29–30
  Wardha Conference of, 211
Indian nationalism, 183
  as anti-colonial, 6
  and education, 28–29, 36, 38, 48, 163–65, 171–75, 180–83, 185–89, 191, 196, 207–08, 210–11, 216, 219, 221–23
  intensification of sentiment, 258–64
  missionary education and, 181
  rise of, 4, 5
  and writings on education, 3, 22
Indian Office Committee, 249
Indian Universities Act, 1904, 39, 225–27, 264, 268
  drafting of bill, 244
Indian Universities Commission, 241–44, 264
indigenous education system, and colonial education system, 270
indigenous schools, in Punjab, 270–72
  religious content in, 271
Industrial Training School, 60
inspection, rule by, 284–85
inspector of schools, in Punjab, 284–85
institutional and symbolic construction, sources for inspiration for, 216–21
International Labour Organization, 218
Islam, 3
Iyakannu, I. N., 60
Iyer, G. Subramanya, 159

Jacobian influence, 23
Jadhav, D. G., 64
Jadhav, Narendra, 77, 82
Jadhav, Raibhan, 56
Jagjivan Ram, Babu, 58
Jaibai Choudhary Junior College, Mopla, 52
Janata High School, Pune, 57
Jatav Pathshala Primary School, Agra, 61
Jataveer, Manikchand, 60
Jawaharlal Nehru University, New Delhi, 74
Jayaseelon, M., 60
Jervis, T. B., 151
Johnston, Rev. James, 255
Jones, Kennerh W., 127, 294
Joshi, Anandibai, 33, 91, 99, 106, 108, 113–14
Joshi, Gopalrao, 99
Jowett, Benjamin, 237
Justicialismo (political party in Argentina), 202

Kabirpanth, 54
Kali, Ayyan, 59
Kamble, Shivram Janab, 31, 50–51
Kamala Nehru Hostel, Pune, 57
Karnik, H. R., 65
Kaur, Bibi Balwant, 142

Kaur, Bibi Harnam, 122, 134, 144, 147
Kaur, Bibi Raminder, 142, 145
Kaur, Bibi Sharan, 142
Kaur, Gurbaksh, 138
Kaur, Roop, 143
Kautilya, 5
Kerschensteiner, Georg, 221
Khalsa College, Bombay, 63–64
Khan, Syed Ahmad, 34, 156, 158–59, 161, 167, 175, 266
  opposition to Deccan Agriculturists Relief Act, 166
Khandare, Janoji, 48
Khandale, R. G., 47
Kharsedji, Francina, 100
Kharsedji, Sorabji, 100
Kipling, Rudyard, 8, 191
Kishwar, Madhu, 146
Kshirsagar, R. K., 55, 59, 62
Krishnaswamy, 60
Kumar, Krishna, 22–29, 283
Kumar Ashram, Meerut, 60
Kureel, Piarelal, 60

Lahore Singh Sabha, 125–26, 133, 139, 141
Lakshmi, K. Vijaya, 79
Lalinkar, P. L., 56
lande schools, in Punjab, 292
language teaching, in Punjab, 294–95
landlords, opposition to free and compulsory education, 154–56
Lansdowne, Viceroy, 230
  on problem of unemployment, 258
Law, Edward, 267
Le Bon, Gustave, 262
Lee-Warner, William, 43
  Citizen of India by, 235
Leitner, G. W., 123–24, 126, 284, 295, 297
Leitner Report, 126
Lewis, Thomas, 179
Lewis, Commissioner for North-Western Provice, 242
Locke, John, 11
Long, Rev. James, 9, 10
London Missionary Society, 177, 179
  parent committee, 162
Lucas, Rev. Bernard, 192
Lumbini Cultural Centre, Mumbai, 84–85
Lumbini Study Centre, Mumbai, 87
Lytton, Viceroy, 154

Macaulay, Thomas Babington, 12–15, 247, 262–63
  minute of 1835, 14, 256
Maclean, vice-chancellor of Calcutta University, 232, 236
Maconachie, John, 192
Madhavi, Bipin Bihari, 97
Madras Sanitary Commission, of 1886, 288n
Madrasa education, 161–62
Mahad Satyagraha (1927), 64
Mahanubhav sect, 54
Mahar community, 46, 47–49, 53–54, 57
Maharaja of Baroda, 172
Maharani Indumati Boarding, Kolhapur, 57
Mahatma Phule Hostel, Pune, 57
Maine, Henry, 248

Majid, Nawab Abdul, 171
Makesar, V. D., 56
Malabari, Behramji, 116
Malaviya, Madan Mohan, 52
male children, preference for, 104–07
Mandalik, Vishwanath Narayan, 154
  opposition to Bengal Rent Bill, 1884, 166
Mang community, 53
Mangu Ram, 61
Malhotra, Anshu, 127
Marathawada University, Aurangabad, 55
marriage, ceremony among Sikhs, 139
  early, of girls and widowhood, 107–11
  reforms, 117
Matashri Ramabai Vidyarthi Ashram, Ratnagiri district, 66
matriculation exams, successful candidates of, 247
Mayo, Viceroy, 154
Mazdur Patrika (newspaper), 53
Mazhar-ul-Haq, 170
M. C. Rajah Hostel, Madras, 60
McCully, Bruce T., 4, 5
Mehta, H. R., 126
Mehta, Pherozeshah, 5, 159
Milind Hostel, Nanded, 56
Milind Mahavidyalaya, Aurangabad, 32, 45, 66, 72, 74–76, 78, 81, 87
Milind Primary School, Nanded, 56
Miller, William, 178, 180
Minault, Gail, 125–26
Minto, Governor-General, minutes of, 23–24
missionaries, education and Indian nation, 9, 37, 176ff.
  and female education, 124
missionary teachers, 176, 179–83, 18–88, 195
Mitra, Dinabandhu, 9
Mitra, Rajendra Lal, 154, 156, 159–61
  on Bengal Rent Bill, 166
  on women's education, 167
Moderates, 160
modern education, 2, 19, 35, 36
  imperialists on growth of, 4
  introduction of, 152
  opposition to, 41
Mondal, Sitanath, 60
Montessori, Maria, meeting with Gandhi, 251
Montgomery, Bishop, 186
Montgomery, Robert, 125
More, Hanumantrao, 56
Morley-Minto reforms, 185
motherhood, early, 107
Mouvat, F. J., 246
Mudholkar, R. N., 170
Mukherjee, Ashutosh, 242, 245
Mukerjee, Peary Mohan
  opposition to compulsory education, 154–55
  on Bengal Rent Bill, 166
Muktab education, 161
Mullick, B., 60
Mulraj, Lala, 286
  on instruction of colonial schools, 280
Mumbai, educational divide in, 82–84

municipalities, Bombay, power of, 162
Munro, Thomas, 151–53
  schools established by, in Madras, 19n
Munshi Ram, Lala, 124
Murugesan, M. Y., 60
Murthy, B. S., 60
Muslim Girls' School, Jullunder, 131
Muslim League, 170–71

Nagappa, S., 60
Nagasena, 78
Nag community, 56
Naik, S. G., 56
Nair, Sankaran, Commissioner of Madras, 242
Nandagavali, Kalicharan, 54
Namasudra community, 60
Naoroji, Dadabhai, 5, 11, 155, 159, 195, 259
  on unemployment, 251–52
Nashik, as educational center, 56
Nashik Temple-entry Satyagraha (1930), 53
'national education', 163–65
National Institute of Social Work and Social Sciences, Orissa, 59
National Institute for Studies in Social, Economic and Cultural Transformation, 84–85
'national schools', establishment of, 165
Nayak, Radhakant, 59
Nehru, Jawaharlal, 223
New Education Fellowship, India, 220–21
Northbrook, Viceroy, 154
  and Lord Curzon, 236
Northcote, Stafford, 236
North-West Frontier Province, creation of by Curzon, 224

Oakley, Edward, 169
Orange, as Director-General of Education, 242, 244
Oriental education, 246
Osmania University, Hyderabad, 76

Packenham-Walsh, Henry, 186
Paine, Thomas, *Rights of Man* by, 20
Pal, Bepin Chandra, 160, 164, 261
Palaniswami, Pandit, 60
Panchal Pandita (journal), 133, 136, 143–45
Partiger, Rev., 183
Parulekar, R. V., 27
Paschim Khandesh Dalit Shikshan Prasarak Mandal, 56
Paswan, Ram Vilas, 61
Patankar, V. S., 65
Patil, Bhaurao, 57
Pawde, Kumud, 80
Pechey, Edith, 98
People's Welfare Society, 55
Perón, Juan Domingo, 37–39, 196–223
  and economic independence, 203
  government of, 197, 203, 207
  Justicialismo (political party) of, 202
  as president of Argentina, 202
  on self-determination, 202
  socio-economic and labour policy of, 217

vocational education under, 222
work policy of, 202, 212, 214
Perry, Erskine, 15
Persian, teaching in Punjab, 279, 287
Phadke, Vasudeo Balwant, 58
Phule, Jotirao, 30, 31, 33–34, 154–55
and the Satyashodhak Samaj, 47
physical and sanitary education, in Punjab, 286–90
Pillai, Madhurai, 60
plague, threat of outbreak of, 261
Plessy v. Ferguson case (USA), 69
political leadership, compulsory education and, 151ff.
Poona, Brahman hegemony in, 30
Poona Girls' School, 167
Power, D. S., 57
Prabhu, Chandrasena Kayastha, 64
Prakash, Dharam, 60
Prasad, Rajendra, 45
Presidency College, Calcutta, 10–11, 246
see also Anglo-Indian Vidyalaya College
Prohibition of Female Infanticide Act, 1872, 93n
proselytisation, threat of, in Punjab, 124–25
provincial educational departments, in British India, 233
Punjab, British annexation of, 41, 124, 126, 271–72
indigenous schools in, 41, 270–72
missionary schools in, 296
transformation of schooling in, 269ff.
women's education in, 150
Punjab schools, equipment supply to, 289–90
medium of instruction in, 292
physical and sanitary education in, 286–90
Punjab Land Alienation Act, 1899, 224
Punjab Textbook Committee, 1877, 275, 277
Punjabi Bhain (journal), 132–33, 143–45
Punjabi, as medium of instruction in Punjab, 131
Puranchand, 60
purdah system, 92n, 104, 118, 245, 296
PWS Arts and Commerce College, Nagpur, 55

Queen's Proclamation (1858), 147, 248, 254

race/racial, divide between Europeans and Indians, 191
religious community and nation, 189–94
Rahman, Tariq, 294
Rai, Lala Lajpat, 160, 164, 166, 261
Rajah, M. C., 62
Rajbhoj, P. N., 57
Rajput clans, female infanticide among, 105–06
Raleigh, vice-chancellor of Calcutta University, 237, 241
Ramabai, Pandita, 32, 33, 91, 103, 106–07, 109, 114
High Caste Hindu Woman, 97
on reforms, 115

Ramabai Ambedkar Boarding, Nashik, 56
Ramabai Ambedkar Girl's School, Nashik, 57
Ranade, Mahadev Govind, 11, 34, 97, 154
  girls' school of, 69
  on women's education, 167
Ranke, Leopold von, 30
Ranuva Ram Primary School, 60
Ravidas temple, Varanasi, 58
Rathnam, Rev. John, 61
Rayat Shakshan Sanstha, 55
Ravi Das High School, Jalandhar, 61
Reddy, M. V. Bhagya, 60
religious identity, education and, in Sikh schools in Punjab, 120ff.
religious instructions, in schools in Punjab, 123, 138–39, 141, 271n, 281–82
Republican Party of India, 56
Ripon, Viceroy, 154–55, 255–56
Risley, H. H., 244
Rohan, P. J., 57
Rohidas Samaj Panchayat, 57
Rose, Mrs, 124
Roy, Raja Rammohan, 10, 11, 15–16, 246
Rudra, Sushil, 191, 194
Rukhmabai, 32, 33, 91, 98, 103, 108–09, 110, 115–16, 118
Rukhmabai Hospital, Surat, 98
Rules for Classification of Educational Institutions, 293
Rupvate, D. T., 57
Ruskin, John, 204, 229
Russia, educated Russians in Tsarist, 267
Sagar, Sundarlal, 61
Said, Edward, 12
Salisbury, secretary of state for India, 254
Salve, Lahujibuwa, 47–48
Samarg Bodhak Nirashrit Samaj, 52
Sambodhi High School, Ahmadnagar, 57
Sanskrit colleges/schools, 11, 19, 23, 292
Sao, Nagnath, 85
Sarmiento, Domingo Faustino, 37
sarvodaya, concept of, 204
sati, practice of, 92, 153, 245
Satyashodhak Samaj, 47
Sayani, Rahmatullah, 159
SC/ST hostels, 79
school(s)
  curricula, 269n
  categories of, 292–93
  monitoring and regulation in Punjab, 284–85
  Oriental education in, 279
  in rural areas, 152, 154–56
  secondary, rise in Calcutta, 256
  transformation of, in colonial Punjab, 269ff.
'sedition', and the school, 183–85
'Sedition Law', 261
Sen, Haimabati, 33, 91, 99–100
  on education, 114–15
Sen, Kunjabehari, 100
Seton-Karr, W., 152
Sevagram, Wardha, 220
Shahare, M. L., 59
Shahu Maharaj, Chhatrapati, 55
Shajanandar, Swami A. S., 61

Shantiniketan, 36, 220
Sharada Sadan, Bombay, 97
Shastri, Tagadi Keshwar, 61
Sherring, Matthew, 193
Shinde, Bapuji Hari, 96
Shinde, Tarabai, 32, 91, 103, 109, 115
  Stri Purusha Tulana by, 96
Shinde, Vithal Ramji, 31, 49–50, 52
Shirke, D. M., 57
Shirtarkar, Sitaram, 57
Shiva Kumar Swamiji, 22
Shivalingaiah, L., 58, 60
Shortrede, Robert, 152
Shri Cokhamela Hostel, Buldhana, 55–56
Shri Gadge Maharaj Backward Class Hostel, Pandharpur, 66
Shri Janoji Free Boarding, Akola, 48
Shudras, 127
Siddharth College, Bombay, 64, 65, 72, 75, 77–78, 80, 87, 89
  library of, 81
Siddharth Educational Society and High School, Mysore, 61
Siddharth Sahitya Sangh, 65
Siddayya, S. M., 61
Sikh community, ceremony for dead among, 140
Sikh diaspora, 133
Sikh *panth*, 143
Sikh schools, education and religious identity in Punjab, 120ff.
Sikhism, 146–47
Singh, Baba Khem, 125
Singh, Bhai Ditt, 126, 146
Singh, Bhai Mohan, 132
Singh, Bhai Takht, 120, 121, 126–29, 134, 142
  biography of, 140
  contribution to female education, 137–38
Singh, Bhai Vir, 121, 132
Singh, Sardar Jagjit, 63–64
Singh Sabha, 42, 121–22
  leaders of, 132
  reforms, 141, 146
skilled labour, 258
slavery, abolition of, 1
Smith, Adam, 10
Smith, Robert Percy, 2
Society for the Propagation of the Gospel, 177
socio-religious reforms, of the nineteenth century, 93
Somavansh caste (of Mahars), 49
Somavansh Hitachintak Samaj, 49
Somavamshiya Mitra (journal), 52
Sorabji, Cornelia, 32, 91, 100, 111–12, 116, 118
  India Calling by, 100
  India Recalled by, 100
  Love and Life Behind the Purdah by, 100
  Purdahnashin by, 100, 103
South Africa
  colleges for black students in, 70
  institutes of higher education in, 31–32, 70, 87–89
South India Buddhist School, Marikuppam, 60
sports culture, in English public schools, 286
Sri Satchidananda Vachan Griha, Mopla (library), 51

Sriniketan Institute for Rural Reconstruction, Shantiniketan, 220
St. Stephen's College, Delhi, 194
Subhedar Savadkar Vidhyarthi Ashram, Mahad, 66
Swadeshi Movement (1903–08), 37, 168, 170, 178, 183–86, 195, 219
  leaders of, 164
syllabus, for female education, 129, 135
  in Punjab, 278–82
symbolic and institutional construction, sustainability of, 222–23

Tagore, Rabindranath, 36, 160, 219, 251
  Gandhi and, 220
Takshashila High School, Nashik, 56
Tat Khalsa image, of Sikhs, 35, 125, 132, 139, 141, 147
Taylor, Rev. V., 9
teachers, of indigenous schools, 274
  status of, 290n
technical training, 257
tehsil schools, 292–93
Telang, Kashinath Trimbak, 11, 154, 158
Temple, Richard, lieutenant-governor of Bengal, 250
textbooks, homogenisation of, 275–78
  policy, 276
Thaware, G. M., 55–56
Thompson, E. P., 290
Thorat, Sukhadeo, 74, 82
Tilak, Bal Gangadhar, 34, 52, 58, 160, 168, 172, 175, 271
  on compulsory education, 157
  on education, 159, 161, 173
  on 'national' education, 164–65
  opposition to Deccan Agriculturists Relief Act, 166
  on female education, 34–35, 129, 167
Tipnis, Surendranath, 64
Tirpude, N. K., 55
Tirpude Institute of Social Work, Nagpur, 55
Tolstoy, Leo, 219
Trevelyan, Charles, 13, 21
Tubb, Rev. Henry, 194
Tyabji, Badruddin, 159
Tyndale-Biscoe, Charles, 179

unaided colleges, in British India, 233
  legal education by, 234
uncovenanted service, selection for posts in British India, 249–50
unemployment, among English educated Indians, 251, 258
United Dalit Students' Forum (UDSF), JNU, 86
United States of America, institutes of higher education in, 87–89
Universities Act, 1904, 188, 245, 247
University of Allahabad, 228–29
  establishment of, 257
University of Bombay, Acts of Incorporation and establishment of, 227–32, 247, 256
University of Calcutta, 43
  Acts of Incorporation and establishment of, 227–32, 245

affiliated colleges of, 232
Curzon's address at, 265
Curzon's confrontation with, 234–37
on higher on higher education, 234
syndicate of, 232
University Grants Commission, 74
University of London, 265
University of Madras, Acts of Incorporation and establishment of, 247
University of Punjab, 130
Act of Incorporation and establishment of, 228, 229, 257
Oriental department of, 229
'untouchables' (castes), 69, 71, 76, 127
attending schools, 48–49
students, 54
treatment of, 46
see also Dalits
Urdu, as medium of instruction, 133, 294
as official language in Punjab, 24, 41
teaching in Punjab, 126, 278

Vadapally, Ealy, 60
Vaid, Bhai Mohan Singh, 121
Vaishya, Muldas, 61
Validating Bill, 226
Varma, Mahadevi, 38, 90–91, 107, 110–11, 114, 117
Ateet Ke Chalchitra by, 102
Shrinkhala ki Kadiyan by, 102, 104
Varnashramadharma, 29
Vedas, 140, 146
Vedic knowledge, 146
Velaskar, Padma, 46n, 63
vernacular literature, in Punjab, 277
vernacular schools, 41
and Anglo-vernacular schools, 294
vernacular teachers, in colonial India, 26–27
viceroy's executive council, election to, 158
Victoria Memorial Hall, Calcutta, 225
Vicziany, Marika, 88
Vidyasagar, Ishwarchandra, 34, 154
Vijapurkar, Vishnu Govind, 165
Vijbhukhandas, Seth Mararbhai, 98
village schools, 292–93
village welfare schemes, 223
Viswanathan, Gauri, 12–19
vocational education, 198–99, 201, 205–11

Wagh, Usha, 58
Wagh, Vilas, 58
Waghmare, L. B., 76, 78
Wardha 'Basic Education' Conference, 1937, 209–11
Watson, F. J., 186
Wauton, Mrs, 299
Wedderburn, William, 6
Wellesley, Governor-General, 23
Westcott, George, 182
White Paper, on Indian Education, 244–45
Whitehall, 242
widows/widowhood, early marriage and widowhood, 107, 111
enforced, 92–93

- problems of, 109–10, 118
- remarriage of, 93, 119

Wilkins, Charles, 8

women
- chastity and domestic work, 136
- condition of, 122–28
- education of, 32–34, 90, 94–95, 167, 169
  - opponents of, 129
  - in Punjab, 295–99
  - *see also* girls' high schools
- maternal mortality, 107
- perception about self and education, 90ff.
- role in society, 93
- seclusion and loss of identity, 93, 102–104
- sexuality, 131–32
- social position of, 93
- social reforms and, 16, 91–94, 115–19
- space for, 95
- traditional roles of, 141–45
- writings by, 91

Wood, Charles, 236

Wood's Despatch (1854), 43, 227–29, 233, 249, 266, 278
- *see also* Educational Despatch

Woodburn, John, Curzon's consultation with, 235–37

Woolf, Virginia, 69

work and education, 212–16

working children, 151

Yajnavalkya, 28
- *Shukla Yajurveda* by, 28
- *Yajnavalkya Smriti* by, 28

Yajurveda, 28

Yohannan, Poykayil, 60

Yugantar Society, 55

Zanana Mission, 299

zilla schools, 292–93